The Yazzie Case

STUDIES IN INDIGENOUS COMMUNITY BUILDING

Lloyd L. Lee and Wendy S. Greyeyes, Series Editors

The Studies in Indigenous Community Building series presents titles that capture how Native peoples today are cultivating their communities, both on the reservation as well as in urban enclaves. The series provides an opportunity for scholars, authors, practitioners, and community members alike to publish works emphasizing how Native and Indigenous peoples are building their communities to sustain their traditional ways of life.

THE YAZZIE CASE

*Building a Public Education System
for Our Indigenous Future*

Edited by Wendy S. Greyeyes,
Lloyd L. Lee, and
Glenabah Martinez

University of New Mexico Press | Albuquerque

© 2023 by the University of New Mexico Press
All rights reserved. Published 2023
Printed in the United States of America

Library of Congress Cataloging-in-Publication Data

Names: Greyeyes, Wendy Shelly, 1978– editor. | Lee, Lloyd L., 1971– editor. |
    Martinez, Glenabah, editor.
Title: The Yazzie case: building a public education system for our
    indigenous future / edited by Wendy S. Greyeyes, Lloyd L. Lee, and
    Glenabah Martinez.
Other titles: Studies in indigenous community building.
Description: Albuquerque: University of New Mexico Press, 2023. |
    Series: Studies in indigenous community building | Includes
    bibliographical references and index.
Identifiers: LCCN 2023013324 (print) | LCCN 2023013325 (ebook) |
    ISBN 9780826365088 (cloth) | ISBN 9780826365095 (paperback) |
    ISBN 9780826365101 (ebook)
Subjects: LCSH: Yazzie, Wilhelmina—Trials, litigation, etc. | Educational
    equalization—New Mexico. | Discrimination in education—New
    Mexico. | Educational change—New Mexico. | Culturally relevant
    pedagogy—New Mexico. | Indians of North America—Education—
    New Mexico. | New Mexico—Trials, litigation, etc.
Classification: LCC LC213.22.N6 Y38 2023 (print) | LCC LC213.22.N6
    (ebook) | DDC 379.2/609789—dc23/eng/20230414
LC record available at https://lccn.loc.gov/2023013324
LC ebook record available at https://lccn.loc.gov/2023013325

Founded in 1889, the University of New Mexico sits on the traditional
homelands of the Pueblo of Sandia. The original peoples of New Mexico—
Pueblo, Navajo, and Apache—since time immemorial have deep
connections to the land and have made significant contributions to the
broader community statewide. We honor the land itself and those who
remain stewards of this land throughout the generations and also
acknowledge our committed relationship to Indigenous peoples. We
gratefully recognize our history.

Cover illustration by Karl Pino
Designed by Felicia Cedillos
Composed in Huronia Navajo

Contents

Part II. The Response

Part III. The Future

Illustrations

Figures

Maps

Tables

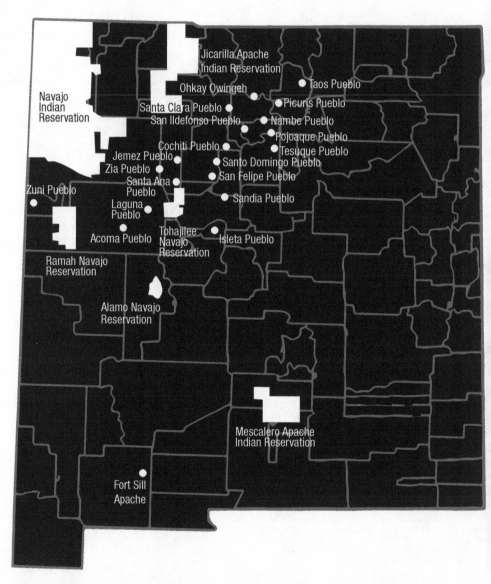

Map 1. New Mexico's nineteen Pueblos, the Navajo Nation, the two Apache tribes, and eighty-seven school district boundaries. Developed by Johnathan Sylversmythe.

Preface

WILHELMINA YAZZIE

The book begins with an interview with Wilhelmina Yazzie, the lead plaintiff in the Yazzie lawsuit. We have kept the integrity of the interview, presenting it with minimal edits.

YAZZIE: I grew up in Casamero Lake, New Mexico, which is the eastern part of the Navajo Nation. I grew up with no running water or electricity, but I'm very thankful that I grew up traditionally, learning Navajo as my first language. I was raised by my grandparents. I had my grandmother until she passed away when I was ten years old. My mother at the time was a single mother and was going to school and working as well, so I spent the first ten years of my life with my grandmother, following her and learning from her and everything. Then, just recently, my mother passed. It's going to be five years this month. My late mother was an educator for thirty years.

She was a Head Start teacher and had gone into preschool teaching and then also secondary elementary school. She'd been teaching for quite a while, and so I was pretty much raised with the sense that education is important, which was very important to her as well as her children. When I say her children, it wasn't just me and my siblings. It was the whole community as her children that she deeply cared about. In her earlier years, I know that she talked about being shipped off to boarding school at Intermountain in Utah, and that's where she attended high school and graduated, and she was the only sibling among her family that graduated from high school and college and then, of course, my uncles, the younger ones. For me, I attended Gallup McKinley County Schools when growing up because I was living in Casamero Lake and the closest school was Smith Lake Elementary, which is closed down now, but that's where I went to school. My first teacher was my mom, of course, because she was a Head Start teacher.

Then from there, I attended Smith Lake Elementary from kindergarten through fifth grade. After that, I went through mid[dle school] and high school and graduated from there, and then I went on to attend college. I started here at UNM Gallup, which I was not prepared for even though it was a branch [sic]. I was not prepared for college, and it took me a while to get into my required classes because there were a lot of pre-reqs and a lot of other classes that I needed to take in order for me to get to those required classes for my degree. Nonetheless, I completed it, and I obtained two degrees, and now I'm currently going back to school at the main campus with online classes at UNM. I'm currently living here in Gallup and working here. I'm a tribal court advocate. I'm able to practice law in Navajo Nation among my people. Also, I'm a paralegal. I've been in the legal field for quite some time. I think it's been about maybe fourteen to fifteen years. Again, with my tribal advocacy and me learning my language and knowing my language, it's a great asset.

I'm very grateful to assist my Diné people and my Diné clients and speak to them in our language. There's so much more meaning and so much comfort when I talk to them in my language. I do have a partner, who is of the Oglala Lakota tribe of South Dakota, and we have three beautiful children. Two boys and one girl. My oldest is Xavier, and then after him is Reese, and then my youngest is Kimimila. Kimimila means butterfly in Lakota. She's five years old and she just started kindergarten. Reese is actually a sophomore in high school now, and my oldest Xavier is in college. He went on to college. A little background on my son Xavier—my son Xavier also grew up in Casamero Lake until we moved to Gallup when he was about eight years old. I was a single parent at the time and commuting to Gallup for work and school—especially with the young child—was pretty hectic, and it was too much, so we moved closer, and we moved into Gallup. He attended the Gallup McKinley County School, public schools as well.

He started at Jefferson with pre-K; unfortunately, at the time, my mom was about to retire, and she wasn't teaching pre-K or Head Start anymore. She was actually teaching second grade. My mom wasn't able to be his first teacher as it was for me, my siblings, my cousins, my other brothers and sisters in the family. Xavier started pre-K at Jefferson Elementary. He stayed there all the way until fifth grade. After that, he went to JFK Middle School and then on to Miyamura High School. He graduated this past year in May from Miyamura; now he's in college. He's very creative and very talented. He loves art, he loves music. He did play sports as well, growing up with the schools, and also with the city leagues. He is such an awesome big brother. He's just overall such a great individual, and I know that as a parent, as a mother, I have been hard on him to make sure that his education is going well. Aside from that, with his peers and all those things that come about when you have children, most of all, he gives me joy and he's my greatest son. That's a little background of Xavier and I.

So, what sparked my decision to join the lawsuit against the state? First of all, going back, I was taught through my traditional teachings that our children are sacred. As a mother, as a Navajo woman, my children, our Indigenous children, are very important. Their future, their education. My mother was a great inspiration in my decision to join the lawsuit. She taught me the importance of what being a woman meant, "what a mother means," and most of all our responsibility, which is a sacred trust to our children—that they're protected, that we guide them in the right direction, that we prepare them for what we call life. Also, my late grandmother also growing up with her even though I was up to ten years old after she left, I do remember that she always stressed to my mother and my aunts, my uncles, and my family members growing up that you have to be tough to be a parent because as a parent, our children are our priority above everything else. We have that responsibility. Just growing up in that matriarchal environment with my grandmother and mother really motivated me, and I knew that I needed to stand up for my children and our Indigenous children. That's pretty much what sparked it. Also, I was moved by the inequities that our children received in the public school system. When I say our children, I mean our Indigenous children, our children of color, our English language learner children, our low-income children, especially our children with disabilities—they're starved of resources in our school, in our public school system. Our children are placed on the last pedestal of everything. Of everything. I experienced it, and I'm sure other families have experienced it. As a person of color or an Indigenous person, there's no equality. There are things that I feel like are provided and given to us just—I'm not sure how to explain it but just to—I don't really want to say it in a way. Well, I guess to shut us up. One way I would say it. Overall, our children are not provided the sufficient education that they have the right to and deserve. That also sparked my decision to join the lawsuit. Going back to experiences that I had with the schools where my son was in third grade at the time when we started discussing the lawsuit and then initiated it. My son is a brilliant and smart boy. However, when he struggled with some subjects in school, there was no academic support. Of course, they had an after-school program, maybe like thirty minutes to an hour, but it was more of an extracurricular activity after-school program; there was no tutoring, there was no assistance and on how to prepare the children to further assist them. I felt like it was more of babysitting, I guess, and I hate to say that. When he went, and I would ask questions, "Did you get help on your math? Did you get help on this?" "Oh, no, we played this, we drew this, we created this." I, as a parent, took the time, after work, to sit down with him to help him look for resources online.

We were fortunate enough to live here in town with Internet access and computers. I'm not like some of my family members that live in the tribal lands who struggle with no Internet, no technology, no other type of resources. I was one of the resources as well, helping them out printing things, searching for things, and just being there for my family. Again, there was no academic support. Then, of course, when it came to the testing and the standardized testing, he always scored below his grade level. Of course, during parent-teacher conferences, I would raise my concerns, and I would ask them, "How do we help him to score above these levels, although he's getting good grades, he's on a roll."

All these things, and a lot of times there were substitute teachers that were there for long periods of time, even months, who didn't teach the curriculum and the subject that they were substituting in because the teacher wasn't available, or the teacher was gone or there was no teacher at all. I think that was one of the biggest barriers was substitute teachers that were there to substitute and look after the children, but not yet really teaching the curriculum that they needed in order to pass these tests. Again, our schools have limited resources, not enough textbooks is another thing that I struggle with. I think I mostly struggle with that in middle school.

My son would have homework, my other son would have homework, and they didn't have a textbook. When I helped them with their homework, it was like, "Okay, where do we get this information? Where is the book?" "Well, the teacher said we couldn't take the books home because there's not enough and if we take it home with it might not come back" sort of thing. Then I would reach out to the teachers and see if we could get copies or make copies. That was another route that I had to go on my own to try to help my children with their homework. I think, middle school, also computer lab, I remember my son telling me that there were three to four students to a computer sharing a computer during a computer class. Some of those days he wasn't able to actually do the actual computer work and just looked on because they were sharing. Not enough textbooks, classroom supplies. I remember teachers giving us a list of things that our children needed to bring. At times, there were old socks, old shirts for the boards. Then, especially now with the pandemic that's happening, there's not enough technology like laptops and tablets for our children, especially those families with more than three kids. No Internet access, no broadband, especially for those that live on our tribal lands.

Parents do reach out to me and call me, my family members, and I have family members that come out an hour and a half away from where they live in order to come to my house to use the Internet to help their children and those types of things, just limited resources. There were limited resources that Xavier and our children were lacking. The substitute teachers who have been there for extended periods of time, not enough counselors to make sure that our children were placed in the right classes and are prepared to be career and college ready.

I know that when he got to high school coming from middle school as an honor roll student, when we first got his class schedule, I know it was an exciting time; he's going into high school. When we got his class schedule there were some classes that we were not sure about. I went to the counselor and asked if Xavier was able to get into any advanced classes because I was pretty confident, and he was confident himself, that he could be in advanced classes, and because he was getting straight As and on the honor roll.

I met with the high school counselor, and she didn't know who my son was or all that. I understand, because she was taking care of over two hundred students. I asked, "How do I get my son into AP classes? How can we do that?" She said, "Well, it depends on his grades and his school records." I said, "Okay. Well, he's always been pretty good, had good grades, straight As, honor roll, whatnot."

Freshman year he went to high school. At that time, my other son was in middle school. He struggled a little bit more than Xavier did, and for him, I always contacted the school principals, counselors, and had to go through different avenues. There were no after-school programs, no language programs for children. A Navajo culture class was limited and sometimes they weren't offered. Our language class was an elective, so our children could elect to take Navajo class or they could take Spanish, French, or any other language class. These resources are worse in our schools on our tribal land. The transportation issues, social services, and just programs that our children need to be academically set, and most of all, no culturally relevant curriculum. There's no inclusion of who we are, our history, and so forth. Just from all of this, every time I contacted the schools there were just excuses. I totally understand some of the teachers, it's out of their hands. Some of them did go out of their way to help our children with their own funding or own resources, but a lot of times teachers were not given enough support to be there for our children.

We have had a lot of support from our legal team. They've always been there to guide us and everything, and they literally fought for us. Our expert witnesses, our advocates, our supporters, and we parents stood up on behalf of our children. We stated our concerns, we stated our experiences, we stated everything that we've been fighting for our children. When this first started, at first from the beginning, I had my doubts, I'll be honest. That is because as an Indigenous person and the history of what my people experienced was not always in our favor. They actually have never been in our favor, but then more parents stepped up and got involved, and that provided more confidence. Most of all, this education lawsuit was for our children, our children's future. I know that there was a lot of preparation and legal stuff going on during the course of the lawsuit. We were deposed, we had depositions. We had to provide documents such as our children's school records, different resources that we use and how we help our children, what they go through. All kinds of stuff. There was a lot of paper trail that I've done: who I talked to, on what day, what time, what kind of response I received, if there was a resolution to it, and how did we go about it. Just those type of things.

During that time, I think a lot of the parents that were involved in this case, we stayed out of the public, but I still advocated on behalf of my children with their education at their schools, and I help other parents. We seek other alternative resources to help our children with their education, making sure that they were on top of their work, that they receive what they needed. Through the course of this legal proceeding, I stayed optimistic because in our Diné traditional ways we have to stay positive. We have to have a mind concept of where we have to keep the balance of harmony, what they call *Hózhó*. We had to keep that balance, we had to stay positive just with prayers and all that. I stayed optimistic for our children.

INTERVIEWER: Are you satisfied with the outcome of the lawsuit?

YAZZIE: Yes, I am. We won the decision [*chuckles*]. We won, proved our case against the state, and we won. I'm forever grateful that the late Judge Singleton ruled in our children's favor. The decision and order we know was pretty lengthy. She had stated everything. Gosh, there was so much that's in the order. I'm just forever grateful that this is the start of something. I can't thank our legal team enough, including our educational experts who also testified on behalf of our children. The outcome came about, we won, and now it's just enforcing of the court order. Working with the state to be there for our children, to provide for our children, to get what they need and deserve, and all that. It's just enforcing the court order.

INTERVIEWER: Why do you think a book like this is important?

YAZZIE: I think a book like this is crucial, and I'm very grateful that this book is being created. It will educate all about what the case is about, the history of what the case is, the current events of the case, and to recognize all those that are involved in changing the education system for our Indigenous children. Changing the narrative and, most of all, what it means, what do our children mean to us. The importance of our children. This book will be about the truth. The truth of the lawsuit, the experiences, all that have been involved. I think this is going to be a great book, and I appreciate everyone that has taken their time and effort in putting this together. I'll be forever grateful to you all and everyone, so *ahéhee'*.

Lastly, last thoughts I may have. My upbringing and my Navajo traditional ways and Navajo being my first language, growing up with my grandparents, in that setting I was taught a lot about our fundamental values of life growing up. My mom was a great influence in all these things. *Child* in the English dictionary, the definition in English is just pretty straightforward. It's a young human being below the age of puberty. That's how a child is defined in English. But when we define a child in our Indigenous language and ways, it has so much more meaning, and it's defined in greater length than this simple descriptive definition that's in English. If you go see an elder or grandparents or parents, a child has a lot of meaning, and our children are of great importance. They are sacred; we view them as sacred. They're beautiful, they're precious, and most of all, they're our future. It's our responsibility that we set them on the right path. In my Navajo way, we say that we set our children on the right path of the yellow corn pollen road, and we prepare them for *iiná*, or life. That's a responsibility for me as a parent. The Navajo language is the teaching that I was taught and, of course, the four directions in my traditional ways. What I would like to see in the future for our Indigenous children and all children of color—all that we have involved in this school suit, English language learners, children with disabilities, low income—is inclusion and equity. Our children have the right to be career- and college-ready. They have the right to be given the academic support, and they're deserving of an equitable education. All children are. We need to be brought up from the low pedestal that they always put our children on—that they put us on. We need to be brought up equally with everyone else. I think that's the main thing about this whole thing, is that we want our children to be included and to receive what they need and what they deserve. As a parent, for me, I try my best at home to guide them and to teach them in my ways and be there for them, even with their education.

Figure 1. Wilhelmina Yazzie (Diné) and her son Xavier at their home in Casamero Lake, New Mexico (population of 518). Mrs. Yazzie initiated the lawsuit against the State of New Mexico in 2014. The Yazzies live fifty-six miles from the Gallup McKinley County School district, which Xavier attended as a third grader. Photo credit Hondo Louis. Funded by UNM's Center for Regional Studies and Native American Studies Department.

An Examination of the *Yazzie* side of the *Yazzie/Martinez* Lawsuit

WENDY S. GREYEYES, LLOYD L. LEE,
AND GLENABAH MARTINEZ

PRESENTLY, NO BOOK ADDRESSES the impact of the *Yazzie/Martinez v. State of New Mexico* case. We seek to address this rift, bringing together the analytical perspectives of educators, policy analysts, attorneys, and professors in a way that will help educators (both preservice and in-service) understand the dilemmas impacting their communities and their own role shaping future policies and curriculum centered on one important aspect: recognizing Indigenous or Native American students as the leaders of New Mexico. We must embrace the motto of the Farmington, New Mexico, Navajo Preparatory School: *Yideeskáágóó Naat'áanii*, meaning "Leaders Now and into the Future." While the main audience we have in mind comprises educators and education leaders, higher education and education policy analysts and advocates will find the book relevant to their work as well.

This volume consists of a collection of essays, witness stories, and photographs meant to educate stakeholders on the significance of *Yazzie/Martinez* and lay the groundwork for a new vision of education in New Mexico for Native American children. It addresses the imperative that future educators understand the disenfranchisement of Native students and the state's impact on American Indian education. In addition, the book includes chapters from legal advocates, providing context and relevancy to the *Yazzie/Martinez* case in ways that should be clear to students and educational leaders. As we highlight the significance of the *Yazzie/Martinez* case, we recognize an urgent need to create a volume unifying the many partners who have played an influential role in both the case and the remedy. Indeed, the story of *Yazzie/ Martinez* unites the space of the courtroom and its impact upon the classroom.

This book is focused on an important court decision with far-reaching implications for educators generally and more specifically the future of Native American education in New Mexico and the United States. We recognize the legal battles around a tribal remedy have been a sore point of contention among state, educational, and tribal leaders. The tribal remedy, a collection of educational recommendations developed by New Mexico tribal leaders and educators that focuses on transformative change, is undermined by rigid educational definitions that rely on the legal definitions of an outdated educational threshold of adequacy. Once the state meets this threshold, it sees no need to exceed existing definitions. This book explores this dilemma. As we have learned, adequate is not sufficient for our Native American students. Particularly within a state that has an active Indian education act, it is appalling that the rhetoric from New Mexican state leadership about supporting tribal sovereignty falls to the wayside when tribal leaders and community members demand improved educational outcomes for their children. We believe that the efforts by state leaders—meaning the secretary of education, public school boards, and school administrators—to continually chip away at the educational hopes for Native American students must be exposed. The counternarratives of students and families resisting state leaders' efforts to reform American Indian education without tribal input must be heard. This is especially evident in the accounts of several witnesses who are part of this book. It is imperative we examine the educational deficiencies and successes within New Mexico's public education system, a process that requires a deep exploration and recognition of the voices of students and families, which are continually dismissed. Native Americans have historical experience with such dismissiveness, and the fight to resist it evidences Native peoples' strength, courage, and persistence. It is the fortitude of a people who will not give up on their children. We hope that this book will bring clarity to our students and educational leaders and inspire action.

We recognize the need to put together a book that captures this pivotal point in time. We also recognize that the lawsuit brought by Yazzie was combined with the Martinez case. For us, the unique cultural and historical experience of our Chicano/a and Hispano/a relatives is undermined through this combined effort. To recognize this unique experience, we have employed the terms *Yazzie/Martinez* case or *Yazzie/Martinez* lawsuit, which allow us to resist the colonial move of clumping the minority experience. We have learned too often that Native people are continually clumped into categories of the minority or classified as "something else." We have chosen this move not out of disrespect but as a recognition that Native people are the stewards of this land, a role held long before the colonial project undermined our tribal sovereignty. Therefore, we respectfully recognize the court's use of *Yazzie/Martinez* as the standard reference point, but we have made the decision to bring the focus of Native American students to the center of our analysis. The *Yazzie* side brings to light the unique historical, colonial, and settler experiences for Native peoples, which are remarkably different from the issues characterizing the *Martinez* lawsuit. This decision was not made lightly by the co-editors, but we are convinced it was the right one, particularly because the book is designed with Native American students in mind.

Constructing Critically Conscious Educational Reform

Scholarship on American Indian education captures the historical twists and turns of both federal and state authorities constructing an education system meant to undermine tribal sovereignty and to assimilate Native American students. Within this literature, educational reform arises as a constant theme. Throughout, the contributing authors point out that educational reform must not make the mistakes of the past. Reform must be conscious and carried out with an awareness of the historical challenges and unique cultural and racial experiences encountered by our Native American students.

This is reflected in the rich canon of works about American Indian education, beginning with the Meriam Report in 1928, titled *The Problem of Indian Administration.*[1] This report is an early recognition of the deficiencies in education across the United States and recommends increased funding for Native American students across all federal and state school systems. Much later, in

2004, Reyhner and Eder (2004) provide a comprehensive review of the history of American Indian education, beginning with the colonial encounter and missionary activity to the period of self-determination when tribes began making decisions to control their schools. In their introduction, they reflect on the dangers of modern education reforms relying upon outcomes assessments, state and national standards, and use of high stakes testing.[2] Their advice for the future of American Indian education is to understand the past failures and successes characterizing Indian education and to focus on supporting the latter.[3] Later still, in the 2015 *Red Pedagogy: Native American Social and Political Thought*, Sandy Grande describes how education was a project designed to colonize American Indian minds as a means of gaining access to Native land, labor, and resources.[4] She provides a thematic account of the historical relationship between schooling and American Indians categorized in terms of eras:

1. The period of missionary domination, from the sixteenth to the nineteenth centuries;
2. The period of federal government domination, from the late nineteenth to the mid-twentieth centuries; and
3. The period of self-determination, from the mid-twentieth century to the present.[5]

Grande stresses that any educational reform must happen in conjunction with the "analyses of the forces of colonialism"; otherwise, it becomes a "bandage over the incessant wounds of imperialism."[6] Collectively, these scholars provide recommendations based on their rich analysis of the historical legacy of Indian education. Vine Deloria Jr. also provides rich insight on Indian education in a booklet of eight essays, *Indian Education in America*.[7] He points out that "Indigenous knowledge . . . was the realization that the world and all its possible experiences, constitutes a social reality, a fabric of life in which everything had the possibility of intimate knowing relationships because, ultimately, everything was related."[8] Deloria's depiction of Indigenous knowledge is contrasted to Western educators devaluing these perspectives because they do not align to Western conceptions of knowledge and science. Deloria examines this conflict and challenges scholars to reconsider the contribution and the knowledge of Indigenous peoples. This statement of recognizing the local knowledge systems within each community is a necessary aspect of decolonizing tribal perspectives and valuing the rhetorical sovereignty of tribal nations in any educational reform. This booklet sets up Deloria's future work, *Power and Place: Indian Education in America*, coedited with Daniel R. Wildcat.[9] Overall, numerous authors (e.g., Brenda J. Child, David Wallace Adams, and Francis Paul Prucha) have written extensively on the history of American Indian education, focusing on the boarding school period.[10] Notable contributions include work on institutional racism and American Indian education (Huff), the rise of the first tribally controlled school system (McCarty and Roessel Jr.), survival in education (Villegas, Neugebauer, and Venegas), the politics of curriculum and instruction in urban public schools (Martinez), decolonizing education (Battiste), Indigenous leadership in education (Aguilera-Black Bear and Tippeconnic III), and American Indian education, critical race theory, and the law (Fletcher).[11] What we find in the extensive collection of works about American Indian education is that the only beneficiaries of the form and function of school are white Americans in all educational systems.

Although Sandy Grande points out that we are experiencing an era of self-determination, the potential benefits of this fact have yet to be reached.[12] The process of taking full control and accountability of school systems is described by John P. Hopkins in *Indian Education for All: Decolonizing Education in Public Schools* and Wendy S. Greyeyes in *The History of Navajo Nation Education: Disentangling Our Sovereign Body*.[13] To resist these limitations to Indian education and the harmful policies as we strive for an adequate education, it is imperative we reconfigure spaces of learning and strategize methods to decolonize these spaces. This work is being accomplished by Teresa McCarty and Tiffany Lee in their 2014 article, "Critical Culturally Sustaining/Revitalizing Pedagogy and Indigenous Educational Sovereignty," and can also be seen in Jeremy Garcia's "Critical and Culturally Sustaining Indigenous Family," Matthew Sakiestewa Gilbert's *Education beyond the Mesas: Hopi Students at Sherman Institute, 1902–1929*, and Leilani Sabzalian's *Indigenous Children's Survivance in Public Schools*, all works that focus on transforming educational curriculum about American Indians.[14] In addition, the authors in the 2020 volume coedited by Alayna Eagle Shield, Django Paris, Rae Paris, and Timothy San Pedro, *Education in Movement Spaces: Standing Rock to Chicago Freedom*

Square, recognize education occurring within social movement spaces and a shift toward viewing the world as a classroom.[15] Another book, coedited by Pedro Vallejo and Vincent Werito, *Transforming Diné Education*, speaks to transforming Diné educational teaching practices.[16] This work brings with it a concerted pedagogical focus on Navajo values as an important element to integrate into teaching. Finally, as we think about educational reform, we want to note other books that are rethinking past educational reform and how it fits into our consciousness as Indigenous defenders of education. The identified publications are revisiting and inspiring a rethinking of the impact of the American Indian educational experience.

Overall, we see the spectrum of existing work on American Indian education as abundant. However, we believe there is still a lot of work to be done. More work must be done to address each state's political and social influences and impact upon public education for Native American students. This is especially true against the backdrop of a global pandemic and social movements occurring nationally that are reconfiguring the meaning of education.

Focusing on the State as a Site of Struggle

The impact of the *Yazzie/Martinez* case must be cast against the historical and colonial backdrop of American Indian education. It has been long known and understood that American Indian children have not been a priority for states. A 2019 National Congress of American Indians report, *Becoming Visible: A Landscape of State Efforts to Provide Native American Education for All*, provides a descriptive analysis of a state survey inquiring into the funding, curriculum, and staffing in each state.[17] Currently, only thirty-five states have federally recognized tribal nations, and of those, twelve have some form of an Indian education act, with California being the most recent to push for developing an act.[18] The report highlights twenty-eight states surveyed, of which twelve have permitted Native American standards, curriculum, and content into their social science area.[19] It is clear that the invisibility and erasure of Native peoples begins in the classroom and perpetuates itself in the state legislative halls.

In New Mexico, the unique tribal terrain includes twenty-four Native

Nations, including the Navajo Nation, nineteen pueblos (the twentieth pueblo, recognized by the All Pueblo Council of Governors in 2009, is located in the Yselta section of El Paso, Texas), and three Apache Nations. In "Indigenous Research Perspectives in the State of New Mexico: Implications for Working with Schools and Communities," Minthorn et al. describe the unique history and sovereign power retained by Native Nations in New Mexico; indeed, tribal sovereignty has endured the colonial effects of Spanish, Mexican, and currently, American states.[20] Although New Mexico continues to control Indian education, tribes have exerted their authority in many unique ways reflected in the New Mexico Indian Education Act (NMIEA), which requires consultation with tribal nations regarding their educational policies. Minthorn et al. explain that "tribal nations are in the position of accepting or rejecting state policies and services they determine to be either beneficial or contrary to the needs or interests of their communities."[21] Although this appears to give tribes an advantage within the game of educational policy, this advantage is still constrained by a colonial institution of power reflected in how states are structured. For example, when tribes demand that schools continue to teach remotely due to the COVID-19 pandemic challenges, they are met with resistance from school leaders, which is discussed by former Navajo Nation president Jonathan Nez in the conclusion of this book.

This book is necessary to understand the role of the state's structure in shaping and forming how decisions are implemented, interpreted, and enforced. We are seeing within this lawsuit the strong convergence of state actors continuing to push their agendas. The state is structured as a three-branch system: executive, legislative, and judicial. The executive branch is the governor, lieutenant governor, and thirty-three departments and offices responsible for executing the laws of the State of New Mexico. One of these departments, the New Mexico Public Education Department (NMPED), is led by a secretary of education. At least three secretaries of education have served in the current administration under Governor Michelle Lujan Grisham: Arsenio Romero (February 2023–Present), who replaced Ryan Stewart (August 2019–July 2021), who replaced Karen Trujillo (January 2019–August 2019). Under the Lujan Grisham administration, an assistant secretary of Indian education position was unstaffed for the first twenty months. Lashawna Tso filled the seat in October 2020 and departed in June 2022. Eleven months later,

KatieAnn Juanico filled the seat in May 2023. NMPED is responsible for carrying out and implementing the policies directed by the secretary of education, which include the regulatory oversight of eighty-nine school districts across New Mexico.[22] The annual Tribal Education Status Report identifies twenty-three districts and seven charters that serve Native public school entities with approximately 35,300 American Indian students. Approximately 5 percent of the statewide district staff is identified as American Indian.[23] The eighteen-member body of the Indian Education Advisory Council serves to advise the secretary of education on American Indian educational matters. They are nominated to serve by their respective Native Nation, pueblo, tribe, or urban Native community. But the advisory group does struggle to fill a quorum for their meetings, and advisements to the secretary of Indian Education are neglected.

The legislative branch is responsible for creating the laws impacting the state. The New Mexico legislature is split into two chambers: the House of Representatives, composed of seventy members who run for reelection every two years, and the Senate, composed of forty-two members who run for office every four years. All legislators must live in the districts they are elected to represent. The state legislature creates bills in the form of legislation. A bill may begin in either chamber, but to become law, it must be passed by both houses and signed by the governor. In the legislature, there are standing educational committees for both the House of Representatives and the Senate that only work during the legislative session. In New Mexico, the legislative session convenes in January each year for sixty days in odd-numbered years and thirty days in even-numbered years. The Legislative Education Study Committee (LESC) is a permanent interim committee made up of both state representatives and state senators. This committee is crucial in shaping educational laws that may become a resolution, memorial, or bill. Major responsibilities of the LESC are:

1. Following up on legislation passed at the regular session;
2. conducting research and study on memorials passed in the regular session;
3. hearing proposals from the secretary or NMPED;
4. hearing from other state agencies on educational issues;
5. drafting an educational budget for the legislature;

6. drafting education legislation;[24] and

7. hearing from tribal educational stakeholders on educational issues.

These critical duties of the New Mexico state legislature shape and influence American Indian education.

Finally, and most critically, the judicial branch of New Mexico serves to interpret the law. The New Mexico Supreme Court is the highest court in New Mexico. It is the final authority on questions of law and can review decisions of the court of appeals as well as district courts. Although the courts are not directly involved in governing education, they have a powerful impact on the education program through specific cases. In *Public Education in New Mexico*, Mondragón and Stapleton highlight several vital educational cases:

1. *Zeller v. Huff* (1949–1950), which removed nuns from teaching in public schools;

2. *Serna v. Portales Municipal Schools* (1965), which indicated students were not being taught in their home language;

3. *Los Alamos v. Wugalter* (1975), which argued the funding received by the federal government to the school district of Los Alamos National Laboratory should not be included in the Equalization Funding Formula; and

4. *Zuni, Gallup-McKinley, Grants Cibola County School Districts v. State of New Mexico* (2000), which argued that because property in the district included nontaxable tribal land, the school districts were not able to bond the district and provide capital outlay funding for needed and adequate facilities.[25]

The *Yazzie/Martinez v. State of New Mexico* (2018) consolidated educational case is imperative to understand because of the number of years of inadequate educational services provided to Native American students.

Recasting Educational Spaces of Learning

Amid the backdrop of the court case, we recognize the many Indigenous and social movements transforming our understanding of the classroom space as a learning arena.[26] The tension between the state and tribes has triggered tribal leaders, educators, and educational activists to find new terrains for learning as the classroom space has come under suspicion with its overregulation and lack of creativity. Activists have found postcolonial sites of learning and growth, and many times these sites exist in the spaces of the kiva, hogan, teepee, and kitchen table. These moves have also happened historically with the establishment of the Rough Rock Demonstration School, the American Indian Movement (AIM) survival schools like Heart of the Earth (Minnesota), and the Navajo Community College (NCC), now known as Diné College (Tsaile, Arizona). Activists from Standing Rock Sioux Tribe (SRST)—David Archambault, Dr. Robert Roessel, and Roessel's wife, Ruth—and AIM activists have reconceptualized educational spaces beyond the classroom in line with the many social movements happening throughout the country, from Standing Rock to Black Lives Matter. The work of Shield et al. in *Education in Movement Spaces* shows that Native resurgence and Black liberation have configured new domains of education, as families bring their children to protest sites to teach and educate them on the meaning of these actions.[27] We are seeing social movements, tribal councils, and virtual spaces transforming how knowledge and ideas are expressed and celebrated. Meanwhile, in state legislatures—the spaces where state laws are made—conservative legislators are attempting to censor critical race theory (CRT) and the teaching of race in social studies in New Mexico. In the urban domain, Renya Ramirez in *Native Hubs: Culture, Community, and Belonging* discusses how the urban space has transformed our understandings of reservation-based Indigenous identities, leading to the development of urban Indian citizenry.[28] Within spaces of Native education, Leilani Sabzalian shows how educators, Native youth, and families enact their survival against state-approved curricula, which continue to perpetuate colonial acts of erasure, silencing, and marginalization of Native peoples within schools.[29] Although New Mexico has led the United States with the country's first Indian education act, it continues to lag in teaching and fully implementing a comprehensive social studies curriculum that includes the dark history of New Mexico's engagement with Native people. Sabzalian's book examines how she approached educators to unlearn these practices of erasure, silencing, and marginalization,[30] as her work both centralizes the public school classroom space and shows how this environment can act as a place of empowerment. Similar works to Sabzalian's project examine a history book's depiction of the Pilgrims and Wampanoags from a Native boy's perspective, the use of Halloween costumes and Native identity, and a discussion with a teacher on the use of a wax museum as part of their teaching. Generally, these studies reconsider the use of more contemporary Native "Sheroes" and the meanings of Native American Heritage Month.

Native American education decision-making and decolonization must move from the kitchen table to the classroom, from the tribal council chambers to state legislative halls, from the chapterhouses to conference rooms, and finally, from Zoom rooms to social media spaces. We must begin decolonizing the classroom space and recognize that education begins where families, students, and tribal leaders unite and create new understandings and spaces of learning.

Within the arena of state legislative spaces, liberal activist legislators have resisted the pushback against CRT and pushed for the continued expansion of ethnic studies programs. In more substantive acts, the New Mexico state legislature approved Research and Public Service Projects (RPSPs) for several ethnic studies programs, and some legislators have utilized their own junior funding sources to supplement programs such as the Native American Studies Department at the University of New Mexico (UNM). Yet there have been setbacks. In 2020 the RPSP that directly addressed *Yazzie/Martinez* was not renewed by the state legislature. In 2021 the Institute for American Indian Education submitted a new RPSP focusing on the need to increase the number of Native American K-12 teachers. The 2022 RPSP was not considered for funding at all. It should be noted that the RPSP process is highly political and dependent on variables such as the state legislators' knowledge of institutions of higher education (IHE), their limited resources, UNM College priorities, and working relationships between key legislative committees and legislators with entities in IHE.

The moves by the state legislature show there are differing attitudes and strategies to determine the best course of action to resolve the disenfranchisement described in the *Yazzie/Martinez* lawsuit. With the many players seeking to determine the remedy for decades of Native American student disenfranchisement, students, activists, community members, and legislators have all become part of the discussion. This book is intended to clarify the significance of *Yazzie/Martinez* from the perspective of the Yazzie plaintiffs and to show the actions of educational leaders as they work to develop their own programs and responses. It is clear we cannot wait for the courts and the state to make a final decision. As the state struggles for a clear-cut remedy, we can hope that it embraces all the demands from the original Native New Mexicans. But it is up to us to make changes for our future and state as we compete against total erasure of the distinctive histories and contributions of Native Americans to this state.

Organization of the Book

The book is divided into three sections: (1) a discussion of the *Yazzie/Martinez* lawsuit, including background and significance; (2) the response from all three branches of state government, tribes, institutions of higher education, and community members; and (3) considerations of the future, focusing on efforts and actions under way to create a better educational system for Native students in New Mexico.

Our book opens with an interview with Wilhelmina Yazzie, the lead plaintiff of the *Yazzie/Martinez* lawsuit. She begins with her story and experience of advocating for her son Xavier Yazzie, a third grader in New Mexico's Gallup McKinley School District. Wilhelmina shares how her son had been earning straight As but scored below grade level on statewide and national achievement tests. She raised concerns to the school and school board. Her objections and concerns were ignored, which led to her lawsuit against the school district in 2014. Wilhelmina's concerns led to the revelation that her son's experience was a result of a deeper systemic issue impacting American Indian education in New Mexico. Other families joined the lawsuit, and the case was won in 2018. Wilhelmina describes the conditions of the school and the responses by the teachers, the principal, and the school board. She also describes what she envisions for the future of education for Navajo and Native American students in New Mexico.

Part 1 of the book focuses on the case's background and significance. The first chapter, by Preston Sanchez, titled "The Legal Significance and Background of the *Yazzie/Martinez* Lawsuit," is a history of the foundational laws activated in this case and the laws shaping American Indian education in New Mexico, as well as education for low-income and English-language learner (ELL) students. This chapter describes the systematic process whereby these laws have been violated or neglected. The chapter also discusses Judge Singleton's ruling and its significance for American Indian education, the response of NMPED, and the importance of the ruling for the future of Indian education in New Mexico.

The second chapter, by Glenabah Martinez, Carlotta Penny Bird, Terri Flowerday, Lloyd L. Lee, Leola Tsinnajinnie Paquin, Nathaniel Charley, and Wendy S. Greyeyes is titled "Post-Summit Report on the *Yazzie/Martinez* Ruling: Action Report." It discusses a summit organized by the Institute for American Indian Education faculty, which reviewed the impact of the case and the role of the University of New Mexico in preparing future educators and educational leaders in the state. The summit report provides a summary of continued concerns and recommendations.

Chapter 3, "Witness Perspective from a Mother and Academic," by Georgina Badoni, describes the barriers to advocating for educational services in a New Mexico public school system. She describes the experience from the point of view of a mother and academic professional and outlines suggestions on how to navigate the system and ensure agency for Native American children. Badoni hopes NMPED will intentionally commit to serving Native American children but describes how the department's lack of accountability and failure to protect her son's Indigenous identity denied him his fundamental right to a college and career-oriented education.

In chapter 4, "The Significance of the New Mexico Indian Education Act in the *Yazzie/Martinez* Case," Carlotta Penny Bird focuses on research and experiences related to Native American student progress. She discusses important questions that arose in the *Yazzie/Martinez* case surrounding the interpretation of the state's Indian Education Act. The chapter details the Indigenous perspective of education the author and others sought to bring into the discussion at the time and how the process moved forward. She describes how, once the decision was made in favor of the plaintiffs, the state's response moved to continue the inequities through state-sanctioned processes and policies. In this regard, it is essential to understand how the educational system in New Mexico continues to counter tribal sovereignty, despite the fact that perspectives from tribal community members are vital and important to the transformation of education for Native students in New Mexico.

Part 2 of the book begins with chapter 5, "The New Mexico Public

Education Department Response: An Analysis of the 2021 Strategic Plan to Resolve the *Yazzie/Martinez* Case," by Wendy Greyeyes. The chapter high-lights the *Yazzie/Martinez* strategic plan matrix developed by NMPED. The plan references the Tribal Remedy Framework in consultation with New Mex-ico tribal leaders and stakeholders. This response comes after NMPED's effort to dismiss the *Yazzie/Martinez* lawsuit. Analysis includes statements by the current secretary of education, the new assistant secretary of Indian educa-tion, and state government–to–tribal government discussions.

Chapter 6, "Navajo Nation's Response to the *Yazzie/Martinez* Case: Implica-tions for Navajo Nation's Educational Sovereignty," by Alexandra Bray Kinsella, a former Navajo Nation Department of Justice attorney, analyzes the meaning of Navajo educational sovereignty and how it is impacted by New Mexico pub-lic schools operating on and off the Navajo reservation. It discusses past actions by NMPED to close schools and the Navajo Nation's authority over schools that intended to remain open during the COVID-19 pandemic. In addition, the chap-ter analyzes the legal tools available to the Navajo Nation to exercise its author-ity over the education of Navajo students, both on and off the reservation. This includes an analysis of a land lease agreement between the Navajo Nation gov-ernment and the school district. This legal analysis provides the backdrop for the legitimacy of the *Yazzie* case and its legacy for the future of education for Native American students in New Mexico.

In chapter 7, "Narratives and Responses to *Yazzie/Martinez*: Tribal Consul-tation and Community Engagement," Natalie Martinez examines the emerg-ing discourse in response to the court ruling. As lawmakers, school districts, tribal leaders, and educators engage in discussions regarding the NMIEA, associated funding opportunities, and legislative actions, *Yazzie/Martinez* has taken on different meanings in various contexts. Although the court case was successful in highlighting the inequities of New Mexico's public education system, the resulting language used in reference to the court decision has become conflated with a new funding stream and mandates often misunder-stood as an additive measure that can be met without foundational restructur-ing of the very systems that created the inequities and continue to reproduce unequal access and opportunities for the groups identified in the court case. In addition to the analysis of the developing narratives surrounding *Yazzie/ Martinez,* this chapter considers the various responses to the court ruling, legislation, and associated funding currently being designed and implemented in the twenty-three Native American–serving school districts in New Mexico. It looks at the process of tribal consultation and community engagement in how these school districts determine the most appropriate course of action to meet the needs of the students identified in the court case.

Chapter 8, "The Department of Native American Studies at the University of New Mexico: Role and Responsibilities with the *Yazzie/Martinez v. State of New Mexico* Education Ruling," by Lloyd L. Lee, focuses on higher education and its role and responsibility to the *Yazzie* remedy. Since 1970 the Native American Studies (NAS) department at UNM has been a fundamental institution in educating the public about Native American history, Indigenous ways of life, and the pertinent challenges all Native Nations face in the United States. In the last fifteen years, over one hundred and fifty students have earned a bachelor's and/or master's degree from NAS. Since 2020, NAS has been engaged in the development of crucial state legislation to transform the education system in New Mexico. The chapter discusses how NAS at UNM is a significant instrument in fulfilling the *Yazzie v. State of New Mexico* education ruling and transforming the public education system in New Mexico.

Part 3 of the book turns to the future, opening with chapter 9, Glenabah Martinez's "The *Yazzie/Martinez* Ruling: The Politics of Culturally Relevant Curriculum." Martinez provides a discussion of the significance of culturally relevant curriculum in the case presented by the legal team representing the plaintiffs in *Yazzie v. State of New Mexico* and the remedies prescribed by Judge Singleton in the consolidated case of *Yazzie/Martinez v. State of New Mexico*, as well as in subsequent motions. One primary question guides this discussion: What can we learn from the court case about the pedagogical value of culturally relevant curriculum in providing Indigenous youth with a uniform and sufficient education for college and career readiness? The chapter highlights primary sources, with attention to the relevancy of the case in motions filed after 2018.

Chapter 10, "The Complexities of Language Learning for New Mexico's Indigenous Students," by Christine Sims and Rebecca Blum Martínez, highlights the unique needs of Native American students learning English while also facing the challenges of maintaining and learning their Native language. These students encounter unique issues unlike the circumstances of other notionally similar student populations, such as immigrants or speakers of other world languages. The implications for appropriate support of New Mexico Native American students are discussed, with specific recommendations for addressing the court's findings in the *Yazzie/Martinez* case.

Chapter 11, "Diné Language Teacher Institute and Language Immersion Education," by Tiffany S. Lee, Vincent Werito, and Melvatha R. Chee, explores a remedy initiative. Namely, they discuss a project aimed at increasing the number of Diné language immersion teachers through a teacher preparation program at UNM called the Diné Language Teacher Institute (DLTI). The purpose of DLTI is to support the unique needs of Diné communities, revitalizing and sustaining their languages by increasing the number of Diné language teachers. As of the fall 2020 semester, UNM's Language, Literacy, and Sociocultural Studies, Native American Studies, and Navajo Language Program offer eighteen hours of coursework and winter and summer institutes with a specific focus on using language immersion methodologies for Diné language revitalization in community and school-based settings. The activities specifically address Diné language immersion teaching that draws upon the tribal strengths of Diné communities, utilizing Diné-centered, community-based (*k'é*) approaches to language teaching methodologies, pedagogies, and research. This chapter summarizes this collaborative project and the status of Diné language today, particularly as a result of Western schooling practices, followed by a strong justification for language immersion education as a compelling remedy for the *Yazzie* ruling. The chapter concludes with a reflection about the program's current successes, challenges, and aspirations.

In chapter 12, "Lessons from the Past: Fifty Years after *Sinajini v. Board of Education of San Juan School District*," Cynthia Benally and Donna Deyhle examine similar legal arguments and court orders—regarding equitable resource distribution, academic opportunities, and the demand for effective educational practices such as bilingual and cultural education—in Utah's *Sinajini v. Board of Education* compared to *Yazzie/Martinez v. State of New Mexico*. Using the example of the *Sinajini* case, they project the trajectory of Indian education in New Mexico if the *Yazzie/Martinez* mandates are not embraced, supported, and well-funded. In 2018 the judge in the *Yazzie/Martinez v. State of New Mexico* case found that the state failed to prepare Native students for colleges or careers. Almost a half-century earlier, in 1974, *Sinajini v. Board of Education* in Utah alleged deprivation of equal educational opportunities. In that consent decree, the court ordered the construction of schools in the Utah portion of the Navajo Reservation, equality in financing between the primarily white and primarily Native portions of the school district, and provisions for bilingual and bicultural education programs. Within eight years, two high schools were built; however, fifty years later the curriculum and language instruction orders remain unfulfilled. Disconcertingly, since the *Yazzie* decision, the State of New Mexico has failed to pass meaningful legislation or create a plan to meet the court orders, suggesting *Sinajini* may be an unfortunate precedent.

In chapter 13, "Promoting Solidarity for Social Justice and Indigenous Educational Sovereignty in the Cuba Independent School District," Leola Tsinnajinnie Paquin, Vincent Werito, Shiv R. Desai, Nancy López, and Karen Sanchez-Griego use storytelling to weave together race and social justice theory, Indigenous education, policy, pedagogy, solidarity, and community well-being amid the backdrop of the COVID-19 and racial injustice pandemics. Cuba Independent School District, which provides schooling to predominantly Native American students from the surrounding Navajo communities, served as a plaintiff in the *Yazzie/Martinez* lawsuit. In 2019 the district's superintendent Dr. Karen Sanchez-Griego began discussions with Vincent Werito on how the district could take steps to move toward social justice and Indigenous education. By early 2020 Leola Tsinnajinnie Paquin, Shiv R. Desai, and Nancy López joined these discussions. As a team, in partnership with the school district, they created distance student learning modules and implemented two sets of virtual professional development series for educators that took place from March to December 2020, which they describe as possible steps going forward.

In the concluding chapter, "Constructing Critically Conscious Race Policy for Our State: The Case for a Re-racialization and Indigenizing of Our Education Policies," Wendy Greyeyes and former Navajo Nation president Jonathan Nez discuss how the NMIEA requires a retooling of policy to strengthen tribal sovereignty and partnerships between the school board and tribal leaders. It is evident that NMPED adheres fully to the Indian Education Act, but much of this top-level decision-making rarely filters to local education agencies. In their conclusion, Greyeyes and Nez call for racial and Indigenized policies imperative to remedy the *Yazzie/Martinez* case, as targeted state policy is necessary for the success of Indigenous-based curricula and the preservation and strengthening of Indigenous languages.

Conclusion

The purpose of this book is to contextualize the continuing disenfranchisement occurring in American Indian education in New Mexico. The *Yazzie/Martinez* case resulted in one of the largest rulings against any state education agency. The First Judicial District Court ruled the State of New Mexico's Public Education Department and secretary of education failed to provide Native American students with a college- and career-ready education. Judge Singleton stated in her ruling that "lack of funds is no excuse" for not providing equitable services and programs for "all at-risk students." Her ruling is a clear signal to NMPED, the secretary of education, and the state that they are responsible for "providing an adequate, sufficient education to at-risk students i.e., socio-economically disadvantaged children, English learners, Native American students, and children with disabilities."

The contributors to this book cover the background and significance of the lawsuit and racial and social politics; provide an overview of the Native American educational system; offer a policy analysis of the NMIEA; discuss comparable cases in Utah and Arizona; analyze the financial cost to recoup a sustainable education system for students; share testimonials from the experiences of expert witnesses; and delve into institutional implications from higher education, K-12 schools, tribal education departments, and students. Finally, this book constructs a new vision and calls for transformational change to resolve the systemic challenges plaguing Native American students in New Mexico's public education system.

Notes

1. Lewis Meriam, *The Problem of Indian Administration* (Washington, DC: Institute for Government Research), 1928.
2. Jon Reyhner and Jeanne Eder, *American Indian Education: A History* (Norman: University of Oklahoma Press, 2004), 11.
3. Reyhner and Eder, *American Indian Education*, 12.
4. Sandy Grande, *Red Pedagogy: Native American Social and Political Thought* (Lanham, MD: Rowman and Littlefield, 2015), 23.
5. Grande, *Red Pedagogy*, 16.
6. Grande, *Red Pedagogy*, 23.

7. Vine Deloria Jr., *Indian Education in America* (n.p.: American Indian Science and Engineering Society, 1991).

8. Deloria, *Indian Education in America*, 10.

9. Vine Deloria Jr. and Daniel Wildcat, eds., *Power and Place: Indian Education in America* (Golden, CO: Fulcrum Resources, 2001).

10. Brenda J. Child, *Boarding School Seasons: American Indian Families 1900–1940* (Lincoln: University of Nebraska Press, 2000); Child, "Homesickness," in *Boarding School Seasons: American Indian Families 1900–1940* (Lincoln: University of Nebraska Press, 1998), 43–54; David Wallace Adams, *Education for Extinction: American Indians and the Boarding School Experience 1875–1928* (Lawrence: University Press of Kansas, 1995); Francis Paul Prucha, *The Churches and the Indian Schools, 1888–1912* (Lincoln: University of Nebraska Press, 1979).

11. Delores J. Huff, *To Live Heroically: Institutional Racism and American Indian Education* (Albany: State University of New York Press, 1997); Theresa McCarty, *A Place to Be Navajo: Rough Rock and the Struggle for Self-Determination in Indigenous Schooling* (Mahwah, NJ: Lawrence Erlbaum Associates, 2002); Robert A. Roessel Jr., *Indian Communities in Action* (Tempe: Arizona State University, 1967); Roessel Jr., *Navajo Education, 1948–1978: Its Progress and Its Problems* (Rough Rock, AZ: Navajo Curriculum Center, 1979); Roessel Jr., "An Overview of the Rough Rock Demonstration Schools," *Journal of American Indian Education* 7, no. 3 (May 1968): 2–14; Malia Villegas, Sabina Rak Neugebauer, and Kerry R. Venegas, *Indigenous Knowledge and Education: Sites of Struggle, Strength, and Survivance* (Cambridge, MA: Harvard Educational Review, 2008); Glenabah Martinez, *Native Pride: Politics of Curriculum and Instruction in an Urban High School* (Cresskill, NJ: Hampton Press, 2010); Marie Battiste, *Decolonizing Education: Nourishing the Learning Spirit* (Saskatoon, SK: Purich Publishing, 2013); Dorothy Aguilera-Black Bear and John W. Tippeconnic III, eds., *Voices of Renewal: Indigenous Leadership in Education* (Norman: University of Oklahoma Press, 2015); Matthew L. M. Fletcher, *American Indian Education: Counternarratives in Racism, Struggle, and the Law* (New York: Routledge, 2008).

12. Grande, *Red Pedagogy*.

13. John P. Hopkins, *Indian Education for All: Decolonizing Indigenous Education in Public Schools* (New York: Teachers College Press, 2020); Wendy S. Greyeyes, *A History of Navajo Nation Education: Disentangling Our Sovereign Body* (Tucson: University of Arizona Press, 2022).

14. Teresa L. McCarty and Tiffany S. Lee, "Critical Culturally Sustaining/Revitalizing Pedagogy and Indigenous Education Sovereignty," *Harvard Educational Review* 84, no. 1 (Spring 2014): 101–24; Jeremy Garcia, "Critical and Culturally Sustaining Indigenous Family and Community Engagement in Education," in *The Wiley Handbook of Family, School, and Community Relationships in Education*, ed. Steven B. Sheldon and Tammy A. Turner-Vorbeck, (Hoboken, NJ: Wiley-Blackwell, 2019), 71–90; Matthew Sakiestewa Gilbert, *Education beyond the Mesas: Hopi Students at Sherman Institute, 1902–1929* (Lincoln: University of Nebraska Press, 2010); Leilani Sabzalian, *Indigenous Children's Survival in Public Schools* (New York: Routledge, 2019).

15.   Alayna Eagle Shield, Django Paris, Rae Paris, and Timothy San Pedro, eds., *Education in Movement Spaces: Standing Rock to Chicago Freedom Square*, Indigenous and Decolonizing Studies in Education (New York: Routledge, 2020).

16.   Pedro Vallejo and Vincent Werito, *Transforming Diné Education: Innovations in Pedagogy and Practice* (Tucson: University of Arizona Press, 2022).

17.   National Congress of American Indians, *Becoming Visible: A Landscape Analysis of State Efforts to Provide Native American Education for All*, Washington, DC, September 2019, https://www.ncai.org/policy-research-center/research-data/prc-publications/NCAI-Becoming_Visible_Report-Digital_FINAL_10_2019.pdf.

18.   AB-1554 American Indian education, 2021–22 Regular Session, California Legislature, https://leginfo.legislature.ca.gov/faces/billNavClient.xhtml?bill_id=202120220AB1554; "The California Indian Education Act Pushes for an Expanded K-12 Social Studies Curriculum," December 14, 2021, https://lacomadre.org/2021/12/the-california-indian-education-act-pushes-for-an-expanded-k-12-social-studies-curriculum/.

19.   National Congress of American Indians, *Becoming Visible*, 19.

20.   Robin Zape-tah-hol-ah Minthorn, Lorenda Belone, Glenabah Martinez, and Christine Sims, "Indigenous Research Perspectives in the State of New Mexico: Implications for Working with Schools and Communities," *Journal of American Indian Education* 58, nos. 1–2 (Spring–Summer 2019): 108–23.

21.   Minthorn et al., "Indigenous Research Perspectives," 112.

22.   John B. Mondragón and Ernest S. Stapleton, *Public Education in New Mexico* (Albuquerque: University of New Mexico Press, 2005), 45.

23.   NMPED, *Tribal Education Status Report (TESR) 2019–2020*, https://webnew.ped.state.nm.us/wp-content/uploads/2021/01/TESR2020.pdf.

24.   Mondragón and Stapleton, *Public Education in New Mexico*, 35.

25.   Mondragón and Stapleton, *Public Education in New Mexico*, 37–38.

26.   The social movements we discuss argue for the removal of racist statues of Christopher Columbus (who led the genocide of Indigenous peoples), Robert E. Lee (a Confederate general who forced his slaves to fight against the emancipation of Black slaves), George Preston Marshall, Henry Benning (a slave owner), and so forth. We also refer to the movement against the Dakota Access Pipeline (NoDAPL) in Standing Rock, South Dakota, the demand to support Missing and Murdered Indigenous Women and Men (MMIWM), and the fight for justice in the wake of George Floyd's murder in 2020.

27.   Shield et al., *Education in Movement Spaces*.

28.   Renya K. Ramirez, *Native Hubs: Culture, Community, and Belonging in Silicon Valley and Beyond* (Durham, NC: Duke University Press, 2007).

29.   Sabzalian, *Indigenous Children's Survivance in Public Schools*.

30.   Sabzalian, *Indigenous Children's Survivance in Public Schools*, 3.

Part I | The Case

Figure 2. Preston Sanchez (Jemez Pueblo, Laguna Pueblo, and Diné) served as the co-lead counsel for *Yazzie v. State of New Mexico*. Photo credit Hondo Louis. Funded by UNM's Center for Regional Studies and Native American Studies Department.

CHAPTER ONE

The Legal Significance and Background of the *Yazzie/Martinez* Lawsuit

PRESTON SANCHEZ

Introduction

In 2018 the landmark *Yazzie/Martinez* decision proved that many years of poor policy implementation, piecemeal reform, and inadequate funding for public education effectively denied New Mexico children an opportunity to succeed in school. New Mexico, in fact, remains at the bottom of the "Kids Count Report," a national ranking of public school systems among the fifty states.[1] At the core of problems identified in *Yazzie/Martinez* is the systematic neglect of New Mexico's "at-risk" student population—that is, poor, English-learner (EL), disabled, and Indigenous students.

The first part of this chapter explores the general issues and findings key to the *Yazzie/Martinez* ruling, including:

1. New Mexico's constitutional duty to maintain a "sufficient education" system;
2. the view that adequate educational opportunities require adequate funding;
3. an overview of school adequacy litigation;
4. New Mexico standards for a sufficient education; and
5. the court's *sufficiency* findings and analysis.

The second part explores *Yazzie v. State of New Mexico* and the specific issues and findings that pertain to New Mexico's Indigenous students, including:

1. the basis of the *Yazzie* lawsuit;
2. an understanding of Indigenous students' unique cultural and linguistic needs; and
3. the significance of New Mexico's Indian Education Act.

Yazzie/Martinez v. State of New Mexico: Enforcing the Education Clause of the New Mexico Constitution

In 2014 the *Yazzie* plaintiffs sued the New Mexico legislature and the New Mexico Public Education Department (NMPED), naming former NMPED secretary Hanna Skandera, on the basis that underfunded schools had denied most children their right to a *sufficient* education, a requirement under article 12, section 1 of New Mexico's constitution.[2] In 2015 Honorable Judge Sarah Singleton of New Mexico's First Judicial District Court consolidated the *Yazzie* plaintiffs' lawsuit with *Martinez v. State of New Mexico*, a similar case brought by the Mexican American Legal Defense and Educational Fund (MALDEF) on behalf of a family of plaintiffs against the same defendants. On June 12, 2017, the consolidated *Yazzie/Martinez* case began a two-month trial, with over one hundred witness testimonies and thousands of documents entered into evidence.

On July 20, 2018, Judge Singleton ruled New Mexico's public school system unconstitutional, finding that it denied "at-risk" students—that is, Indigenous, EL, disabled, and low-income students—their right to a *sufficient* education.[3] A *sufficient* education under New Mexico's constitution, the court held, is one that provides "every student with the *opportunity* to obtain an education that allows them to become prepared for career or college."[4] The court ordered the state "to take immediate steps" to fix the problem.[5] Importantly, the court's ruling made clear: "A *sufficient* education is a right protected by the New Mexico Constitution. As such, it is entitled to priority funding."[6]

NEW MEXICO'S CONSTITUTIONAL DUTY TO MAINTAIN
A SUFFICIENT EDUCATION SYSTEM

Every state has a constitution. Every state constitution but one contains a clause or set of clauses that impose(s) a duty upon state governments to create and maintain a public school system.[7] The New Mexico constitution's education clause states, "A uniform system of free public schools, *sufficient* for the education of all school aged children shall be established and maintained."[8] This constitutional duty belongs to New Mexico's legislative and executive branches, while the duty to interpret the education clause and determine if the state has met its constitutional obligation belongs to the judiciary.[9]

In New Mexico the state legislature must enact laws and determine budget levels for government functions, including public schools.[10] Likewise, NMPED—an executive agency overseen by the state governor—must propose policies, enforce education laws, authorize public school budgets, and determine whether public schools have sufficient funds to operate.[11] Together, these two "State Defendants" are responsible for appropriating money to individual school districts through the State Equalization Guarantee (SEG)—a complex "funding formula" used to calculate operational funding for public schools—and enacting laws that together form the public school system.[12]

State courts must determine—or, in some cases, refuse to hear—whether state governmental duties (particularly funding levels) adequately provide all students with an education that satisfies the state constitution.[13] In doing so, state courts must analyze, in part, whether public education provides students an educational opportunity that keeps up with the ever-changing demands of society.[14] Population movements, changing market and global demands, and historical and political changes, for example, require that students be prepared adequately for shifting societal trends. In *Brown v. Board of Education of Topeka*, 347 US 483 (1954), arguably the most recognizable civil rights case in US history, the US Supreme Court ended public school segregation in a decision that validated educational opportunity as a basic right and essential function to society:

> Today, education is perhaps the most important function of state and local governments. Compulsory school attendance laws and the great

expenditures for education both demonstrate our recognition of the importance of education to our democratic society. It is required in the performance of our most basic public responsibilities, even service in the armed
forces. It is the very foundation of good citizenship. Today it is a principal
instrument in awakening the child to cultural values, in preparing him for
later professional training, and in helping him to adjust normally to his
environment. In these days, it is doubtful that any child may reasonably
be expected to succeed in life if he is denied the *opportunity of an education.* Such an opportunity, where the state has undertaken to provide it, is a
right which must be made available to all on equal terms.[15]

Since then, many state courts throughout the nation have determined
similarly that educational opportunity is both a basic right and an essential
function for maintaining the best economic and political interests of the
state.[16] Washington's supreme court, for example, held that:

[The] State's constitutional duty to provide an "education" goes beyond
mere reading, writing and arithmetic. It also embraces broad educational
opportunities needed in the contemporary setting to equip our children
for their role as citizens and as potential competitors in today's market as
well as in the marketplace of ideas. Education plays a critical role in a free
society. It must prepare our children to participate intelligently and effectively in our open political system to ensure that system's survival. It must
prepare them to exercise their First Amendment freedoms both as sources
and receivers of information.[17]

Similarly, the Massachusetts Supreme Court recognized that "[under] our
republican government, it seems clear that the minimum of this education can
never be less than such as is sufficient to qualify each citizen for the civil and
social duties he will be called to discharge, including . . . the civil functions of
a witness or a juror; as is necessary for the voter in municipal and in national
affairs." It further opined that "our Constitution, and its education clause, must
be interpreted 'in accordance with the demands of modern society or it will
be in constant danger of becoming atrophied and, in fact, may even lose its
original meaning.'"[18]

In *Yazzie/Martinez* the court found that "education is critical for economic and social mobility in the United States, especially for groups that have limited generational mobility or limited resources." Educational opportunity is "even more pressing for students from first-generation, low-income, English Learner status, and diverse backgrounds to have access to educational resources, in an effort to offset the generational poverty that persists among the working poor [. . .] and specifically within Hispanic and Native American communities." A constitutionally adequate education, the court found, must provide high school graduates with the opportunity to acquire the "necessary knowledge and skills to participate in a rapidly-changing, democratic society by successfully transitioning to a postsecondary institution (without needing remedial coursework) and/or entering the workforce and competing in the labor market."[19]

ADEQUATE EDUCATIONAL OPPORTUNITY REQUIRES ADEQUATE FUNDING

Like *Yazzie/Martinez*, many school adequacy (also generally referred to as "education adequacy") cases are premised on the theory that inadequate school funding correlates with inadequate educational opportunity for students to achieve state-mandated standards. The court held, for example, that "at-risk students are the school children whose lives [. . .] are directly affected by New Mexico's education system and its funding decisions" and that the "the overall [public school] appropriation is insufficient to fund the programs necessary to provide [. . .] all at-risk students [. . .] an adequate education."[20] Many state courts nationwide, in fact, have found that public education systems cannot faithfully function to achieve their constitutional obligation without reliable and adequate funding sources.[21]

In short, the better schools are financed, the better students' chances are at educational success.[22] Case in point: it is common for affluent families to invest tens of thousands of dollars on private school education for their children, which in turn guarantees many essential ingredients for student success, such as smaller student-teacher ratios, high academic expectations, take-home textbooks, time for on-task learning, and rigorous curricula. The reasoning for adequate public school funding is no different.

Importantly, the greater the concentration of high-needs (i.e., "at-risk") students, the greater the funding need for programs and services that correspond to their comprehensive educational needs. For example, the court found that "effective programs for English Learner (EL) students must have qualified [EL] teachers—meaning bilingual-certified or an endorsement in Teaching English to Speakers of Other Languages (TESOL)." However, New Mexico schools, serving one of the largest percentages of English Learners nationally, suffer from a shortage of qualified EL teachers.[23] The reason, in part, is that school districts across the state lack adequate funding to recruit, hire, and retain enough EL educators to meet EL student needs.[24] In addition, state law requires EL educators to receive ongoing training and professional development—another expense that schools struggle to afford.[25] Yet, without qualified EL instructors in the classroom, both academic proficiency and English language proficiency among EL students have suffered dramatically.[26]

When schools lack adequate funding for basic resources to meet student need, high-needs students suffer the greatest harm. Indeed, money matters. Schools serving high-need students require greater funding. Thus, the amount of state funding allocated to public schools—and whether it is sufficient to give high-need students an opportunity at educational success—is a primary focus of school adequacy litigation.

SCHOOL ADEQUACY LITIGATION

Wielding the inherent power of New Mexico's constitution, both the Yazzie and Martinez plaintiffs challenged whether "public education," including the "funding formula and the implementation of programs to meet statutory mandates which are designed to achieve the constitutional requirement," were constitutionally *sufficient.*[27]

Yazzie/Martinez is not alone in the realm of school adequacy litigation. For many decades now, plaintiff parties around the nation have sued their state governments for violating their state constitution's education clause, arguing that underfunded schools deprive public school students of the basic resources necessary for an adequate education. Essential to many school adequacy cases is evidence of inadequate state funding for basic resources and, generally, a showing that underfunded schools correlate with glaring academic failure among high-need students.[28]

In many cases, state courts will develop or adopt a legal standard to measure overall "inputs"—teacher quality, curriculum, programs, services, etc.—against overall "outputs"—test scores, graduation rates, college enrollment, etc. Generally referred to as the "input to output ratio," a strong showing of evidence may lead courts, such as the *Yazzie/Martinez* court, to "presume that inadequate inputs caused the inadequate outputs."[29]

In *Rose v. Council for Better Education*, Kentucky's landmark case, the state supreme court ruled public schools "constitutionally deficient."[30] The court defined an "efficient system of common schools" as written in the Kentucky constitution's education clause to mean that public schools must afford all students an opportunity to develop and demonstrate the following seven capacities:

(i) oral and written communication skills [. . .]; (ii) [. . .] knowledge of economic, social, and political systems to enable the student to make informed choices; (iii) [. . .] understanding of governmental processes to enable the student to understand the issues that affect his or her community, state, and nation; (iv) [. . .] self-knowledge and knowledge of his or her mental and physical wellness; (v) [. . .] grounding in the arts to enable each student to appreciate his or her cultural and historical heritage; (vi) [. . .] training or preparation for advanced training in either academic or vocational fields [. . .]; and (vii) [. . .] levels of academic or vocational skills to enable public school students to compete favorably with their counterparts in surrounding states, in academics or in the job market. [31]

Evidence of inputs to outputs measured under the "*Rose* standard" showed that "students in property poor districts receive inadequate and inferior educational opportunities as compared to those offered to students in the more affluent districts [. . .] and [a] substantial difference in the curricula offered in the poorer districts contrasts with that of the richer districts, particularly in the areas of foreign language, science, mathematics, music, and art." Achievement test scores in the poorer districts were "lower than those in the richer districts and expert opinion clearly established that there is a correlation between those scores and the wealth of the district." In fact, "only 68.2 percent of ninth grade students eventually [would] graduate from high school." Also, "student-teacher ratios [were] higher in the poorer districts."[32]

Many state courts have developed or adopted an adequacy standard identical or similar to that of *Rose*, including Massachusetts, Kansas, North Carolina, Washington, Texas, and South Dakota.[33] In each case, the standard is tethered to the state's constitutional duty to provide students with an adequate educational opportunity.

NEW MEXICO STANDARDS FOR A SUFFICIENT EDUCATION

Notably, the *Rose* standard focuses largely on the demonstration of traditional academic skills—reading, math, and writing—that understandably are essential student-outcome measures used by most public schools nationwide. However, while increased funding for programs and services is important for improving outcomes among high-needs students, a typical response for doing so is often academic remediation. Little attention, if any, is paid to students' linguistic and cultural needs. In fact, history shows that educational systems have treated students' cultural and linguistic heritage as shortcomings. The infamous 1800s notion of "kill the Indian, save the man," for example, is a firm reminder that school systems intentionally desecrated traditional Indigenous identity in favor of Americanized values.[34]

Unlike other school adequacy cases, the *Yazzie/Martinez* ruling focuses emphatically on New Mexico students' unique cultural and linguistic needs. At trial, the court heard persuasive testimony by local experts and witnesses that education systems that build upon students' cultural and linguistic aptitudes actually improve self-confidence and inclusion—and therefore learning—in the classroom, especially among culturally diverse students.[35] The court's decision also cites crucial state education laws as legal authority that recognize multicultural student needs, including the following statute: "*The key to student success in New Mexico* is to have a multicultural education system that [. . .] [*sic*] attracts and retains quality and diverse teachers to teach New Mexico's multicultural student population; integrates the cultural strengths of its diverse student population into the curriculum [. . .]; [and] recognizes that cultural diversity in the state presents special challenges for policymakers, administrators, teachers and students."[36] Vital to the court's adequacy analysis was determining whether state defendants had met their duties to comply with the laws that support multicultural student needs.

For the above reasons, the court boldly rejected the mainstream *Rose* standard as "inappropriate" and developed one that better reflects New Mexico's multicultural identity. In doing so, the court paid great deference to New Mexico laws, finding that "the legislature has already adopted statutory provisions which appropriately define adequacy for purposes of this litigation."[37] Unlike *Rose*, the court's adequacy standard in *Yazzie/Martinez* is fundamentally built on the laws that require education to be responsive to students' multicultural and multilingual identities, as well as on legislation pertaining to the needs of low-income, English learners, and disabled students.[38] In effect, the court used its newly developed standard to measure inputs to outputs and, ultimately, to determine "whether the State, primarily through the New Mexico Public Education Department (NMPED), [had] met its [constitutional] obligation."[39]

Several of the significant education laws integrated into the court's adequacy standard include New Mexico's Indian Education Act (NMIEA), the Hispanic Education Act (HEA), and the Bilingual Multicultural Education Act (BMEA). These laws were meant to build on students' cultural and linguistic aptitudes through "equitable and culturally relevant learning environments, educational opportunities and culturally relevant instructional materials."[40] They also impose specific legal duties upon state defendants, including duties to provide schools grant funding, furnish technical assistance and support, collect student data, and monitor program effectiveness.[41]

THE COURT'S "SUFFICIENCY" FINDINGS AND ANALYSIS

At trial, in 2017, more than one hundred testifying witnesses, including academic and financial experts, offered their observations and analyses regarding the root causes of failing outcomes trending in New Mexico schools. In over six hundred pages of fact findings, the court attributed "dismal" student outcomes to the state's glaring failure to ensure that schools overall have enough resources necessary to provide "at-risk" students a *sufficient* education.[42]

Ultimately, Judge Singleton rejected the state defendants' theory that incompetent school leadership, excess poverty, family dysfunction, bad teachers, and disengaged students were to blame.[43] Rather, years of inadequate state funding for basic resources, court findings show, meant that provided resources were nowhere near enough to offset challenging student needs.[44]

In fact, thousands of *Yazzie/Martinez* findings reveal the in- and out-of-school needs of New Mexico's Indigenous, disabled, EL, and low-income student populations. For example, these "at-risk students," the court found, "begin school with certain disadvantages that are not the making of the school system. These disadvantages may include poor nutrition, lower parental resources and involvement, challenging home environments, high mobility rates, and fewer out-of-school educational opportunities."[45] Importantly, the court found that many New Mexico students have unique cultural and linguistic needs that go unmet throughout their entire K-12 education.

In New Mexico, one of only six majority-minority states in the nation—with Latinx and Native American students comprising 50 percent and 11 percent of all students statewide, respectively—a significant need among many students is the melding of traditional academic learning with students' cultural and linguistic aptitudes.[46] For instance, several New Mexico studies, reports, and articles attribute the core barriers for educating Native students to a "lack of culturally and linguistically academic programming" and "difficulties [. . .] developing academic programming that matches Native learning styles and needs."[47]

Ongoing efforts by the state to transform public schooling in a way that meets multicultural students' needs, however, have proved insufficient. The *Yazzie/Martinez* findings show that New Mexico textbooks "continue to marginalize Native Americans and Hispanics." In social studies, for example, "the economic, political and historical contributions made by Indigenous peoples to New Mexico [and United States] history are absent or minimal," resulting in "students developing a limited perception about the role that Native Americans play in State and Federal government."[48] The court found that the exclusion of Indigenous views, values, and history from the curriculum not only violates state law but also creates a distrust and disconnect felt by many Native students toward public schooling today.[49]

Under the NMIEA and BME statutes, NMPED must "ensure equitable and culturally relevant learning environments, educational opportunities and culturally relevant instructional materials for American Indian students enrolled in public schools."[50] Both laws, in fact, impose administrative duties on NMPED's Indian Education Division (IED) and Language and Culture Bureau (LCB)—the two NMPED agencies responsible for NMIEA and BMEA enforcement—to ensure school district compliance.[51] However, the failure by NMPED to deliberately administer both laws communicates to school districts that compliance is optional.

Indeed, there is no shortage of court findings proving the state's utter failure to meet NMIEA and BMEA requirements over many years; most apparent are its failure to consistently provide school districts with (1) technical assistance and support and (2) adequate funding to implement both laws in their entirety.[52] Most districts can count on one hand the number of times they received visits or communication from NMPED.[53] From a big-picture perspective, NMPED lacks adequate capacity and expertise to provide programmatic assistance and statutory support to schools serving Native and EL students.[54] IED staff, for instance, suffer from "ongoing vacancies" and constant leadership turnover, while the LCB "has never evaluated whether the funding that school districts receive is enough to implement effective programs for ELLs."[55]

Moreover, court findings also show that out-of-school challenges undermining educational *sufficiency* are more frequent in New Mexico's rural areas, where most Indigenous students live.[56] Unpaved roads, for example, make it difficult during the winter season to transport students to and from school, "which directly impacts student attendance." Even worse, without reliable transportation or at-home Internet, students miss out on early childhood, after-school, and extended learning opportunities. An additional challenge to rural districts is the cost to maintain or replace worn-out school buses when annual state transportation funds are woefully inadequate.[57]

Despite the many unmet in- and out-of-school needs that impair educational opportunity for most New Mexico students, NMPED officials and state lawmakers do not dispute that (1) "children from low-income families *can* and do learn and achieve at high levels if given the proper support and intervention"; (2) "ELL students *can* perform at the same level as non-ELL students with the proper training, instruction, and background"; and (3) "all New Mexico students, including [. . .] Hispanic students, Native American students, and students with disabilities *can* learn at high levels" if given "quality programs and interventions."[58] Indeed, the *Yazzie/Martinez* ruling is a reminder that "no education system can be sufficient for the education of all children unless it is founded on the sound principle that every child can learn and succeed."[59]

The court identified many basic resources necessary to address the unmet needs for "at-risk" students in New Mexico. For example:

- ◆ **Multicultural Education.** "Providing a multicultural and bilingual education to preschoolers is an important part of preparing a child to be successful." One aspect of multicultural education is "culturally responsive pedagogy." This involves both recognition of the different cultural skills, strengths, and capacities and close relationships between teachers and students. However, multicultural education "requires structured and sustainable learning environments and opportunities for students, a framework rather than just temporary experiences." New Mexico currently lacks a "multicultural education framework."[60]
  Early Childhood Education. "Prekindergarten provides economically disadvantaged, ELL students, and students of color with educational opportunities that enhance cognitive and social development and enable these children to start kindergarten ready to learn." However, about "one-third of all four-year-olds statewide lacked access to *any* PreK program."[61]
- ◆ **High Quality and Diverse Teachers.** "Highly effective teachers are key to improving proficiency . . . [They] need to be allocated to schools serving the most at-risk students." Equally important is "teacher diversity for students from historically underrepresented backgrounds because they can serve as role models for students, often living in the same community and having a shared cultural experience." However, "schools with high rates of student poverty or other education needs have persistent, serious difficulty recruiting and retaining qualified, skilled [and diverse] teachers."[62]
- ◆ **Literacy Programs.** Only one in four New Mexico children read at grade level by third grade. "It is critical that children be proficient readers by the end of third grade in order to be successful for fourth grade and beyond." To that end, "[evidence-based] literacy programs and

practices [. . .] are essential to ensure that low-income students learn
how to read at grade level."[63]

+ **Smaller Class Sizes.** "Students, [including ELs], who [struggle] academically or socially benefit from smaller class sizes—which are associated with higher achievement, higher earnings, higher high school
graduation rates, and higher college completion rates—because they
get more differentiated instruction from their teachers." Due to school
district class-size waivers, however, "class sizes are 7–10 percent larger,
and students get less individualized attention from teachers."[64]

+ **Language Acquisition Programs.** EL needs include "qualified bilingual-certified or TESOL-endorsed teachers" and "a program to assist
[them] in acquiring English proficiency and to allow [them] to participate comparably with other students in the core curriculum within a
reasonable time period."[65]

+ **Summer and After-School Programs.** Summer school addresses "student performance by providing opportunities for elementary students
to be exposed to both academic and other enrichment activities in
order to be prepared for the next school year, keeping them on track
for graduation." It "can also reduce summer learning loss and close the
achievement gap for at-risk students in the early grades."[66]

Yazzie/Martinez v. State of New Mexico—Ensuring a Sufficient Education for New Mexico's Indigenous Children

If any lesson can be drawn from the boarding school era, it is that education
undeniably shapes student identity. Whose identity and how it is being shaped
by public education, however, is an underlying issue explored by the *Yazzie/
Martinez* ruling.

In most school adequacy cases, courts have generally considered whether
public education is effectively shaping students academically for future college and career prospects and instilling them with mainstream, democratic
values. However, from Judge Singleton's viewpoint, the tribal home experience for most Native students "is left at the doorstep of the school."[67] New
Mexico textbooks, for example, provide copious examples of Western/

European history while the Indigenous narrative is mostly ignored.[68] Even worse, schools still lack an Indigenous curriculum to integrate into social studies, history, and other core subjects, despite NMIEA requirements and NMPED's repeated promises to create one.[69] For many Indigenous communities, public education in New Mexico cannot be sufficient if schooling is not responsive to Indigenous values, views, language, culture, and identity.

THE BASIS FOR THE YAZZIE LAWSUIT:

According to Wilhelmina Yazzie, the *Yazzie* plaintiffs' lead witness, Gallup-McKinley County Schools ("Gallup Schools") could not provide her son Xavier with the basic skills and tools he needed to transition seamlessly from middle to high school. When the *Yazzie* case was filed, he had little to no access to advanced classes, bilingual courses, or after-school programs, and his classrooms lacked basic supplies, computers, and textbooks.[70] Most troubling, the state's mandated curriculum neglected Xavier's Navajo (Diné) culture, language, and history—a current reality for most Indigenous students statewide.

New Mexico is home to nineteen Indian pueblos, the Jicarilla Apache Nation, Mescalero Apache Tribe, Fort Sill Apache Tribe (recognized in 2014), and the Navajo Nation—the largest federally recognized tribe. Each of the twenty-three sovereign nations maintains a complex system of traditional culture, language, leadership, and governance.[71] In New Mexico, Native people—from both the tribal and urban communities, including a fraction from other states—comprise about 11 percent of both the total state and public school populations.[72]

Like Xavier, a majority of New Mexico's thirty-four thousand Indigenous students attend school in one of twenty-three public school districts, out of eighty-nine total.[73] Mostly located on or near tribal lands, these "Indian Education" districts—an NMPED term to describe schools that serve significant numbers of Indigenous students—receive some federal funding supports, including Impact Aid and Johnson O'Malley funds, to help offset several social inequities affecting students in comparable environments. Gallup and Cuba Schools—two of six *Yazzie* school district plaintiffs—struggle with rural-specific conditions, including depleted road infrastructure and scarce Internet access.[74]

Moreover, "dismal" academic outcomes across the state affect most Indigenous students. From 2007 to 2016, between 62.4 percent and 71.1 percent of Native American fourth graders were not proficient in reading and 66.5 percent to 74.8 percent were not proficient in math.[75] Similarly, 51.7 percent to 69.4 percent of all Native eleventh-grade students were nonproficient in reading, and 67 percent to 74.9 percent were nonproficient in math.[76] In 2015—when the Partnership for Assessment of Readiness for College and Career exam (PARCC) was introduced—86.5 percent and 89 percent of Native American fourth graders were nonproficient in both reading and math, respectively, while math and reading scores among eighth and eleventh graders fared no better.[77] From a narrower view, student outcomes in both Gallup Schools (serving the most Native American students statewide, approximately nine thousand) and Zuni Schools (serving the highest percentage, approximately 99 percent) have often fallen below the state average.[78] It is no surprise then that about 50 percent of all Indigenous students who attend New Mexico colleges must enroll in remedial, noncredited courses.[79]

Even worse are outcomes among New Mexico's Native American English Learners (NAEL). During the trial, NMPED data showed that "less than 2 percent of ELs" in five Indian Education districts scored at "grade-level" on state mandated exams, while 0 percent demonstrated English language full proficiency on state assessments.[80]

Numerous factors play into these terrible outcomes. For instance, court findings show that teachers new to the Indian Education districts are often "unfamiliar with the Native American populations" and "experience difficulty adapting to the isolated community and finding housing."[81] The result is a revolving pattern: teachers come and go in one or two years, while vacancies go unfilled. For example, losing teachers "during the middle of the school year" forced Cuba Schools, serving mostly Navajo students, to rely on "long-term substitutes."[82]

For the Gallup district, scarce state funding proved disastrous for its thirty-four schools and 11,300 students (80 percent Native American). Facing tough decisions when funds for reading specialists, tutors, and professional training ran dry, Gallup Schools sacrificed several high school elective courses in order to pay for three reading coaches to improve literacy in over half its schools.[83] Further, it made no difference that Gallup Schools had only enough funds to offer either summer school or after-school programming, because scant transportation funds limited the participation of students residing remotely in the Navajo Nation.[84]

Grants, Zuni, and Magdalena Schools all struggle similarly to afford the necessary programs and services corresponding to Native student needs. In Grants Schools, for example, mostly "Native American children who live on the reservation" are deprived of access to after-school tutoring due to unreliable transportation. Zuni's elementary schools offered zero academic-based, after-school programs. And, sadly, Magdalena Schools had only one counselor and a part-time social worker to help the many students who experience "domestic abuse, neglect, [and] homelessness."[85]

For most Indian Education districts, inadequate state funding for early childhood programs limits participation among Native children despite a growing need. Grants Schools, for example, received only enough state funds to expand existing pre-K programs, but not enough to offer one in the area where most Native children reside.[86] Also, a common need among New Mexico's working families is a "full-day" early childhood program for their preschool-aged children; half-day programs require parents to pay out of pocket for additional childcare.[87] It makes no fiscal sense, however, for districts to operate a state-funded "full-day PreK program" when the state allocation is not enough to fully cover reliable transportation, facility space, and qualified staff for all eligible children district-wide.[88]

Underfunded schools are just one of several problems undermining educational sufficiency for New Mexico's NAEL students. For many NAELs, their use of English does not always comport with the "academic" English required in schools.[89] When educators fail to recognize that a linguistic challenge is not synonymous to a reading/cognitive challenge, NAELs often—and mistakenly—are given remedial instruction designed to help struggling readers, resulting in their stunted academic growth.[90] In a survey of six Indian Education districts with high numbers of NAELs, for instance, NAEL students were given remedial reading programs rather than intensive language supports; in each case, staff failed to know the difference.[91] Because "many [NAEL] students have not been exposed to the English language," court findings show that New Mexico's Indigenous students lacking EL teachers qualified to meet their unique linguistic needs are often misidentified as needing special education programming.[92]

UNDERSTANDING INDIGENOUS STUDENTS' UNIQUE CULTURAL AND
LINGUISTIC NEEDS

The *Yazzie* plaintiffs' Indian education experts bridged every aspect of K-12 education to the unique but unmet needs of New Mexico's Indigenous children. As Indigenous youth begin transitioning into tribal leadership roles and communal responsibilities, court findings show, it is important for them to learn and know their cultural traditions, histories, languages, and tribal governance systems.[93] New Mexico's Native American students must not only graduate from high school proficient in the core academic subjects but must also be proficient in the laws, codes, rules, and traditions that will allow them to be of service to their tribal communities.[94] For that reason, "it is important to provide long-term investment and educational opportunities for Native American students," the court found, "because they will be the future leaders of their tribal communities."[95]

Indigenous experts and educators agreed that a *sufficient* education for Indigenous students must include a "culturally relevant education that blends both academic learning" with a "traditional-based learning system that incorporates traditions, cultural norms, community relations, hands-on learning, language, civic duties, and community development."[96] As the following summary indicates, it also requires strong relationships and collaboration with tribal communities:

> An early childhood learning program centered on cultural roots; culturally-relevant curriculum and [trained] teachers trained to deliver it (pre-K to grade 12); a cultural competency program for non-Native American teachers and administrators to develop a belonging in indigenous communities; education staff privy to Native American student needs; [culturally responsive] instructional materials; tribal language program that also incorporates the English language; positive school district and tribal relations; and state funding and technical assistance to support Native American student success and education.[97]

Typically, Indigenous children's unique needs are treated as add-ons or ignored in public schooling altogether.[98] This systematic neglect, the court found, is tied historically to federal assimilation policies and boarding schools. The

court also found that the NMIEA, if fully implemented, exists to end assimilation practices and "improve [Native] student outcomes."[99] To do so requires
teaching and learning to be done through an Indigenous lens, with Indigenous input and Indigenous leadership. These recommendations face a sober-
ing challenge: in New Mexico, where only 2 percent of teachers are Native
American, most Native students may never see a Native teacher in their
lives.[100]

Thus, in order to administer a sufficient education system that responds
fully to the constitutional rights of New Mexico's Indigenous students, New
Mexico leaders must commit to fully enforcing NMIEA and enacting the
transformative changes called for by the *Yazzie/Martinez* ruling.

NEW MEXICO'S INDIAN EDUCATION ACT IS THE FOUNDATION OF A SUFFICIENT EDUCATION

The court held that NMIEA is "the standard of an adequate education for
Native American students," and "a failure to comply with it amounts to a violation of the constitution's adequacy clause."[101] In essence, the NMIEA is a
vessel by which a sufficient education in New Mexico must be delivered and
administered.

The court deeply understood the historical forces within educational institutions that stripped away rather than reinforced Indigenous culture and the
resulting disconnect between public schooling and Indigenous communities.
One profound court finding reflects this viewpoint:

> New Mexico's Native American students share a legacy of historical trauma
> and a set of well-recognized, but chronically unmet, educational needs. It is
> important to be knowledgeable of this legacy so as to appreciate the need
> to meet the requirements of the [NMIEA].[102]

In a nutshell, federal boarding schools were created in the late 1800s to
"destroy Native American religious and cultural identity" and force Native
people to assimilate to American culture. During this assimilation era, Indigenous children throughout the United States were forcibly removed from their
ancestral lands by federal agents and placed in boarding schools, often

hundreds of miles away from their homes. In essence, the classroom is where Native boys and girls learned to reject their traditional identity, culture, language, and values and reap the physically and emotionally traumatic consequences.[103]

Court findings show that boarding school atrocities—as documented by two national reports—deeply affected New Mexico's tribal communities. The Meriam Report of 1928—prepared by Lewis Meriam and the Brookings Institute of Washington, DC—documented multiple decades of boarding school abuse experienced by Native children, which court findings show included the self-humiliation of having "to cut their [own] hair and change their style of clothes and beliefs."[104] Similarly, the 1969 Kennedy Report documented long-term trauma resulting from forced assimilation practices on Indigenous communities since boarding schools commenced. Notably, between 1940 and 1960, the US government deployed a full assault against tribes to repeal their "federal recognition status" and "eliminate them and their communal rights to federal trust land." Known as the Termination Era, everything cultural—including language—was "prohibited in schools." The impact on tribal communities, according to *Yazzie* expert testimony, was "a disconnect from and distrust of state institutions, such as public schools."[105]

Yazzie witnesses testified to the "devastation caused by federal assimilation policies," causing New Mexico lawmakers to rethink the glaring inequities marginalizing Native students in public schools. Some state leaders proposed a framework founded on traditional Indigenous values to guide policy decisions.[106] The resulting framework for developing public school programs, curriculum, and services intended for Native children—done in collaboration with tribal leaders—emerged as the NMIEA (2003). Since its inception, the act—if fully implemented and funded—is meant to improve academic success among American Indian students.[107]

In summary, the NMIEA requires the state to ensure that (1) culturally relevant learning environments, educational opportunities, and instructional materials are provided to students; (2) NMPED supports and assists school districts with substantive guidance; (3) NMPED studies and develops effective educational systems for Native students; and (4) government-to-government relationships between the state and tribes are maintained.[108]

A vital role to both the management and administration of Indian education is played by NMPED's Indian education assistant secretary, who serves as "both a voice of tribal leadership and directs Indigenous education policy." The NMIEA requires the assistant secretary to "provide assistance to school districts and New Mexico tribes in the planning, development, implementation and evaluation of curricula in native languages, culture and history designed for tribal and nontribal students as approved by New Mexico tribes."[109]

Court findings show, however, that the NMIEA goal "has not been realized in most [Indian Education] districts." In fact, the entire Indian Education Division, including the assistant secretary, have suffered from on-and-off vacancies over the past decade. The ripple effect, in part, is that public schools receive little to no technical assistance and support for Indian education and that, furthermore, "government-to-government relationships needed to achieve the statutory goals under the [IEA]" have failed.[110]

A dive into Indian education's assimilationist history often begs the question: What, if anything, has changed? Nearing one hundred years since the Meriam Report, fifty years since the Kennedy Report, and twenty years after NMIEA's passage, public education in New Mexico still does not correspond to the unique and comprehensive needs of its Native student population.

Beyond inadequate public school funding, institutional barriers in state government also impede educational progress for Indigenous students, families, and tribal communities at large. In 2021 derogatory statements about Indigenous education made by certain legislative and executive leaders, for example, disrupted long-standing state and tribal relations.[111] At best, those statements reflect a lack of commitment to and understanding of Indigenous culture; at worst, they reflect racist and paternalistic principles that will continue to undermine educational opportunity for New Mexico's Indigenous children.

Conclusion

Nearly five years after the *Yazzie/Martinez* ruling, the state has not made meaningful progress to comply with the court's decision and order. The question of how best to remedy education for New Mexico children demands the greatest attention by state leaders. An understanding of relevant education laws and adequacy standards, as well as issues identified by the *Yazzie/Martinez* findings, comprise the baseline. What must come next is long-term, comprehensive planning and targeted investments that directly address opportunity gaps for New Mexico's "at-risk" students, as well as transforming the issues in public schooling that money alone cannot fix.

In 2021 members of the state legislature passed House Memorial 26, entitled "Develop Education Plan for Yazzie Lawsuit."[112] House Memorial 26 provides a detailed framework mandating New Mexico's executive and legislative branches to work cooperatively to develop a comprehensive plan "jointly in consultation with the *Yazzie* and *Martinez* Plaintiffs and attempt to resolve the case." This plan, it states, must "build on existing plans and recommendations developed by education and tribal community stakeholders and researchers."

As for existing plans and recommendations, the Tribal Remedy Framework developed by tribal leaders and advocates provides a detailed framework of programs, services, and supports that respond to both the court's findings on Indian education and NMIEA.[113] Further, the *Yazzie* Remedy Framework developed by the Transform Education New Mexico coalition provides short- and long-term remedies to address the major systemic issues identified in the court's decision.[114]

Student Learning Objectives

1. Students will understand the role that each of the three state governmental branches play in providing NM students with a sufficient education.
2. Students will comprehend the connection between a multicultural education and improved learning among culturally diverse students.
3. Students will understand the significance and meaning of school adequacy.

Discussion Questions

1. Who are the plaintiffs and the defendants?
2. What is the claim made by the plaintiffs against the defendants?
3. How does the court define a "sufficient education"?
4. Why is the term *sufficient* so important to the *Yazzie/Martinez* case?
5. What is the tension caused by the phrasing "sufficient education" and "adequate education"? Why is this clarification necessary?
6. What were Judge Singleton's responsibilities and duties as the judiciary in the *Yazzie/ Martinez* litigation?
7. Why is adequate funding for public schools necessary to provide New Mexico students a sufficient education?
8. How does the history of Indian education currently impact the way public education in New Mexico is administered? What needs to change, if anything?
9. What is the significance of the New Mexico Indian Education Act to the education of Native American students?

Notes

1. "New Mexico KIDS COUNT Profile," New Mexico Voices for Children, July 20, 2021, https://www.nmvoices.org/archives/11728. The Annie E. Casey Foundation's Kids Count Report measures children's well-being in six categories in all fifty states.

2. Comprising the *Yazzie* plaintiffs are Wilhelmina Yazzie, a Navajo mother from Gallup, New Mexico—also *Yazzie*'s lead family plaintiff—and her son Xavier Nez, along with four families from Grants, Albuquerque, Gadsden, and Peñasco and six school district plaintiffs from Cuba, Rio Rancho, Santa Fe, Moriarty-Edgewood, and Lake Arthur.

3. New Mexico courts have interpreted "sufficient" to mean "adequate, enough, equal to the end proposed, and that which may be necessary to accomplish an object." *Nissen v. Miller*, 1940-NMSC-055, ¶ 10, 44 N.M. 487.

4. Decision and Order at 24–25. See http://nmpovertylaw.org/wp-content/uploads/2018/07/Order-DECISON-2018-07-20.pdf.

5. Decision, 2–4, 9–10, 66, 74–75.

6. Decision, 56.

7. Decision, 4.

8. N.M. Const. art. XII, § 1.

9.   See *State v. Nunez*, 2000-NMSC-013, ¶ 48, 129 N.M. 63; *State v. Gutierrez*, 1993-NMSC-062, 55, 116 N.M. 431. ("It is the role of the judiciary, and not the legislature to interpret the constitution.")

10.   The legislature has the right to determine "necessary" appropriations for educational institutions, created by existing law, and to provide therefore in the general appropriation bill, authorized to do so by Const. art. 4, § 16, permitting the inclusion of "expenses required by existing law." *State ex rel. Lucero v. Marron*, 17 N.M. 304 (1912).

11.   N.M. Stat. Ann. § 22-8-14; §§ 22-2-1, 22-2-2, & 22-8-4; N.M. Const. art. XII, § 6.

12.   Report of the Legislative Finance Committee to the Forty-Seventh Legislature, first session, January 2005 for fiscal year 2005–2006, vol. 1, at 22. See https://www.nmlegis.gov/Entity/LFC/Documents/Session_Publications/Budget_Recommendations/2006RecommendVolI.pdf.

13.   Decision and Order at 8–9. "[W]hen a citizen sues the state on the theory that the state has failed to fulfill its constitutional obligation to provide for adequate education, the judiciary has the institutional duty to interpret the education clause to determine whether the state has complied with its constitutional obligation."

14.   "Public education" means education that is publicly financed, tuition-free, accountable to public authorities, and accessible to all students. See Nancy Kober, "Why We Still Need Public Schools: Public Education for the Common Good," Center on Education Policy, Washington, DC, 2007.

15.   *Brown v. Bd. of Ed. of Topeka, Shawnee Cty., Kan.*, 347 U.S. 483, 493, 74 S. Ct. 686, 691, 98 L. Ed. 873 (1954), supplemented sub nom. *Brown v. Bd. of Educ. of Topeka, Kan.*, 349 U.S. 294, 75 S. Ct. 753, 99 L. Ed. 1083 (1955).

16.   *Gannon v. State*, 298 Kan. 1107, 319 P.3d 1196 (2014); *Campaign for Fiscal Equity, Inc. v. State*, 100 N.Y.2d 893, 801 N.E.2d 326 (2003); *Columbia Falls Elementary Sch. Dist. No. 6 v. State*, 2005 MT 69, 326 Mont. 304, 109 P.3d 257; *Leandro v. State*, 346 N.C. 336, 488 S.E.2d 249 (1997).

17.   *McCleary v. State*, 173 Wash. 2d 477, 516, 269 P.3d 227, 246 (2012).

18.   *McDuffy v. Secretary of Executive Office of Educ.*, 415 Mass. 545, 619–20 (Mass. 1993).

19.   Findings of Fact (FOF), 642–43, 648. See http://nmpovertylaw.org/wp-content/uploads/2019/01/Courts-Findings-of-Fact-and-Conclusions-of-Law-2018-12-20.pdf.

20.   Decision, 3, 45, 50–51, 53. See http://nmpovertylaw.org/wp-content/uploads/2018/07/Order-DECISON-2018-07-20.pdf.

21.   *Gannon v. State*, 298 Kan. 1107, 319 P.3d 1196 (2014); *Campaign for Fiscal Equity, Inc. v. State*, 100 N.Y.2d 893, 801 N.E.2d 326 (2003); *Columbia Falls Elementary Sch. Dist. No. 6 v. State*, 2005 MT 69, 326 Mont. 304, 109 P.3d 257; *Leandro v. State*, 346 N.C. 336, 488 S.E.2d 249 (1997); *McCleary v. State*, 173 Wash. 2d 477, 516, 269 P.3d 227, 246 (2012).

22.   FOF, 2250, 2255.

23.   FOF, 298, 304, 327–28, 676. See http://nmpovertylaw.org/wp-content/uploads/2019/01/Courts-Findings-of-Fact-and-Conclusions-of-Law-2018-12-20.pdf.

24.   See generally FOF, 353, 361, 363, 367–68, 370, 372, 434, 726.

25. FOF, 305.

26. See generally FOF, 244, 874–89.

27. Decision, 5. See http://nmpovertylaw.org/wp-content/uploads/2018/07/Order-DECISON-2018-07-20.pdf.

28. CFE II, 100 N.Y.2d at 903, 801 N.E.2d at 328 (holding that a "plaintiff in an adequacy case must prove that the state provided inadequate inputs and then must correlate these failures to inadequate outcomes").

29. Decision, 12.

30. *Rose v. Council for Better Educ., Inc.,* 790 S.W.2d 186 (Ky. 1989).

31. *Rose v. Council for Better Educ., Inc.,* 212

32. *Rose v. Council for Better Educ., Inc.,* 196–97.

33. E.g., *Gannon v. State,* 298 Kan. 1107, 1170 (Kan. 2014); *McDuffy v. Secretary of Executive Office of Educ.,* 415 Mass. 545, 618 (Mass. 1993); *Leandro v. State,* 346 N.C. 336, 347 (N.C. 1997); *McCleary v. State,* 173 Wn.2d 477, 483 (Wash. 2012); *W. Orange-Cove Consol. I.S.D. v. Alanis,* 107 S.W.3d 558, 563 (Tex. 2003); *Davis v. State,* 2011 SD 51, P14 (S.D. 2011).

34. Rebecca Blum Martínez and Preston Sanchez, "A Watershed Moment in the Education of American Indians: A Judicial Strategy to Mandate the State of New Mexico to Meet the Unique Cultural and Linguistic Needs of American Indians in New Mexico Public Schools," *American University Journal of Gender, Social Policy and the Law* 27, no. 3 (2019): 321–22, 325.

35. FOF, 65, 322, 328, 443, 456–62, 465, 672, 674, 2953.

36. NMSA 1978 § 22-1-1.2 & NMSA1978 §22-23A-1.

37. Decision, 13.

38. Decision, 17–24

39. Decision, 13.

40. N.M. Stat. Ann. § 22-23-1.1.

41. FOF, 379–80, 539–54, 3019–28, 3066–72.

42. See generally Findings of Fact and Conclusions of Law.

43. FOF, 1–2, 2111.

44. See generally Findings of Fact and Conclusions of Law.

45. FOF, 1, 797–811.

46. New Mexico Public Education Department, *School District Report Card 2016–17: Albuquerque Public Schools,* July 12, 2018, 1, available at https://webed.ped.state.nm.us/sites/conference/2017%20District%20Report%20Cards/Forms/AllItems.aspx.

47. Martinez and Sanchez, "A Watershed Moment," 335–37.

48. FOF, 463.

49. Decision, 27–28; see also FOF, 458–63, 508.

50. N.M. Stat. Ann. § 22-23-1.1; and N.M. Stat. Ann. § 22-23A-2.

51. N.M. Stat. Ann. § 22-23-4; and N.M. Stat. Ann. § 22-23A-5.

52. FOF, 297, 303, 376, 382–89, 426–30 (BMEB failures), 539–605 (NMIEA failures).

53. FOF, 425–31.

54. FOF, 606, 619.

55. FOF, 383–86.

56. Sarah Dewees and Benjamin Marks, "Twice Invisible: Understanding Rural Native America," Research note, First Nations Development Institute, April 2017, 5, available at https://www.usetinc.org/wp-content/uploads/bvenuti/WWS/2017/May%20 2017/May%208/Twice%20Invisible%20-%20Research%20Note.pdf.

57. FOF, 81, 92, 182, 197, 198, 229, 362, 2151–57.

58. FOF, 2. See http://nmpovertylaw.org/wp-content/uploads/2019/01/Courts-Find-ings-of-Fact-and-Conclusions-of-Law-2018-12-20.pdf.

59. Decision, 17, citing NMSA 1978 § 22-1-1.2 (2015).

60. Decision, 32; see also FOF, 65, 468, 574, 3019–28; see generally 461–75.

61. Decision, 30 (finding that "in FY 2017, full-day pre-K was estimated to be available to only 3,641 four-year-olds out of a total population eligible of 12,278 four-year olds."); see also FOF, 66, 89–90.

62. FOF, 668, 674.

63. FOF, 236, 239, 242, 244; see generally FOF, 252–65.

64. FOF, 215–16, 219, 223; see generally FOF, 224–35.

65. FOF, 302, 304. See also Martinez and Sanchez, "A Watershed Moment," 323. ("Moreover if students are allowed to study in a substantive dual language program, where both the native language and English are supported and developed through academic content, children will outperform those in monolingual programs. It is important to remember that for the most part, individual bilingualism reflects the bilingualism of the communities in which bilinguals live. Therefore, schools and other public institutions must consider the families and communities when developing educational policies.")

66. FOF, 183.

67. FOF, 510.

68. FOF, 463.

69. FOF, 464, 467–68, 475, 585.

70. FOF, 2565–70.

71. FOF, 480, 482, 487.

72. FOF, 481.

73. Albuquerque Public Schools, Aztec Municipal Schools, Bernalillo Public Schools, Central Consolidated Schools, Cuba Independent Schools, Dulce Independent Schools, Española Public Schools, Farmington Municipal Schools, Gallup-McKinley County Schools, Grants-Cibola County Schools, Jemez Mountain Public Schools, Jemez Valley Public Schools, Los Lunas Public Schools, Magdalena Municipal Schools, Peñasco Independent Schools, Pojoaque Valley Public Schools, Rio Rancho Public Schools, Ruidoso Municipal Schools, Santa Fe Public Schools, Taos Municipal Schools, Tularosa Municipal Schools, and Zuni Public Schools.

74. FOF, 619.

75. FOF, 947, 950,

76. FOF, 949, 952.

77. FOF, 1007, 1009–13, 1015–18.
78. FOF, 517, 1869–98, 2115.
79. FOF, 661.
80. FOF, 665–66, 333.
81. FOF, 702–3.
82. FOF, 702.
83. FOF, 261.
84. FOF, 95–97.
85. FOF, 198, 207, 283.
86. FOF, 91, 202.
87. FOF, 4, 6–11, 50.
88. FOF, 67, 69, 70, 72–74, 91–93.
89. Numerous studies have revealed that many students from marginalized groups come to school with ways of using English that are distinct from those required in schools. See Martinez and Sanchez, "A Watershed Moment," 321; Mary J. Schleppegrell, *The Language of Schooling: A Functional Linguistics Perspective* (New York: Lawrence Erlbaum, 2004).
90. FOF, 409–11.
91. FOF, 349–64. See also "Public School Districts of Bernalillo, Cuba, Gallup, Jemez Valley, Grants, and Zuni," 346.
92. FOF, 305, 306, 308, 325, 328, 335, 371.
93. FOF, 483, 486, 493, 512–13.
94. FOF, 512, 515, 518.
95. FOF, 495.
96. FOF, 513. Additionally, the court identified: state and school district collaboration with tribes to develop an educational plan; culturally relevant teacher trainings; teachers who understand students' community, language, and culture; pedagogical methods relevant to Native students; culturally relevant and responsive curriculum; a Native American teacher pipeline; and family engagement.
97. FOF, 522.
98. FOF, 526.
99. FOF, 530–31, 536–38.
100. FOF, 326, 607.
101. Decision, 28.
102. FOF, 496.
103. FOF, 497–502.
104. FOF, 501.
105. FOF, 504–9.
106. FOF, 531–35.
107. Fiscal Impact Report for SB 115, 2003 legislative session. ("Historically, Indian students have scored low on standardized tests and have consistently underachieved in the public schools, a phenomenon attributed primarily to linguistic and cultural

differences. This bill addresses that issue and provides mechanisms intended to improve the success rate of Indian students in public schools.") See https://www.nmlegis.gov/Sessions/03%20Regular/firs/sb0115.pdf.

108.   N.M. Stat. Ann. § 22-23A-1.

109.   FOF, 459.

110.   Decision, 28–29.

111.   Dan McKay, "Top Legislative Staffer Who Was Censured Quits," *Albuquerque Journal*, September 1, 2021, https://www.abqjournal.com/2425258/gudgel-top-legislative-staffer-submits-resignation.html; see also Andrew Oxford, "Pueblo Leaders Decry Public Education Chief's 'Manifest Destiny' Comment," *Santa Fe New Mexican*, December 22, 2017, http://www.santafenew mexican.com/news/education/pueblo-leaders-decry-public-education-chief-s-manifest-destiny-comment/article_da7cd5bf-4102-5f2f-9bfo-c5692dc49e73.html.

112.   See New Mexico State Legislature website, https://nmlegis.gov/Legislation/Legislation?Chamber=H&LegType=M&LegNo=26&year=21.

113.   See "Tribal Remedy Framework," Native American Budget Policy and Institute, University of New Mexico, https://nabpi.unm.edu/tribal-remedy-framework.html.

114.   See "Resources," Transform Education New Mexico, https://transformeducationnm.org/resources/.

Figure 3. The Gallup McKinley County School District is located in Gallup, New Mexico. With a population of 21,493, Gallup sits on the border of the Navajo Nation and Zuni Pueblo. Photo credit Hondo Louis. Funded by UNM's Center for Regional Studies and Native American Studies Department.

CHAPTER TWO

Post-Summit Report on the *Yazzie/Martinez* Ruling

Action Report

GLENABAH MARTINEZ, TERRI FLOWERDAY,

LLOYD L. LEE, LEOLA TSINNAJINNIE PAQUIN,

WENDY S. GREYEYES, NATHANIEL CHARLEY,

AND CARLOTTA PENNY BIRD

ON MAY 15, 2020, the Institute for American Indian Education (IAIE) at the University of New Mexico hosted a virtual summit, the purpose of which was to address the impact of the *Yazzie/Martinez v. State of New Mexico* ruling on the current state of Indian education. The summit provided updates on the legal issues and a legislative perspective by expert speakers, followed by small- and large-group discussion among all attendees.

The mission of IAIE is to support the community's intergenerational well-being and educational outcomes of Indigenous peoples by cultivating professionals through community engagement and collaborative partnerships. IAIE has six guiding principles: Educator Preparation, Leadership, Curriculum, Language and Culture, Family and Life Preparation, and Individual and Community Health and Wellness. The institute is composed of Indigenous faculty from the College of Education and the Department of Native American Studies, professional staff, and a seven-member advisory council.

Through the IAIE, the faculty and members developed a report that found five areas of major concern from the public and developed six aligned recommendations. Since the completion of the report, the IAIE has shared this document with the New Mexico Public Education Department (NMPED), stakeholders, tribal leaders, parents, teachers, and students. It is evident that there is still much work to be completed in advocating for this work. Throughout this report, we note that the concerning trends we document continue to permeate the system, from the state education agency to the classrooms.

Background

In July 2018 Judge Sarah Singleton of the First Judicial District Court of New Mexico ruled that the state, NMPED, and the state's secretary of education are failing to provide Native American students with a college- and career-ready education. Judge Singleton stated in her ruling that "lack of funds is no excuse" for failing to provide equitable services and programs for "all at-risk students." The ruling was a clear signal to NMPED, the secretary of education, and the state that they are responsible for "providing an adequate, sufficient education to at-risk students i.e., socioeconomically disadvantaged children, English learners, Native American students, and children with disabilities." While legislation during the 2019 and 2020 session sought appropriations to fund tribal and school efforts to transform the education system in the wake of this ruling, it fell short in many areas.

On March 13, 2020, NMPED and the state filed a motion to dismiss *Yazzie/ Martinez v. State of New Mexico*. The timing of the motion to dismiss coincided with the emergence of the COVID-19 pandemic, which blindsided tribal leaders and educational stakeholders focused on safety and remote instruction delivery. One must question the extent of the state's commitment to government-to-government relationships. Meanwhile, NMPED contends they are working to address Judge Singleton's order, and the *Yazzie* plaintiffs filed an opposition to the motion to dismiss on May 1, 2020. The motion hearing was scheduled for June 29, 2020, in Santa Fe, New Mexico, at which time the motion to dismiss was denied.

Process

The summit consisted of two large-group sessions and seven breakout rooms for participants to meet in smaller groups. 124 individuals registered, including IAIE faculty, staff, and advisory council members. Each breakout session had seven to ten participants, plus the facilitator and notetaker. A majority of the registrants were school administrators (27 percent), followed by higher education (17 percent) and tribal education representatives (15 percent). Other registrants included tribal leadership, representatives from educational organizations, funders, educators, and students.

The first part of the meeting centered on two presentations by attorney Gail Evans and New Mexico House District 65 Representative Derrick Lente. Ms. Evans, lead counsel for the *Yazzie v. State of New Mexico* case, presented an overview of the case, ruling, and the subsequent motion to dismiss. Representative Derrick Lente of Sandia Pueblo, representing Pueblo and Navajo constituents, provided an overview of his legislative proposals to address *Yazzie/Martinez* and his experience as a legislator.

The second part of the summit focused on communal discussions through breakout sessions that considered two questions:

1. Are the remedies in Judge Singleton's ruling being met? What else is needed to not only comply with the ruling but to transform public education for American Indians in the state?
2. Are equity councils a sufficient response (relief) to the *Yazzie/Martinez* court decision?

IAIE sought to provide a communal format allowing stakeholders to offer their perspectives and listen to statewide concerns from teachers, policy makers, administrators, and higher education representatives. The breakout sessions allowed participants to reflect on the information presented and then share their own experiences in the wake of the judge's ruling on *Yazzie/Martinez*.

Results and Conclusions

After analyzing participant comments and questions, IAIE identified the following common themes:

FUNDING IS A MAJOR CONCERN

- Insufficient timing for grant applications, limited time frames for implementation, and competitive grants among districts and tribes results in returning large, unspent funds to the state.
- The grant process is piecemeal and does not adequately create transformative change necessary to sustain the education of Native American students.
- Federal funding sources (i.e., Impact Aid, Title Funding, Johnson O'Malley) earmarked for Native American students are diverted to other school priorities that do not meet the students' direct needs.
- Lack of adequate guidance for tribal education directors and/or school administrators hinders the navigation of the many requirements, as do the competing directives to apply for state grants.
- NMPED needs to be accountable.
- School readiness assessments are being pushed upon school districts that are expected to complete them without adequate NMPED guidance.
- School staff, such as tribal liaisons and directors, are expected to create comprehensive plans with limited resources and guidance.
- School boards are expected to create transformative long-term plans with limited short-term grant funding.
- No assistant secretary of Indian education has been selected to advocate for Native American students.
- NMPED's reliance on equity councils to examine and determine the plans for student success is seen as questionable, ineffective, and redundant.
- Equity councils are at odds with current school policies and tribal sovereignty.
- NMPED's focus on quantified assessment measures of student progress institutionalizes racial disparities.

COMMUNICATION MUST BE INCLUSIVE

- Community input is needed to actualize the *Yazzie/Martinez* ruling.
- Honest communication includes providing families and communities with the tools and understanding needed to elicit meaningful conversations and feedback.
- Student input is essential to the planning for resources, instruction, funding, and professional development so that educators can better serve the students.
- COVID-19 has highlighted and increased disparities and a lack of access to technology.
- NMPED outreach must be comprehensively inclusive of parents, community, tribal/local/regional leadership, elders, and educators.

EDUCATOR PREPARATION NEEDS TO BE IMPROVED

- Educators are not prepared to work effectively with culturally and racially diverse students.
- Recognizing, valuing, and honoring student identities is key.
- Education leaders at all levels need to be prepared to conduct equity audits and to identify the gaps and assist tribal communities.
- Undergraduate and graduate programs need the resources and institutional support to be able to adequately prepare educators and leaders.

CURRICULUM AND INSTRUCTION MUST BE CULTURALLY RESPONSIVE

- There is a lack of guidance and support for culturally responsive teaching.
- Curricula and lessons do not validate or affirm the home culture and language of Native American families.
- Better communication with parents and students is needed to elicit true partnerships, conversations, and feedback.
- Effective culturally responsive pedagogies need to be recognized.

Recommendations

IAIE developed a set of six recommendations in response to the concerns raised by the summit attendees. These recommendations are directed to NMPED, the secretary of education, and the state.

Need for Sustainable Funding. NMPED must ensure that grants and funds directed to school districts allow sufficient time to apply for, implement, and execute these funds and create long-term and sustainable solutions defined under the *Yazzie/Martinez* ruling. The summit stakeholders define the long-term goal as creating transformational change that resolves the systematic issues plaguing Native American children. The summit stakeholders discourage the reliance on grants as an adequate source of additional funding. Grants do not create long-term action, and funding must be guaranteed over an extended period to create long-term strategic action. The discrimination against Native American children cannot be fixed within one fiscal year. IAIE recommends long-term and sustainable funding.

Hold NMPED Accountable. As the state education agency, NMPED must be held solely accountable in addressing and resolving the *Yazzie/Martinez* orders. The schools are not the defendants; the state must be held directly accountable. In response to the lawsuit, the state mandated "equity councils" to address Judge Singleton's ruling. This is not a suitable response as it decentralizes the role of NMPED and places pressure on the schools. The equity councils are not funded by the state and their effective implementation would require school districts to seek voluntary participation from community members. In addition, the state expects school districts to form fifteen-member equity councils to develop guidance for how schools can make education culturally appropriate and assess how they will serve at-risk students. Many educational leaders and stakeholders question the effectiveness of the "equity councils" as a tool to solve the lack of infrastructure, materials, instruction, and funding within New Mexico's public education classrooms. IAIE wants to see a statewide strategy to resolve the challenges articulated by the ruling with annual measurable goals. IAIE recommends a means to measure a ten-year overview of NMPED's progress on all elements of Judge Singleton's order.

Intensify Communication Outreach. NMPED must improve their outreach to all stakeholders to educate everyone on their approaches and strategies to resolve the *Yazzie/Martinez* ruling. Based on the concerns raised by the summit participants, IAIE recommends that NMPED, in partnership with tribal leaders, hosts monthly town halls through social media and other online tools to detail the progress of the *Yazzie/Martinez* ruling. Government-to-government biannual meetings are not adequate venues to engage in dialogue with all stakeholders. IAIE recommends these updates be recorded and made accessible on NMPED's website. In addition, NMPED must publish a monthly newsletter widely distributed in local, tribal, and school district newspapers describing the progress of NMPED in meeting these needs.

Improve Educator Preparation. NMPED must increase their advocacy for state legislators to improve and expand educator preparation at Higher Education Institutions (HEI). Education leaders at all levels need to be prepared to conduct equity audits to identify the gaps and assist tribal communities. These equity audits will inform actions toward resolving the disproportionately low numbers of culturally competent and highly qualified teachers working in rural tribal communities. IAIE recommends expanding funding opportunities for future teacher pipelines from the most rural communities to HEIs. This data will serve as a baseline metric of the annual progress of NMPED's effort to assist HEIs' effort to eliminate vacancies throughout the state.

Increase Support for Curriculum and Instruction. NMPED must provide resources to teachers for developing culturally sensitive curriculum and instruction. Stakeholders would like to see a report on best practices occurring within all schools serving Native American students. This report will support the ability of faculty and educational stakeholders to determine how to support schools. Most if not all eighty-seven school districts in the state serve Native American students. NMPED needs to analyze the efficacy of effective programs that can create authentic school/tribal partnerships with shared resources.

Critical Review of Existing Laws. NMPED must review and revise existing policies to determine alignment with the *Yazzie/Martinez* ruling. A critical review of the existing laws and their alignment with Judge Singleton's order is sorely needed. A report to show how existing statutes, laws, and appropriated funding meet or do not meet the order is warranted. NMPED must provide a meaningful solution that allows schools under its purview to comply with state and federal laws regarding the education of Native Americans and English-language learners, including the New Mexico Indian Education Act, Bilingual Multicultural Education Act, and other relevant laws and policies. IAIE also recommends the inclusion of case studies providing evidence of how policy is currently enacted and funded at the school level, specifically for the schools serving Native American students.

Follow-Up Summit

The IAIE hosted a follow-up summit in June 2021 to discuss the progress of the responses to the *Yazzie/Martinez* case. The summit focused on the New Mexico state legislative process and the types of *Yazzie/Martinez*–related legislations initiated by state leaders. Since Judge Sarah Singleton's ruling on *Yazzie/Martinez v. State of New Mexico* in 2018, legislation has been introduced to implement educational remedies. However, numerous significant bills to carry out these remedies in 2019, 2020, and 2021 have not reached the governor's desk for signature.

The purpose of the 2021 IAIE summit, titled "Looking to 2022: Finding Strategies That Work," was to reexamine and refine a framework of legislative strategies that would maximize IAIE's advocacy, resources, and educational capacity and better serve our children in New Mexico.

As already mentioned, on March 13, 2020, NMPED and the state filed a motion to dismiss *Yazzie/Martinez v. State of New Mexico*. Particularly given the coincidence of the filing coinciding with the explosion of COVID-19, the timing distressed the Native community. The state's motion to dismiss the case relied heavily upon "trusting the state government (PED), legislators, and the governor to fix the state's school system," which they have proven unable and unwilling to do despite their constitutional obligations.[1] On June 29, 2020, First Judicial District Court judge Matthew Wilson denied the state's motion and noted "that the state's by its own admission was not fulfilling its constitutional duty to provide a sufficient education to all students."[2] Additionally, at the request of the *Yazzie* plaintiffs, on April 30, 2021, Judge Matthew Wilson ordered the state to address technology and broadband connectivity issues in rural and tribal areas that were adversely impacting students and their learning during remote schooling caused by the pandemic. Finally, in the 2021 legislative session, tribal and school efforts were again made to address the issues of *Yazzie/Martinez* and again these efforts fell short in many areas.

Legislation from the 2019, 2020, and 2021 sessions of the New Mexico State Legislature were reviewed by IAIE faculty with technical assistance from IAIE staff and consultation with UNM government relations director Dr. Barbara Damron. Dr. Wendy S. Greyeyes organized the data from the 107 legislative actions (including 82 bills, 23 memorials, and 2 resolutions) into Excel spreadsheets and inserted documents into the Atlas.ti qualitative data analysis software to construct a listing of themes and trends. From the coding and analyses, five primary codes/themes were identified:

College and Career Ready

Culturally Relevant Courses

Community Preparedness for College and Career Ready

New Mexico Public Education Department Planning and Preparedness

Yazzie/Martinez Education Funding Disparity

Of the 107 legislative actions reviewed, the following bills from the Senate and the House of Representatives in 2021 responded to the *Yazzie/Martinez* lawsuit:

1. **College and Career Ready:** SB 337 (Workplace Preparation School Programs) and HB 87 (Yazzie Lawsuit Higher Education Funding)
2. **Culturally Relevant Courses:** HB 86 (Native American Library, Internet & Education) and SB 337 (Workplace Preparation School Programs)
3. **Community Preparedness for College and Career Ready:** HB 86 (Native American Library, Internet and Education) and HB 87(Yazzie Lawsuit Higher Education Funding)
4. **NMPED Planning and Preparedness:** SB 337 (Workplace Preparation School Programs) and HB 219 (Biliteracy Development Framework Task Force)
5. *Yazzie/Martinez* **Education Funding Disparity:** HB 6 (State Equal-

ization Guarantee Distributions) and HB 116 (Additions to 3-Tiered Teacher Licenses)

At the summit, the following questions guided the communal discussions:

1. What thoughts and questions were raised for you from the legislation analysis and panel commentaries?
2. What strategies, along with legislation, should we focus on in 2022 to address the *Yazzie/Martinez* ruling?

Drawing on data collected from the breakout sessions, the following recommendations were identified:

There is a need for improved communication. Specifically, there is a lack of awareness of information, initiatives, and interaction among all members of the tribal community regarding the issues and remedies of *Yazzie/ Martinez*. Additionally, the voices of all members of the tribal and educational communities are inconsistently heard. Therefore, a more detailed and comprehensive plan for communicating among the twenty-three Native Nations, educational participants, and external stakeholders such as policy makers and community leaders should be implemented so that all stakeholders are heard from and higher levels of unity and collaboration are achieved.

There is a need for greater unity among the twenty-three Native Nations and stakeholders. Voice, vision, and leadership should be interwoven to ensure all tribal leadership, Native communities, and education stakeholders are working to achieve the remedies. Tribal leadership needs to engage with parents and community members regarding the remedies for which Native Nations are advocating. Common objectives among all twenty-three Native Nations and stakeholders need to be developed to create a unified legislation. With the help of their communities and Native Nations, the tribal leadership should consider developing one unified legislation to achieve remedies.

There is a need for a unified approach in developing legislation and engaging the legislature. To begin this process, a review of the intent and purpose of the lawsuit could be beneficial. Next, legislation put forward should reflect a unification of purpose and commitment to specific goals.

One story, one narrative, addressing key remedies set forth in the *Yazzie/ Martinez* ruling, should be advanced under the leadership of one or two primary legislators. Finally, there is a need for participation from tribal leaders, communities, educators, and all stakeholders in the development of legislative actions.

There is a need to engage all stakeholders. Engagement is critical in the process of educational reform and specifically in implementing the remedies outlined by Judge Singleton in her 2018 ruling. Parents, educators, administrators, tribal leaders, equity councils, and other stakeholders from the twenty-three Native Nations, rural regions of the state, and urban settings all have an investment in achieving educational equity and equality. Multiple approaches in engaging all stakeholders are critical to presenting a unified front to ensure that legislation reaches the governor's desk. The voices and perspectives of all these actors are foundational to realizing transformation that addresses present and future challenges.

The full report from the 2021 summit is available on the website of the University of New Mexico's Institute for American Indian Education.[3]

Student Learning Objectives

- Students will be able to assess whether the remedies in Judge Singleton's ruling are being met and supply evidence to support their conclusions.
- Students will be able to provide examples of actions that could be taken to bring public education into compliance with the *Yazzie* ruling and transform education for American Indian students in the state.
- Students will be able to think critically and explain ways in which the *Yazzie* ruling might be applied to education outside of New Mexico.

Discussion Questions

1. After reviewing the five key themes (funding is a major concern; NMPED needs to be accountable; communication must be inclusive; educator preparation needs to be improved; curriculum and instruction

must be culturally responsive), determine which one should be addressed first. Why?

2. After reviewing the recommendations (critical review of existing laws; increase support for curriculum and instruction; improve educator preparation; intensify communications outreach; hold NMPED accountable; address the need for sustainable funding), determine which ones might best be addressed by:

    a. Classroom teachers. Why? What could be done?

    b. District administrators. Why? What could be done?

    c. College faculty and students. Why? What could be done?

    d. Public education officials. Why? What could be done?

    e. Communities. Why? What could be done?

3. Might the *Yazzie* ruling have implications for equity in public education outside of New Mexico? If so, in what ways?

Notes

1.   New Mexico Center on Law and Poverty, "Yazzie/Martinez Education Lawsuit Moves Forward!" June 29, 2020, http://nmpovertylaw.org/2020/06/yazzie-martinez-education-lawsuit-moves-forward/.

2.   "Education Legislative Study Committee," prepared by Joseph W. Simon, July 14, 2020, https://www.nmlegis.gov/handouts/ALESC%20071520%20Item%203%20-%20 Brief%20-%20Martinez%20and%20Yazzie%20Lawsuit.pdf.

3.   Institute for American Indian Education, University of New Mexico, *2021 Post-Summit Executive Report*, May 2021, https://iaie.unm.edu/news-events/summit/2021-iaie-post-summit-report6236.pdf.

Figure 4. Statue of a Navajo Code Talker from World War II located at the entrance of the Gallup Cultural Center. Artist is the late Oreland Joe (Navajo/Ute). The city of Gallup is described as the "most patriotic city" in the United States. It has also been described as a racist border town, with a population that is 36.5 percent white and 44.1 percent American Indian (according to the American Community Survey 2019). It is also a city with a handful of millionaires living in mansions who have profited off of the Navajo and Zuni peoples. Navajos and Zunis continue to drive to Gallup for the variety of shops and restaurants due to limited access to groceries and supplies in their communities. Photo credit Hondo Louis. Funded by UNM's Center for Regional Studies and Native American Studies Department.

CHAPTER THREE

Witness Perspective
from a Mother and an Academic

GEORGINA BADONI

The child starts school and leaves with a pinch of pollen
on top of her head and her tongue.
This is done so the child will think clearly,
listen quietly, and learn well away from home.
The child leaves home with prayers and good thoughts.
It has been this way for centuries among us.
This is how we were raised.
We were raised with care and attention
Because it has always been this way.
It has worked well for centuries . . .

—LUCI TAPAHONSO, "IT HAS ALWAYS BEEN THIS WAY"

ONE CONSIDERABLE CHALLENGE PRESENTLY threatening Native families
is the agency and visibility of Native parents within the New Mexico public
education system. Native American parents are the primary advocates asserting students' access to equitable education. However, even with the landmark
ruling of *Yazzie/Martinez v. State of New Mexico*, public schools continue to
exclude Native students and parents from educational processes and decision-
making.

As a parent, I share my firsthand encounter with the barriers to educational
equity in the New Mexico public school system and tell my story as a mother

pleading for support services for my son. As an academic professional, I disclose how my positionality opened opportunities to assist other struggling families. Lastly, I offer suggestions on how to navigate and ensure agency for Native American children.

This chapter will use the expression "parent/parenting" to represent the extended family members taking care of Native American children. We know that in Native American societies family members take responsibility for our children. It is common among Indigenous families for nonparental family members to take the primary caregiver role. Also, the use of the term "mothers" is not contingent on a relationship to biological children. Native American women have become "mothers" in other ways, such as adopting or caring for children. In short, in Native American communities, roles are interchangeable, not biologically defined.[1]

I am a mother first and an educator second. When I introduce myself to a class or larger groups, I always begin with my role as a mother. In Diné culture, motherhood presupposes a standing of autonomy and authority.[2] Our Creation stories affirm our roles and responsibilities blessed by the Holy People. This raises the question: If we are given a powerful position as mothers, why are our roles and voices disregarded when protecting our children in schools? My role as a mother shapes me as an advocate for all Native American children, especially in the New Mexico public education system.

We moved to southern New Mexico in 2019 from Seattle. I accepted a tenured position with New Mexico State University as an assistant professor in Native American studies. Before school started, I attempted to reach out to the Las Cruces Public School District to connect to the Native education program. I left several voice messages and emails, hoping someone would answer. Because there are twenty-three federally recognized Native Nations in New Mexico, I assumed the district must have a Native American education program. We came from a school district with such an education program that provided services for our son; we hoped for a similar program to provide community connection and to ease the challenges of my son's transition. Even though I had little knowledge about the schools or programs available for Native American students in New Mexico, we decided to enroll our son in our neighborhood school.

My son's new school picture captured his uneasy body language: shoulders hunched forward, eyes closed tightly, no smile, but a scrunched face refusing to react to the camera (fig. 5). I interpreted his appearance in the photo as new school nerves and silently reassured myself it would get better. As the days continued, we noticed little change in his demeanor: he struggled to get ready for school and not once did he talk about his teacher, classmates, new friends, or what he was learning. The growing concern for his lack of interest in school and disheartened attitude compelled me to meet with his classroom teacher. The meeting offered no comfort but did raise more fears and revealed our son was an invisible Native American student at his new school. Sadly, most people in the United States do not know a Native American person.[3] There is little awareness of Native American peoples existing in contemporary life. The lack of awareness creates an invisibility and fuels biases against our Native American children. In turn, these biases on the part of teachers and administrators hold back Native American students in K-12 education by limiting their rights to equitable education, cultural identity, and self-worth.[4]

My son would start every morning by reluctantly dragging his bag down the hall toward the front door, physically sinking in the car seat, and slowly dropping his head as we got close to the school. To ease our pain, I adopted a

Figure 5. Georgina Badoni's photograph of her son. Photo credit Georgina Badoni.

routine. Ten minutes before we got in the car in the morning, I would begin emotionally uplifting him for school. As I walked him into the school, down the hall, and to class, I spoke in a cheerful voice, speaking positively about nonsense to ease him into his morning. I dug deep to comfort his pain and mine. As I left him, he appeared so broken and lost, I would cry in my car on the way to campus, overwhelmed by responsibility and regret. This experience added to my guilt of taking my son away from a school and city he had grown attached to.

As we went through these trials and tribulations with my son's school, I decided that I could offer my services to the school to facilitate Native American students' support. Before becoming an academic, I had worked as a Native education consulting teacher with the Seattle Public Schools Native Education Program, providing advocacy for our Native youth, parents, and communities. There, I offered academic, cultural, and social support and led after-school programs for Native American youth. In addition, I gave professional development presentations to Seattle school teachers on issues like culturally relevant curricula, cultural appropriation, identity safety, and implementation of state-required Native American history. Believing I could help and giving an account of my previous work with Seattle schools, I reached out to my son's classroom teacher and principal to offer my teaching and student support services. Based on my experience with school leaders, their response was predictable. They stated that they do not have that many Native students. When I asked for the student demographics of Native American/Alaska Native student enrollment in the school and the district, they did not have the data. Their lack of knowledge of their own student demographics revealed another layer perpetuating the invisibility of Native students in statistical representation.[5] The lack of data on the Native American category means it is often marked with an asterisk, indicating roughly less than 1 percent of the student population.[6] Stephanie A. Fryberg and Sarah S. Townsend (2008) find student invisibility to be a purposeful act designed to exclude certain groups so that the majority can continue to advance.[7] In this case, the leadership purposefully dismissed my parental involvement due to the low number of Native American students.

The school declined my assistance, giving the impression that they had no interest in fostering culturally responsive teaching and would rather maintain the social and cultural norms of the mainstream group. Every morning, upon arrival at the school, we were greeted by a large office tapestry asserting the six pillars of Character Counts—core ethical values intended to "transcend cultural, religious, and socioeconomic differences."[8] As an educational model intended to make a positive impact on schools, community, and youth, Character Counts mean to develop decision-making skills and foster a growth mindset. The six pillars of Character Counts are:

Pillar 1: Trustworthiness
Pillar 2: Respect
Pillar 3: Responsibility
Pillar 4: Fairness
Pillar 5: Caring
Pillar 6: Citizenship[9]

It is evident in the listing of these pillars that they do not include cultural responsiveness. Graham Hingangaroa Smith (1990) describes how the dominant group in the United States controls and influences knowledge and culture. For example, these gatekeepers practice cultural prejudice supporting the dominant culture and pay little attention to the matters impacting the minority group.[10] Similar to the boarding school period, the dominant group continues to maintain control of academics and excludes the history, language, and culture of Native peoples.[11]

A common misconception of Native American parents' participation in their children's education is lack of interest: they allegedly do not care.[12] This misconception is commonly held by school officials. In a 2008 study conducted by Mackety and Linder-VanBerschot, Native American parents and students are described as feeling unwelcome and intimidated, raising questions about cultural competency, racism, and discrimination that, in the end, discourage parental engagement in children's schooling.[13] The report indicated that Native American parents with an adverse personal history lack the confidence to interact with school staff because of the fear of making a mistake. Some parents communicated feeling discouraged by unwelcoming school-sponsored events where they were met with intimidating stares, excluded from discussions on how to work with their children's school, and interrupted and corrected by non-Natives. Also, the parents' personal histories with boarding schools contributed to their hesitation to engage with schools. According to the study, Native families were restricted from any involvement in their children's boarding school education:

> The bottom line was that parents resented boarding schools, both reserva-
> tion and off-reservation, because they severed the most fundamental of
> human ties: the parent-child bond. The reservation school, by taking the
> child for months at a time, was bad enough; the off-reservation term of
> three to five years was an altogether hellish prospect, especially if the child
> had been shipped off without the parent's consent.[14]

Still, Native American families have been able to continue their parental responsibilities despite this colonial trauma.

My husband and I would talk about solutions like switching schools for our son; we floated the idea of both of them returning to Seattle, where I would join them when the academic year ended. These possibilities became a reality when I got a call from the principal telling me that our son was suspended for fighting. It was near the end of the school day when the elementary staff called to say that my son spent most of the day in the office from an incident that had occurred that morning. I asked why he was not allowed to return to the classroom or why we did not get called earlier. They struggled and fumbled over words to give me a response. I called my husband to pick up our son and went to the school to meet with the administrators.

During our meeting, I was told our son was involved in a fight with another student. They admitted that no one witnessed the fight, but in the version from the other student involved, our son had physically attacked him for no reason. Based on the one-sided account of the situation, the school placed my son, a first grader, on suspension. I asked if the other student would be reprimanded as well, and they said no. When I asked the principal whether the school practiced social justice, she hesitantly responded yes. I continued to demand an equitable resolution, like bringing the students together to work through the issue, since blame and alienation are not characteristics of social justice work. Social justice gives everyone affected by wrongdoing a chance to address the harm; yet our son and family did not receive an equitable, proactive disciplinary response. When I got home, I asked my son what had happened, and he said the other student had jumped on his new backpack repeatedly. My son asked the boy to stop, but he did not listen, so he reacted physically to get him to stop.

The following day I met with the school administrators to discuss the discipline policy and the reentry plan. At that time, I was informed that my husband would not be allowed on the school campus for six months. The day before, my husband had picked up our son before I met with the principal. Being upset with the school's suspension of a first grader, he voiced his frustrations during that time. The school staff and security took my husband questioning their course of action as a threat and banned him from the school premises for half a year. They said if our son needed to be picked up during school hours, I would be the only one authorized on campus; if I were not available, my husband would be allowed on campus with a school security escort.

Native families have been pleading for communication from their children's schools since boarding schools. During that era, Native "parents often bitterly complained that they were left in the dark."[15] Many wrote letters to school officials asking for the school's policies, but these went unanswered. Federal agencies seized guardianship over Native American children and parents were denied any say in terms of their children's educational rights. Even as Native American parents surrendered authority to federal agents and school officials, they were expected to be compliant and silent, giving up agency.[16]

Garry Hornby (2011) presents a compelling case that the gap in the relationship between school professionals and parents impacts student education outcomes. According to Hornby, parental involvement improves students' attitudes, behaviors, and attendance. For the teachers, parent involvement means better relationships, improved classroom climate, and more confidence.[17] Despite the encouraging results of successful parent-school relationships, issues continue to exist across the US educational system. Hornby suggests negative attitudes toward parents by school professionals are due to the lack of training the latter receive on how to work with parents. He proposes that schools work with trained professionals to learn how to communicate with parents successfully as part of teacher professional development or implement evaluations of parental communication to identify areas of strength or improvement.[18]

Some studies indicate that different outcomes in the relationship between parents and schools are related to difference in social class. Erin McNamara Horvat, Elliot B. Weininger, and Annette Lareau, for example, look at social class variations; specifically, the ways social networks influence how parents address school problems.[19] Social networking differs among families from different classes, resulting in different schooling outcomes. Middle-class families use social networking ties established through children's organized activities, teacher contact, and professional relationships to mobilize collectively and use available resources to influence the outcome of their children's educational pathways. Working-class or low-income families are more likely to remain connected to smaller kinship and have fewer ties to professionals and resources to assist with schooling concerns.

In the case of our son's school, the school district policy stated they would not tolerate the rights of others being attacked and that hostile or offensive conduct by any student would result in disciplinary action such as suspension. According to the National Center for Education Statistics, the suspension rate of American Indian/Alaska Native students is higher than that of white students by 5 percent, Hispanic students by 6 percent, and Asian/Pacific Islander students by 3 percent. However, it is lower than the suspension rate of Black students by 13 percent.[20] American Indian/Alaska Native students are more likely to be suspended and expelled at higher rates than African American students.[21] Students who have been suspended from school are at higher risk of dropping out of school. Particularly concerning is the fact that such suspensions feed into the school-to-prison pipeline. School districts enforcing discipline policies that disproportionately impact students of color generate pathways from schools toward future incarcerations.[22] Indeed, the lack of educational services, zero-tolerance policies, and suspensions or expulsions result in students dropping out or becoming part of the penal system, raising the possibility that they eventually end up in activities leading to imprisonment.[23]

Jeremiah Chin, Brian McKinley Jones Brayboy, and Nicholas Bustamante (2018) identify the school-to-prison pipeline as "rooted in the history of colonization and assimilation through boarding schools."[24] If we recognize that the current prison system was developed based on boarding school ideologies—such as removing students from homes for assimilation purposes and then oppressing them to conform—then we can see that disciplinary policies have replaced the abuse endured in boarding schools.[25] In the context of increased school violence and concern for student safety and disruption to the school day, many schools have adopted policies that employ suspension and expulsion as retribution and a way to deal with behavioral issues. In terms of Native students, the inequalities in services and supports contribute to school discipline issues. Schools too often use suspension to discipline behaviors that stem from the student's educational experiences.

Our family felt like we were blamed for the conflict; we felt disempowered, and our faith in the school diminished. At that moment, I knew our son would not be returning. He was harmed by a school that failed to provide state-directed cultural and identity support. We withdrew him from school the next day with no hesitation. After doing so, we were reluctant to enroll him in another school within the district. We revisited the idea of returning to the Pacific Northwest and the school, community, and jobs we had left. Then, a colleague shared a flyer of an Indigenous-focused charter school that recently opened in our area. I immediately drove to the school to check if they were accepting students. As I drove up to the school, the students, teachers, staff, and administrators gathered in a circle to start the morning greeting by acknowledging the sacred direction with offerings. At that moment, I knew this was our school. The morning greeting resembled the way the Diné recognize the sacred direction during prayers and ceremonies.

My roles as a mother and an academic are intrinsic to how I view my son's school, its leadership, and the historical context of school systems in the United States and New Mexico. As a Diné mother, my status is valued within our culture. To an outsider, the importance of my responsibility means very little. The Diné woman's status is from her clan affiliation at birth. Her biological children take her clan as their primary connection and become "born into" the mother's clan and "born for" the father's clan.[26] Changing Woman, the most revered deity and a symbol of maternal power, created the Diné people's clan system. As birth mother to the Hero Twins, who freed the world of monsters to create a life for the Diné people, Changing Woman is the supreme mother, encompassing intellect, kindness, and nurturing characteristics. She is the model Diné women aspire to become.[27]

Native children are at the center of Native communities; indeed, they are viewed by most Native societies as the sacred center of family or community. When colonizers became aware of this importance attached to children, they forced their removal, gaining control over families. If Indigenous communities value women as the mothers of the next generation of Native children, the children themselves are valued because they represent the future.[28] Maria Campbell explains:

> When the colonizers started to break that circle down, one of the things that the missionaries saw was that the women were so strong. They could not quite understand what was happening, but they knew that if they moved the children out of the center of the community and removed them from the women and elders, they would win.[29]

Native women were valued as the keepers of knowledge and the source of culture and wisdom.[30] Native women were the primary focus in the efforts to silence Native voices because they held political status, spiritual influence, and kept tribal societies together.[31] And by removing the children from their mothers, elders, and communities and placing them in boarding schools, missionaries succeeded at overpowering Native peoples.

My position as an academic gives me access to the State of New Mexico's education decision-makers and leaders. Native education representatives would not return my calls or emails as a parent urgently seeking support for my Diné son, but I did get responses to those emails I sent as a faculty member with my credentialed signature. Here, I utilized my positionality and privilege of educational achievement and social access.[32] As Indigenous mother and academic Robin Zape-tah-hol-ah Minthorn affirms, "we are always Indigenous in these positions and when we interact with others, we have an opportunity to educate and dismantle the systemic structures that have rendered our people invisible."[33] I drafted an email to the school district superintendent and New Mexico public education leadership to share our narrative and request a meeting to start the conversation about how my son's former school district could serve Native American students better. A month after withdrawing my son from school, I met with the superintendent of Las Cruces Public Schools to begin our conversation. After our meeting, I looked forward to hearing from the district about beginning the intentional work we discussed. Over a year later, the school district reached out to me to discuss implementing the state mandate requirements in response to *Yazzie/Martinez v. State of New Mexico.* I was invited to collaborate with southern New Mexico educators on a professional development series addressing culturally and linguistically responsive teachings for our administrators, teachers, and supporting staff. The professional development included the history of the Native American education system and how to implement culturally relevant teachings.

As part of the *Yazzie/Martinez v. State of New Mexico* case, every district and charter school in New Mexico must respond to the mandates in the lawsuit. One of the mandates is the establishment of equity councils at district and charter school levels. These councils are made up of school staff, parents, community members, and experts who develop and advise on culturally and linguistically responsive (CLR) approaches to improving the academic achievements of Native students. CLR teaching is widely approved among tribal communities, Native education leaders, and scholars.[34] Culturally responsive teaching has been described as bridge building between the students' cultures to the school environment. Cornel Pewewardy and Patricia Cahape Hammer (2003) explain, "Building such a bridge requires a degree of cultural literacy often absent in mainstream classrooms, where the vast majority of AI/AN students are taught by non-Native teachers."[35] Castagno and Brayboy believe this as well:

> Becoming a culturally competent educator is a constant learning process that requires flexibility and adaptability on the part of the educator depending on the students and contexts with which they are working. [. . .] The awareness, knowledge, and skills required are not often the focus of typical teacher education programs, nor have most of the White, middle-class women who become teachers in the United States grown up with this background. Thus, becoming a culturally competent educator requires additional time and energy devoted to this important goal.[36]

Culturally responsive teaching requires a shift in outlook on curriculum and instruction. To create an inclusive classroom, educators must foster an environment reflective of students' identities and cultures, adopt a caring teaching style, and show respect for diversity.[37] This includes strengthening relationships between schools and Native students, parents, and Native communities in a way that integrates Native language and knowledge systems into the curriculum.

Another crucial matter that needs attention is the racism prevalent in schools and directed at Native students and families. As pointed out by Castagno and Brayboy, culturally responsive teaching "rarely includes discussions of racism and how racism might relate to the need for and the effectiveness of culturally responsive educational practices."[38] The mentioned study conducted by Mackety and Linder-VanBerschot revealed that students experience racial harassment in schools. Rather than trying to understand the Native students' reactions (verbal or physical) to racial slurs from classmates, schools identify the Native students as the source of behavioral problems. Native students are harassed to the point of fighting, then are made to take the blame for the conflict and duly experience the consequences. Schools and teachers need to become reflective practitioners and question their own beliefs about Native students for change to transpire. For the partnership between schools, parents, and students to thrive, our education structures need to meet the needs of our Native families.

At the same time, Native parents cannot depend entirely on educators for solutions, as they rarely seek to understand and connect to the students' lives. Expanding on this thought, Native parents must take the initiative in advocating for students, but civilly. Finding your voice and exercising it is not always easy. Many families have challenged the educational system for their children's rights and have been disappointed by the outcome. Students have bravely attempted to take matters into their own hands and fight for equity, but their concerns go unanswered. These experiences justify our speaking up and speaking out against oppressive incidents.

Advocacy requires a planned approach. As advocates, we must remain calm and respectful. Even though protecting our children's well-being is most important, staying calm during the communication process will bring about results. If we react with anger and threats, our efforts for justice will stall. The following suggestions are strategies I put into practice as a Native education consultant advocating for Native students and my son. First, have a calm conversation with your student; ask questions for clarity. If you have a younger child (as I did), ask multiple times what happened. Staying calm and using careful language when questioning young children is essential; raising your voice could end the dialogue. Next, reach out to the school staff by phone and by email. Include all school staff involved; if your student has an IEP (individualized education plan), involve the SPED (special education) team. If your school has a truancy officer or parent liaison, request their presence. Once you have connected to all individuals involved for a team meeting, be prepared with paper and pen to write down the names of those present, including job titles and contact information like emails and phone numbers. Be an active listener and collect all details like dates, locations, and who was involved. Especially in incidents resulting in suspensions or expulsions, ask about the district's policy. Speak with confidence and intention when asking questions to convey your concerns better and get clarity on opposing views. Using your notes, construct an email or speech to the person(s) you are in touch with about your concerns, including school staff involved. Give adequate time for a response, but if you do not receive one, reach out to experts in the Native education profession.

If you have questions or need additional support, the following are suggestions for Native families to seek support from professionals in the Native education field:

- Native Education Programs: Look for Native American educators or representatives from your school district's Native education programs.
- State's Office of Indian Education Programs: Speak to a member of the Indian Education Advisory Council who advises the state Secretary of Education, Assistant Secretary of Indian Education, and the New Mexico Public Education Department about essential issues in Native communities.
- Universities: Reach out to Native American education programs/Native American education departments/Native American Studies departments.
- Native Organizations: Seek local nonprofits/tribal education offices.
- National Indian Education Association: Get in touch.

For parents who would like to build relationships with their student's school, Mackety and Linder-VanBerschot offer strategies that encourage parent involvement in school organizations, activities, and programs. They write:

> Parents seemed to be more comfortable and likely to participate in schools that offered various fun, informal social opportunities for parents and families to get to know school staff and each other. Formal and policymaking opportunities (such as school boards, parent-teacher organizations, and Johnson-O'Malley committees) had minor participation among American Indian parents. [. . .] Parents liked general activities that were open to everyone, but especially appreciated cultural events targeted to American Indian families. [. . .] One school was reported to offer a community supper one night each week for families. Another school offered a resource night for families to inform and connect them to community services.[39]

Increasing parent involvement with children's schools can be successfully accomplished by adjusting types of communication with parents like phone calls, newsletters, flyers, and emails. Schools need to be aware that some Native families do not have access to the Internet, phones, or computers to stay informed on their child's academic progress or teacher contact.[40] Also, parents should be contacted promptly before the students fall behind in school or show signs of struggling. Parents are willing to partner with schools to determine children's needs if teachers hold a genuine caring attitude of interest and respect. Often parents associate school communication with only negative reasons. While schools often reach out to parents about their children's behavior problems or disciplinary issues, parents appreciate when teachers recognize students' success or show that they are interested in their well-being and safety. Teachers' involvement with the Native community requires becoming informed of student lives and extending themselves to assist students and families by advocating and accommodating.

On the first day at our new school, my son and I were both nervous for the same reason, wondering how this school would treat him. I internalized additional anxiety, knowing that if this school did not work out, we would be moving again, causing more disruption and displacement. Gradually, I started to see the joy in his face; he was smiling and laughing again. His head was raised, and his shoulders pulled back with confidence. After school, he willingly shared details of his day, talking about his friends by name and telling me what he learned in class. There was no need to persuade or groom him into attending school; he found his place.

The school acknowledged his cultural understanding and reinforced it with a curriculum that motivated him to participate and eagerly share. School staff intentionally incorporated Indigenous languages with all students, but they also spoke Diné to my son. Although he is not fluent, speaking his first language at school supports linguistic preservation. One day he wore his moccasins to school, and I thought he would not have done this at his previous school. In a 2013 study, Stephanie A. Fryberg, Rebecca Covarrubias, and Jacob A. Burack show that the expression of cultural identities without fear of judgment or mistreatment and having a sense of belonging can result in a student successfully experiencing identity safety.[41] The school understood the importance of community members' involvement in the schooling process and invited our family to share our language and knowledge as part of the curriculum and cultural awareness. True, the transition was difficult for him at times. But when he did have rough moments at school, he was not labeled as the problem student. With a caring teacher and a principal that understood his trauma, he was able to develop trusting relationships. School staff and students that resemble him contribute to the positive outcomes and his desire to stay at the same school.

While I have shared our struggles and challenges within the New Mexico public school system, our experience is not new or unique. Native parents seek educational opportunities for their children that are safe, caring, equitable, and culturally supportive, demands that have burgeoned since the time of boarding schools. With a secure Diné identity that began in a home with a loving and protective relationship between mother and son, my boy—with a solid, positive Native identity—rejected colonial efforts to break him. Like many Native children, his act of resiliency was identified as a behavioral issue, and he was forced out of his school. As a Diné mother and academic, I began speaking out for my son when his access to a sufficient education was threatened in the New Mexico public school system. Now, his school assists parents in navigating educational, support, and advocacy services for their Native students.

Student Learning Objectives

1. Students will understand and apply different ways to advocate for Native American youth and families.
2. Students will describe the barriers experienced by Native American families and explain why student advocacy is essential in New Mexico public education.
3. Students will examine the roles of Native women within Native American education and analyze the impact on education systems.

Discussion Questions

1. Compare the ideas of Native American boarding school systems to the current New Mexico Native American education climate. Where might they be parallel, and where do they diverge?
2. If your family experienced similar events, what approach would/did you take if this was your child?

Notes

1. Kim Anderson, *A Recognition of Being: Reconstructing Native Womanhood* (Toronto: Sumac Press, 2000), 171.
2. Jennifer Nez Denetdale, "Representing Changing Woman: A Review Essay on Navajo Women," *American Indian Culture and Research Journal* 25, no. 3 (2001): 1–26.
3. Maria Elena Campisteguy, Jennifer Messenger Heilbronner, and Corinne Nakamura-Rybak, "Research Findings: Compilation of All Research," First Nations Development Institute, June 2018, https://www.firstnations.org/wp-content/uploads/2018/12/FullFindingsReport-screen.pdf.
4. Campisteguy, Heilbronner, and Nakamura-Rybak, "Research Findings."
5. Heather J. Shotton, Stephanie J. Waterman, and Shelly C. Lowe, eds., *Beyond the Asterisk: Understanding Native Students in Higher Education* (Sterling, VA: Stylus, 2013), 1–24.
6. Shotton, Waterman, and Lowe, *Beyond the Asterisk.*
7. Stephanie A. Fryberg and Sarah S. M. Townsend, "The Psychology of Invisibility," in *Commemorating Brown: The Social Psychology of Racism and Discrimination*, ed. Glenn Adams et al. (Washington, DC: American Psychological Association, 2008), 173–93.

8. "The Six Pillars of Character," Robert D. And Billie Ray Center at Drake University, accessed January 4, 2022, https://charactercounts.org/about-character-counts/.

9. "The Six Pillars of Character."

10. Graham Hingangaroa Smith, "The Politics of Reforming Maori Education: The Transforming Potential of Kura Kaupapa Maori," in *Towards Successful Schooling*, ed. Hugh Lauder and Cathy Wylie (London: Routledge, 2012), 73–87.

11. David Wallace Adams, *Education for Extinction: American Indians and the Boarding School Expereince 1875–1928* (Lawrence: University Press of Kansas, 1995); Tsianina K. Lomawaima and Teresa L. McCarty, *"To Remain an Indian": Lessons in Democracy from a Century of Native American Education* (New York: Teachers College Press, 2006).

12. Carol Robinson-Zañartu and Jauanita Majel-Dixon, "Parent Voices: American Indian Relationships with Schools," *Journal of the American Indian Education* 36, no. 6 (Fall 1996): 33–54.

13. Dawn M. Mackety and Jennifer A. Linder-VanBerschot, *Examining American Indian Perspectives in the Central Region on Parent Involvement in Children's Education* (Washington, DC: US Department of Education, 2008).

14. Adams, *Education for Extinction*, 209–38.

15. Brenda J. Child, "Homesickness," in *Boarding School Seasons: American Indian Families 1900–1940* (Lincoln: University of Nebraska Press, 1998), 43–54.

16. Lomawaima and McCarty, *"To Remain an Indian,"* 43–66.

17. Garry Hornby, *Parental Involvement in Childhood Education: Building Effective School-family Partnerships* (New York: Springer, 2011), 17–25.

18. Hornby, *Parental Involvement in Childhood Education*.

19. Erin McNamara Horvt, Elliot B. Weininger, and Annette Lareau, "From Social Ties to Social Capital: Class Differences in the Relations between Schools and Parent Networks," *American Educational Research Journal* 40, no. 2 (2003): 319–51.

20. Jill Fleury DeVoe and Kristen E. Darling-Churchill, *Status and Trends in the Education of American Indians and Alaska Natives: 2008* (Washington, DC: National Center for Education Statistics, 2008).

21. Troy A. Enid et al., *A Roadmap for Making Native America Safer: Report to the President and Congress of the United States* (Washington, DC: Indian Law and Order Commission, 2013).

22. Jeremiah Chin, Brian Mckinley Jones Brayboy, and Nicholas Bustamante, "Carceral Colonialisms: Schools, Prisons, and Indigenous Youth in the United States," in *Handbook of Indigenous Education*, ed. Elizabeth Ann McKinley and Linda Tuhiwai Smith (Singapore: Springer 2019), 575–604.

23. NCAI Research Policy Center, *School-to-Prison Pipeline Infographic* (Washington, DC: National Congress of American Indians, 2019), https://www.ncai.org/policy-research-center/research-data/prc-publications/School-to-Prison_Pipeline_Infographic.pdf.

24. Chin, Brayboy, and Bustamante, "Carceral Colonialisms."

25. Chin, Brayboy, and Bustamante, "Carceral Colonialisms."

26. Mary Shepardson, "The Gender Status of Navajo Women," in *Women and Power*

in Native North America, ed. Laura F. Klein and Lillian A. Ackerman (Norman: University of Oklahoma Press, 2000), 159–76.

27.   Carol A. Markstrom, "North American Indian Perspectives on Human Developmemt," in *Empowerment of North American Indian Girls: Ritual Expressions at Puberty* (Lincoln: University of Nebraska Press, 2008), 46–84.

28.   Anderson, *Recognition of Being*, 157–79.

29.   Anderson, *Recognition of Being*, 161.

30.   Kay G. McGowen, "Weeping for the Lost Matriarchy," in *Make A Beautiful Way: The Wisdom of Native American Women* (Lincoln: University of Nebraska Press, 2008), 53–68.

31.   Devon A. Mihesuah, *American Indians: Stereotypes and Realities* (Atlanta, GA: Clarity, 1996).

32.   Marisa Elena Duarte, *Network Sovereignty: Building the Internet across Indian Country* (Seattle: University of Washington Press, 2017).

33.   Robin Zape-tah-hol-ah Minthorn, "Indigenous Motherhood in the Academy, Building Our Children to Be Good Relatives," *Wicazo Sa Review* 33, no. 2 (Fall 2018): 62–75.

34.   Angelina E. Castagno and Bryan McKinley Jones Brayboy, "Culturally Responsive Schooling for Indigenous Youth: A Review of the Literature," *Review of Educational Research* 78, no. 4 (2008): 941–93; Cornel Pewewardy and Patricia Cahape Hammer, "Culturally Responsive Teaching for American Indian Students," *ERIC Digest*, December 2003, https://files.eric.ed.gov/fulltext/ED482325.pdf.

35.   Pewewardy and Hammer, "Culturally Responsive Teaching."

36.   Castagno and Brayboy, "Culturally Responsive Schooling," 941–93.

37.   Pewewardy and Hammer, "Culturally Responsive Teaching."

38.   Castagno and Brayboy, "Culturally Responsive Schooling," 950.

39.   Mackety and Linder-VanBerschot, *Examining American Indian Perspectives*.

40.   Mackety and Linder-VanBerschot, *Examining American Indian Perspectives*.

41.   Stephanie A. Fryberg, Rebecca Covarrubias, and Jacob A. Burack, "Cultural Models of Education and Academic Performance for Native American and European American Students," *School Psychology International* 34, no. 4 (August 2013): 439–52.

Figure 6. Students at a bus stop on their way to Gallup McKinley County School District in New Mexico, the fifth largest district in the United States. The district serves six communities that are 29 to 103 miles away from the central office. School buses travel over 2.5 million miles annually, of which over 300,000 miles are on unpaved roads. New Mexico was established on the homelands of over twenty-three different Tribal Nations and Pueblos. Out of the thirty-three counties in New Mexico, twelve are labeled as rural according to the United States Department of Agriculture. Photo credit Hondo Louis. Funded by UNM's Center for Regional Studies and Native American Studies Department.

CHAPTER FOUR

The Significance of the New Mexico Indian Education Act in the *Yazzie/Martinez* Case

CARLOTTA PENNY BIRD

Introduction and Preliminary Questions Considered for the Case

In 2014 discussions began among attorneys from the New Mexico Law and Poverty Center (NMPLC), and witnesses were contacted to assist in building a lawsuit filed on behalf of students, parents, and school districts that included Native Americans. The suit filed against the New Mexico Public Education Department (NMPED) also named the governor and legislature for their failure to provide "at-risk students with a sufficient education."[1] The plaintiff's claim that the state was not providing sufficient education referenced inadequate services for Native American children in the state's public schools. The witnesses contacted were professional educators and advocates who were asked to present testimony on the children's behalf.

The initial picture of Native American student achievement considered in the suit was based on state-reported standardized test scores, demographics of attendance and dropout rates, and rates of graduation. The witnesses were asked to consider general questions that included: What are the services and opportunities needed for Native American students to increase student achievement and what research is there to support this? With these questions in mind, the witnesses began to identify issues and factors that would present more holistic indicators for demonstrating Native American student achievement. As expert witnesses, they were permitted to state opinions based on their own experiences, that of their colleagues, and available research on the education of Native American students. It was important for the witnesses to demonstrate what was necessary to educate Native American students for success in the schools and in their communities.

Initial discussions and questions focused on how "Indian education" was defined and the kinds of indicators used to identify it. As a start, the funding sources and federal grants earmarked for Native American students attending public schools were considered, as these sources defined Indian education according to the data required to report to the public. The usual requirements were tied to indicators such as standardized test scores on reading and math assessments—in English only—along with attendance and/or dropout rates in the schools. The state's Indian Education Act (NMIEA) required the state and school districts to report on:

1. student achievement as measured by a statewide test approved by the department, with results disaggregated by ethnicity;
2. school safety;
3. graduation rate;
4. attendance;
5. parent and community involvement;
6. educational programs targeting tribal students;
7. financial reports;
8. current status of federal Indian education policies and procedures;
9. school district initiatives to decrease the number of student dropouts and increase attendance;
10. public school use of variable school calendars;
11. school district consultations with district Indian education committees, school-site parent advisory councils, and tribal, municipal, and Indian organizations; and
12. Indigenous research and evaluation measures and results for effective curricula for tribal students.[2]

The reporting requirements of the NMIEA included the indicators from the federal grant sources with additional indicators that could show a school district working with the local Native American communities. For instance, by reporting on "public school use of a variable school calendar," a school/district would be able to demonstrate its work with a local pueblo community to observe days important to the cultural ways of the community and show that the local school did not require students to be in attendance, while staff could participate in school or district professional days.

The option to consider the NMIEA as the means to determine the standards that would ask NMPED questions about the "deliverables" for Native American students developed as talk continued about the NMIEA. The questions considered related to the purposes stated in the IEA and whether there was evidence to show they were being addressed. NMPED required school districts to submit annual reports and data that could be accessed for compiling this evidence. The data was public information that could be studied to exhibit how funds were budgeted and how they were being utilized for Native American students' educational programs and services. The Law and Poverty Center requested the data and worked with professional consultants to review it.

With a focus on the Indian Education Act, the expert witnesses were asked to think about the following: What was the purpose of the NMIEA? What was the history of education for Native American students that led to today's situation? What is a sufficient education, and what is essential and basic to Native American student success? There had to be consideration of definitions of success and who was defining success, and whether success was to be viewed only from the point of view of an academic paradigm. These questions brought about remembered stories and experiences that the witnesses could share and build upon.

Key concepts began to form regarding a more expansive way to demonstrate what Native American students needed to succeed. These included ideas that education must be useful and meet the needs of the community; that language, culture and traditional values that have survived and strengthened the people must be taught; that leadership requires Native languages be understood and spoken to build the relationships of people and nations; and that knowledge of relationships and interdependence are essential to teachers and other education professionals working with Native American students. With these concepts in mind, the formulation of Native American standards of student success from a tribal perspective were then considered. This prompted a look at how tribes were expending their own funds and resources to supplement early childhood, elementary, secondary, and postsecondary education with programs related to their priorities.

In the effort to define what "Indian education" meant and the indicators of student success based on data required by state and federal education agencies, lawyers and consultants reviewed the many documents containing an abundance of statistical measures and data published by organizations like Kids Count, the National Assessment for Educational Progress (NAEP),[3] and the many annual reports published by the State Education Department (SDE) of New Mexico and later NMPED. There was no doubt in the minds of policy makers reviewing these statistical reports, based on years of standardized assessments, that Native American students were not "achieving" in the education system of the state. However, the onus for this was put upon the children and their families rather than recognized as a failure of the education system. In the minds of the public, there was something wrong with Native American students because they failed to make progress compared to other racial groups in the same schools. In short, the system was failing Native American students and had to be transformed into an environment that saw these students as valued members of their communities and schools.

Understanding the New Mexico Indian Education Act as the "Standard"

To understand the implications of the law protecting Native American students in New Mexico, it is important to return to 2003, when the legislators passed, and Governor Richardson signed into law, the NMIEA to address long-standing issues and concerns impacting the education of American Indian students within the state's public schools. This was long-awaited legislation, as several previous efforts failed to be enacted, although the need had been brought to the awareness of policy makers with the establishment of the Indian Education Unit in what was then the SDE. This later became the Public Education Department in 2003, the same year the NMIEA was established. Past experiences and ties to tribal communities provided an important perspective to the functions of the newly established Indian Education Division staff and assistant secretary of education for Indian education working to implement the NMIEA within a restructured state system. The assistant secretary of education for Indian education recalls:

> As a student I learned to leave my language and "Puebloness" at the door of the classroom because it was not valued, and much less understood. As a parent seeing my children provided an inadequate learning environment because we lived on the reservation, advocating to find the best teachers for them became a responsibility. As an education assistant I worked alongside teachers who did not know the students they were there to teach, nor did they make an effort to get to know them; but taught from textbooks and curricula that the school had adopted from district and state resources that were far removed from the community of the students. As a teacher, I saw students struggle to understand the reason for being in a school that saw them as deficient; therefore, it was imperative to share experiences and knowledge that the students could relate to as "fellow learners." As one of very few Native American education administrators, I was determined to address the foregoing issues and saw with frustration the difficulty most principals and district administrators had in communicating with Native American parents, tribal leaders, and degreed Native American teachers and staff. Many administrators had worked their way up through a system that rewarded uniformity and following state rules and policies, rather than building relationships by sharing ideas, perspectives, and inviting recommendations.[4]

The NMIEA was envisioned to begin addressing the unmet needs of Native American students attending the state's public schools. While federal dollars had been provided to public schools for these students since the 1930s and 1950s (Johnson-O'Malley and Public Law 874),[5] this was the first time that funds were appropriated from the state's coffers specifically for the needs of Native American students. Over several decades Indian educators, parents, and tribal leaders had become dissatisfied with the services provided in many public schools as they saw their children dropping out of school, being shamed by other students and teachers, and receiving less resources. Additionally, they had little to no say in the decisions made by the schools and districts regarding the education of their children. When Native American legislators attempted to provide amelioration through legislation, they did not receive widespread support among their peers until the passing of the NMIEA in 2003.

The NMIEA opens with a statement of eleven purposes meant to guide the steps necessary for public schools to begin addressing the inequities of educational services and long-standing needs of American Indian children attending the public schools serving tribal communities. Although schools were expected to report on requirements and standards defined by NMPED, the tribes and Indian educators saw the NMIEA as a first step in the right direction.[6] In this section the purposes are explained based on how we, the first staff responsible for bringing the legislation to life, understood the steps that had to be taken to transform education for Native American students in New Mexico. This understanding recently contributed to the *Yazzie/Martinez* lawsuit that aimed to address the state's failure to follow through on these stated purposes.

The purpose of the NMIEA is to:

> A. Ensure equitable and culturally relevant learning environments, educational opportunities and culturally relevant instructional materials for American Indian student enrolled in public schools.

The first important words here are "ensure equitable." "Equitable" indicates that it was necessary to provide more resources for the priorities that became clearer as dialogue with American Indian communities increasingly characterized the operations of NMPED. For instance, in the past, no education funds had gone directly from the SDE to the tribes. With the establishment of NMPED and the NMIEA, a direct funding mechanism was developed through the Memorandum of Agreements (MOA) between the tribes and NMPED for those tribes that chose to receive funds from the state to fund Native language efforts in their communities and schools. When the Requests for Proposals (RFP) were issued, it was understood and recognized that the amount of funds required to implement plans for language maintenance and support depended on the status of language efforts within each tribe. Under subsequent administrations, however, an arbitrary amount was determined by NMPED to fund tribes and schools in *equal* amounts for the projects that met NMPED specifications.

The next words to comprehend are "culturally relevant learning environments." We thought this would be easily understood by the schools; however,
in a study contracted by the Eight Northern Indian Pueblo Council (ENIPC)
from NMPED in 2007, researchers found that many teachers, schools, and districts did not provide culturally responsive learning environments. The
researchers stated that "cultural responsiveness is more than being sensitive
and aware of students' cultural background. It is also recognizing how cultures are contextually based, and necessitates educators becoming culturally
competent in order to meaningfully and appropriately incorporate students'
cultural and linguistic background into their teaching."[7] This finding supported the tribes' priority for the development of teacher preparation programs, preferably for faculty from their own communities, that would increase
and expand teachers' skills to better serve their students.

The first purpose ends with reference to "educational opportunities and
culturally relevant instructional materials." From the perspective of many
schools, the inclusion of cultural studies in tribal communities would limit
children from gaining experiences necessary for success in the present-day
world. When seen from the Native perspective, culturally relevant instruction
would provide more sustenance and foster resilience for children to achieve
greater outcomes for the benefit of themselves and their communities. If the
schools and state included the knowledge, wisdom, skills, and resources from
tribal communities in the development of instructional materials and curricula, the options for student success would greatly increase. Students and
teachers who seek cultural competency understand this approach.

B. Ensure maintenance of native languages.

This is a short and clear statement, but the realization of NMPED's obligation
to assist tribes in this area was complex. First, there had to be a recognition
that the state has no authority over Native American tribes in New Mexico,
much less over the languages still being spoken. As sovereign entities, the
tribes are not governed by legislated mandates of the state unless there is a
formal agreement stipulating the purposes and established procedures for
how the state and tribes are to relate. Thus, "The responsibilities for meeting
the purposes of the IEA was [sic] clearly on NMPED and the public school

system to implement as state agencies."[8] Not only did the NMIEA establish the responsibilities of the state but it also created a Division of Indian Education, an assistant secretary of education position, and an Indian Education Advisory Council to provide leadership and guidance for the development of relationships with the tribes. Discussions among this leadership group amplified the necessity to make clear to NMPED that for the first time, they had to coordinate efforts with the tribes. In order to do this and provide the process to distribute funds directly to the tribes, the MOAs developed between the tribes and NMPED upheld the sovereign status of the tribes to determine who would teach their language, how the language would be taught, what would be taught, and where it would be taught. Then, as this process became tribally defined, the tribes determined who would receive language instruction.

The MOAs represent a documented acknowledgment by the state that tribes have knowledge, expertise, and authority to develop procedures for certifying language teachers and determining who could teach Native language and culture to their children rather than leaving this responsibility to an outside entity or authority. This provided the means to include elders and knowledgeable people from the community to work in the schools as teachers, thus forming a valuable link between home and school. The process and procedures were tribally developed, and it was at the discretion of the tribe whether they were shared with NMPED. To facilitate these efforts, NMPED recognized and accepted the letters submitted by tribal leaders and authorities requesting certification for the teachers who were selected to work in the schools. The support of the secretary of education and the governor of New Mexico paved the way for other state officials to accept and assist in the developing partnerships for the education of Native American children. In later administrations, these intents were diminished by administrators who lacked the history, understanding, and intentions of the IEA.

> C. Provide for the study, development and implementation of educational systems that positively affect the educational success of American Indian students.

The first such study is referenced above and was contracted to ENIPC in 2007, who then subcontracted with the University of New Mexico (UNM) faculty to conduct a statewide research project to gather the educational perspectives of Native students, parents, community members, and teachers. These stakeholders identified, described, and defined authentic instructional practices and curricula to the faculty known as the Indigenous Education Study Group (IESG).[9] This collective of sharing experiences, beliefs, and values created a vision for what it means to have a system that provides opportunities for success to American Indian students.

The IESG began each focus group discussion with stakeholders by asking participants to describe the attributes of an "educated Native person." This was an important starting point as there was an unstated assumption that if one became educated, they no longer would be accepted in the community; indeed, being called a "schoolboy" or "schoolgirl" was insulting. The researchers found that "educated Native persons strengthened cultural identity by promoting and supporting strong Native American values, traditions, culture and language; served as role models and mentors for students; provided a foundation for life-long learning; worked with schools and tribes to create bridges to successful postsecondary opportunities and career development in building the capacity of their communities."[10] The IESG study found examples of successful language programs; curricula that were relevant and sustaining to Native students; teaching strategies and methods that encouraged innovation and problem solving in the context of tribal communities; factors influencing accountability indicators that would result in positive outcomes; school climates that were inviting and welcoming to Native students and their families; successful relationships that developed opportunities for collaboration among students, teachers, school staff, and tribal communities; and a vision of schools that nurtured and inspired student learning. The IESG reported these findings back to NMPED, communities, and schools that participated in the study with hopes that recommendations from the study would contribute to the implementation of the IEA.

In 2006 the state legislature's Legislative Finance Committee requested staff in the Legislative Finance Council (LFC) to conduct a "performance audit" to "determine if the 2003 provisions and resultant Public Education Department (PED) and Indian Education Division (IED) implementation activities and uses of the Indian Education Fund were appropriate to address the Native American achievement gap."[11] While there were some inherent weaknesses and biases in the quick study, the one indisputable statement was that "the reality that the 23 school districts serving 97 percent of the Native American population are focused on the state standards and tests which concentrate on core academic requirements of NCLB [adopted by the state in 2003]."[12] The study further stated that "for practical purposes there is little, if any additional time, resources, or incentives for school district administrators, school principals and teachers to grapple with expanding the curriculum to make it culturally and linguistically relevant for Native American students."[13] This finding was later corroborated by the IESG study.

> D. Ensure that the department of education partners with tribes to increase tribal involvement and control over schools and the education of students located in tribal communities.

This purpose has become more important today, as more tribes consider the establishment of charter schools or contracting Bureau of Indian Education (BIE) schools. Enactment of this purpose in schools serving Indian children provides a means for tribes to participate on equal footing in important decisions affecting the education of their children.

An example is the Navajo Nation's efforts toward this purpose within two years of establishing IEA legislation. The requirement for more tribal "control over schools" caused some debate within NMPED because the department's authority was absolute when it came to public schools. For its part, the Navajo Nation had legislated its own Sovereignty in Education Act, whereby the nation asserted its right to control schools serving their children. The Navajo Nation is the largest tribe in New Mexico and has a land base that extends into Arizona and Utah. Within this context, the Navajo Nation pushed its agenda for education sovereignty by discussing this initiative with all three state education agencies. The tribe also asked federal level officials to consider its Department of Diné Education (DODE) at the same level as a state education agency (SEA). In 2005, when the Navajo Nation amended title 10 of the Navajo Nation Education Code, it did so with the intent of initiating greater authority over and partnerships with all schools serving Navajo children. Tribal leaders stated their responsibility to do so as "the Navajo Nation has the authority and inherent right to exercise responsibility to the Navajo people; has authority to prescribe and implement education laws and policies; recognizes the legitimate authority of the actual education provider; and will work cooperatively with all education providers."[14] The state did not recognize the Navajo Nation's tribal sovereignty in all the ways that is described here in title 10. Relying solely on IEA funds, the state provided minimal resources to the Navajo Nation primarily to address NMPED priorities for Navajo language assessments for students enrolled in bilingual classes and to certify Navajo language teachers. It is still hoped that the analysis of student data may lead to the construction of tribally developed indicators for showing Navajo student progress in schools.

    E. Encourage cooperation among the educational leadership of Arizona, Utah, New Mexico, and the Navajo Nation to address the unique issues of educating students in Navajo communities that arise due to the location of the Navajo Nation in those states.

This purpose would seem to support the efforts of the Navajo Nation, for example, to have more say in the education of their children. However, issues ranging from school transportation and school boundaries to the determination of how much influence the DODE has on the schools has seen continuous discussion, even at the postsecondary level, wherein some institutes of higher education (IHE) across the three states began coordinated efforts toward professional development and teacher education courses to increase the number of Navajo teachers. The staff within the Indian Education Division of NMPED participated in and facilitated many of these initial discussions among the three states and DODE in the beginning stages of NMIEA's implementation.

With the human and material resources that have been developed by DODE, the Memorandums of Understandings (MOU) established with individual school districts have functioned as the way to influence the education of Navajo children. With MOUs in place, the Navajo Nation has provided support for the schools teaching their children through increased materials and curricula for language instruction; technical assistance to schools and districts; professional development for teachers; and workshops to assist in the certification of Navajo language teachers in all schools serving Navajo students.

F. Provide the means for a formal government-to-government relationship between the state and New Mexico tribes and the development
of relationships with the education division of the Bureau of Indian
Affairs [Bureau of Indian Education] (BIE) and other entities that
serve American Indian students.

This was seen as an important part of the NMIEA from the beginning because
several Native communities have children enrolled in both federally operated
BIE schools and state public schools. The mobility of students between the
two systems of education was both a source of conflict and opportunity. When
the NMIEA was enacted, the government-to-government (G2G) meetings
served as active work sessions where information was shared in two-way discussions that often resulted in recommendations to be acted upon by NMPED.
One of these was developing a working relationship between public and BIE
schools serving the same communities. Professional development opportunities were planned and implemented to encourage teachers and administrators
in these schools to consider transition activities and share data critical to student learning.

While NMPED continued conducting semiannual G2G meetings, these
became venues for promoting state policies rather than facilitating a voice for
the tribes. For example, at a meeting in winter 2021, state plans were provided
to tribal leaders for comment with little or no time to consult with their tribal
staff or educators regarding the merits of those plans. Even with the adoption
of the State Tribal Collaboration Act,[15] the meetings involved one-way communication where the state informed the tribal representatives of its latest
initiatives and plans with little feedback from the tribes.

G. Provide the means for a relationship between the state and urban
American Indian community members to participate in initiatives
and educational decisions related to American Indian students residing in urban areas.

This purpose responded to the increasing number of Native American children living in towns and attending schools in Albuquerque, Gallup, Farmington, and Rio Rancho. While schools in these areas were eligible to apply for

grants from the NMIEA funds, it proved challenging to determine the needs of these children, whose parents had chosen to enroll them in these schools for various reasons. Most often the family had chosen to move their residence to a location where employment or higher education was available. The legislators responded to this challenge by increasing the number of IEAC members from urban communities from one to three. This provided representation from Albuquerque, Gallup, and Farmington to advise on matters pertaining to the education of children residing in those towns.

> H. Ensure that parents; tribal departments of education; community-based organizations; the department of education; universities; and tribal, state, and local policymakers work together to find ways to improve educational opportunities for American Indian students.

This purpose was meant to involve a wide range of stakeholders in the provision of education for Native children through active ongoing services, technical assistance, and collaboration. An example of the type of collaboration envisioned was the work expected in the development of a statewide Native American history curriculum, to be advanced and facilitated by the Museum of Indian Arts and Culture (MIAC). MIAC sought to be more of a presence in and resource to tribal communities with its many holdings available for teachers and students in the classroom. Individuals invited to participate in this task force included representatives from tribal departments of education, knowledgeable parents and community members, IHE faculty, and tribal leaders. It was an important project considered seriously by tribal community members who questioned the intentions of the state and expressed their concern about the state's willingness to be honest in the telling of their history. They wanted a document that would "set the record straight" about events that impacted and shaped their lives and communities. The need for this curriculum was evidenced by students and parents participating in the IESG study. Students especially decried the old texts that referred to American Indians in the past tense in very brief sections of the social studies textbooks, otherwise erasing them from the narrative entirely. Then, when they saw the names of their parents or aunts and uncles in the books' lists of users, this added insult to injury, as it vividly demonstrated the lack of funding to provide them with new educational material. The hope was to distribute the history curriculum to all eighty-nine school districts in New Mexico and provide workshops with a resource guide for teachers to utilize.

I. Ensure that tribes are notified of all curricula development for their approval and support.

This purpose was to set precedence for curricular work at the state level, beginning with the history curricula referred to in purpose H. Importantly, it was to provide how any curricula adopted for teaching Native American students and the materials and resources to support such instruction would be reviewed and approved by the tribes before being implemented in the classroom. However, tribes and their representatives have been effectively excluded in decision-making regarding the content of instruction or the pedagogy utilized at the schools their children attend. Many decisions at state and school district levels have not been presented to tribes. The many programs that have been instituted without tribal approval or consent have yet to be documented but include distance education, textbook selection, materials, resource development, etc. As the work on implementing the NMIEA continues, with changes in both tribal and state personnel, this area requires particular attention, especially with state and local administrators prone to seeking expertise outside of New Mexico and through private contractors unfamiliar with the needs of Native American students.

An IEAC member observed that the "ongoing 'modern' problem contradicting Native self-determination occurs when Native learners are forced to wear a Western lens that makes Native culture appear backwards, stagnant, or lacking. Often the Western or modern lens is more concerned with power, control, hierarchy, materialism, enterprise, conquest and domination—values that historically subjugated Native people and rendered Native knowledge marginal and inconsequential."[16]

J. Encourage an agreement regarding the Bureau of Indian Affairs [BIE] and state assessment programs so that comparable information is provided to parents and tribes.

This was achieved early in the implementation of the IEA, as the need for accurate and reliable data sharing among state and BIE representatives, schoolteachers, and administrators was seen as vitally important by the two educational agencies. Presentations and discussions were conducted at G2G meetings where state and BIA officials viewed the data alongside tribal leaders and representatives who then provided feedback on the benefits and challenges that would accrue if an agreement was reached. Regional training sessions were conducted where public school and BIE teachers participated together, with similar questions and concerns. They questioned the selection of programs that were limited to narrow interpretations of "research-based models" recommended to address standards-based reform in their "low-performing schools." These programs did not seem to address the high expectations and success indicators envisioned by Indian students, parents, grandparents, mentors, and educators who advocated for quality and equity in the learning systems.

    K. Encourage and foster parental involvement in the education of Indian students.

This purpose has been important to all schools, as it reflects both state and federal laws mandating the involvement of parents and parent groups (e.g., school boards, school advisory councils, and parent-teacher associations in the past, and now NMPED mandated equity councils). In several tribal communities this became a complex issue, as tribal leadership was responsible historically for speaking on behalf of families in their community. Then, in cultural contexts, the parents may not be the ones responsible for the children's education. Often, this responsibility was with grandparents or other respected elders who ensured the children were properly educated. In today's school environment, these notable relations may not be acknowledged or given respect. In the complexities of individual families who have legal authority and responsibility ascribed to them by the state, the important extended family may not be understood. This is yet one more challenge to be addressed.

    With the prescriptive mandate by NMPED for school districts to establish equity councils (EC), the means for parent and community involvement became more complicated. The questions regarding responsibility and authority for decision-making remained unsettled as the role of the councils was unclear with respect to the school districts' other policy and decision-makers. Every school was required to have an advisory council and every program had an advisory committee; further, it was now the responsibility of the local school board and superintendent to work with all these interests in making the financial and programmatic decisions for all students in the district they were elected to serve. This new mix of parents, tribal leaders, teachers, and administrators now had the responsibility to ensure Native American children were served equitably.

The previous detailing of the purposes and related intents of the 2003 NMIEA became critical to the understanding of the *Yazzie/Martinez* lawsuit and the determinants of standards and deliverables in the purpose statements, beginning with the words *ensure* and *provide*.

Indigenous Perspectives to be Considered

From the tribal perspective, the NMIEA should work to hold NMPED accountable for the education of American Indian students in its schools. The idea that tribes hold schools and educational agencies accountable and responsible has yet to be addressed by NMPED and BIE. In the words of a tribal education director from a northern pueblo, "Indian children need to be given the opportunity to pursue their dreams. Schools need to be held accountable for those who do not succeed."[17]

The NMIEA brought hope for change in the schools and classrooms Native American children attended. Expectations were expressed that efforts would be directed in a positive and constructive manner toward the needs of these students. For those who were fortunate to be in the schools and districts working to serve all students, there was a sense that they would finally receive the support needed for doing the "right thing." Indigenous teachers looked forward to not closing their doors when using their language and culture to teach the children. While education is very important to the tribes, of equally high priority is the survival of their Native languages and culture. Sacrificing the latter for the sake of school success is not acceptable in their understanding of education for their children. Tribes see their children requiring additional resources, more meaningful learning experiences, enriched curricular content, and respectful relationships with those who teach them.

Deficit-focused education programs missed the message of Native communities and did not provide enriched educational experiences. These communities experience all the stress of an ever-changing world that continues to press upon their people, and some maintain that current social problems can only be understood in the context of historical trauma related to waves of colonization. Researchers are examining the causal relationship between historical trauma and issues related to human rights abuses and social problems. Resiliency theory research from the fields of psychology and sociology is identifying the tools that students and educators may employ to build stronger support systems for Native children. This can be manifested in education as exemplified by the work of Hawaiian and Alaska Natives, who have recognized this challenge and developed educational curricula centered on key values and philosophies from their own cultures. Unfortunately, institutionalized oppression of Indian people is not just a historical artifact—it persists in contemporary life. As Dorothy E. Aguilera writes, "The oppression of assimilationist educational systems is what indigenous students and communities reject, not education itself."[18]

Perspectives from tribal community members are vital and valuable to the transformation of education for American Indian students in New Mexico. At a meeting of the All Pueblo Council of Governors (APCG), with the *Yazzie/Martinez* lawsuit and discussions between NMPED representatives on the agenda, a Zuni tribal councilman explained, "Language is us. Our hearts, our soul has been given to us from time immemorial."[19] He asked the governors to do more to set the context for what languages mean to pueblos and other tribes. A state legislator supported this comment by saying, "We aren't going to be foreigners in our own land; we won't let our languages be threatened."[20] A retired legislator attending the meeting reminded NMPED officials that there has to be "consultation and agreement."[21] The New Mexico Tribal Language Consortium (NMTLC) shared their recommendations for language instruction in schools, which included resources for program and student success and elevating the status and salary of Native language teachers. They concluded with the statement, "If language is important, we have to build the infrastructure to assist tribes."[22]

Did the State Implement the NMIEA to Address
the *Yazzie/Martinez* Ruling?

Once the state district court ruled on the lawsuit in favor of the plaintiffs in 2018, the state's response was to file an appeal and continue their inequitable practices through state-sanctioned processes and policies. It is essential to understand how the educational system in New Mexico continued to maintain its stance and authority in countering tribal sovereignty.

- In recent NMPED administration, the push appeared to be toward charter and private for-profit schools, with less being done to create joint or coordinated efforts with tribes in the education of their children. This prompted one state legislator to amend the NMIEA with language requiring districts to be more accountable in how they budget and program services for Native American children as intended by the tribal-state MOAs, which were developed to share responsibility, especially in the teaching of Native languages.[23]
- The state contacted an outside entity, the Learning Policy Institute, to study and recommend what needed to be done to address the *Yazzie/ Martinez* ruling, even as recognized and respected educators in New Mexico offered their own recommendations.[24]
- NMPED called for a revision of NMIEA statutes in March 2020 just as schools were closing doors and tribal leaders were protecting their communities in response to the COVID-19 crisis. The proposed revisions presumed authority over the tribes and followed a format that was difficult to read and understand, thwarting comments from many tribal representatives. No response was given to the written comments the NMTLC submitted opposing the proposed changes.[25]
- There was a lack of tribal consultation when the assistant secretary of Indian education referred to plans for reviewing and standardizing 520 Certification during the La Cosecha Conference in November 2020. This was interpreted as ignoring the tribes' authority in determining who teaches their languages.[26]
- The Tribal Education Alliance (TEA), in partnership with Transform Education New Mexico (TENM), developed legislation carried by leg-

islators in the 2019, 2020, and 2021 sessions that would support tribal education departments, Native language instruction, libraries, and technology infrastructure. NMPED did not support these legislative initiatives during committee hearings.[27]

Conclusion

The NMIEA was enacted as a response to growing concerns that the State of New Mexico and New Mexico public schools failed to recognize the unique cultural, linguistic, and educational needs of American Indian students living in both urban and reservation communities. The intent and purpose of the NMIEA was to ensure equitable and culturally relevant learning environments for Native students in public schools; develop and implement positive educational systems; enhance the opportunities for students and aid in the development of culturally relevant materials for use in New Mexico schools; develop strategies for ensuring the maintenance of Native languages; increase tribal involvement and control; create formal government-to-government relationships between the tribes and state; and increase parental involvement in schools. Compliance with the NMIEA is overdue and necessary to sufficiently educate Native American students in New Mexico public schools.

Toward this end, greater effort must be made to acknowledge student success and definitions of sufficiency that support healthy and prosperous Native communities. Amendments made to the NMIEA in 2019 require districts to develop systemic frameworks that include programs, services, culturally relevant activities, and professional development based on the needs and priorities determined in the schools for Native American students.[28] In addition, the plaintiffs in the *Yazzie/Martinez* case called for a state plan to address the issues presented on behalf of the children attending public schools, citing the NMIEA as the standard.[29] The state and schools must develop these plans, allocate funding and resources, implement culturally appropriate methods and strategies, and determine success in coordination with the tribes in New Mexico, as envisioned by the NMIEA, to transform education for the benefit of all Native American students.

Student Learning Objectives

1. Students will be able to determine differences in the interpretation and implementation of the New Mexico Indian Education Act from enactment in 2003 to 2021.
2. Students will discuss the multiple meanings of culturally appropriate instruction and provide examples of expectations in preparation for work in schools serving Native American children.
3. Students will develop examples of enriched education activities that would be considered appropriate for Native American students.
4. Students will compare and contrast how Native tribes/nations define successful students and how the New Mexico Public Education Department defines sufficient, adequate, and uniform education.

Discussion Questions

1. What was the purpose of the New Mexico Indian Education Act? Is it still meaningful to educators as they consider the development of educational programs for Native American students?
2. How does the author consider the New Mexico Indian Education Act be used as a guide for schools serving Native American students? How would you propose to utilize it as a reference for yourself and other educators?
3. How are the meanings of culturally relevant, linguistically relevant, and multicultural education interpreted? How would you utilize your understanding of these terms in developing a program or curriculum that would increase student learning?
4. What is the tension caused by the phrasing "sufficient education" and "adequate education"? Why is this clarification necessary?

Notes

1. *Yazzie/Martinez vs. New Mexico*, no. D-101-CV-2014-00793 (First Judicial Court 2018).

2.   Indian Education Act of 2003, chapter 22, 23A NMSA (amended 2007 and 2019).

3.   Annie E. Casey Foundation, *Kids Count Data Book: State Trends in Child Well Being* (Baltimore: Annie E. Casey Foundation, 2014–2020) (reported specifically on the well-being of children); National Center for Education Statistics, *The Nation's Report Card*, National Assessment of Education Progress, 1983–2019, nationsreportcard.gov (based on standardized test scores).

4.   Carlotta Penny Bird, author's personal statement to the New Mexico Law and Poverty Center, 2016.

5.   The Johnson-O'Malley Act of 1934 and Public Law 81-874 of 1950 are two of oldest federal funds made available for Native American students attending public schools. Prior to the availability of this funding, these students attended Bureau of Indian Affairs day schools and boarding schools. P.L. 874 is also known as Impact Aid and is now Title VII of the Every Student Succeeds Act (ESSA).

6.   Carlotta Penny Bird, "Building Partnerships for Native American Languages: A Study of MOA between State and Tribes" (PhD diss., University of New Mexico, 2007), 6.

7.   Theodore Jojola et al., *Indian Education in New Mexico, 2025* (Ohkay Owingeh, NM: Indigenous Education Study Group, 2010).

8.   Bird, "Building Partnerships."

9.   Jojola et al., *Indian Education in New Mexico.*

10.   Jojola et al., *Indian Education in New Mexico.*

11.   G. Christine Chavez et al., *Quick Response of Implementation of Indian Education Act,* New Mexico Legislative Finance Committee, Report #06-04, 2006, 1.

12.   Chavez et al., *Quick Response,* 12.

13.   Chavez et al., *Quick Response,* 12.

14.   Navajo Nation Sovereignty in Education Act of 2005, the Navajo Nation Education Code Title X (as amended), Navajo Nation Tribal Council, 2005.

15.   New Mexico State-Tribal Collaboration Act (STCA, effective on December 31, 2009). The STCA requires every state agency to develop and implement a policy to promote positive government-to-government relations with tribes in New Mexico. The Indian Affairs Department is responsible for oversight, monitoring, and assisting with annual review and training of state personnel.

16.   Larry W. Emerson, *Indigenization: A Working Definition for American Scholars and Collaboration Program* (San Diego, CA: San Diego State University, 2005).

17.   New Mexico Tribal Education Summit, December 19, 2005. At this one-day forum, New Mexico tribes/nations presented education issues and concerns to then governor Richardson and state agencies. The summit was jointly facilitated by the New Mexico Public Education Department Indian Education Division and the Indian Affairs Department.

18.   Dorothy E. Aguilera, "Who Defines Success: An Analysis of Competing Models of Education for American Indian and Alaska Native Students" (PhD diss., University of Colorado, 2003).

19.   Wilfred Eriacho Sr., Zuni Tribal Council, All Pueblo Council of Governors meeting, July 20, 2017.

20.   Derrick Lente, representative, New Mexico State Legislature, All Pueblo Council of Governors meeting, July 20, 2017.

21.   Richard Miera, retired representative, New Mexico State Legislature, All Pueblo Council of Governors meeting, July 20, 2017.

22.   Virgie Bigbee, president, New Mexico Tribal Language Consortium, All Pueblo Council of Governors meeting, July 20, 2017.

23.   Indian Education Act of 2003, chapter 22, 23A NMSA (amendments authorized in 2007 and 2019).

24.   Jeanie Oakes et al., *Improving Education the New Mexico Way: An Evidence-Based Approach* (Palo Alto, CA: Learning Policy Institute, 2020).

25.   Virgie Bigbee, president, New Mexico Tribal Language Consortium, letter response to proposed revisions to the statutes governing the implementation of the NMIEA, March 16, 2020.

26.   Gwen Warniment, deputy secretary of education for teaching, learning and assessment, presentation on "Dual Language as a Touchstone for the State of New Mexico" at La Cosecha Conference in Santa Fe, NM, November 5, 2020. Author's personal notes documented for NMTLC.

27.   Transform Education New Mexico (TENM) and Tribal Education Alliance (TEA) bills HB 52, HB 84, HB 85, HB 86, HB 87, and HB 135, presented at legislative committee hearings during the 2021 regular session.

28.   Indian Education Act of 2003, chapter 22, 23A NMSA (amended in 2019).

29.   *Yazzie/Martinez vs. New Mexico*, no. D-101-CV-2014-00793 (First Judicial District Court 2018).

Part II | The Response

Figure 7. The New Mexico State Legislative Senate discussing House Bill (HB) 60—Native American Language Certificate Salaries—through the New Mexico legislative webcast. Pictured standing is Senator Benny Shendo Jr. (Democrat, District 6, Jemez Pueblo), explaining to Senator William E. Sharer (Republican, District 1) the intent behind HB 60. Pictured alongside Honorable Shendo are House Representative Derrick J. Lente (Democrat, District 65, Sandia Pueblo) and Regis Pecos (Cochiti Pueblo). HB 60 passed in the Senate by Yay 34 and Nay 0 on February 15, 2022. Photo credit New Mexico State Legislature webcast.

CHAPTER FIVE

The New Mexico Public Education Department Response

An Analysis of the 2021 Strategic Plan to Resolve the Yazzie/Martinez *Case*

WENDY S. GREYEYES

Introduction

How can an organization identified as a culprit that perpetuates the disenfranchisement of students be the same entity to construct its own remedy? The consolidated *Yazzie/Martinez* lawsuit created just that circumstance:[1] increased accountability means the organization must find remedies that may be extreme, thus rendering them incapable of implementation. This issue was brought up among Native American professors as we discussed the actions taken by the State of New Mexico to resolve the *Yazzie/Martinez* educational suit. Our Native faculty discussed how the legislative moves and fixes were ineffective and too far removed from tribal communities. One of my colleagues stated their community was already enacting homegrown resolutions stemming from their community values. Still, although this response is important to Native communities, the state should ultimately be held responsible. Native communities should not be fixing the state's problem, yet this creates a complex dynamic because the students in these school systems are *our* children. The state is not invested in American Indian children. This has been repeatedly proven. Even now, as the question of critical race theory hits the state legislative debate floors, some New Mexico politicians continue to downplay its necessity. A systematic restructuring of the entire educational system needs to occur statewide, not just as isolated pockets of community action. The results of the *Yazzie/Martinez* case reveal the issues affecting American Indian education to be systemic and structural. Change must be pursued from the top down to effectively solve the lack of responsiveness to Native students by educational institutions. But it is evident that very little is understood about how state and federal policies feed into local communities.

At the state level the implementation arm of policy action belongs to the executive branch. The laws are very clear regarding how funding should be expended, and policies provide direction. The response to the *Yazzie/Martinez* ruling from the state, specifically from the New Mexico Public Education Department (NMPED), was to create a strategic action plan. Strategic plans build upon expectations of stability in the present in order to forecast outcomes. They identify and attempt to organize goals, actions, timelines, and eventually, outcomes. As we examine the remedies arising in response to the *Yazzie/Martinez* lawsuit, we must situate the role of the strategic plan and its historical significance. We must question the underpinnings of a strategic plan that may come under the guise of an action plan or a long-term plan. The tenor of the vocabulary and terms may shift, but ultimately, the strategic plan is driven by the state itself.

In this chapter, I (1) explore the history of strategic planning in order to understand its historical and bureaucratic significance, particularly in light of NMPED's response to the *Yazzie/Martinez* ruling; (2) examine the role of strategic plans in education and educational settings; (3) provide an analysis of the proposed NMPED strategic plan; and (4) conclude with a discussion on what is needed to transform the education of Native American students in the state.

History of the Strategic Plan: The Myth of Planning

There is a Western belief that strategic planning holds the key to the future, just like the mythical fortune teller's crystal ball. The belief is that by planning and organizing all the moving parts of a bureaucratic system toward specific goals, the outcomes will be fulfilled. The underlying premise is if you control the actions of the people, then the outcomes will be in your favor. In essence, the people in the bureaucracy endure a process of assimilation in order to fulfill the goals. Adherence to strategic planning relies on the workers within the bureaucracy trusting its legitimate action, meaning they must have a belief in "the legality of enacted rules and the right of those elevated to authority under such rules to issue commands."[2] The bureaucracy is, in essence, a community, an organization, a grouping of people who are the agents carrying out and acting upon the strategic plan. However, it is important to understand challenges to these assumptions about bureaucratic rule. The ideal types of legitimate authority are described by Max Weber, a classic theorist focused on the study of bureaucracies.[3]

Max Weber's analysis of the three ideal types of legitimate authority provides a deeper understanding of how a legal, authority-driven structure is validated by its workers. This is critical to understand why people follow these systems, which Weber describes with the following terms: legal authority, traditional authority, and charismatic authority. [4]Actions of the legal type rely on the acceptance of colonized conceptualizations of a rationalistic legalism. The idea of rationality as the driver of bureaucracy is premised on a set of stable actions undertaken by the organization's workers. In contrast, traditional authority is premised on the idea that leaders are given positions of power based on their lineage, similar to a monarchical distribution of power. People therefore follow the leadership based on the inherited status and lean on this form of leadership with a "belief in the sanctity of immemorial traditions."[5] For its part, charismatic authority is dependent on a person's skillfulness in articulating issues and ideas so that people are convinced to follow their leadership and support the implementation of their goals. The charismatic leader relies on the "devotion to the exceptional sanctity, heroism or exemplary character of an individual person."[6] Weber's discussion of traditional and charismatic leaders was intended to contrast with modern society's version of legal authority, which is dependent on a set of conditions to create a system of domination within a bureaucratic structure. Namely, the organization's leaders must be "personally free and subject to authority only with respect to their impersonal official obligations, [the structures of authority] are organized in a clearly defined hierarch of offices, [and] candidates are selected on the basis of technical qualifications."[7] The importance of clarifying *why* people follow and adhere to a system helps to explain the bureaucratic relationship to the people the bureaucracy ostensibly serves. This type of bureaucratic chain is found in churches, hospitals, the military, some governments, and corporations.

Understanding the roots of bureaucracy is key to deconstructing institutions like NMPED, a state education agency utilizing a bureaucratic system to organize its actions. It is critical to also recognize that this adherence to a legalistic authority stems from widespread belief in its advantages. Bureaucratic effectiveness is a great human accomplishment but also one of the most oppressive structures in our world. As Weber describes it, the effectiveness of the bureaucratic mechanism historically helped to push capitalism into a new era of output and routinization. Indeed, in his view, "[bureaucracy] is superior to any other form in precision, in stability, in the stringency of its discipline, and its reliability."[8] The bureaucratic system is a powerful structure pushing the goals and agenda of capitalism into our daily lives.

When Weber published his analysis of the rise of bureaucracy and its rational justifications in 1914, the industrialization of American economic life was pushing forward, characterized by theories of the division of labor, assembly lines, and Fordism that stemmed from an understanding of the positive effects of bureaucracy. During this period, schools taught young American Indians agricultural and industrial skills as well as the English language, which ultimately was intended to bring them into the fold of a capitalistic wage labor system. Jon Reyhner and Jeanne Eder highlight this process: "Taken altogether, an impartial view of the situation warrants the belief that sometime in the near future it is fair to presume that, with the aid of such industrial, agricultural, and mechanical schools as are now being carried on, the Indian will be able to care for himself, and be no longer a burden but a help to the Government."[9]

In the 1950s strategic planning was viewed as a critical corporate function in larger companies, such as General Electric Company (GE). The work of William Ocasio and John Joseph shows how early integrative strategic planning was originally called long-range planning.[10] Their 2008 study of GE from the 1940s to the 2000s provides a glimpse into both its rooted nature as a capitalistic structure and the evolution of strategic planning. Ocasio and Joseph describe that although language and labels change, ultimately the underlying roots of strategic planning are at work within corporate structures. The authors provide a basic definition of strategic planning: "We define strategy as a framework, either implicit or explicit, that guide's an organization's choices of action. We interpret this definition broadly and view strategies as planned and emergent, resulting from strategic design, the evolution of a pattern of decisions, or a combination of the above."[11] Specifically, they identify planning as based on three conditions:

1. Articulation of goals and objectives for planning;
2. establishment of a division of authority and responsibility for planning, implementation, and control; and
3. development of standardized planning procedures.[12]

In the same article the authors point out that these strategic actions were borrowed from the US War Department during World War II. The military enacted them in order to cope with the vast number of people operating within the ranks of their organization.[13]

In another study Ansoff examined whether companies that undertook strategic planning outperformed non-planning companies. The evidence reveals mixed outcomes. At present, the study of strategic planning research, according to Whittington and Cailluet, has become less popular owing to the rationalistic and detached perception of strategic planning; it is increasingly seen as missing the role of intimacy and intuition. This view is emphasized by Henry Mintzberg's "Crafting Strategy," which brought about a different awareness of strategic planning and its shortcomings. Still, Whittington and Cailluet contend strategic planning has never stopped but has taken on new forms.[14]

The ebbs and flows of strategic planning have a rich and deep history among organizational analysts. The history of strategic planning as a component of bureaucracy helps us better understand the educational domain. To boil down the argument: Organizational analysts have developed these Eurocentric systems in order to perpetuate the myth of objectivity to increase efficiency. It is applicable to our specific case as we consider how other systems of power perpetuate this myth, such as the New Mexico Public Education Department, formerly the State Education Department discussed by Carlotta Penny Bird in chapter 4.

History of Educational Strategic Plans

According to Robert H. Beach and Ronald A. Lindahl, the earliest educational planning began around the period of World War I and II.[15] Soldiers used their military training and applied the tools of strategic planning to indoctrinate recruits. In the models described by Beach and Lindahl, the strategic plan was broken into processes—the design process and implementation (change). They describe how "a school will examine its capacity and willingness to plan, implement and institutionalize the proposed change(s)."[16] To implement these processes, schools would do the following after World War II:

- Assess the scope and feasibility of change
- Provide administrative support for change
- Address the organizational culture and climate
- Develop leadership and staff skills
- Assess institutional history and current involvement with change efforts
- Clarify the vision, goals, and objectives
- Observe innovations in other settings
- Provide access to consultants
- Recognize time constraints[17]

Later, Beach and Lindahl added additional items to the list, seeking to investigate educational institutional goals through a set of questions:

- Where are we?
- Where do we want to go?
- What steps must we take in order to get there?
- What time and resources will we need to take those steps?
- How will we measure our progress or success?

Although Beach and Lindahl focus strictly on the school site, it is important to point out that State Education Agencies (SEAs) were established in

1965 with the creation of the Elementary and Secondary Education Act (ESEA). This was the first time the federal government pushed states to actively become uniform in structure and increased national oversight of all kindergarten-to-twelfth-grade education systems in the United States. Although historically the federal government had been heavily involved with American Indian education, according to the Center for American Progress (CAP), "Title V of ESEA marked an explicit attempt to equip states to implement expansive new federal legislation by providing federal support to strengthen state education agencies' administration of the new law."[18] The centralizing elements of the 1965 ESEA reconstituted the educational system and placed the burden upon states to set up SEAs. Although the CAP points out that no state education agency looks similar, they have identified several concerns about SEAs, as expressed by former and current chief state officers from thirteen states. In the study, the CAP finds SEAs to be overly focused on compliance, pointing out that SEAs were simply responsible for administering state and federal funds with a focus on law compliance and less on helping schools increase student achievement. Second, there is a lack of transparency. SEAs receive millions in public funds annually, and it is unclear how agencies spend this money and how they function. Specifically, the CAP study points out that state education websites are difficult to navigate to acquire this information. Third, federal funding can hinder SEA operations. Federal funding comes with an unsurmountable number of rules and restrictions that constrain the SEAs' flexibility. Finally, there are bureaucratic obstacles to reforming the SEAs. State governments have rigid rules around hiring, pay scales, and civil service laws preventing state chiefs from hiring talented staff.[19]

These findings highlight some of the challenges affecting state education agencies and contributing to the culture of stagnation built into the institution of state education agencies. It is imperative that we deconstruct these institutions if tribal educational leaders and stakeholders are to know whether strategic planning goals are not met by the state education agency—in this case, NMPED. Holding the SEA accountable means also recognizing its strengths and limits.

The history of New Mexico's governance over education is a unique one compared to other state education agencies. Education researchers John D. Mondragón and Ernest S. Stapleton show public education in New Mexico existed in 1891, even before the state was formalized.[20] The authority and power of the state's oversight comes from the New Mexico State Constitution, which identifies the secretary of public education, appointed by the governor, as a cabinet level position. The secretary is responsible for the operation of public schools. In addition, the Public Education Commission, the governor, and the legislature also have roles in the operation of schools, specifically in financing and managing public schools.

Mondragón and Stapleton point out the tension among the different levels of government, comprising the local, state, and federal agencies.[21] The question is "Who's in charge" among these three entities? In the case of New Mexico, there is also the added governing body of tribal governments. The tension stems from educational law changes, funding, rule-making authority, and other decisions. This is an added institutional pitfall that must be factored into any strategic decision-making.

Overall, this section of the chapter is intended to understand the role of NMPED and the complex institutional terrain that must be navigated in its case to implement a tool such as strategic planning. Planning is an integral part of NMPED's culture; however, as much as NMPED may aim for the stars, they are still bridled by federal, local, and tribal expectations. There is also the added layer of attitudes and grounded beliefs that is harder to capture. Recent efforts to develop revised social studies standards that include the history of Native peoples have been met with resistance. Many view these changes in the standards as a strategy to impose critical race theory. Evidently, some political ideologies continue to hold that Native peoples' history is not part of New Mexico's history. In what follows, I examine New Mexico's proposed strategic plan as a remedy to the *Yazzie/Martinez* ruling.

New Mexico's Strategic Plan as Remedy

On August 9, 2021, a draft action plan (the strategic plan) was released to the public. The plan included NMPED's responses to Judge Singleton's decision in the consolidated *Yazzie/Martinez v. State of New Mexico* case; it emphasized this was only a draft action plan, with heavy, italicized markings. In it the authors from NMPED describe the many collaborators, including "the

Governor, multiple state agencies, Children's cabinet, tribal leadership, legislators, student group representatives, individuals, institutions, organizations,
advocacy groups, community-based organizations, school and charter school
leaders, boards of education, higher education, and professional organizations." They also included select portions of the Tribal Remedy Framework
(TRF) and Improving Education the New Mexico Way Learning Policy Institution.[22] The TRF was a project organized by tribal leaders to identify priority
areas as a collective voice. (A deeper analysis of the TRF is developed in chapter 8 of this book by Lloyd L. Lee.)

Overall, the plan is extremely ambitious, though it does not address some of
the structural issues affecting NMPED. It includes a variety of stakeholders,
such as grassroot players, making it very diverse , though it is unclear how these
voices will be equally heard. The effort to construct a strategic plan that effectively captures the diversity of voices must be met with caution. To provide
some refined structure, the plan's authors aligned it to a four-pillar framework.

In table 1, I discuss the four pillars, NMPED's response under these pillars,
and my analysis of the action plan, and I provide a synthesis of the action plan
used to collect information from stakeholders. The draft plan is clearly a document still at its genesis stage. As stakeholders' comments on the plan mate-
rialize, there will be changes to future documents. At this stage, however, an
analysis of the plan reveals some major issues that make it an unreliable and
untargeted response to the *Yazzie/Martinez* ruling. Here, I provide a point-by-
point analysis of these problematic areas.

1. It is not clear why the pillars do not indicate which departments are
    directly responsible for implementing each plan. For example, under
    the first pillar, the action plan identifies five strategies to fulfill its first
    goal: (1) recruitment, (2) high quality teacher preparation, (3) induction
    for early career teachers, (4) growth-oriented professional learning, and
    (5) leadership development for principals, district leaders, and school
    boards. Among the agencies listed in the plan, it is unclear which
    agency or department is accountable for fulfilling the strategies. (Spe-
    cifically, the departments and agencies mentioned are the New Mexico
    Public Education Department, the Department of Cultural Affairs,
    the Indian Affairs Department, Early Childhood Education and Care

Table 1. The Four Pillars of NMPED's Action Plan for Responding to the *Yazzie/ Martinez* Lawsuit. Published August 9, 2021.

FOUR PILLARS	NMPED RESPONSE	MISSING OR CONCERNING ELEMENTS
1. Creating a Vibrant Educator Ecosystem	Under the first pillar, the action plan identifies five strategies to fulfill its first goal: 1. Recruitment (p. 10); 2. High Quality Teacher Preparation (p. 11); 3. Induction for Early Career Teachers (p. 12); 4. Growth-Oriented Professional Learning (p. 13); 5. Leadership Development for Principals, District Leaders, and School Boards (missing).	Pillar 1 is incomplete, with the fifth strategy missing. Accomplishments listed in the appendix do not make it clear how the fourteen accomplishments link back to the five strategies. Data points are incorrect. For example, under vacancies listed, the year 2018 shows 740 while 2020 shows 571. This action plan released in 2021 does not give updated data that shows that the vacancy increased to over 1,000 based on a draft analysis presented to the NM State Legislature on September 21, 2021, during the Legislative Finance meeting in the Senate Chamber.* In addition, it is imperative that a baseline is described to show progress. The 2020 New Mexico Tribal Education Status Report shows 5 percent of statewide district staff are American Indian.† In order to establish benchmarks for the plan, the baseline must be clarified for how many teachers are Highly Qualified, how many are Highly Effective, and the number of Native teachers in teacher pipelines. Many of the strategies are situated in the future tense and need additional data and timeline clarification.
2. Whole Child and Culturally Responsive Education	Under the second pillar, the action plan identifies five strategies through: 1. Deeper Learning (pp. 15–16); 2. Community-based Culturally and Linguistically Responsive Instruction (pp. 17–18); 3. Social Emotional Learning (p. 19); 4. Positive School Climates and Proactive Support (pp. 19–20); 5. Enrichment, Extracurricular, and Out of School Time Programs (pp. 20–21). As described, the pillar promises increased academic outcomes and attention to the social-emotional, cultural, linguistic, and enrichment needs of all students.	Pillar 2 describes an additional comprehensive Yazzie/Martinez plan to address Whole Child Education (p. 48) as part of its accomplishments. It is not clear if this is the same document or why there is a separate response plan. The concept of culturally responsive education is not clarified in the accomplishment section. Which of these accomplishments are linked to the five pillars? Echoing points made in relation to pillar 1, benchmarks are critical, especially because special attention is being paid to students with disabilities, Native American students, English language learners, and economically disadvantaged students.
3. Pathways and Profiles	Under the third pillar, the action plan identifies five strategies: 1. Graduate Profiles (pp. 22–23); 2. Reimagined system of College and Career Preparation (pp. 23–24); 3. Experimental Learning Opportunities (pp. 24–25); 4. Culture of College and Career Readiness (missing); 5. School Redesign (missing). As described, the pillar promises increased graduation rates and increased opportunities for applied experiential learning.	This pillar is incomplete, with two strategies missing. Under the accomplishments, the goal establishes a 2 percent graduation rate goal. This is the first time a benchmark is established. Accomplishments listed in the appendix do not make it clear how the five accomplishments link back to the five strategies (p. 49).

| 4. Asset-Based Supports and Opportunities | Under the fourth pillar, the action plan identifies seven strategies: 1. Strategic Resource Allocation (p. 26); 2. Closing the Digital Divide (p. 27); 3. Community Schools (p. 27); 4. Health Services & High-Quality Nutrition (pp. 27–29); 5. Student Attendance (p. 29); 6. Extended Learning Opportunities (p. 30); 7. Family and Community Engagement (pp. 30–31). As described, the pillar promises the removal of external barriers and provision of equitable access to services for students to be able to thrive in educational settings regardless of their demographics, income level, or disability level. | This pillar identifies accomplishments on pp. 48–49, but needs to be reorganized to follow pillar 3. There are data points that reference the COVID-19 pandemic, but it is not clear how this links to resolving the *Yazzie/ Martinez* lawsuit. Accomplishments listed in the appendix do not make it clear how the thirteen accomplishments link back to the five strategies (pp. 48–49). |

Note: Missing means there is no narrative or analysis included in the strategic plan.

* Julia Goldberg, "NM Grapples with 'Staggering' Teacher Shortage," Santa Fe Reporter, September 22, 2021; New Mexico State Legislature, "2021 Legislative Finance Meeting," September 21, 2021, http://sg001-harmony.sliq. net/00293/Harmony/en/PowerBrowser/PowerBrowserV2/20210922/-1/67947.

† New Mexico Public Education Department, 2019–2020 Tribal Education Status Report, November 2020, https://webnew.ped.state.nm.us/wp-content/uploads/2021/01/TESR2020.pdf, p. 6.

Department, Human Services Department, Higher Education Department, and Department of Information Technology (pp. 32–46).)

2. It is not clear which entity within NMPED will be responsible for the implementation of the strategic plan.

3. The timeline for implementation is unclear.

4. It is not clear how the funding amounts listed under appendix A on pp. 47–65 address the overall unmet need of students with disabilities, Native American students, English-language learners, and economically disadvantaged students.

5. Throughout the body of the strategic plan, baseline data is not provided, although metrics are used to show measurable outcomes. For example, the current number of students with disabilities, Native American students, English-language learners, and economically disadvantaged students identified throughout the strategic plan is unclear.

These five issues demonstrate the major gaps in this planning stage of the document. The myth of strategic planning as being the most efficient and effective pathway toward enacting transformative change is evident here. Judge Singleton released her decision in June 2018; this draft plan was only announced in August 2021. The delay of three years of planning and preparation in NMPED's response shows external stakeholders that the State Education Agency may not be the best actor to resolve the immediate needs of Native American students. As actions by NMPED continue to be delayed, the needs of 8.7 percent of American Indian and Alaska Native students in New Mexico continue to be unmet, perpetuating Indigenous disenfranchisement.[23] Transformative educational change and cultural shifts will take a long time, especially in a very large state education agency.[24] It is evident the stakeholders must be part of the conversation to create structural and organizational shifts.

REORGANIZING NMPED

NMPED needs to reexamine its own bureaucratic structure and consider ways to transfer more power and authority to local decision-makers. NMPED staff serving American Indian and Alaska Native students have endured high turnover; it takes extended periods to fill key Native education positions. For example, in 2019 the Indian Education Advisory Council (IEAC) prioritized one of their advisories to include the hiring of key personnel to fill vacant positions. The organizational chart for NMPED showed at this time five vacant positions (fig. 8).

Indeed, NMPED's team has struggled to fill critical positions. Kara Bobroff carried out two sets of duties, as both deputy secretary and acting assistant secretary of Indian education. The department finally filled the assistant secretary position in October 2020, one year after her departure. The position of assistant secretary is a key position within NMPED; however, the job is highly political, as reflected in former interim assistant secretary Kara Bobroff's departure the same week that First Judicial District Judge Matthew Wilson denied a motion by the State of New Mexico to dismiss the *Yazzie/Martinez* lawsuit. The inability to adequately staff these New Mexico Indian Education positions, totaling eight roles intended to serve the tribes and

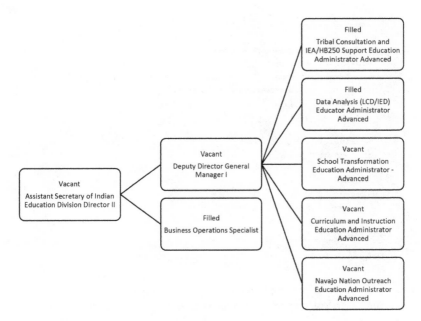

Figure 8. Indian Education Department Organizational Chart, New Mexico Public Education Department (NMPED), October 2019. Council Meeting, November 14, 2020. Indian Education Advisory Council Quarterly Meeting. Information provided by the New Mexico Public Education Department

pueblos within the entirety of New Mexico, is a small sampling of the continued inefficiency of a large bureaucratic system. The actions of one administration also do not necessarily transfer to new administrations, and typically, high ranking decision-makers within NMPED will leave after a new governor's administration starts. This adds another limitation to the action plan devised by NMPED.

DISCONNECTED LEADERSHIP

A potential partner for NMPED is the state legislature, a complex system impacting two critical elements: funding for programs and initiatives at NMPED and regulatory and statutory changes to existing educational law. The legislative response to *Yazzie/Martinez* leaves one with an overwhelming

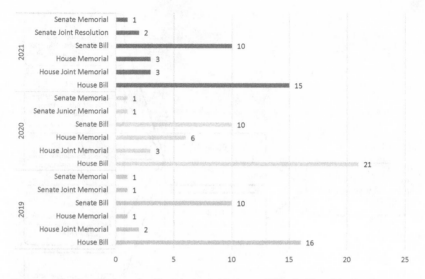

Figure 9. The distribution of 107 legislative initiatives within the New Mexico State Legislature that reference or mention "Yazzie/Martinez Lawsuit." Produced June 10, 2021.

sense of the creation of too many measures. One critic described it as "producing lots of legislation until one sticks." In response to Judge Singleton's orders, the legislature initiated 107 separate pieces of legislation, shown in figure 9.

The figure shows the rapid action of the state legislature in trying to resolve the *Yazzie/Martinez* lawsuit. Unfortunately, many of these legislative actions did not directly address the lawsuit, a majority did not pass, and very few made it to the governor for a signature. This further contributed to the delays in responding to the needs of Native American students. The rush of action during this period does not reflect a strategic state action, as many new entities and players emerged to fend for their own public schools or were very specific in addressing the needs of their students. The State of New Mexico has many leaders but no cohesive singular decision-maker. The state also has many players working to address the issue of student disenfranchisement, but ultimately, the bureaucratic process is a hindrance to bringing fast-paced relief to students. The creation of structural and cultural change will take a dedicated leader to remove the *who is in control* issue.

Conclusion

As demonstrated in this chapter, the bureaucratic system, conceived and described by Max Weber as the most efficient system in human history, is clearly shown to be a myth. In essence, to adequately transform the system, there is a need for a new form of organization wherein tribes and pueblos are the decision-makers, with the added element of building stronger schools operated by tribes and pueblos. Although many tribally controlled schools and bureau-operated schools are not permitted to be built by the federal government due to a moratorium, public schools should be returned to tribal nations, who should operate their own school systems.

NMPED is a cumbersome, large bureaucratic structure attempting to manage a school system like the military manages its soldiers, as noted earlier. The state must consider ways of decentralizing the system and empowering tribal governments to be the drivers of their own educational structures.

It is also clear the bureaucratic response to the *Yazzie/Martinez* lawsuit is extremely delayed and not a durable or responsive system capable of meeting the immediate needs of students identified in the lawsuit. The report *State Education Agencies as Agents of Change* proposed a set of recommendations to resolve the structural limitations for an SEA like NMPED.[25] These include the following:

+ The state should reduce hiring constraints for both the SEAs and schools in order to allow decision-makers to hire talented teachers and staffing.
+ The state should continue to increase salaries for teachers to induce more individuals to become teachers.
+ The state should give authority to take over low-performing schools and school districts.
+ The federal government should provide political cover to drive improvement.
+ The federal government should grant flexibility around federal rules and regulations.

When considering these recommendations, federal and state rules and systems seem to have failed to achieve efficiency. I believe it is imperative to educate tribal leaders and educational stakeholders on the historical roots of NMPED, which is encumbered by rigid federal rules and regulations. This is a common theme even for tribal nations as they navigate their own administrative systems. Optimally, the adoption of the report's recommendations could alleviate the bureaucratic hindrances besetting NMPED, allowing it to become a durable and responsive organization.

Student Learning Objectives

1. Students will understand the history and purpose of strategic planning.
2. Students will understand the New Mexico strategic plan.
3. Students will understand the bureaucratic barriers impacting NMPED's strategic planning.

Discussion Questions

1. What is the myth of strategic planning?
2. What are the bureaucratic barriers impacting NMPED's strategic planning?

Notes

1. The lawsuit is titled the *Yazzie/Martinez* lawsuit. Given that this chapter is about Native Americans, I have intentionally reversed the labeling to read "*Yazzie/Martinez* lawsuit." See *Yazzie/Martinez v. State of New Mexico*: July 20, 2018, Decision and Order, prepared by the Legislative Education Study Committee, https://www.nmlegis.gov/handouts/ALESC%20081518%20Item%2012%20.1%20-%20Brief%20-%20Decision%20and%20Order-Yazzie%20and%20Martinez%20v%20State%20of%20NM.pdf.
2. Guenther Roth and Claus Wittich, *Economy and Society: An Outline of Interpretative Sociology* (Berkeley: University of California Press, 1978), 215.
3. Roth and Wittich, *Economy and Society*, 215.
4. Roth and Wittich, *Economy and Society*, 220, 227, 241.

5.   Roth and Wittich, *Economy and Society*, 215.

6.   Roth and Wittich, *Economy and Society*, 215.

7.   Roth and Wittich, *Economy and Society*, 220.

8.   Roth and Wittich, *Economy and Society*, 223.

9.   Jon Reyhner and Jeanne Eder, *American Indian Education: A History* (Norman: University of Oklahoma Press, 2004), 76.

10.   William Ocasio and John Joseph, "Rise and Fall—or Transformation? The Evolution of Strategic Planning at General Electric Company, 1940–2006," *Long Range Planning* 41, no. 3 (June 2008): 248.

11.   Ocasio and Joseph, "Rise and Fall," 250.

12.   Ocasio and Joseph, "Rise and Fall," 250.

13.   Ocasio and Joseph, "Rise and Fall," 250–51.

14.   Richard Whittington and Ludovic Cailluet, "The Crafts of Strategy: Special Issue Introduction by the Guest Editors," *Long Range Planning* 41, no. 3 (June 2008): 241.

15.   Robert H. Beach and Ronald A. Lindahl, "A Discussion of Strategic Planning as Understood through the Theory of Planning and its Relevance to Education," *Educational Planning* 22, no. 2 (2015): 6.

16.   Beach and Lindahl, "Discussion of Strategic Planning," 6.

17.   Beach and Lindahl, "Discussion of Strategic Planning," 6.

18.   Cynthia G. Brown et al., *State Education Agencies as Agents of Change: What It Will Take for the States to Step Up Education Reform*, Washington, DC: Center for American Progress, July 27, 2011, 7.

19.   Brown et al., *State Education Agencies*, 3.

20.   John B. Mondragón and Ernest S. Stapleton, *Public Education in New Mexico* (Albuquerque: University of New Mexico Press, 2005), 28.

21.   Mondragón and Stapleton, *Public Education in New Mexico*, 30.

22.   Draft Action Plan for Response to Judge Singleton Decision: *Yazzie/Martinez v. State of New Mexico*, New Mexico Public Education Department, August 9, 2021, email received by Assistant Secretary of Indian Education on August 15, 2021, 3.

23.   NMPED, *Tribal Education Status Report Guidebook* (TESR), 2020, 7.

24.   NMPED, *Tribal Education Status Report Guidebook* (TESR), 2020, 7.

25.   Brown et al., State Education Agencies.

Figure 10. New Mexico state representative Derrick J. Lente (Democrat, District 65, Sandia Pueblo) has been a strong advocate defending the *Yazzie/Martinez* tribal remedy framework initiatives through the state legislature. Photo credit Hondo Louis. Funded by UNM's Center for Regional Studies and Native American Studies Department.

CHAPTER SIX

Navajo Nation's Response to the *Yazzie/Martinez* Case

Implications for Navajo Nation's Educational Sovereignty

ALEXANDRA BRAY KINSELLA

The Navajo Nation specifically claims for its people and holds the government of the United States responsible for the education of the Navajo People, based upon the Treaty of 1868 and the trust responsibility of the federal government toward Indian tribes. The Navajo People also claim their rights as citizens of the states within which they reside to a non-discriminatory public education.

—*SECTION §1(D), NAVAJO SOVEREIGNTY IN EDUCATION ACT OF 2005*

Introduction

This chapter analyzes Navajo educational sovereignty and how it is impacted by New Mexico public schools operating within and around the Navajo Nation.[1] Looking to the *Yazzie/Martinez v. State of New Mexico* decision, this chapter proposes that culturally relevant education requires stronger government-to-government consultation mechanisms and increased recognition of tribal sovereignty through investment in tribal education departments in New Mexico.[2] Specifically, the chapter discusses the Navajo Nation's authority over schools that opened during the COVID-19 pandemic and corresponding governance disputes. In addition, the chapter analyzes the legal tools available to the Navajo Nation to support its authority over the education of Navajo students. Ultimately, the chapter examines the potential development of Navajo Nation educational sovereignty, exploring the nation's options for enhancing its control over the provision of education of all Navajo students under the jurisdiction of the Navajo Nation. This legal analysis will provide a context for the future development of education laws and policies in New Mexico in accordance with the mandates set forth by the *Yazzie/Martinez* decision.

Foundations of the *Yazzie/Martinez* Decision

The *Yazzie/Martinez* decision creates a historic opportunity to dismantle the colonial legacy at the heart of education in New Mexico today. The decision calls for transformative change in the provision of education, with a particular emphasis on the need to elevate the interests of at-risk students, including Native students. The Navajo Nation has an especially great interest in the *Yazzie/Martinez* decision, given the presence of twenty-four New Mexico state schools operating within its territorial boundaries and the enrollment of over 27,275 Navajo children in the New Mexico public school system.[3] The *Yazzie/Martinez* decision illuminates a path forward to enhance tribal influence over education in the State of New Mexico by restructuring the New Mexico Public Education Department (NMPED) educational model toward one indelibly responsive to direct tribal input and decision-making.

The court in *Yazzie/Martinez v. State of New Mexico* was asked to determine if New Mexico is fulfilling its constitutional obligation to provide a sufficient education for children characterized as at-risk.[4] At-risk children are defined as children who are English-language learners, Native American, disabled, or from economically disadvantaged homes.

In determining whether the state's education for at-risk students is constitutionally sufficient, the court assessed the adequacy of educational inputs and whether they correlated to inadequate student outputs. The court evaluated the sufficiency of the state's provision of education by examining instructional material, quality of teaching, programs, and services necessary to make at-risk students college- or career-ready. The court found these inputs were insufficient and furthermore ascertained that, when coupled with poor student outputs as measured by performance on standardized tests, graduation rates, and college remediation rates, most of New Mexico's at-risk children finish each school year without the basic literacy and math skills needed to pursue postsecondary education or a career.

The court determined the state failed to provide the programs and services necessary for at-risk students to learn and thrive in accordance with the New Mexico constitution. The court further found that the State Equalization Guarantee (SEG) funding formula, which provides about 89 percent of state and local funding for schools, uses calculations that are insufficient to fund the programs necessary to provide all at-risk students with the opportunity to receive an adequate education. Ultimately, the court concluded that the State of New Mexico violated the equal protection clause, the education clause, and the due process clause of the New Mexico constitution by failing to provide at-risk students with a uniform, statewide system of free public schools sufficient for their education. The court directed the state to provide necessary funding and ensure students receive the programs and services needed for success.

The *Yazzie/Martinez* decision heralds a defining moment in a long struggle to reform New Mexico public education and compels the State of New Mexico to ensure that all students receive a sufficient and culturally inclusive education reflective of New Mexico's rich history and diverse population.

New Mexico Education Policies Addressing Native Americans

Of particular importance to the many tribal communities in New Mexico is the *Yazzie/Martinez* court's discussion of NMPED's failure to fulfill its constitutional obligations to Native students. The court looked to existing laws within the state to highlight the gaps in the provision of education for Native students. One such law is the New Mexico Indian Education Act (NMIEA) of 2003.

NMIEA purports to provide students with a culturally relevant education through the cooperation of schools, tribal communities, and the state. The three primary purposes of the act are to ensure equitable and culturally relevant learning systems, maintain Native languages, and support tribal involvement and control over schools.[5] In an effort to institutionalize the provision of equitable education for Native American students in New Mexico, the NMIEA created the Indian Education Division of NMPED as well as the Indian Education Advisory Council (IEAC), two offices intended to promote the unique needs of Native students. Ultimately, the NMIEA set forth a foundation to guide how the state, school districts, and charter schools should collaborate with tribal governments on education matters.[6]

Two essential elements of the NMIEA are the emphasis on tribal input and involvement in the education of Native students and the creation of a mechanism for establishing a formal government-to-government relationship between the state and New Mexico tribes. Consultation is widely considered the bedrock of building effective and transformative intergovernmental relationships, and when tribes have strong education departments, they are better able to meaningfully contribute to constructive dialogue on education matters. Although international standards assert more stringent and robust principles for Indigenous peoples' consultation rights, the NMIEA does bring tribal consultation to the table.[7]

The *Yazzie/Martinez* court affirmed that the NMIEA is "premised on the idea that culturally relevant education is to be produced through the cooperation of the schools and the tribal communities";[8] it further found that this goal has not been realized. The court cited the failure of NMPED to staff crucial positions within the Indian Education Division as evidence of its violation of the NMIEA's statutory requirement to develop government-to-government relationships.

Importantly, the *Yazzie/Martinez* court asserted that the NMIEA "sets forth the legislative determination of what constitutes a constitutionally adequate education for Native American children in New Mexico public schools."[9] The court went on to state that "failure to comply with the NMIEA amounts to a violation of the constitution's adequacy clause."[10] Therefore, in accordance with the *Yazzie/Martinez* decision, compliance with the NMIEA is arguably a state constitutional requirement, and any violation of the NMIEA amounts to a violation of the New Mexico state constitution. While actual enforcement of the NMIEA as a constitutional right is yet to be seen, this assertion potentially creates an enforcement right under the NMIEA that did not exist before.

Although not expressly discussed by the *Yazzie/Martinez* court, New

Mexico is also governed by the New Mexico State-Tribal Collaboration Act, which promotes positive and collaborative government-to-government relationships between the state and the twenty-three Native Nations of New Mexico. The State-Tribal Collaboration Act requires any state agency to make reasonable efforts to collaborate with Native Nations in the development and implementation of policies, agreements, or programs of the state agency that directly affect American Indians or Alaska Natives.[11] While this act does not mention education specifically, it does indicate legislative intent for collaboration between the state and Native Nations where any state agency operation directly affects tribes.

Ultimately, while the New Mexico legislature passed several laws promoting tribal collaboration, the state failed to uphold these laws, as evidenced and affirmed by the *Yazzie/Martinez* case. This lack of implementation became especially apparent during the COVID-19 pandemic.

Disputing Governments and the COVID-19 Pandemic

A MAZE OF AUTHORITY

The COVID-19 pandemic has had a lasting and measurable impact on the Navajo Nation's ability to ensure safe and accessible education to all students in the Navajo Nation. Navajo students attending schools on or proximate to the Navajo Nation's boundaries are served by five different and independent school systems: public schools (Arizona, New Mexico, and Utah), BIE-operated schools, BIE grant (tribally controlled) schools, charter schools, and parochial schools. The five different categories of schools, operated by different sovereigns including the Navajo Nation, the states of Arizona, New Mexico, and Utah, and the federal government, create a dizzying and sometimes unclear landscape of authority over the provision of education.

During the first and most devastating wave of the COVID-19 pandemic in the United States to date, many schools located in the Navajo Nation sought guidance from the Department of Diné Education (DODE) about how to safely reopen their schools while complying with both the directives of the Navajo Nation and the often-conflicting directives of their respective state governing bodies.[12] Many schools in the Nation are operated by local school boards but funded by state education departments, including the Arizona Department of Education, NMPED, and the Utah State Office of Education. Each of these three education departments, in turn, had to comply with their respective state regulations regarding the reopening of schools during COVID, regulations that continue to shift as the pandemic continues. It is the position of the Navajo Nation that its jurisdiction takes precedent when it comes to the health and safety of the Navajo people in all institutions within its territorial boundaries, including schools.[13]

NAVAJO NATION AUTHORITY OVER EDUCATION ON THE NAVAJO NATION

The COVID-19 pandemic highlighted the complexity and prejudice embedded in the provision of education in New Mexico state schools in the Navajo Nation. Specifically, local school districts in New Mexico operating schools within the territorial boundaries of the Navajo Nation challenged the Navajo Nation's jurisdiction and authority to make decisions related to operations of those schools during the pandemic. The nation required all schools to remain closed to in-person learning and to only provide remote instruction given the high rate of COVID-19.

The Navajo Nation is a sovereign government whose authority predates the federal constitution.[14] With this sovereign authority, the Navajo Nation can issue public health orders to protect the safety and well-being of its tribal members.[15] In exercise of this sovereignty, the executive and legislative branches of the Navajo government passed resolutions, executive orders, and public health orders directing the closure of nonessential activities in the Nation, including the closure of schools for in-person learning.[16] The Navajo Nation Office of the President and Vice President (OPVP) issued Executive Order no. 010-20, on November 13, 2020, declaring a state of emergency in the Navajo Nation and ordering the closure of government offices and related entities. The order explicitly supported the closure of all schools on the Navajo Nation and further empowered the Navajo Nation Board of Education (NNBOE) to continue to provide guidance on the closures. Executive orders have the force of law in the Navajo Nation.[17]

On September 3, 2020, in response to the immense impact of COVID-19, the

NNBOE exercised its executive authority by passing Resolution NNBESE-664-2020, requiring all schools located in the Navajo Nation, including Public Law 100-297 grant schools, Public Law 93-638 contract schools, BIE-operated schools, public schools (including charter schools), private schools, parochial schools, higher education institutions, early childhood programs, and all after-school programs, to provide virtual or online learning options only, without face-to-face instruction, until the Navajo Nation deemed it safe to return to in-person learning. This resolution limited on-reservation school reopening plans to virtual and distance learning tools only. The Navajo Nation Council further passed Resolution CO-84-20 on October 26, 2020, which opposed in-person instruction at all schools intending to reopen within the Navajo Nation amid COVID-19.

SCHOOL DISTRICT RESISTANCE TO REMOTE LEARNING

Despite these resolutions, executive orders, and public health orders, several school districts expressly refused to acknowledge the legitimacy of the Navajo Nation's sovereign authority over schools located within its territorial boundaries by leaving schools open for in-person learning.[18] Given the varying directives from state education agencies and tribal education departments, school districts felt emboldened to take decisions regarding the health and safety of students into their own hands.

In response to the many tribal public health orders and emergency declarations related to COVID-19, the State of New Mexico, through Secretary of Education Ryan Stewart (served September 2019 to August 2021), issued a memorandum to all New Mexico superintendents and charter leaders requesting Local Education Agencies (LEAs) conduct regular consultation meetings with local tribes in accordance with the New Mexico State-Tribal Collaboration Act and the NMIEA.[19] While the Navajo Nation did partake in consultation meetings with a few local school districts, these meetings generally resulted in unchanged, opposing positions without fostering meaningful compromise. Ultimately, the school districts continued providing in-person learning and resisted any significant shift in their policies in the direction of complying with the Navajo Nation health directives.

Many of the school districts that remained open in the Navajo Nation challenged both the authority of the Navajo Nation to determine if they could open their schools to in-person learning and the authority of the State of New Mexico when the state expressed support for tribal public health orders. Indeed, while the Stewart memorandum cited the New Mexico State-Tribal Collaboration Act and the NMIEA, the school districts correctly declared that these acts do not create any right of action against a state agency or a right of review of an action of a state agency. This fact highlights the importance of implementing stronger requirements for tribal consultation and collaboration in New Mexico when it comes to decisions directly affecting the education of Native students. The *Yazzie/Martinez* decision opens the door for such reform.

Navajo Nation Sovereignty in Education

NAVAJO NATION SOVEREIGNTY IN EDUCATION ACT (2005)

Robust tribal education departments lead to greater tribal input into state governance decisions regarding education. In 2005 the Navajo Nation Council passed the Navajo Sovereignty in Education Act, asserting a renewed commitment to the provision of education for all students in schools located in the Navajo Nation. The law details the organizational reforms needed for establishing self-governance over education matters and a series of initiatives necessary for improving the education of Navajo youth.

The Sovereignty in Education Act established the Navajo Nation Board of Education (NNBOE) and the Department of Diné Education (DODE) and confirmed the commitment of the Navajo Nation to the education of the Navajo people.[20] The NNBOE is responsible for monitoring the activities of BIA-funded schools and local community school boards serving the Navajo Nation. The DODE is responsible for implementing and enforcing the educational laws of the Navajo Nation; it carries out the policies passed by the Navajo Nation Board of Education. The Navajo Nation Sovereignty in Education Act empowers DODE and NNBOE to work together as entities within the executive branch of the Navajo government to exercise oversight responsibilities for all schools serving students in the Navajo Nation.

One of the key components of the law was the directive to develop an educational and accountability plan that recognizes Navajo language and culture and infuses it into schools' curriculum and instruction. The Sovereignty in Education Act was a major step forward for the cohesive governance of schools across the Navajo Nation.

DINÉ SCHOOL ACCOUNTABILITY PLAN

As previously described, Navajo students attending schools in or proximate to the Navajo Nation's boundaries are served by five different and independent school systems. Importantly, federal student accountability laws, as set forth in the Every Student Succeeds Act (ESSA), have not adequately supported Navajo students in these varying school systems across the Nation.[21] For instance, most Navajo students in BIE-operated schools fail to meet proficiency standards in mathematics, reading, and science.[22] Part of the discrepancy in the provision of education under ESSA for Native students is attributable to the limited role allotted to tribal education departments.

A tribal education department (TED) is the agency, department, or instrument of an eligible Indian tribe that is primarily responsible for supporting Native American students' elementary and secondary education.[23] A state education agency (SEA) is the state board of education or other agency or officer primarily responsible for the state supervision of public elementary schools and secondary schools.[24] The BIE also serves as an SEA when it comes to oversight of bureau-funded schools under ESSA.[25] While TEDs operate in a capacity similar to SEAs in that they develop and administer educational policies, collect and analyze student data, set academic standards, and create assessments and curricula,[26] they do not enjoy the same level of autonomy over education in schools on tribal lands. Indeed, TEDs occupy the outskirts of the federal education framework, as opposed to serving a central role in the Nation-wide administration of education services.

In order to receive Title I funding under ESSA, SEAs and the BIE must submit accountability plans to the federal Department of Education.[27] If approved, the states and the BIE then redistribute the funding to local education agencies (LEAs), such as school districts and BIE schools. LEAs can also directly apply for grant funding via Indian Education Formula Grants. The Navajo Nation, given the many states and entities operating schools within its territorial boundaries, must work to support school compliance with

multiple accountability plans—many of which are poorly designed—to provide the pervasive, culturally relevant education needed for Navajo students
to thrive.

In an attempt to streamline and take ownership over the accountability
assessment of all students on the Nation, the Navajo Nation submitted an
Alternative Accountability Proposal to the US Department of Education and
the secretary of the Department of the Interior in 2013, titled the "Diné School
Accountability Plan." The plan sought the creation of a single set of standards
by which all Navajo students and schools can be held accountable, and in so
doing, replace the accountability plan administered by the BIE.[28] To this end,
the Navajo Nation developed a curriculum and instructional plans for implementing educational standards in ways that address the needs of Navajo students and their communities.[29] Since the plan was submitted in 2013, the
Navajo Nation has only received provisional approval for it, despite strict
deadlines for approval on the part of the federal government.[30]

The organizing philosophy of the Navajo plan invokes the intent of the
Navajo Sovereignty in Education Act: to highlight Diné Studies standards and
hold schools accountable to teaching Navajo language and cultural subject
matter.[31] The Diné Studies standards include five subject areas: Navajo language, culture, history, government, and *k'é* (character).[32] These five areas
exemplify crucial tenets of Navajo history and tradition and express the
importance of place-based learning. Inclusion of these five subject areas into
the accountability plan reflects the Navajo Nation's belief that the loss of
Navajo language and culture threatens the Diné way of life.

The Diné School Accountability Plan addresses culturally significant gaps
in the provision of federally funded education for Navajo students and is an
essential step toward the increased organizational capacity of the Navajo
Nation tribal education department, DODE.

EXPANSION OF THE NAVAJO NATION'S TRIBAL EDUCATION DEPARTMENT

The *Yazzie/Martinez* decision elevates the essential role of culturally relevant
education for the success of Native American students. While the Navajo
Nation's accountability plan is an important step toward strengthening tribal

influence over the education of Navajo students, it is limited in its ability to augment tribal input in the actual policy and programmatic decision-making of NMPED regarding schools on tribal land.

In accordance with the Navajo Nation's goal of assuming greater ownership over the provision of education for all students in the Navajo Nation, the BOE and DODE have mapped out several options for enhanced tribal input in the education of Navajo students. One option is for the Navajo government to assume control over all thirty-one BIE schools in the Navajo Nation via a 638 contract with the BIE.

Under the Indian Self-Determination and Education Assistance Act (ISDEAA) of 1975, also known as Public Law 93-638, a 638 contract is one with the federal government wherein a tribe may enter into a legal agreement to take on responsibilities typically performed by the federal government. The inherent goal of the tribe assuming control over the function contracted is to foster long-term self-governance.[33] Under a 638 contract, the government must reimburse the tribe the money it spent on the federal program; however, tribes are also eligible for administrative overhead costs. Such a contract allows the tribe to gain experience in managing a formerly federally operated program or function and to develop staff while building its own infrastructure. While 638 contracts enhance tribal management and control over their own assets, they remain under the purview of the BIE, retaining many financial and governance barriers to which SEAs are not subject.

The BOE and DODE are also exploring the option of contracting with the US Department of Education to assume direct oversight authority over all BIE schools in the Navajo Nation. Such a contract with the federal Department of Education poses a potentially complicated and monumental leap for the Navajo Nation and its exercise of educational sovereignty over bureau-operated schools. Typically, the US Department of Education directly oversees SEAs, while the Department of Interior oversees the BIE, which then works with tribal education departments. For the Navajo Nation, through its tribal education department, to act as an SEA by contracting directly with the US Department of Education for ESSA funding poses a potential restructuring of the legal and financial landscape for tribal education. Unlike 638 contracting for federal services, direct tribe-to–Department of Education contracting of this magnitude does not fall neatly within the existing federal legal landscape.

The Navajo Nation is exploring ways to strengthen educational services for Navajo students, ways that are both established and unprecedented. In so doing, the Navajo Nation hopes that its increased capacity will enhance its position for more meaningful government-to-government consultation with NMPED.

Tribal Consultation

The *Yazzie/Martinez* court emphasized the essential role of government-to-government consultation in upholding the state constitutional mandate of adequate education for all students in New Mexico in accordance with the NMIEA. As the twenty-three Native Nations of New Mexico maneuver to implement the *Yazzie/Martinez* decision, turning to international standards of tribal consultation helps to illuminate best practices and serves as a guide for approaching tribal input in public education systems in New Mexico.

From a tribal government perspective, respect for self-determination and sovereignty establishes an inherent right to consultation on all matters related to tribal self-governance.[34] Article 4 of the United Nations Declaration on the Rights of Indigenous Peoples (UNDRIP) states, "Indigenous peoples, in exercising their right to self-determination, have the right to autonomy or self-government in matters relating to their internal and local affairs." The declaration goes on to affirm:

> Indigenous peoples have the right to participate in decision-making in matters which would affect their rights, through representatives chosen by themselves in accordance with their own procedures, as well as to maintain and develop their own indigenous decision-making institutions.[35]

UNDRIP asserts the internationally acknowledged and accepted legal principle that Indigenous peoples have an inherent right to self-determination and a corresponding right to be involved in decision-making in all matters affecting tribal nations.

While NMPED involves the twenty-three Native Nations in New Mexico in formal consultation meetings each year, these meetings fail to integrate tribal input in meaningfully transformative ways. Considering international standards and the *Yazzie/Martinez* decision, the NMIEA opens the door for government-to-government engagement wherein all governments at the table have leverage on the outcome of discussions. In the realm of education, tribes must be at the table not only to offer opinions on decisions and policies set forth by NMPED but also to offer concrete recommendations and input that foundationally inform the educational system in New Mexico. In the wake of *Yazzie/Martinez*, tribes can work to strengthen the language of the NMIEA and the State-Tribal Collaboration Act to create a right of action or other compliance mechanism to ensure meaningful state-tribal consultation moving forward.

True consultation begins at the roots, not the branches: To transform education in New Mexico, tribes must be robust and essential participants in NMPED decision-making processes. Only tribal governments, tribal education departments, and tribal community members are positioned to offer the input needed to realize the culturally responsive education called for by the *Yazzie/ Martinez* decision.

Yazzie/Martinez and the Navajo Nation: A Pivotal Opportunity

The call to action in the *Yazzie/Martinez* case to transform public education thundered across New Mexico, raising the question: How can Native Nations seize this opportunity to influence, inform, and transform education for Native students today? There is a resounding consensus that direct tribal input into NMPED decision-making must be at the heart of any education reform.

Enhancing tribal consultation measures in state legislation and strengthening tribal education departments are two avenues for increasing Native Nations' influence over education in New Mexico. The twenty-three Native Nations can unify to galvanize state compliance with the NMIEA and the State-Tribal Collaboration Acts and can further lobby for increased enforcement mechanisms in future tribal consultation legislation. Tribes such as the Navajo Nation may also consider creative avenues for increasing the reach and input of their tribal education departments to assume greater control in ensuring culturally relevant education in schools within their territories.

The passage of the Navajo Sovereignty in Education Act illustrates the Navajo Nation's plan for building the laws, policies, and infrastructure necessary to realize sovereignty in education. The Navajo Nation's efforts can serve as a guide for other tribal education departments to assert their own culturally based education frameworks and accountability plans for schools operating on or near their respective tribal lands.

The *Yazzie/Martinez* decision exposes the legacy of colonial violence still central to the public education system in New Mexico. The Navajo Nation, joined by the other twenty-two Native Nations of New Mexico, is poised to dismantle the harmful remnants of the boarding school era and to rebuild a model education system sensitive to the wisdom, beauty, and brilliance of Native peoples.

Student Learning Objectives

1. Students will be able to recognize best practices for tribal consultation and evaluate whether NMPED legislation regarding tribal collaboration meets these standards.

2. Students will be able to analyze the Navajo Nation's approach to building educational sovereignty and adapt this approach to the unique situations of other Native Nations.

Discussion Questions

1. How do the *Yazzie/Martinez* decision and the COVID-19 pandemic expose weaknesses in the existing New Mexico legislation regarding tribal consultation?

2. What are some creative ways that tribes can strengthen their tribal education departments to have greater influence over the public education system in New Mexico?

3. Why are tribes uniquely affected by state-run education systems? How did the COVID-19 pandemic highlight this impact?

Notes

1.   This chapter relies heavily on input from Dr. Kalvin White and Dr. Patricia Gonnie, Department of Diné Education. The chapter further benefited from comments provided by attendees of the University of New Mexico Summit on Educational Sovereignty, April 2021. Throughout the chapter, the author uses the words "tribal," "Native," "Indigenous," and "American Indian and Alaska Native" interchangeably. This editorial decision stems from the variety of terms used in relevant tribal, state, federal, and international laws, policies, and regulations, as well as the terms used by Native Nations themselves.

2.   *Whilhelmina Yazzie and Louise Martinez et al. v. State of New Mexico*, First Judicial District, July 2018.

3.   Navajo student count for SY2020–2021, Navajo Nation Profile, Indian Education Division, September 2021.

4.   This section is informed by the New Mexico Supreme Court decision in *Yazzie Martinez v. State of New Mexico*, July 20, 2018.

5.   New Mexico Legislative Finance Committee, Program Evaluation Unit, *Progress Report: Indian Education Act Implementation*, January 2021.

6.   New Mexico Legislative Finance Committee, *Progress Report*, January 2021.

7.   United Nations Declaration on the Rights of Indigenous Peoples, art. 19, G.A. Res. 61/295, art. 19 [hereinafter "UNDRIP"]. See also Organization of American States, "American Declaration on the Rights of Indigenous Peoples," art. VVIII, para. 2, https://www.oas.org/en/sare/documents/DecAmIND.pdf.

8.   *Yazzie Martinez v. State of New Mexico*, July 20, 2018, 28.

9.   *Yazzie Martinez v. State of New Mexico*, July 20, 2018, 28.

10.   *Yazzie Martinez v. State of New Mexico*, July 20, 2018, 28.

11.   New Mexico State-Tribal Collaboration Act, New Mexico Statutes, chapter 11, article 18, section 4(C), 2011.

12.   As of this writing on January 9, 2022, there were 42,622 reported cases of COVID-19 in the Navajo Nation, with 1,593 confirmed deaths from the virus. The Navajo Nation Department of Health Website monitors COVID-19 reporting and is available at https://www.ndoh.navajo-nsn.gov/covid-19.

13.   Official statement from the Navajo Nation Office of the President and Vice President in response to NMPED's attempt to appeal the *Yazzie/Martinez* decision.

14.   The Navajo Nation has two treaties with the United States, one ratified in 1849 and another in 1868, which recognize and affirm the sovereignty of the nation.

15.   The *Montana v. United States* decision limited tribal civil jurisdiction over nonmembers, requiring tribes to affirmatively prove: (1) the nonmember has a "consensual relationship" with the tribe or a member, or (2) the nonmember's actions would be catastrophic to the existence of the tribe. *Montana et. al. v. United States et al.*, Supreme Court of the United States, March 24, 1981. For a deeper discussion of the jurisdictional

landscape regarding tribal public health orders, see Paul Spruhan, "COVID-19 and Indian Country: A Legal Dispatch from the Navajo Nation," *Of Note* (blog), *Northwestern University Law Review*, May 5, 2020.

16.   The Navajo Nation Commission on Emergency Management (CEM) declared a public health state of emergency, due to COVID-19, on March 11, 2020. CEM 20-03-11. OPVP passed several executive orders on the state of emergency, including EO 011-20, EO 012-20, EO 002-21, and EO-003-21, December 3, 2020. The Navajo Nation Public Health Emergency Order no. 2020-003 on March 20, 2021, issued a stay-at-home order requiring all individuals in the Navajo Nation to remain in their homes unless traveling for emergencies or to perform "essential activities."

17.   Navajo Nation Code, 2 N.N.C. § 1005(C)(14).

18.   While many school districts were reported as remaining open in violation of Navajo Nation orders, the Navajo Nation specifically met with both Central Consolidated School District and Gallup McKinley School District to reach an agreement about public safety in schools located in the Navajo Nation.

19.   Secretary Ryan Stewart, "Memorandum: Expansion of In-Person Learning—Tribal Consultation," January 29, 2021, State of New Mexico, Public Education Department.

20.   Sovereignty in Education Act, Navajo Nation Council Resolution, CJY-37-05.

21.   President Barack Obama reauthorized the Elementary and Secondary Education Act (ESEA) in 2015, signing into law the Every Student Succeeds Act (ESSA), an updated national education law and commitment to promote equal opportunity for all students.

22.   *Navajo Nation Alternative Accountability Workbook*, submitted to the US Department of Education, Office of Elementary and Secondary Education, and the US Department of Interior, September 2013, https://www.navajonationdode.org/wp-content/uploads/2021/01/NN_DSAP_Final.pdf.

23.   DODE serves as the Navajo Nation Tribal Education Department.

24.   IDEA Statute, part B, subpart A, section 300.41, description available at https://sites.ed.gov/idea/regs/b/a/300.41#:~:text=State%20educational%20agency%20or%20SEA,Governor%20or%20by%20State%20law.

25.   White House, Office of the Press Secretary, Executive Order 13592, "Improving American Indian and Alaska Native Educational Opportunities and Strengthening Tribal Colleges and Universities," December 2, 2001.

26.   Dawn M. Mackety et al., *American Indian Education: The Role of Tribal Education Departments*, Institute of Education Sciences, May 2009, available at https://sites.ed.gov/whiaiane/files/2012/04/The-Role-of-Tribal-Education-Departments.pdf.

27.   US Department of Education, "Improving Basic Programs Operated by Local Education Agencies (Title I, Part A)," available at https://www2.ed.gov/programs/titleiparta/applicant.html.

28.   *Navajo Nation Accountability Workbook*.

29.   *Navajo Nation Accountability Workbook*.

30.   ESSA, Title VI Indian, Native Hawaiian, and Alaska Native Education; SEC. 6116.

[20 U.S.C. 7426] (f) PLAN APPROVAL. "Within 90 days after the receipt of an entity's plan by the Secretary, the Secretary shall inform the entity, in writing, of the Secretary's approval or disapproval of the plan. If the plan is disapproved, the entity shall be informed, in writing, of the reasons for the disapproval and shall be given an opportunity to amend the plan or to petition the Secretary to reconsider such disapproval."

31. *Navajo Nation Alternative Accountability Workbook.*

32. Department of Diné Education Accountability Plan, available at https://www.navajonationdode.org/school-accountability/.

33. Indian Self-Determination and Education Assistance Act, Public Law 93-638, available at https://www.bia.gov/sites/bia.gov/files/assets/bia/ots/ots/pdf/Public_Law93-638.pdf.

34. UNDRIP serves as an international consensus on the basic rights of Indigenous peoples. UNDRIP recognizes "in particular the right of indigenous families and communities to retain shared responsibility for the upbringing, training, education and well-being of their children, consistent with the rights of the child." See United Declaration on the Rights of Indigenous Peoples, preamble, 2007. UNDRIP further asserts a right to education: "Indigenous peoples have the right to establish and control their educational systems and institutions providing education in their own languages, in a manner appropriate to their cultural methods of teaching and learning. Indigenous individuals, particularly children, have the right to all levels and forms of education of the State without discrimination." UNDRIP, article 14, 1&2.

35. UNDRIP, article 18 (2007).

Figure 11. Navajo Nation president Jonathan Nez, Second Lady Phefelia Nez, Miss Navajo Nation Niagra Rockbridge, and Kiva Club students at the 65th Nizhoni Days Powwow, May 1, 2022. Photo credit Wendy S. Greyeyes.

CHAPTER SEVEN

Narratives and Responses to *Yazzie/Martinez*

Tribal Consultation and Community Engagement

NATALIE MARTINEZ

Introduction

This chapter examines the emerging narratives in response to the 2018 *Yazzie/Martinez* court ruling through an overview of responses to New Mexico's most significant court case on education (herein, the court case).[1] The discussion provided here considers the sociopolitical landscape affected by the ruling and the shifting relationships between New Mexico's Indigenous Nations, schools, and lawmakers, as well as the potential impact on students, using the conceptual frames of co-optation and hegemony. The *Yazzie/Martinez* case highlighted the inequities of New Mexico's public education system. However, the short-term responses by New Mexico Public Education Department (NMPED) and public school districts have been fragmentary.

In what follows, I present an overview of meanings associated with *Yazzie/Martinez* in the discourse around Native American education and examples of misapplications, misinterpretations, and misunderstandings of the court mandates. The critique presented in this chapter discusses the focus on superficial change at the school district level, rather than foundational restructuring of the public school system.

This chapter also considers various responses to the court ruling, legislation, and associated funding currently being designed and implemented in the twenty-three Native American–serving school districts in New Mexico. It looks at the role of tribal consultation and community engagement in determining the most appropriate course of action to meet the needs of the students identified in the court case.

The "Adjectivication" of *Yazzie/Martinez*

CO-OPTATION PRACTICES

In the case of the consolidated Yazzie and Martinez lawsuit, the phrase "Yazzie/Martinez" has become an adjective. This form of discursive transformation can occur by appending a suffix to an event, a thing, a person, or a concept to create a novel way of identifying something. As in the "adjective + ication" example here, transforming a term into an adjective has a similar effect. In New Mexico education spheres, we see the emergence of the practice of describing new programs, processes, and funding with adjectives like "Yazzie/Martinez."

This is similar to what Heine et al. describe as "a cognitive-communicative operation whereby some fragment of linguistic discourse is transferred from one domain of discourse to another."[2] The practice of affixing "Yazzie/Martinez" in an adjectival manner promotes co-optation. Heine et al. state, "Cooptation leads to the transfer of linguistic material from one domain or plane of discourse to another."[3] In this example, the shortened court case title—*Yazzie/Martinez*—becomes the catch phrase. "Yazzie/Martinez" is the modifier linked to nouns such as "money," "program," "initiatives," "policies," etc. The transfer of meaning from the domain of the court case to the domain of performance indicates some measure that meets student needs with specific efforts. One example of this practice can be seen in the Albuquerque Public Schools framework for equity, which includes diversity work with their "Yazzie/Martinez Committee" or "Yazzie/Martinez funding" to describe legislative appropriations at the school and district level to address the needs of student groups identified in the court ruling.[4]

Beyond discourse, co-optation has become a corruptive practice in civil rights and social justice movements. In political theory co-optation exists as an ideological strategy based on the notion of soft power.[5] Co-optation occurs through attraction rather than coercion and is aligned with the principle that the competition for strategic positioning of preferred ideologies is won by "taking advantage of the opportunity to co-opt" uncertainty or novelty.[6] The effort by the *Yazzie/Martinez* plaintiffs embodies the social justice movement behind the court case.

In a 2016 article, Esposito and Romano look at the process through which movements, such as Black Lives Matter (BLM), are hijacked by what they term "benevolent racism."[7] They find that such processes deflect the examination and interrogation of hegemonic systems of oppression. Through this phenomenon, co-opting groups frame their efforts as altruistic, thus avoiding the need to examine their complicity in producing or maintaining systems of oppression. Simultaneously, the original group might frame external voices as an amplification strategy for the movement. The process of co-optation hijacks and replaces the deeper intentions of the movement with misaligned messaging, commodification, and shift in focus.

Adjectivication becomes an apparatus that resembles a shell game co-opting the movement. It capitalizes on momentum, perhaps by pointing out funding proposal deadlines or rushing to outline checklists of NMPED requirements, and then shifts the focus toward superficial measures, such as promoting "Yazzie/Martinez activity" happening in school districts, thus obscuring the systemic injustices the movement originally attempted to uncover. The foundational structures, such as institutional racism, in New Mexico's schools are thereby masked because surface efforts produce the appearance of addressing identifiable problems. These tangible "solutions" offered to ameliorate problems can then be combined and counted as additive measures completed by schools and paid for with "Yazzie/Martinez funding," but the question remains whether *structural* changes resulted.

Another example is Indigenous land acknowledgements that have become a widespread, albeit co-opted practice; nothing of substance changes, and the individuals or institutions who acknowledge the original inhabitants of the land do nothing to challenge settler-colonial harm. These actors engage in superficial "Yazzie/Martinez-ing" that allows them to feel good about identifying as "an ally" by offering hollow words while checking the box titled "Land Acknowledgement" in order to appear *woke*, in social justice terminology.

A similar example is the NMPED's institution of school district "equity councils," whose purpose is to "focus on equity challenges, build skills and knowledge, and catalyze local actions focused on equity" as practical goals.[8] The committee acknowledges "equity challenges," and the school district and committee members can engage in discussion and tout the wokeness of talking about "Yazzie/Martinez issues." If the goal is to affect meaningful change, the institution of these committees as advisory bodies rather than policy-making ones is problematic.

In a 2019 study, Sosanya Jones examines diversity and inclusion trends in public institutions. She states that such institutions "co-opt the language of change and inclusion while sidestepping the difficult and uncomfortable challenge of specifically addressing race and racism."[9] Jones's framework includes an analysis of how diversity itself is acknowledged, embedded, and explained within the institutions. She considers the practice of representation: When employed as a co-optation device, it appears "as tokenism, where the diverse 'other' becomes a symbolic tool and cultural capital for organizations."[10] New Mexico institutions must tangibly measure efforts to meet the *Yazzie/Martinez* final judgment, and so offices of diversity and equity have emerged. Native American teachers and culturally and linguistically responsive (CLR) pedagogy and curriculum are now trendy. These practices are well-intended efforts to meet the expectations of the ruling but always fall short when offered piecemeal. As Jones concludes, further study of the role of diversity work within institutions must occur to examine the underpinnings of how "diversity has become a commodified asset for institutions of higher education and diversity professionals are hired to create, facilitate, and/or support diversity and inclusion efforts to signal institutional value in this area."[11]

HEGEMONY

There is clear evidence of hegemony in the nearly twenty-year-old state statute NMIEA that still has its merit debated, remains underfunded, and is the legislative centerpiece of the *Yazzie* plaintiffs' demand for constitutional rights. The power of the state has undercut the relevance of the New Mexico Indian Education Act (NMIEA), and only through legal action via the *Yazzie/Martinez* case has it become an important factor in meeting the constitutional rights to a fair and sufficient education for marginalized students in New Mexico.

The pattern of superficial adherence to the spirit of the law can be seen in other arenas. Proposing meaningful change to deeply rooted state institutions such as schooling produces pushback when systems of power are unmasked and critiqued. Jones points out:

> Engaging in the work of promoting change for greater diversity and inclu-
> sion means combating resistance to change. However, within an environ-
> ment where diversity and inclusion are embraced as a value but are used
> to circumvent addressing race and racism, it can be difficult to determine
> when diversity professionals are actually engaging in change efforts to
> promote greater diversity and inclusion for all and when they are being
> used to co-opt an agenda that touts a value without any real commitment
> to change.[12]

In such instances, hegemony operates to maintain power and control afforded by the status quo, as Michael Apple describes, through "a continual process of compromise, conflict, and active struggle to maintain hegemony" that also influences proposed changes to the ways schools operate and per-form education. Apple stresses the nature of schools as a direct arm of the state, with an operational motive to uphold dominant culture by legitimizing the knowledge and customs of groups that maintain power by promoting "norms, values, dispositions, and culture that contribute to the ideological hegemony of dominant groups."[13] Through their exercise of agency, individuals and groups can assert power to affect change, much like the *Yazzie/Martinez* plaintiffs. They effectively challenged the status quo of New Mexico's insufficient education system and brought momentum to a movement that will have lasting ramifications for learners whose experiences have been marginalized by the public school system.

Resistance to commitment for structural changes to how New Mexico educates its public-school children was evident in pushback from the State of New Mexico and its educational arm, NMPED, by their motion to dismiss the court case in 2020, based on the claim that the state had met the mandates. In the motion to dismiss, filed at the onset of a global COVID-19 pandemic that shut down major operations, NMPED enumerated its efforts to prove it satisfied the ruling and declared that it also aimed at "raising up the general education system as a whole for all students." [14] The court denied the motion, according to Judge Wilson's statement in the *Santa Fe New Mexican*, claiming state jurisdiction over the matter "until there are long-term comprehensive reforms implemented by the state." [15] The court's insistence on the push for foundational restructuring of the inequitable systems supports the original findings "that New Mexico's educational system has been failing students for years." [16] The *Yazzie/Martinez* case clarifies that reform and restructuring at the foundations of public education must occur to address the needs of learners in New Mexico and to correct the injustices resulting from decades of intentional neglect.

In their 2020 reply brief, the *Yazzie* plaintiffs refer to the "Systemic Neglect of Native American Students," repeatedly characterizing New Mexico's public education system as "broken" and one that "requires comprehensive educational reform that demonstrates substantial improvement of student outcomes." As the *Yazzie* plaintiffs assert in their reply brief, anything less than full, systemic restructuring in support of full implementation of the NMIEA "reflects a grave misunderstanding about the comprehensive approach necessary to redress the 'broken' education system for Native students." [17]

The attempt to dismiss the case indicates an attempt to maintain the status quo by securing hegemonic power. The reality is that New Mexico's public schools need equity, diversity, and inclusion practices embedded structurally. Until the efforts to dismantle the structural inequality that fueled the *Yazzie/Martinez* plaintiffs' decision to sue are acknowledged and owned, these practices will exist in hidden conflict, co-opted to deflect historical legacies of racism and hegemonic power.

Policy Requirements and Responses

NMPED

In response to the mandates of the court ruling, NMPED established an "Identity, Equity, and Transformation Team." NMPED launched several initiatives on the heels of the court decision and mandated that school districts in the state adhere to their responses, including establishing equity councils, assessing schools for readiness, using CLR statewide, and using the state's data reporting system to collect more information from districts to track the populations specified in the court ruling.

According to NMPED, this "four-pronged approach" in response to the *Yazzie/Martinez* case will address the decades-long systemic inequities in New Mexico's public schools that have pervaded the system since its inception. In its assurances to the public, and especially to the parties most affected by the lawsuit, NMPED stated that their response plan "will create an effective and equitable system of supports for all students focused on root-cause analysis, equity-focused leadership and continuous improvement, and culturally and linguistically responsive curriculum and pedagogy."[18] The issues inherent in this "deal" are that much of the work of recreating this system is left to the school districts, which are financially reliant upon the state for funding. However, the very funding structure would benefit from continuing to receive public funds generated by the same students named in the plaintiff groups: Native American, English-language learners, those with disabilities, and those who are economically disadvantaged—sometimes all in the same person. At the onset of these requirements, Torres-Velasquez, Sleeter, and Romero pointed out that "these changes appear to be unfunded mandates for districts that continue to express funding needs and for teachers who have not studied bilingual or multicultural education."[19]

Funding is a structural impediment to meeting the Yazzie/Martinez final ruling. In his comparative analysis of New Mexico's legislative appropriations between 2008 and 2020, economic researcher Steve Barro explained the impact of concurrent legislative mandates that rely on the same funding allocation (2020).[20] Barro detailed how New Mexico school districts were ostensibly "forced" to expend funds set aside for addressing the *Yazzie/Martinez* case to cover teacher salary increases that were also legislated at the same time. This analysis supports the "unfunded mandate" argument presented earlier and offers another example of how co-optation can undercut the goals of a movement. Barro characterized this legislated obstruction as "perverse, considering that Judge Singleton's decision in the *Yazzie/Martinez* case—the main impetus for increased 2019–20 funding—focused on the urgent need to do much more for the state's low-income, non-English-proficient, and other at-risk students."[21] By its action to address two equally pressing needs for education in one allocation, the legislative body conflated its obligations to meet both distinctly, thus co-opting crucial appropriations of funds and forcing districts to resolve another inequity on their own.

The mandates set forth in the final judgment by Singleton have far-reaching, comprehensive effects, and yet the state contended in its 2020 request to dismiss the lawsuit that it had "complied with both the spirit and the letter" of the court order. The state claimed that its efforts to address inequities raised by the *Yazzie/Martinez* case resolved the matter and asserted that the state "passed legislation, increased funding, improved accountability, and added and reformed programs aimed at providing an adequate education system for at-risk students by targeting at-risk students generally and raising up the general education system as a whole for all students." Of particular interest in these claims is the inclusion of "the general education system as a whole for all students"—another example of co-optation.[22] In this instance the state deflects its complicity in the perpetuation of systemic inequalities by co-opting its efforts to include "all students" absent of race, class, ability, or status—what Jones described as "side-stepping" more complex issues.[23]

SCHOOL DISTRICTS EQUITY COUNCILS

School districts were instructed to select equity council members in a short timeframe and to complete the work of developing in-depth discussions about race, inequity, and deficiencies within their districts without ample training or guidance. In July 2020 New Mexico's governor also created a "council for racial justice," which further taxed the pool of available experts who might be asked to serve on district equity councils. Top-down policy instructions for the districts that direct equity councils to do the work of assessing the districts included a general idea of what would constitute such a council: "district and charter staff, people from the school community that are experts in meeting the educational, social, and emotional needs of at-risk students, and members of the student groups that compose at-risk students." The first task of the councils was to complete the readiness assessment. NMPED described the assessment tool as one "meant to support Equity Councils and district and charter school leadership in having meaningful and productive conversations about current services and programs that impact at-risk students."[24]

Feedback from districts reported at the Institute for American Indian Education Summit (IAIE) in 2020 indicated these mandates are not fully funded; rather, they are haphazard and stand as dictates without support from NMPED for implementation, clarity, and follow up. Major conclusions by Martinez et al. from participant feedback at the 2020 summit cited a lack of leadership from NMPED; inadequate competitive funding to address the vast needs of students and districts; a lack of support for much of the required action; and overreach into the purview of districts and tribal sovereignty.[25]

Participants in the 2020 education summit commented on their experiences with equity councils, indicating frustration with the process, member selection, and overall operation of the councils, as reported in the IAIE post-summit report. The report also concluded that the "reliance on equity councils to examine and determine the plans for student success is seen as questionable, ineffective and redundant."[26] Anecdotal evidence from education colleagues and community members reveals that many were inundated with requests to serve on equity councils, and in some instances, districts merely renamed their existing committees "equity councils" while keeping membership the same.

SCHOOL DISTRICT RESPONSES

A few public school districts in New Mexico had already begun the process of elevating social justice initiatives at the administration level before the 2018 ruling. For example, Albuquerque Public Schools (APS) with its Office of Equity, Instruction, Innovation, and Support established itself as a forerunner in the development of strategic planning to address issues of inequity prior to the *Yazzie/Martinez* court ruling. The scope of this project included professional development, policy study, realigning curricular frameworks, and systemic alignment. APS began in 2014 to build a "framework of equitable access to high quality culturally responsive instruction for all students, aligned instructional and assessment practices in regular and special education, bilingualism and biliteracy, and opportunities for all to develop critical racial, ethnic, and cultural competencies."

The district partnered with several social justice, anti-racism, culturally responsive pedagogy organizations to promote educator practices through professional development opportunities outlined in the "Equity Plan." They also supported legislation through NM House Bill 250 (2019) to conduct needs assessments for American Indian students and report that efforts to support similar legislation for African American students are under way. Whether these efforts are productive remains to be seen, as APS has a history of glossing over race-based challenges, an issue highlighted in the Families United for Education (FUE) open letter to Albuquerque Public Schools. According to their letter, FUE worked with organizations such as the Anti-Racism Training Institute of the Southwest and People's Institute for Survival and Beyond and "organized Undoing Racism and Community Organizing workshops for members of the APS School Board and the larger community for the past twelve years with little and reluctant support, participation, and follow through from the district as a whole."[27] Still, as a purported leader in New Mexico's school districts in promoting social justice and anti-racism practices, and as New Mexico's largest, most diverse district, with over sixty-five hundred Native American students, APS has the potential to set the tone for other districts to emulate.[28]

Other larger school districts have also implemented operational changes. In 2021 Santa Fe Public Schools established the Equity, Diversity and Engagement Department, which highlights two initiatives: the Superintendent's Diversity and Equity Council and the Executive Equity Council, both "created to ensure that SFPS is in alignment with current NMPED efforts and meets as needed throughout the year" and adheres to the fifteen-member limit "per PED guidelines." Meanwhile, Las Cruces Public Schools consolidated nine preexisting programs and departments under the umbrella of the Division of Equity, Innovation, and Social Justice, whose goal is to "support and serve all, by ensuring equitable access to learning by continually evolving through innovation promoting social justice and cultural diversity."[29]

Overall, there have been mixed reviews on how well these district initiatives have been implemented and received. Referring to both the IAIE 2020 and 2021 education summits, community stakeholders remained concerned in their observations about school district responses and expressed keen awareness that the responsibilities for carrying out NMPED's mandates resulting from the *Yazzie/Martinez* case fall on district personnel and communities without any real guidance. Evidence of those community responses in 2020 included commentary that "school readiness assessments are being pushed upon school districts to complete without adequate Public Education Department guidance. School staff such as tribal liaisons and directors are expected to create comprehensive plans with limited resources and guidance."[30] These community stakeholders also expressed concerns over NMPED and school district communication with communities and families; they recommended ways to strengthen their engagement, such as more frequent outreach using more accessible social media outlets.

Under the direction of the February 2022–January 2023 secretary of education, Dr. Kurt Steinhaus, a New Mexico educator appointed to the position in September 2021, NMPED appears to be reaching a wider stakeholder audience with its outreach efforts. NMPED acknowledged, in its 2021 Equity Council Brief, the need to provide more guidance to districts, as well as strengthen the support networks for equity councils by providing a mentoring network called "the Support Hub." Community stakeholder voices are included in the 2021 brief, which indicates positive movement in addressing equity issues at the local level, such as the inclusion of more parents, tribal leaders, students, and school communities engaged in the work of the equity councils. These voices hold promise for the possibilities of structural change in our schools, as one school district leader with whom I spoke reflected on the recent concerted efforts by NMPED to offer trainings as well as maintain regular email communication and site visits. This school leader also noted that monthly opportunities for tribes and their education departments to engage in face-to-face meetings with Secretary Steinhaus demonstrate commitment to strengthened relationships and meaningful reform.

Government-to-Government Collaboration

Educational policy has historically made its way to the courtroom and the legislative arena, especially when the needs of students are not being met. Protections under the law for intended beneficiaries of public education have warranted pressure from the law to ensure compliance and equitable implementation. The *Yazzie/Martinez* case is monumental in New Mexico because it opened the platform to protect students' rights to education and to mandate that the state meet its constitutional obligations to provide a sufficient public education to its students who are Native American, English-language learners, living with disabilities, and/or economically disadvantaged. Inherent in the larger body of complaints raised in the lawsuit and long-standing grievances from New Mexico's sovereign nations has been the lack of true and meaningful collaboration and consultation on a government-to-government platform with the State of New Mexico.

MEANINGFUL TRIBAL CONSULTATION AND SOVEREIGNTY

The practice of consultation is a formal, sanctioned process intended to uphold government-to-government relationships between Indigenous nations and federal or state offices such as the US Department of Education and NMPED.[31] In many ways its intent has also been subject to co-optation.[32] Briefly, co-opted "consultation" with tribes as an informal practice has been used to describe meetings where decision-making representatives are present or not; it can also refer to notices given to Indigenous nations via post or email. In many instances, "consultation" is completely removed from its legal intent, thus co-opting and circumventing the intended formal consultation process and conveying the appearance of consent. As with many practices that have been legally codified, the need for consultation always arises from some insufficiency or inequity, such as that with the *Yazzie/Martinez* case. Miller presents case after case of historical validation from across the United States to assert his observation that most tribal governments experience frustration with the consultation process.[33] Although his argument centers on the federal consultation process, any government agency relationships that rely on tribal consultation also engage in similar practices, as often relayed in personal conversations with tribal elders and tribal officials. Miller presents narratives from many Indigenous nations that characterize tribal consultation as merely pretense, box-checking, and hoop-jumping to support decisions that have already been made prior to "consulting." Miller refers to various testimonies from Indigenous Nations and leaders who declare that what often counts as tribal consultation has not given "tribes a real voice in decisions that vitally affect them."[34] At this level of co-optation, decision-making rights of Indigenous nations have been usurped to serve the interests of the state that claims to serve them. The *Yazzie* plaintiffs unmask this duplicitous consultation practice in their 2020 reply brief when they report that "more than half of all focus districts, the family plaintiffs, and several New Mexico tribes, submitted affidavits in this case showing that those efforts are nothing more than lip service and have no real effect."[35]

With updated mandates resulting from the *Yazzie/Martinez* ruling calling for meaningful collaboration, self-reported evidence from school districts indicates more frequent efforts to engage in real and meaningful dialogue with the Pueblo Nations, Navajo Nation, and Apache Nations in New Mexico using the formal consultation process. Through the strengthening and assertion of government-to-government meetings with the State of New Mexico on a biannual basis, the power of collaboration with the All Pueblo Council of Governors, and the exercise of sovereign authority by the Navajo Nation, the Jicarilla Nation, and the Mescalero Nation in the political arena, tribal consultation represents a resolute challenge to existing hegemonic structures. School districts are requesting that their concerns be added to the formal agendas of tribal councils and liaisons, and tribal education directors are being included in the process of consultations. Community outreach and engagement is occurring more formally from districts to tribal nations, but there is still work to be done to make these efforts truly collaborative and bilateral.

Convergence of Strength for Improved Education

THE NMIEA AND *YAZZIE/MARTINEZ*

The efforts to meet the culturally responsive and academic needs of Indigenous students and strengthen the NMIEA have helped to provide substance upon which to build the case in support of the *Yazzie* plaintiffs.[36] With the passage of the NMIEA in 2003, New Mexico's Indigenous Nations have made more consistent efforts to establish a seat at the decision-making table. The *Yazzie/Martinez* final judgment is the strongest reinforcement of the NMIEA and has the potential to restructure the hegemonic institution of schooling in the state. The work of legislators, such as State Representative Derrick Lente of Sandia Pueblo, can advance school reform by leveraging the combined strength of the NMIEA and the *Yazzie/Martinez* case.

According to the New Mexico legislative archive (nmlegis.gov), since the *Yazzie/Martinez* findings of fact and conclusions of law in 2018, New Mexico's legislative body has made more than forty attempts to enact policy in direct response to the court findings. Of these attempts, two have since been signed into law, two memorial resolutions have been signed and distributed throughout the legislature and executive bodies, twenty-two have been postponed indefinitely (Action Postponed Indefinitely or API), and twenty were still being considered in committee as of late 2021.

"*Yazzie/Martinez* Money"

Much of the legislation introduced since the court case included requests for programmatic funding. Legislative allocations have fallen short in providing adequate funding to overhaul the system, but pockets of funding are offered in unconventional and unequal ways. Seeking out "*Yazzie/Martinez* money" to fund culturally relevant initiatives, also identified as "*Yazzie/ Martinez* programming," is a phenomenon that has become embedded in the ways we navigate schooling in New Mexico under the new system brought about through the efforts of the *Yazzie/Martinez* court case.

There is potential for Indigenous nations to reclaim their educative processes and to develop systems of educating their own children in meaningful ways through the availability of funds under the NMIEA and associated "*Yazzie/Martinez* funding." One Pueblo Nation, for example, has used the competitive grant award to supplement the initial process of building the Nation's language and culture curriculum, beginning with pre-K, as a central component of its K-8 academic approach through the development of instructional materials and professional development for its teachers. These efforts must be sustained to see a lasting impact with learners over time and with vertical curricular alignment. With competitive grants, however, the funding to sustain such programming becomes tenuous.

NMPED disseminates these funds using a request for applications (RFA) system, a competitive grant process. Generally, the RFA process is enacted statewide and submissions are scored, thus creating a process dependent on the decisions of the public education department of the state to expend *"Yazzie/Martinez* funds." There are inherent concerns with making such monies available through a competitive process as opposed to an equitable process divided between Indigenous nations. For example, the Indian Education Act funding RFA disseminates between seventy-five-thousand to one-hundred-thousand dollars to qualifying Indigenous nations or tribal education departments or between fifty-thousand and ninety-thousand dollars to school districts and lead education agencies that serve high populations of Indigenous students.[37]

The problem with the process is that it pits Native Nations against one another and against public school districts to vie for funding that should be appropriated by the legislature more equitably. The process also severely limits the options of tribes and districts in their programming use. If the funding is intended to be used for teachers, it is generally acknowledged that one full-time teacher's annual salary with benefits would use the entire amount of the grant. Structural change in schools cannot occur with the addition of one teacher. This is yet another example of how adjectivication works in concert with co-optation—the school can jump on the bandwagon by hiring a Navajo Language teacher using its fifty-thousand dollar competitive *"Yazzie/Martinez* grant"* and check the box to indicate that it has met its CLR requirements, all without having to change anything structurally and at most impacting only fifteen to twenty students.

Conclusion

The new discourses that developed following the *Yazzie/Martinez* court ruling represent both the comprehensive nature of the court case and the longstanding, endemic, and conflicted nature of inequitable public education in New Mexico. "Yazzie/Martinez" has taken on different meanings in various contexts through the process of co-optation when used to describe the practices, funding, and legal ramifications of the lawsuit.

New Mexico's twenty-three Native American–serving school districts have responded to the court ruling, legislation, and associated funding currently being designed and implemented across the state in vastly different ways. Through legislative efforts and the counterhegemonic exertion of tribal sovereignty, the processes of tribal consultation and community engagement have taken shape in more comprehensive ways across New Mexico's school districts. The promise of learning through different lenses offers hope that "a culturally responsive curriculum has the capacity to strengthen students' sense of cultural and ethnic self which in turn impacts their achievement."[38] This supports the findings of Judge Singleton in her estimation of what New Mexico's schools must do to dismantle the systemic, structural inequalities for our most vulnerable populations of children. It took a monumental court battle to finally uncover for the general public the disparities that children who are economically disadvantaged, English-language learners, Native American, and/or living with disabilities have known for years. In the juxtaposition of allies and accomplices, Judge Sarah Singleton exerted her considerable privilege and influence to truly stand up against the oppressive system of schooling in New Mexico as her lasting legacy. May she rest in peace as we take up and continue the fight for justice in education.

Student Learning Objectives

1. Students will explain how the co-optation of "Yazzie/Martinez" has masked the issues addressed in the court case related to the institution of schooling.

2. Students will interpret the role of hegemony in the limits on expression of the New Mexico Indian Education Act.

3. Students will demonstrate understanding of the relationship between the legislative process and school policy regarding the New Mexico Indian Education Act.

4. Students will explain the role of Tribal Consultation as a formal process in shaping education for Indigenous learners.

Discussion Questions

1. In what instances can co-optation help other Indigenous rights movements? In what ways can co-optation hinder the movements? Can you identify examples of co-optation?

2. Why did it take a court case to demand that the State of New Mexico address the rights of learners in New Mexico despite several laws (NMIEA, Bilingual Education Act, Hispanic Education Act, etc.) already enacted?

4. How does the New Mexico Public Education Department operate as an arm of the state government and what is its obligation to its citizens?

5. In what ways does the process of tribal consultation support educational sovereignty for New Mexico's Indigenous nations?

Notes

1. *Martinez et al. v. State of New Mexico et al.*, no. D-101-CV-2014-00793 and no. D-101-CV-2014-02224, Final Judgment and Order (NM February 14, 2019). Initial court decisions were made in 2018, prior to the final judgment: "Final judgment in this case is entered in favor of the Martinez and Yazzie Plaintiffs and against the Defendants in accordance with the Court's July 20, 2018 Decision and Order and the Court's December 20, 2018 Findings of Fact and Conclusions of Law" (2).

2. Bernd Heine et al., "Cooptation as a Discourse Strategy," *Linguistics* 55, no. 4 (2017): 813.

3. Heine et al., "Cooptation as a Discourse Strategy," 815.

4. In professional development work, the author has engaged in planning discussions where school personnel seek to contract training sessions using "*Yazzie/Martinez* funding."

5. Donald J. Kochan, "You Say You Want a (Nonviolent) Revolution, Well Then What? Translating Western Thought, Strategic Ideological Cooptation, and Institution Building for Freedom for Governments Emerging out of Peaceful Chaos," *West Virginia Law Review* 114, no. 3 (Spring 2012): 897–936.

6. Kochan, "You Say You Want a (Nonviolent) Revolution?," 898.

7. Luigi Esposito and Victor Romano, "Benevolent Racism and the Co-Optation of

the Black Lives Matter Movement," *Western Journal of Black Studies* 40, no. 3 (Fall 2016): 161–73.

8.   New Mexico Public Education Department, "Equity Council Brief," Summer 2021, p. 3, author archive.

9.   Sosanya Jones, "Subversion or Cooptation? Tactics for Engaging in Diversity Work in a Race-Adverse Climate," *Journal of Educational Leadership and Policy Studies* 3, no. 2 (January 2019), p. 2, https://files.eric.ed.gov/fulltext/EJ1233799.pdf.

10.   Jones, "Subversion or Cooptation?," 7.

11.   Jones, "Subversion or Cooptation?," 22.

12.   Jones, "Subversion or Cooptation?," 2.

13.   For a comprehensive sense of Apple's contribution to this field, see his collected works in Michael Apple, *Knowledge, Power, and Education: The Selected Works of Michael W. Apple* (New York: Routledge, 2013).

14.   See note 1.

15.   Dillon Mullan, "State Moves to Dismiss Yazzie/Martinez Lawsuit," *Santa Fe New Mexican*, March 17, 2020, https://www.santafenewmexican.com/news/local_news/state-moves-to-dismiss-yazzie-martinez-lawsuit/article_99ec76a8-6865-11ea-bf86-1b6eec7938c7.html.

16.   *Martinez et al. v. State of New Mexico et al.*, no. D-101-CV-2014-00793 and no. D-101-CV-2014-02224, Yazzie Plaintiffs' Response to State's Motion to Dismiss (NM May 1, 2020).

17.   See note 14.

18.   NMPED, "Equity Council Brief."

19.   E. Diane Torres-Velásquez, Christine E. Sleeter, and Augustine F. Romero, "Martínez v. State of New Mexico and Multicultural Education: Divide and Conquer? We Don't Think So!," *Association of Mexican American Educators Journal* 13, no. 3 (December 2019): 175.

20.   Barro detailed how New Mexico school districts were ostensibly "forced" to expend funds set aside for addressing the *Yazzie/Martinez* case to cover teacher salary increases that were also legislated at the same time.

21.   S.M. Barro, "New Mexico's 2019–20 Education Funding Still Less Than in 2007–08," 4.

22.   See note 1.

23.   Jones, "Subversion or Cooptation?"

24.   NMPED, "Readiness Assessment: Purpose of the Martinez/Yazzie Readiness Assessment Tool," April 21, 2020, https://webnew.ped.state.nm.us/bureaus/yazzie-martinez-updates/readiness-assessment/.

25.   Institute for American Indian Education, *2020 Post-Summit Executive Report*, University of New Mexico, May 2020, pp. 2–4, https://iaie.unm.edu/docs/iaie_post_summit_report_final_2020v3.pdf.

26.   IAIE, *2020 Post-Summit Executive Report*, 3.

27.   Families United for Education, "Open Letter to APS," June 15, 2020, available at

https://docs.google.com/forms/d/e/1FAIpQLScD4NUhNHm1Bam0mKYUa_
TLpaBMa5PuDFHvrQJpgC1JADm6kw/viewform.

28.   Albuquerque Public Schools, *2020–2021 Tribal Education Status Report*, September 2021, https://www.aps.edu/indian-education/documents/tesr.

29.   Roberto Lozano, "Las Cruces Public Schools: Addressing Educational Equity for All Students," *Las Cruces Sun News*, August 29, 2020, https://www.lcsun-news.com/story/news/education/lcps/2020/08/29/lcps-addressing-educational-equity-all-students/5667452002/.

30.   IAIE, *2020 Post-Summit Executive Report*.

31.   National Congress of American Indians, "The List of Federal Tribal Consultation Statutes, Orders, Regulations, Rules, Policies, Manuals, Protocols and Guidance," January 2009, https://www.ncai.org/resources/consultations/list-of-federal-tribal-consultation-statutes-orders-regulations-rules-policies-manuals-protocols-and-guidance.

32.   US Department of Education, *Tribal Leaders Speak: The State of American Indian Education, 2010 Report of the Consultations with Tribal Leaders in Indian Country*, 2010, www2.ed.gov/about/inits/ed/indianed/consultations-report.pdf.

33.   Robert J. Miller, "Consultation or Consent: The United States' Duty to Confer with American Indian Governments," *North Dakota Law Review* 91, no. 1 (October 2015): 37–98.

34.   Miller, "Consultation or Consent," 67.

35.   Miller, "Consultation or Consent," 32.

36.   Indian Education Act, [22-23A-1 to 22-23A-8 NMSA 1978], https://webnew.ped.state.nm.us/wp-content/uploads/2019/03/NM-Indian-Education-Act-1.pdf.

37.   See NMPED, *Request for Application*, Indian Education Act Funding RFA # 21–92400–00002, April 16, 2021.

38.   Torres-Velásquez, Sleeter, and Romero, "Martínez v. State of New Mexico and Multicultural Education," 182.

Figure 12. Contributing authors on the University of New Mexico campus are photo-graphed before a professional development session hosted by the Institute for American Indian Education. From top left to right: Lloyd L. Lee, Wendy S. Greyeyes, Tiffany S. Lee, Glenabah Martinez, Nancy Lopez, Shiv R. Desai. From bottom left to right: Christine Sims, Georgina Badoni, Leola Tsinnajinnie Paquin, and Cynthia Benally. Not pictured: Wilhelmina Yazzie, Preston Sanchez, Carlotta Penny Bird, Alexandra Bray Kinsella, Natalie Martinez, Rebecca Blum Martínez, Donna Deyhle, Vincent Werito, Karen C. Sanchez-Griego, President Jonathan Nez, Terri Flowerday, and Nathaniel Charley. Photo credit Hondo Louis. Funded by UNM's Center for Regional Studies and the Native American Studies Department.

CHAPTER EIGHT

The Department of Native American Studies at the University of New Mexico

Role and Responsibilities with the Yazzie/Martinez v. State of New Mexico *Education Ruling*

LLOYD L. LEE

Introduction

In July 2018 New Mexico First Judicial District Judge Sarah Singleton ruled that the State of New Mexico, the New Mexico Public Education Department (NMPED), and the state's secretary of education, named as the defendants in the combined *Yazzie/Martinez v. State of New Mexico* education suit, are failing to provide Native American students with a college- and career-ready education. Judge Singleton's ruling was a clear signal to NMPED, the secretary of education, and the State of New Mexico they are responsible for "providing an adequate, sufficient education to at-risk students i.e., socioeconomically disadvantaged children, English learners, Native American students, and children with disabilities."[1] Singleton's ruling, a six-hundred-plus page document of court findings, facts, and conclusions, states the evidence showed at-risk students—including Native American students—are not receiving a college- and career-ready education in the public education system of the State of New Mexico.

In the court findings, Singleton discusses the New Mexico Indian Education Act (NMIEA) of 2003. One of the purposes of this act is to "ensure that parents; tribal departments of education; community-based organizations; the department of education [public education department]; universities; and tribal, state, and local policy makers work together to find ways to improve educational opportunities for Native American students."[2] The act clearly articulates that universities, including academic departments, are to be involved in improving the educational opportunities for Native American students. Judge Singleton added that she expects the University of New Mexico and the university's Native American Studies department to be a part of transforming the public education system and meeting the court's ruling.

In several testimonies, witnesses discussed providing Native American students with a culturally relevant education with Native and non-Native teachers getting the necessary training, adequate resources, and help with lesson planning and curriculum development. Judge Singleton wrote, "New Mexico and PED have failed to ensure that the following resources are sustainable and systemic: a pipeline program to increase the number of Native American teachers; teachers that have access to culturally-relevant training; and a curriculum and pedagogy that is culturally relevant and responsive to Native American student needs."[3] Further, the evidence presented in the consolidated *Yazzie/Martinez* education case shows higher education should work alongside elementary and secondary education providers to build an equitable public education system in the State of New Mexico.

This chapter reviews the Native American Studies Department (NAS) at the University of New Mexico, discusses the NAS portion of House Bill 87 legislation to meet the *Yazzie/Martinez* ruling, and wraps up with a discussion on the future of NAS in relation to the education ruling.

Department of Native American Studies

The Native American Studies center at the University of New Mexico (UNM) in Albuquerque, New Mexico, was founded in 1970. Native American students at UNM had advocated for a Native American studies program and center since Kiva Club, a Native student group, was formed in 1952. The students wanted a place on campus to help with tutoring, counsel students attending the university, provide information on UNM to Native American students, and help with the students' transition from home to college. The students wanted a communication link between the university and Native peoples in Albuquerque, across the State of New Mexico, and the country. They also wanted a library specifically designed as a research and study area. The Indigenous students believed a Native American Studies center would make them feel more involved and less isolated at school. In their view, Native American Studies programming provided the opportunity to study the Indigenous experience and employ resources at UNM to help resolve the challenges Indigenous peoples face in the state and across the country.

Over the past fifty-two years Native American Studies has grown from a student center to an academic department in the College of Arts and Sciences offering a minor, a bachelor of arts (BA), an accelerated online bachelor of arts, and a master of arts (MA) graduate degree. Since 2005, 169 students have graduated with an NAS BA or MA degree.[4] Many NAS alumni have furthered their education by acquiring a graduate or professional degree and/or working in a tribal community or organization. The department also offers a dual credit course with the Albuquerque Public School District. Since the semester of spring 2016, on average 260 UNM students take a Native American Studies course each fall and spring semester.[5] These numbers reflect sustained growth since the minor was approved in 1999 and the major in 2004.

NAS is a small academic department with four full-time faculty, one senior student program specialist, and a department administrator. The department also has two to three adjunct faculty teaching each semester. Much of the NAS faculty research focuses on Native American education. Faculty conduct research projects in Indigenous languages and revitalization, secondary education curriculum, education policy, tribal education department capacity building, or educational leadership. NAS also collaborates with the Institute for American Indian Education.

The NAS BA program educates students about the Native experience, with significant attention to the complex history and intercultural heritage of New Mexico and the United States. NAS also collaborates with Indigenous communities and immerses students in a Native Nation building framework. The undergraduate program has two areas of concentration: (1) leadership and building Native Nations and (2) Indigenous learning communities. Students can declare an NAS minor or major in one of the concentration areas and need to complete thirty-six credit hours for an NAS major and twenty-four hours for a minor. Major students are required to take six core courses: NATV 1150: Introduction to Native American Studies; NATV 2110: Sociopolitical Concepts in Native America; NATV 2140: Research Issues in Native America; NATV 300: Research Methods in Native American Contexts; NATV 351: Individual Study or NATV 352: Internship; and NATV 474: Seminar: Applying Traditions of Native American Philosophy. They are also required to complete twelve credits of a NAS concentration area and six credit hours of NAS upper division courses (300 or 400 level). For a minor, students are required to take five core courses except for the Individual Study or Internship and nine credit hours of NAS upper division courses. The NAS accelerated online bachelor's program is designed for students to take eight-week online courses in the fall and spring semesters to complete the required thirty-six credit hours of the NAS major. Students can only major in the online degree program with the Leadership and Building Native Nations concentration. The course requirements are the same as an in-person major.

The NAS MA program is for students who hold a bachelor's degree in NAS or an NAS-related field. The graduate degree focuses on Indigenous leadership, self-determination, and sustainable community building. Students are required to complete a minimum of thirty credit hours, with eighteen of those credit hours from core courses and twelve hours from the focus section. The core courses are NATV 550: Indigenous Nations and Sustainable Communities Seminar; NATV 555: Native American Policy and Community Building; NATV 560: Research Method and Practice in Indigenous Scholarship; NATV 570: Indigenous Thought and Ethics; and NATV 590: Project of Excellence. The focus courses are NATV 502: Education, Power, and Indigenous Communities; NATV 522: Indigenous Community Approaches in Restorative Justice; NATV 524: Principles of Leadership in Indigenous Contexts; NATV 530: Gender and Indigenous Leadership; NATV 535: Issues in Contemporary Native Leadership; and NATV 540: Indigenous Economies, Sustainability, and Environmental Protection. Students can also petition for up to six credit hours of elective courses in a related non-NAS discipline.

The Native American Studies Department teaches and addresses Indigenous epistemologies conducive to culturally relevant curricula, culturally responsive pedagogy, and Indigenous languages. For example, NAS teaches NATV 474: Applying Traditions of Native American Philosophy Seminar, where the content focuses on creating a grounded philosophical understanding of Native American traditions of thought upon which students can draw as they apply their knowledge in future educational and professional work. The NATV 570: Indigenous Thought and Ethics course also introduces graduate students to the diverse theoretical and contextual perspectives in the NAS field through an examination of some of the most significant present-day scholarship and reflects Native-centered ethics and objectives.

NAS is a pivotal entity in the effort to ensure the State of New Mexico provides Native American students, socioeconomically disadvantaged students, English language learners, and children with disabilities with a college- and career-ready education. This is particularly important in an environment where the *Yazzie/Martinez* case has shown the state's abject failures in this area.[6]

HOUSE BILL LEGISLATION

During the 2019, 2020, and 2021 New Mexico state legislative sessions and the special 2020 legislative session, appropriations to fund school efforts to meet the *Yazzie/Martinez* ruling fell short. Numerous education stakeholders advocated to the New Mexico state legislature to focus on the totality of Native American education, including language, early childhood, elementary, secondary, infrastructure, curriculum, tribal education departments, and higher education. Professor Wendy S. Greyeyes from UNM researched and found 107 bills, memorials, and resolutions referencing the *Yazzie/Martinez v. State of New Mexico* case. Out of the 107 pieces of legislation, only one bill focused on the state's higher education system, House Bill (HB) 87.

HB 87 came about through several discussions starting in 2018. Following the education ruling in 2018, numerous Native Nations, tribes, pueblos, educational entities, and individuals helped put together a tribal remedy framework (TRF), a comprehensive plan for meeting the educational needs of Native American students in New Mexico. The TRF outlines a transformation of the New Mexico public education system in the areas of governance, funding, programming, and services. Several state legislative bills based on the TRF were developed and submitted for approval in the 2020 and 2021 legislative sessions.

The framework has been endorsed by the leadership of the Navajo Nation, Mescalero Apache Tribe, Jicarilla Apache Nation, and the twenty pueblos. The TRF proposal is aligned with the *Yazzie/Martinez v. State of New Mexico* ruling and the Indian Education Act of 2003. It proposes a set of solutions placing tribes, pueblos, and Native Nations at the center of education planning, programming, and infrastructure. The following describes the core elements of the framework:

- **Share responsibility and increase tribal education sovereignty.** Elevate the role of tribal education departments and build capacity by creating a pipeline for Native professionals and partnering with Native higher education institutions and programs; share education resources more equitably by providing recurring state funding for tribal education departments; formalize collaboration between tribes and school districts; and establish Native technical assistance centers to support tribal education departments and schools.
- **Community-based education, created by and centered on tribal communities.** Invest in tribal libraries as community education centers; invest in early education programs developed and delivered by tribal communities; sustain and scale up tribal community–based student support services; and enable public schools to coordinate and contract with tribes in providing students with social and health supports.
- **A balanced culturally and linguistically relevant education that revitalizes and sustains the strengths of children and their communities.** Address institutional racism, develop trauma-informed practices, and implement Indigenous justice models to end the marginalization and school pushout of Native children; establish Indigenous curriculum development centers and expand Native language programs by adding a Native language factor to the school funding formula and distribute funds to tribes; invest in a pipeline for Native teachers, staff, and educational leaders and ensure pay equity for Native language teachers; and provide tuition waivers for tribal students.[7]

House Representatives Derrick J. Lente (District 65) from Sandia Pueblo,

Georgene Louis (District 26) from Acoma Pueblo, and D. Wonda Johnson (District 5) from the Navajo Nation sponsored HB 87 in the 2021 legislative session.[8] HB 87 asked for recurring appropriations to state institutions of higher education and tribal colleges to increase the base budgets of various units and programs to help the State of New Mexico meet the *Yazzie/Martinez v. State of New Mexico* education ruling. The institutions listed in the bill include UNM, New Mexico Highlands University, New Mexico State University, Northern New Mexico College, Navajo Technical University, A:shiwi College, Diné College, and Southwestern Indian Polytechnic Institute.

The central focus of HB 87 is improving the educational system through Indigenous knowledge and expertise. The bill assists UNM, higher education institutions in New Mexico, NAS at UNM, and other academic programs in increasing the capacity of schools, improving school district performance, and supporting tribes to meet the needs of Indigenous students. UNM, NAS, and the other higher education institutions have Indigenous faculty who can train teachers, create curricula and pedagogy, develop Native American language revitalization programs, provide behavioral health support, and aid schools struggling to serve Native American students. HB 87 leverages the wealth of Indigenous academic expertise to improve pre-K to 12 education in the state. The bill involves over $26,200,000 in recurring investments. It was not approved by the New Mexico legislature in the 2021 session. It was introduced again in the 2022 session and remains unapproved.

The NAS funding component in the bill covers a variety of areas. First, it allocates $705,000 for student support services, including undergraduate scholarships, doctoral fellowships, and assistantships; second, $100,000 for a graduate program coordinator for graduate advising, planning, recruiting, and outreach; third, $1,220,000 for conducting research on Native American education, supporting existing faculty positions, and adding new faculty; fourth, $155,000 for technology systems upgrades; fifth, $380,000 for training elementary and secondary education teachers at sites across the state in NAS curriculum development and implementation; and sixth, $250,000 to include early childhood education as part of the department's curriculum, partnerships, and graduate program. The increased base budget focuses on the expansion of the degree programs and the creation of school curriculums examining Native American history, education, language, way of life, and other pertinent topics.

The increase in the NAS base budget in HB 87 emphasizes the need to support undergraduate and graduate students. Currently, NAS has over eighty students who minor and major at the undergraduate level and fifteen graduate students.[9] The technology allocation focuses on updating current office computers, renovating the NAS library to provide synchronous Zoom/remote capability, and provide laptops for students to use for their research and Projects of Excellence. In terms of curriculum development envisioned under HB 87, the department will partner with the Institute for American Indian Education in the College of Education and Human Sciences to develop a curriculum and materials development center. NAS faculty will offer workshops and teacher trainings and create other needed resources. Along with curriculum development, HB 87 envisions research support for NAS faculty to examine the trends of Native American education in New Mexico and to assess the effectiveness of the remedies implemented to transform the state's public education system.

A graduate coordinator will do advisement, planning, recruiting, and outreach. New faculty will also be needed. Currently, the department has four full-time faculty. In order for all three degrees to be sufficiently taught and covered, the department believes four additional faculty members are needed. Additionally, the department will develop two visiting faculty one-year fellowships and initiatives with Native Nations, groups, and/or organizations such as the National Congress of American Indians and the National Indian Education Association. The initiatives are designed to be a way for students, faculty, and Indigenous communities, groups, and organizations to work together to help resolve the challenges Indigenous peoples face in the state, across the country, and around the world.

The increase base budget funding for NAS and all the higher education institutions mentioned in HB 87 is fundamentally more than just about money. It is about creating, sustaining, expanding, and committing to a deep relationship between the state, tribes, pueblos, Native Nations, Native American students, and public education students, as well as advocating for a college- and career-ready education system for all New Mexico children and students.

Future of NAS in Conjunction with the *Yazzie/Martinez* Ruling

In 2018 NAS submitted a Research and Public Service Project (RPSP) proposal to the State of New Mexico. Through RPSPs, colleges and universities may submit research or public service projects to the state legislature for funding. The projects should be conducted separately from those receiving regular institutional funding designated by the legislature to all colleges and universities in the state. Each New Mexico higher education institution reviews all proposals and determines which department or program will be put forth to the state for RPSP funding. The NAS department submitted a proposal on supporting their graduate students' Projects of Excellence; establishing partnerships with Indigenous communities, groups, and/or organizations in the state; and cultivating internship sites for undergraduate students. Specifically, through the Project of Excellence part of the curriculum, NAS graduate students are required to work with an Indigenous community, group, or organization on a research project to complete their master's degree work. Each student is required to work on their project for two semesters, work that often lays the groundwork for the students' continued engagement after graduation. Indeed, several students who have graduated with their NAS MA are continuing to work with their project community, group, or organization.

Since the NAS MA program started in 2018, ten students have graduated in 2020 and 2021. Seven of them went to schools in New Mexico. Each of these seven students is from an Indigenous community and school impacted by the *Yazzie/Martinez v. State of New Mexico* case. Our students represent a direct link to Indigenous communities, school districts, and schools impacted by the education ruling. NAS is building the necessary human capacity through undergraduate and graduate students to meet the *Yazzie/Martinez v. State of New Mexico* education remedies outlined in the TRF.

The RPSP proposal focuses on student supplies, technical equipment, stipends, travel, and faculty support. The department's RPSP was approved by the university and submitted to the state legislature. The state legislature approved and funded it in the 2020 legislature session. While the original amount was set at $200,000, the department ultimately received $180,000.

Because of the COVID-19 pandemic, the New Mexico legislature reduced the entire state budget in the summer of 2020 by 6 percent, affecting all RPSP projects. Still, even with the reduction, the NAS RPSP has helped graduate and undergraduate students with their Projects of Excellence and internships.

Along with the RPSP approval, NAS submitted a doctoral degree proposal in January 2020, which was approved by all the appropriate university departments and units by December 2021. The NAS department received approval in 2022 and launched the doctoral program in the fall 2023 semester with a first cohort of five doctoral students.

The NAS doctoral degree envisions doctoral candidates who will become academic leaders and/or policy researchers for tribes, pueblos, Native Nations, and/or Indigenous communities. The approach will be interdisciplinary and the candidates will become proficient advocates and ethical researchers. The focus of the doctoral program will encompass the following areas:

- *Critical Indigenous Thought.* Critical Indigenous thought will focus on theorizing and articulating views on issues impacting Native peoples. It will challenge the traditional fields of education, ethnic studies, linguistics, law, anthropology, sociology, American studies, history, English, political science, and philosophy.
- *Healthy Sustainable Community Building.* Sustainable community building will focus on research work targeting policy development and implementation in Native communities. Sustainability will capture the continuation of the Native community's goals and needs.
- *Comparative Studies in Native Government, Policy, Identity, and Sustainability.* Comparative studies will examine the differing trajectories of Native governments, policy, identity, and sustainability.[10]

Doctoral students will be required to complete sixty-six credit hours, including a dissertation. The department will advocate for the need to do doctoral research in the area of education, paying close attention to the *Yazzie/Martinez v. State of New Mexico* remedy approach. However, the doctoral program will not require students to focus on education. Regardless, this option will benefit from an increased base budget and new initiatives with Native Nations, tribes, pueblos, groups, and organizations, which together will enhance the opportunity for doctoral students to engage in community-based education research projects. NAS will be training future academic professionals and policy researchers, whose skills and expertise will benefit the state's public education system in the long term.

Conclusion

The NAS Department at the University of New Mexico is in its fifty-second year of existence. It is the only Native American Studies department in New Mexico to offer a bachelors, an online bachelors, masters, and a doctoral degree. Since its inception, 169 students have graduated with an NAS BA or MA degree. Many of the undergraduate students have gone on to graduate school or found work in their own community, tribe, pueblo, Native Nation, or Indigenous organization. The impact NAS has on the education of students in New Mexico and across the country is evident and documented. NAS is a fundamental element in establishing a transformative public education system in New Mexico.

The *Yazzie/Martinez* education ruling is an opportunity for the state to change the public education system to ensure all New Mexico students recieve a college- and career-ready education. NAS at UNM is an integral department that can help in this process. The NAS faculty demonstrate its meaningful and positive impact for Indigenous and non-Indigenous peoples and communities in New Mexico, across the nation, and globally. The department's expertise is clear and the development of human capacity (i.e., teaching of students) will help usher in a transformative public education system designed to help New Mexico students be college and career ready.

Student Learning Objectives

1. Students will explain the history of Native American studies at the University of New Mexico.
2. Students will evaluate the Native American Studies Department's role in a call for transformational change resolving the systemic issues plaguing Native American students in New Mexico's public education system.

Discussion Questions

1. How has Native American studies at the University of New Mexico developed over the past fifty-two years?

2. How do higher education and NAS help to develop an equitable New Mexico public education system?

3. Outline how NAS advances Indigenous epistemologies in its courses.

Notes

1. *Yazzie/Martinez v. State of New Mexico*, Courts Findings of Face and Conclusions of Law, 2018-12-20; 553.

2. *Yazzie/Martinez v. State of New Mexico*, no. D-101-CV-2014-02224, 2019.

3. *Yazzie/Martinez v. State of New Mexico*, Courts Findings of Fact and Conclusions of Law, 2018-12-20; 143.

4. Catherine Montoya, "Native American Studies Graduates," email to author, University of New Mexico, 2021.

5. Montoya, "Native American Studies Graduates."

6. *Yazzie/Martinez v. State of New Mexico*, Courts Findings of Fact and Conclusions of Law, 2018-12-20; 149.

7. Tribal Education Alliance, *Pathways to Education Sovereignty: Taking a Stand for Native Children Summary Report*, December 2020.

8. HB 87, First Sess. of 2021 (NM 2021), https://www.nmlegis.gov/Legislation/Legislation?Chamber=H&LegType=B&LegNo=87&year=21.

9. Catherine Montoya, "Native American Studies Enrollment," email to author, University of New Mexico Office of Institutional Analytics, 2021.

10. Native American Studies Department, UNM, Doctoral Degree Proposal, January 2020.

Part III | The Future

Figure 13. Andrea Thomas (Diné), a highly recognized teacher, teaching her third-grade students in the Central Consolidated School District. During the COVID-19 pandemic teachers had to migrate from face-to-face to an online teaching platform. Governor Michelle Lujan Grisham ordered all public schools to be closed from March 2020 to March 2021, with limited opening in fall 2021. Here, Mrs. Thomas is using the Zoom platform to teach her third graders. Photo credit Hondo Louis. Funded by UNM's Center for Regional Studies and Native American Studies Department.

CHAPTER NINE

The *Yazzie/Martinez* Ruling

The Politics of Culturally Relevant Curriculum

GLENABAH MARTINEZ

Introduction

This chapter is a discussion of the significance of culturally relevant curriculum in the case presented by the legal team representing the plaintiffs in *Yazzie v. State of New Mexico* and the remedies prescribed by Judge Singleton in the consolidated case of *Martinez and Yazzie v. State of New Mexico* (henceforth *Yazzie/Martinez*) as well as in subsequent motions. One primary question guides this discussion: What can we learn from the court case about the pedagogical value of culturally relevant curriculum in providing Indigenous youth with a uniform and sufficient education for college and career readiness?

Six primary sources are reviewed for their treatment of culturally relevant curriculum as they apply to K-12 Indigenous students who attend public schools in New Mexico: Court's Findings of Facts and Conclusions of Law and Order re Final Judgment (2018), *Yazzie* Plaintiffs' Notice to the Court of Case Status (2019), Motion and Memorandum for Entry of Order of Satisfaction of Injunction and Dismissal of Action (2020), *Yazzie* Plaintiffs' Response to State's Motion to Dismiss (2020), *Yazzie* Plaintiffs' Expedited Motion for Further Relief Concerning Defendants' Failure to Provide Essential Technology to At-Risk Public School Students (2020), and the New Mexico Indian Education Act (1978, amended 2007). The ensuing discussion of the pedagogical utility of culturally relevant curriculum is grounded in evidence-based testimony and depositions by scholars, researchers, educators, parents, and school administrators.

Culturally Relevant Curriculum

A description of culturally relevant curriculum is provided in the discussion of Blum Martínez's testimony on Native American English learners in the Court's Findings of Facts and Conclusions of Law and Order re Final Judgment:

> A rigorous and well-designed culturally relevant curriculum has a positive impact on students. "Culturally relevant" describes "a condition where programs or services are planned, designed, implemented, and evaluated respecting and accounting for the client's cultural and linguistic values and heritage." The terms "culturally relevant," "culturally responsive," and "culturally appropriate" have very similar meanings, and are used interchangeably. Ex P-2881 at 7. Such curriculum should include units of study, courses, or programs that are centered around the knowledge and perspectives of an ethnic or racial group, reflecting narratives and points of view rooted in lived experiences and intellectual scholarship of that group. P-2795, paragraph 36. It is important for schools to provide ELL students a language program that is relevant to their culture, in order to help them develop their linguistic abilities and improve their self-efficacy and self-esteem.[1]

Culturally relevant curriculum appears in the New Mexico Indian Education Act (NMIEA), where the primary duties of the assistant secretary for Indian education are described:

> The assistant secretary for Indian Education shall, among other things: provide assistance to school districts and New Mexico tribes in the planning, development, implementation and evaluation of curricula in native languages, culture and history designed for tribal and nontribal students as approved by New Mexico tribes, develop or select for implementation a challenging, sequential, culturally relevant curriculum [to provide instruction to tribal students in pre-kindergarten through sixth grade to prepare them for pre-advanced and advanced placement coursework in grades seven through twelve].[2]

In this instance, culturally relevant curriculum is described as a deliverable by the state's Indian Education Division. The NMIEA is central to the arguments presented by the plaintiffs.

There are references to culturally relevant curriculum in the depositions and testimonies by superintendents and principals. The deposition of Laguna scholar and educator Dr. Natalie Martinez reinforces its importance in the education of Indigenous youth:

> Schools must provide Native American students, including Native American English learners, the same quality of education that is provided to non-Native American students by incorporating into the classroom a culturally relevant curriculum that contains the historical contributions made by indigenous people; opportunities for cross-cultural experiences, where Native American and non-Native American students can interact meaningfully; and opportunities for Native American parents to engage in their child's education.[3]

Similarly, Hayes Lewis, superintendent of Zuni Public Schools, emphasizes the need for improvement in delivery of culturally relevant curriculum:

> [New Mexico Public Education Department] has not developed a culturally-relevant [sic] curriculum; instead, the contemporary instructional materials and curriculum that are currently in place fail to capture the life, history, and social-legal issues that indigenous people have experienced in New Mexico. Thus Native American students have not learned about their tribal histories in school.[4]

Martinez and Lewis recognize the importance of culturally relevant curriculum in teaching Indigenous students. Both identify culturally relevant curriculum as a means for teaching Indigenous history that is meaningful to students and their families.

School administrators from districts that serve Indigenous Nations and their children provided testimony on their experiences and observations as it relates to culturally relevant curriculum. Superintendent Space of Grants Cibola County Schools and Superintendent Lewis of Zuni Public Schools provided testimony on resources, programs, and services necessary to create the unique cultural pedagogical conditions for meeting the needs of Native

Americans enrolled in New Mexico public schools. Six of the eight conditions relevant to this point are presented in the Findings of Fact and Conclusions:

   a. An early childhood learning program that focuses on their cultural roots;
   b. A culturally-relevant [sic] curriculum from Pre-K to grade 12, which requires a blend of contemporary standards within a curriculum that focuses on language, culture, cultural protocols, and orientation;
   c. A strong cultural competency program, throughout the year, that allows for non-Native American teachers and administrators to have a sense of belonging in an indigenous community;
   d. Education staff that understand the needs of Native American students and are trained to deliver a culturally relevant curriculum;
   e. Instructional materials that are specific to meet the cultural needs of Native American students;
   f. A tribal language program, which is useful for both teaching students their tribal language and for incorporating the English language.[5]

Crucial to the resources, programs, and services necessary to effectively implement a culturally relevant curriculum are funding and a culturally competent teaching force. The testimony of four superintendents led to the conclusion that "districts that serve high concentrations of Native American students lack sufficient resources, including funding, to provide the programs and services necessary to meet the unique cultural and linguistic needs of their Native American students."[6] School districts listed as not employing culturally relevant curriculum include Grants Cibola County Schools and Magdalena Public Schools. According to the testimony, support for Indigenous students with culturally relevant curriculum is absent at Gallup McKinley County Schools and Santa Fe Public Schools. Professional development is also identified as necessary for effective pedagogy in teaching Indigenous students. Superintendent Space emphasizes the point that Grants Cibola County Schools are in dire need of professional development on culturally relevant curriculum for teachers of Pueblo students.

Marsha Leno and Wilhelmina Yazzie also provide powerful depositions of their observations and experiences as plaintiffs and parents of Indigenous students. Leno of Zia Pueblo describes her disappointment with Los Alamitos

Middle and Cubero Elementary schools, regarding their lack of a culturally relevant curriculum and culturally competent teachers:

> Both of the schools where Plaintiff children attend lack Native American teachers; additionally, they lack teachers that are sensitive to their culture, traditions, and tribal affiliation; and teachers who have an ability to make learning relevant to their experiences as Native Americans. Marsha observed that, while Plaintiff children's teachers are generally good, they fail to understand Plaintiff children's unique cultural and linguistic needs.[7]

Plaintiff and parent Wilhelmina Yazzie describes the schooling experience of her son, who was a seventh grader:

> At the time of Wilhelmina's deposition, XN was in 7th grade at John F. Kennedy Middle School [. . .], which is located in the Gallup McKinley County School district. [. . .] The majority of children in XN's classes are Native American, which includes both Navajo and Pueblo students. XN, who is practicing to learn both English and Navajo at home, does not have access to bilingual language classes, including Navajo.[8]

The discussion on the importance of providing culturally relevant curriculum culminates in the section "Conclusions of Law" of the Court's Findings of Facts and Conclusions of Law and Order re Final Judgment. The first line states, "The New Mexico's Public School System Violates the Education Clause, Article XII, Section 1, of the New Mexico Constitution."[9] The NMIEA is described under the subsection "Sufficiency Standard." Fourteen directives to the assistant secretary of Indian Education are listed. Five directives are aligned with the concept of culturally relevant curriculum.[10] The state must:

b. provide assistance to school districts and New Mexico tribes in the planning, development, implementation and evaluation of curricula in native languages, culture and history designed for tribal and non-tribal students as approved by New Mexico tribes;

c. develop or select for implementation a challenging, sequential, culturally relevant curriculum to provide instruction to tribal students

    in pre-kindergarten through sixth grade to prepare them for pre-
    advanced placement and advanced placement coursework in grades
    seven through twelve; [. . .]

d. provide assistance to school districts, public postsecondary schools
    and New Mexico tribes to develop curricula and instructional materi-
    als in native languages, culture and history in conjunction and by
    contract with native language practitioners and tribal elders, unless
    the use of written language is expressly prohibited by the tribe;

e. conduct indigenous research and evaluation for effective curricula for
    tribal students; [. . .]

1. develop curricula to provide instruction in tribal history and govern-
    ment and develop plans to implement these subjects into history and
    government courses in school districts throughout the state;

m. ensure that native language bilingual programs are part of a school
    district's professional development plan, as provided in Section 22-
    10A-19.1 NMSA 1978.[11]

Judge Singleton's rationale for her ruling is presented in Court's Findings of
Facts and Conclusions of Law and Order re Final Judgment. Her ruling states
that the educational clause of the New Mexico Constitution was violated and
key provisions of the New Mexico Indian Education Act were not met. Judge
Singleton points out that the state by law already recognizes the value of
multicultural education, as found in the New Mexico Bilingual Multicultural
Education Act:

    While this Act focuses largely on language education, it also supports
    equitable and culturally relevant learning environments, educational op-
    portunities and culturally relevant instructional materials for all students
    participating in the program. Section 22-23-1.1 (K). The Act also encourages:
    (1) using the cultural and linguistic backgrounds of the students in a bilin-
    gual multicultural education program; (2) providing students with opportu-
    nities to expand their conceptual and linguistic abilities and potentials in a
    successful and positive manner; and (3) teaching students to appreciate the
    value and beauty of different languages and cultures. Section 22-23-1.1 (L)[12]

The Final Judgment and Order was filed on February 14, 2019. It reads, in part, "An injunction is hereby issued enjoining the Defendants to take immediate steps, by no later than April 15, 2019, to ensure that New Mexico schools have the resources necessary to give at-risk students the opportunity to obtain a uniform and sufficient education that prepares them for college and career."[13]

On June 18, 2019, the *Yazzie* Plaintiffs' Notice to the Court of Case Status was filed by the plaintiffs' legal team from the New Mexico Center on Law and Poverty. They point out that the "Court was quite clear about what needed to be done," yet the defendants fell short in addressing the remedies presented by Judge Singleton.[14] One of the exhibits attached to the notice is the Platform of Action: Yazzie Proposed Remedies. Two of the six sections of the platform address culturally relevant curriculum: "Multicultural and Equitable Foundation" and "Instruction-Curriculum, Materials, Extended Learning, and Enrichment."

On March 13, 2020, the State of New Mexico et al. defendants filed a Motion and Memorandum for Entry of Order of Satisfaction of Injunction and Dismissal of Action. In this motion, they assert that "the public education system currently in place in New Mexico is substantially different from the system in place during trial."[15] The defendants argued that they "complied with both the spirit and the letter of this Court's injunction" and "respectfully request that this Court recognize this compliance and dismiss this action."[16] The phrase "culturally relevant" surfaces in their discussion of compliance: (1) culturally relevant pedagogy, (2) culturally relevant plan, and (3) culturally relevant schools. This is drawn from the affidavit of Deputy Secretary of Identity, Equity and Transformation and Acting Assistant Secretary of Indian Education Kara Bobroff. One notable reference to culturally relevant curriculum appears in the affidavit:

The Indian Education Division (IED) has adopted a process for tribal review and approval of social studies curricula that emphasizes ongoing consultation with the state's Nations, tribes, and pueblos. Ultimately, [the Public Education Department] selected the Indian Pueblo Cultural Center's Indigenous Wisdom Curriculum to share with local school districts and charter schools; the department plans to continue reviewing documentaries for potential inclusion in the curriculum, if appropriate. The IED also assesses other, open-source curricula from both local tribes and national sources, to make available to local school districts and charter schools.[17]

The Indigenous Wisdom Curriculum referenced by Ms. Bobroff is the first edition of the K-12 curriculum on the complex political, social, cultural, and economic history of the Pueblo Nations of New Mexico between 1912 and 2012.

Two months later, on May 1, 2020, the legal team responded to the state's motion to dismiss. In Yazzie Plaintiffs' Response to State's Motion to Dismiss, they provide nine arguments describing in detail how the State of New Mexico fails to comply with the court's ruling: "A. Instructional Materials and Technology," "B. Native American Students," "C. Necessary Curricula and Programs," "D. ELL Students," "E. Students with Disabilities," "F. Low-Income Students," "G. Quality of Teaching and Related Issues," "H. Educational Outputs," and "I. Funding and Accountability."[18]

Under section B, "Native American Students," it was pointed out that "the State has not come close to meeting the requirements of the NM Indian Education Act, providing culturally relevant instructional materials to all Native students, and providing essential technology to all Native students. In fact, Defendants continue to go without an Assistant Secretary of Indian Education—a key position to ensure that the Indian Education Act is fulfilled."[19] Ten *Yazzie* plaintiff exhibits are attached to the plaintiffs' response, including the New Mexico Tribal Yazzie/Martinez Remedy Framework and statements issued by the All Pueblo Council of Governors and the Mescalero Apache tribe:

All Pueblo Council of Governors press release (March 27, 2020): Our Native children deserve justice and the right to an equitable education, similar to the one afforded to non-Native students. This means complying with the NM Indian Education Act as well as other laws that require a culturally responsive curriculum, a well-trained teacher workforce, language preservation, appropriate consultation with tribal communities and especially now during the COVID-19 pandemic, broadband infrastructure. (Chairman J. Michael Chavarria, All Pueblo Council of Governors)

Mescalero Apache Tribe Letter to NM Governor Lujan Grisham (April 30, 2020): In two legislative sessions, the State of New Mexico has failed to make any meaningful targeted investments for our children ... no comprehensive investment to address culturally relevant curriculum and instructional material development, no explicit language for Native teacher development, administrators and educational leader capacity building. (President Gabe Aguilar, Mescalero Apache Tribe)[20]

On June 29, 2020, First Judicial District Judge Matthew Wilson denied the motion to dismiss the ruling:

The state cannot be deemed to have complied with this court's order until it shows that the necessary programs and reforms are being provided to all at-risk students to ensure that they have the opportunity to be college and career ready. There is a lack of evidence in this case that the defendants have substantially satisfied this court's express orders regarding all at-risk students. The court's injunction requires comprehensive educational reform that demonstrates substantial improvement of student outcomes so that students are actually college and career ready.[21]

The motion to dismiss was filed by the state just as the COVID-19 pandemic was having a devastating effect on K-12 schools. On March 13, 2020, Governor Lujan Grisham ordered public schools to close for three weeks starting on March 16. On March 27 she extended school closures through the remainder of the 2019–2020 academic year. Schools transitioned to distance learning, which required that students and teachers have access to the Internet and electronic devices. Disparities in access to resources and parental/guardian engagement, as noted in *Spotlight* on June 10, 2020, meant "that at-risk children [would] likely start the upcoming school year farther behind than their more affluent peers."[22] The New Mexico Public Education Department (NMPED) convened a task force to develop guidelines for reopening in the 2020 fall semester, but reentry did not occur until April 5, 2021. The COVID-19 pandemic and challenges brought on by remote instruction had a catastrophic impact on many New Mexicans, as many did not have access to basic technology and the Internet. Disparities between urban and rural, rich and poor, and white and nonwhite existed prior to the pandemic, but the problems were exacerbated as COVID-19 spread across the state.

A 2020 state-sponsored study, *The Internet Connectivity on Tribal Lands: Guidance Document*, reports that "80 percent of people who live in Indian Country in New Mexico do not have consistent access to high-speed broadband internet, according to information obtained from US Senator Martin Heinrich's office."[23] The 2020 documentary produced by the New Mexico Center on Law and Poverty, the Native American Budget and Policy Institute at the University of New Mexico, and Jonathan Sims, *When Access Is Remote: The Digital Divide for Native Students*, presents the narrative of Mr. Kelly Maestas, a bus driver for the Cuba Independent School District.[24] Mr. Maestas describes his daily route of over one hundred miles to deliver meals, homework, and supplies to families residing in rural Navajo Nation lands during the period when schools were closed. Students who did not have access to the Internet at home had to go to the parking lots of libraries to attend their classes and to complete their school assignments. These conditions, along with the state's failure to make meaningful progress to comply with the *Yazzie* case's ruling, led to another court action.

On December 15, 2020, the *Yazzie* legal team filed a motion: Yazzie Plaintiffs' Expedited Motion for Further Relief Concerning Defendants' Failure to Provide Essential Technology to At-Risk Public School Students:

> The Yazzie Plaintiffs move this Court for an Order granting immediate relief from Defendants' failure to provide all at-risk public school students—especially in rural districts serving predominantly Native American students—with essential technology necessary for them to have access to a constitutionally sufficient education through remote learning during the COVID-19 pandemic. Defendants' failure to urgently implement this Court's prior orders and provide these students with essential technology has caused and continues to cause them to be denied a sufficient education required by the State Constitution and ordered by this Court. These students have already suffered grievous harm from the State's decade-long constitutional violations. Now, the failure to provide them essential tech access during the pandemic has resulted in them falling even farther behind. Therefore, Plaintiffs seek an Order from this Court requiring the State to immediately ensure all at-risk students in New Mexico, especially those living in rural districts serving predominantly Native American students,

are provided digital devices and remote access to high-speed internet, along with the funding necessary for the districts to provide tech support sufficient to ensure that these devices and internet access remain stable and reliable.

Plaintiffs have conferred with Defendants and they oppose this motion. Because of the urgency of the relief sought, Plaintiffs request that this motion be decided on an expedited schedule.[25]

The arguments in this motion present a portrait of education during the pandemic as a "deterioration of educational opportunity."[26] They describe access to the Internet and electronic devices as "gatekeepers" preventing uniform and sufficient education. The affidavits of superintendents from school districts (Cuba, Peñasco, Grants Cibola County, Zuni, Jemez Valley, and Gallup McKinley County) convey a common need for technology and concern about the impact that lack of access to technology has on learning. Although there are no direct references to culturally relevant curriculum or pedagogy in this motion due to the urgency of addressing the acute need for technology, Navajo Nation president Jonathan Nez's testimony before the United States House of Representatives Committee on Energy and Commerce on July 8, 2020, emphasizes the importance of culturally relevant curriculum in remote instruction:

> As discussed above, many Navajo households do not have access to fixed broadband internet, which in turn affects a vast majority of Navajo students. With the closure of schools this past spring semester, parents, teachers and school administrators saw the need for fixed internet access in every home so that students could continue their important studies. This lack of internet access made it very difficult for schools to deliver academic programs outside the classroom, seriously jeopardizing Navajo students' education. Technological infrastructure is essential to ensure Navajo students are able to exercise their right to all forms of the levels of education. The United States must, in conjunction with the Navajo government, take effective measures to ensure that students who reside within the borders of their Tribal Nation have the same access to distance learning methods as their urban counterparts via fixed internet.

The move to distance learning illuminates the need for the Navajo Nation to continue providing education in the Navajo language in keeping with Navajo cultural methods of teaching and learning. Investing in culturally appropriate distance learning resources is essential for the continued cultural education of Navajo youth. National funding should support and strengthen schools' ability to nurture language and cultural development for students through remote instruction. There is a great need to invest in the development of Navajo cultural resources for the continuous learning of Navajo students in order to ensure that the Navajo Nation can control the provision of education in a culturally appropriate and responsive way.[27]

On April 30, 2021, First Judicial District judge Matthew Wilson ruled that the state was obligated to provide an adequate education. At-risk students and teachers of at-risk students, Judge Wilson maintained, must be provided with digital devices and Internet access. On May 18, 2021, Judge Wilson issued a ruling for his order to take effect immediately. On the same day, the state's secretary of education Ryan Stewart sent a memo to tribal leaders to discuss the April 30 court ruling.

In summary, the journey of the *Yazzie/Martinez v. State of New Mexico* case and related court actions demonstrate the urgency of addressing educational equity and equality. Culturally relevant curriculum is one of many key points that anchor the arguments, testimony, and depositions presented by both the plaintiffs and defendants.

Discussion

Michael Apple describes curriculum as "never simply an assemblage of knowledge, somehow appearing in the texts and classrooms of a nation."[28] Rather, power (economic, political, and sociocultural), ideology, and selective traditions operate as major factors in the way a state legislates and mandates what counts as knowledge in K-12 public education. While much more can be stated here about the political nature of curriculum and schooling, for the purposes of the present discussion, ideology is best described as a system of ideas, beliefs, fundamental commitments, or values about social reality. Selective traditions, according to Raymond Williams, refer to "someone's selection, someone's vision of legitimate knowledge and culture, one that in the process of enfranchising one group's cultural capital disenfranchises another's."[29] Official knowledge as a product of power, ideology, and selective traditions is embodied in state standards, curriculum, instruction, assessment, and policy. However, it is important to emphasize that Indigenous peoples have not and do not passively accept the dominant narratives embedded in public education curriculum and pedagogy, as articulated in the testimonies, depositions, and affidavits presented thus far. Indigenous peoples are fully aware of the connection between historical injustices and present-day manifestations of oppression, especially in the realm of education.

The history of Americanization and deculturalization of Indigenous peoples through education is established in the testimony by Dr. Joseph Suina, former governor of Cochiti Pueblo and professor emeritus in the College of Education and Human Sciences at the University of New Mexico. In his testimony he provides the court with a comprehensive historical overview of Indian education from 1879 to the 1950s, to explain the disconnect between public schools and Native communities:

From the late 1940s into the 1960s, Federal Indian Policy took a new direction, known as the Termination Era [. . .] During this time [. . .] everything cultural, including language, was prohibited in the schools. [. . .] The implementation of the United States termination efforts has had a long-term, ongoing effect on New Mexico's tribal communities, including a disconnect from and distrust of state institutions, such as public schools, where Native American values are not respected. [. . .] In addition to historical trauma, forced assimilation practices on tribal communities has caused a disconnect between tribal communities and federal and state public schools. [. . .] For Native Americans tribal home experience is left at the doorstep of the school, and, currently, tribes are looking to find that connection.[30]

Dr. Suina concludes this section of his testimony with the statement that "the history of forced assimilation polices on tribal communities in New Mexico requires the system of education to meet the unique cultural and linguistic needs of indigenous students."[31] The testimony of Dr. Suina illustrates the political nature of curriculum, instruction, and policy by underscoring the ethical responsibility of the state to comply with the NMIEA and the rulings of Judge Singleton and Judge Wilson.

New Mexico's Indigenous students in K-12 public schools and their teachers are the direct beneficiaries of culturally relevant curriculum. Natalie Martinez and Hayes Lewis note the importance of critical perspectives of history in general and notable contributions of Indigenous peoples in the narratives of tribal, state, and national histories. Joseph Suina echoes this by asserting the need for public schools to "provide long-term investment and educational opportunities for Native American students, because they will be the future leaders of their tribal communities."[32] A culturally relevant curriculum that is critically oriented serves the interest of all students and citizens across the state. As noted by Walker, "critically oriented and culturally relevant pedagogies have the potential to foster critical thinking, identity development, and equity. [. . .] By linking CRP [culturally relevant pedagogy] with curricula focused on identity, presence, and intentionality, practitioners promote learning that is engaging, empowering, and personal."[33]

Montana's Indian Education for All program is one example where Indigenous knowledge is central to the curriculum of all K-12 students across the state. According to Juneau and Juneau, Montana's students "will translate their Indian Education for All knowledge into a stronger capability to deal with a global society made up of thousands of cultural groups."[34] External entities also place a pedagogical value on culturally relevant curriculum. One example is Advancement Via Individual Determination (AVID).

The New Mexico Alliance for College and Career Readiness is a consortium of fourteen school districts and superintendents that has entered into partnership with AVID, whose College and Career Readiness Framework recognizes the importance of cultural relevancy. The AVID website provides an explanation of how cultural relevance fits into their framework. According to the site, students need:

- Rigorous Academic Preparedness: In a culturally relevant learning

environment, students must develop collaboration skills to build rela-
tional capacity and respect the diverse experiences of others.

◆ Opportunity Knowledge: Students in culturally relevant learning environments develop high expectations for themselves, allowing them to
apply their learning, demonstrate knowledge and achieve success, and
feel more in control of their future.

◆ Student Agency: Culturally relevant learning environments empower
student voices and engender self-advocacy and leadership.[35]

Clearly, culturally relevant curriculum has significant pedagogical value for
all students.

Can a court decision such as the one rendered in *Yazzie/Martinez v. State
of New Mexico* effectively transform K-12 curricular knowledge from one that
reflects a dominant master narrative to one that is culturally relevant? After
all, New Mexico sits on unceded aboriginal lands of the Navajo Nation, the
Mescalero Apache Nation, the Jicarilla Apache Nation, and nineteen Pueblo
Nations. NMPED deputy secretary Kara Bobroff identifies the Indigenous
Wisdom Curriculum as one measure for addressing the need for culturally
relevant curriculum. The Indigenous Wisdom Curriculum presents a complex
political, social, cultural, and economic history of the Pueblo Nations of New
Mexico between 1912 and 2012. At the same time, it does not provide the rich
histories of the Navajo, Jicarilla, and Mescalero Peoples for K-12 educators and
their students, resulting in an incomplete narrative of state history.

A search of the NMPED website was conducted as part of the investigation
into the progress made by the state to effectively address Judge Singleton's
ruling. Two curriculum projects—the Indigenous Wisdom Curriculum and
Native Knowledge 360—are listed on the state's "Culturally and Linguistically Responsive Instruction" webpage. As described earlier, the Indigenous
Wisdom Curriculum was developed by the Indian Pueblo Cultural Center in
Albuquerque, New Mexico. Native Knowledge 360 is a program that includes
curriculum developed by the National Museum of the American Indian in
Washington, DC. There are no references on the website to culturally relevant
curriculum initiated and developed by the state to show compliance with the
court ruling and the NMIEA.

Conclusion

What can we learn from the court case about the pedagogical value of culturally relevant curriculum in providing Indigenous youth with a uniform and sufficient education for college and career readiness? The testimonies, depositions, affidavits, and statements from the Navajo Nation, Jicarilla Nation, Mescalero Nation, All Pueblo Governors Council, and the Tribal Remedy Framework recognize the pedagogical value of culturally relevant curriculum for K-12 Indigenous students. The authors of the NMIEA acknowledge the importance of culturally relevant curriculum and pedagogy and compliance with this act as central to the rulings and remedies of the case. At the national level there is a call for action to improve the quality of and access to Native American curriculum.

In 2019 the National Congress of American Indians released a report entitled *Becoming Visible: A Landscape Analysis of State Efforts to Provide Native American Education for All.* The executive summary presents the purpose of the report, which aligns with the basic arguments presented by the *Yazzie* plaintiffs.

> Native Americans are unfortunately invisible to many. Most Native Americans likely have attended or currently attend a school where information about Native Americans is either completely absent from the classroom or relegated to brief mentions, negative information, or inaccurate stereotypes. This results in an enduring and damaging narrative regarding Native peoples, tribal nations, and their citizens. Even though some exceptional efforts are happening around the country to bring accurate, culturally responsive, tribally specific, and contemporary content about Native Americans into mainstream education systems, much work remains to be done.[36]

The results of this report are based on an extensive review of literature, interviews, and surveys of thirty-five states with federally recognized tribal nations:

- Almost 90 percent of states surveyed said they have *current efforts underway to improve the quality of and access* to Native American curriculum;
- A majority of the states surveyed indicated that *Native American edu-*

cation is included in their content standards, but far fewer states *require* Native American education curriculum to be taught in public schools;

♦ Less than half of the states reported that *Native American education curricula is required* in their state and that it is *specific to tribal nations* in their state;

♦ Barriers to providing Native American educational content in class-rooms include the lack of *access to curricula,* lack of adequate *funding and state support* for staff, technical assistance, professional develop-ment and evaluation, and lack of *policies to expand Native American curriculum* beyond social studies/history subject areas;

♦ Current avenues for advancing adoption of Native American curricula include state legislation mandating collaboration between state educa-tion agencies and tribal nations, state legislation empowering or requir-ing state education agencies to develop curriculum, and state education agency policy to develop culturally responsive guidelines for local dis-tricts.[37]

The concept of culturally relevant curriculum is central to the results of this report, aligning it with the arguments presented by the *Yazzie* plaintiffs and legal team.

The report concludes by providing a tool kit for implementation of Native American education curricula. In the section that addresses curriculum devel-opment, eight states are listed as "Native American Education Curriculum State & National Resources." New Mexico is not listed. Should we be sur-prised? No, we should not be taken aback or surprised. Nor should we hope to be listed as a model in any report when two parents and plaintiffs in the *Yazzie/Martinez* lawsuit, Marsha Leno and James Martinez, point to the lack of change three years after the 2018 ruling in a 2021 letter to the editor:

We are part of the Yazzie/Martinez lawsuit because New Mexico's children deserve a gold-standard education: one that embraces the unique assets of all students and gives them the best chance to be successful. It's been over three years since the court found the state is violating students' constitu-tional right to a sufficient education, but little has changed. We're frustrated by the state's inaction.

For generations, our state has starved our education system, and children suffer because of it. Our culture and traditions are still not recognized by the schools and our languages aren't part of the curriculum. There [is] not enough tutoring or transportation. There's not enough professional support for our teachers or resources for children with disabilities. Even though many of our students lost much during the pandemic, there's not enough socio-emotional, behavioral and mental health support.

It is time we start aiming for the gold standard education our children deserve.[38]

By all indications of the lack of action taken by the state thus far to carry out the ruling by Judge Singleton and subsequent rulings on motions by Judge Wilson, we should not expect to see New Mexico listed as a model of Native American education. However, there are calls to action from New Mexico that can inform our relatives across Native Nations who are seeking to transform curriculum:

- Learn about the historical and current conditions of K-12 and postsecondary education in your state as they relate directly to Indigenous Nations.
- Ask if the schools and state educational system are preparing Indigenous youth to be future leaders of their respective Nations.
- Interrogate the quality, accuracy, and inclusiveness of Indigenous-centered content in state standards, state-adopted textbooks, and teaching resources.
- Question the preparation of preservice educators in elementary, secondary, special, early childhood, and physical education in working with Indigenous youth, families, communities, and Nations.
- Update knowledge on statistics of certified Native American teachers, paraprofessionals, administrators, and support staff, as well as state initiatives to increase their numbers.
- Evaluate the quality of in-service professional development for certified teachers, administrators, and support staff on addressing their knowledge and skills to work effectively with Indigenous students.
- Check on schools, districts, and the state education agency for mean-

ingful compliance with the state's Indian Education Act or other state mandates.

♦ Check on provisions and directives by the state and school districts of essential technology and culturally relevant curriculum and pedagogy for Indigenous students and their families, particularly during the COVID-19 pandemic.

♦ Engage in public action to promote educational reform that directly affects Indigenous students, families, communities, and nations.

Student Learning Objectives

1. Students will identify and explain the historical significance of culturally relevant curriculum in the *Yazzie/Martinez* case and motions filed after 2018.

2. Students will compare and contrast the perspectives presented in testimonies and depositions that center on culturally relevant curriculum.

Discussion Questions

1. Why is curriculum significant in the *Yazzie/Martinez v. State of New Mexico* case and ruling?

2. What did you learn from the depositions and testimonies about the significance of culturally relevant curriculum?

3. Do you agree with Dr. Suina that "the history of forced assimilation polices on tribal communities in New Mexico requires the system of education to meet the unique cultural and linguistic needs of indigenous students" and that this has led to a disconnect between public schools and Native communities in New Mexico? Why or why not?

4. In the discussion, the author addresses the political nature of curriculum and schooling. In what way do "selective traditions" and "official knowledge" relate directly to the *Yazzie/Martinez* case?

Notes

1. *Martinez v. State of New Mexico*, Court's Findings of Fact and Conclusions of Law and Order re Final Judgment, no. D-101-CV-2014-0079, 2018 WL 9489382 (NM Dist. Ct. Dec. 20, 2018), at 80.
2. Indian Education Act, NMSA §22-23A-1 to 22-23A-11 (1978, 2007): A-5E.
3. *Martinez*, Findings of Fact and Conclusions, 2018 WL 9489382, at 130.
4. *Martinez*, Findings of Fact and Conclusions, 2018 WL 9489382, at 162.
5. *Martinez*, Findings of Fact and Conclusions, 2018 WL 9489382, at 141–42.
6. *Martinez*, Findings of Fact and Conclusions, 2018 WL 9489382, at 162.
7. *Martinez*, Findings of Fact and Conclusions, 2018 WL 9489382, at 498.
8. *Martinez*, Findings of Fact and Conclusions, 2018 WL 9489382, at 492.
9. *Martinez*, Findings of Fact and Conclusions, 2018 WL 9489382, at 533.
10. The enumeration corresponds with the letter designated for each directive.
11. *Martinez*, Findings of Fact and Conclusions, 2018 WL 9489382, at 555–56.
12. *Martinez*, Findings of Fact and Conclusions, 2018 WL 9489382, at 124–25.
13. *Martinez v. State of New Mexico*, Final Judgment and Order, no. D101-CV-2014-00793 (NM Dist. Ct. February 14, 2019), at 304.
14. *Martinez v. State of New Mexico*, Yazzie Plaintiffs' Notice to the Court of Case Status, no. D-101-CV-2014-00793 (NM Dist. Ct. June 28, 2019).
15. *Martinez v. State of New Mexico*, Defendants' Motion and Memorandum for Entry of Order of Satisfaction of Injunction and Dismissal of Action, No. D-101-CV-2014-0079, 2020 WL 10223954 (NM Dist. Ct. March 13, 2020), at 50.
16. *Martinez*, Defendants' Motion and Memorandum, 2020 WL 10223954, at 51.
17. *Martinez*, Defendants' Motion and Memorandum, 2020 WL 10223954, at 87.
18. *Martinez v. State of New Mexico*, Yazzie Plaintiffs' Response to State's Motion to Dismiss, no. D-101-CV-2014-0079, 2020 WL 10223956 (NM Dist. Ct. May 1, 2020), at 9–29.
19. *Martinez*, Yazzie Plaintiffs' Response, 2020 WL 10223956, at 11.
20. *Martinez*, Yazzie Plaintiffs' Response, 2020 WL 10223956, at Yazzie Plaintiffs Exhibit.
21. New Mexico Center on Law and Poverty, "Yazzie/Martinez Education Lawsuit Moves Forward," news release, June 29, 2020, https://www.nmpovertylaw. org/2020/06/29/yazzie-martinez-education-lawsuit-moves-forward/.
22. New Mexico Legislative Finance Committee, Program Evaluation Team, *Spotlight*, "Learning Loss due to COVID-19 Pandemic," June 10, 2020, available at https://www. nmlegis.gov/Entity/LFC/Documents/Program_Evaluation_Reports/Spotlight%20-%20 Learning%20Loss%20Due%20to%20COVID-19%20Pandemic.pdf.
23. NMPED, *Internet Connectivity Concerns on Tribal Lands: Guidance Document*, June 25, 2020, available at https://webnew.ped.state.nm.us/wp-content/ uploads/2020/04/Revised-Tribal-Guidance-Document_FINAL_6.25.2020.pdf.
24. Native American Budget and Policy Institute, New Mexico Center on Law and Poverty, and Jonathan Sims, "'When Access Is Remote': The Digital Divide for Native Students," YouTube video, https://www.youtube.com/watch?v=9MMAXc1GXSA.

25. *Martinez v. State of New Mexico*, Yazzie Plaintiffs' Expedited Motion for Further Relief Concerning Defendants' Failure to Provide Essential Technology to At-Risk Public School Students, no. D-101-CV-2014-0079, 2020 WL 10223955 (NM Dist. Ct. Dec. 14, 2020), at 2–3.

26. Martinez, Yazzie Plaintiffs' Expedited Motion, 2020 WL 10223955, at 3.

27. "Addressing the Urgent Needs of Our Tribal Communities: Full Committee Hearing before the United States House of Representatives Committee on Energy and Commerce, 116th Cong. (2020) (statement of Jonathan Nez, president of the Navajo Nation), 9. See https://energycommerce.house.gov/sites/democrats.energycommerce.house.gov/files/documents/Testimony-Nez-Tribal%20Communities%20Hearing_070820.pdf.

28. Michael W. Apple, *Knowledge, Power, and Education: The Selected Works of Michael W. Apple* (New York: Routledge, 2013), 1.

29. Raymond Williams, quoted in Glenabah Martinez, *Native Pride: Politics of Curriculum and Instruction in an Urban High School* (Cresskill, NJ: Hampton Press, 2010), 59.

30. *Martinez*, Findings of Fact and Conclusions, 2018 WL 9489382, at 134–37.

31. *Martinez*, Findings of Fact and Conclusions, 2018 WL 9489382, at 138.

32. *Martinez*, Findings of Fact and Conclusions, 2018 WL 9489382, at 134.

33. Anthony Walker, "Culturally Relevant Pedagogy, Identity, Presence, and Intentionality: A Brief Review of Literature," *Journal of Research Initiatives* 4, no. 3 (2019): 10.

34. Carol Juneau and Denise Juneau, "Indian Education for All: Montana's Constitution at Work in Our Schools," *Montana Law Review* 72, no. 1 (Winter 2011): 124.

35. Advancement Via Individual Determination, "Cultural Relevance," https://www.avid.org/cultural-relevance.

36. National Congress of American Indians, *Becoming Visible: A Landscape Analysis of State Efforts to Provide Native American Education for All*, Washington, DC: September 2019, https://www.ncai.org/policy-research-center/research-data/prc-publications/NCAI-Becoming_Visible_Report-Digital_FINAL_10_2019.pdf, 6.

37. National Congress of American Indians, *Becoming Visible*, 7.

38. Marsha Leno and James Martinez, "3 Years after Ruling, Kids Deserve First-Rate Education," *Albuquerque Journal*, September 5, 2021, https://www.abqjournal.com/2426063/letters-218.html.

Figure 14. During the COVID-19 pandemic it became evident that infrastructure needs across the Navajo reservation were severely deficient. Navajo Tribal Utility Authority (NTUA) workers are seen installing a water line to address water scarcity on the Navajo Nation. Photo credit Hondo Louis. Funded by UNM's Center for Regional Studies and Native American Studies Department.

CHAPTER TEN

The Complexities of Language Learning for New Mexico's Indigenous Students

CHRISTINE SIMS AND REBECCA BLUM MARTÍNEZ

Introduction

The *Yazzie/Martinez v. State of New Mexico* consolidated lawsuit brought to light many of the educational injustices that have characterized the history of New Mexico's Native American students and those who are in the process of learning English. These groups were among the plaintiffs represented in the case who, according to the First Judicial District Court judge, were not provided a sufficient and uniform education. Moreover, the court found that the state had failed to comply with the New Mexico Bilingual Multicultural Education Act and the New Mexico Indian Education Act (NMIEA). Each of these acts had been established by the New Mexico state legislature to protect the rights of these students and to guide the state and school districts in developing educational programs appropriate to their unique cultural and linguistic needs.

Underlying the complaint of both groups was the issue of languages: the English, Spanish, and Indigenous languages present in students' lives. In this chapter we take up the issue of Indigenous languages and English. We begin by emphasizing the critical role language plays in all our lives for nurturing, communicating, belonging, and—most especially for students—learning both at home and at school.

In section 1 we discuss the decisive role that language plays in sustaining and cultivating Indigenous world views, values, and concepts, and the danger that language loss poses for Indigenous peoples. Efforts to teach Indigenous languages to younger generations both at school and at home are highlighted.

Section 2 analyzes the status of Indigenous students as English learners (ELs) as designated by the federal government. The discussion reveals the complex linguistic profile of many New Mexico Indigenous students and the lack of understanding of this situation by both teachers and administrators. Suggestions for addressing the needs of Indigenous students in English are provided.

The Role of Language

Language is the means by which we communicate with each other as human beings. Through language we are able to express our feelings, ideas, and concepts. Language is key to a child's cognition and growth.[1] For the purposes of this chapter, Indigenous languages are also crucial to the teaching and learning of values and beliefs and the continuation of culture. As noted by the *Yazzie/Martinez* plaintiffs, developing the knowledge and skills that are transmitted through Indigenous language is especially important for students' participation in their cultural communities and preparation for future roles as leaders in their respective tribes.[2]

Children learn languages naturally from those around them. As they are cared for by and interact with their caregivers, they learn the ways of using language from them. Language socialization has been defined as "both socialization through language and socialization to use language."[3] In Indigenous communities there have always been ways of socializing children into new concepts, new ways of thinking, and new ways of using language. This process occurs through daily use and practice of the language within the family, with siblings and relatives, and with other members of the language community. Socialization of children also involves observation and listening to older, fluent speakers using the language in public and in different contexts. Mentoring by elders or other adult members on the use of language in ceremonial and other formal settings is also part of children's learning as they mature into adolescence and adulthood.

For many Indigenous people, language for communicative purposes, developing a sense of cultural identity, and intergenerational transmission of rich oral traditions has been key to children's learning in their own communities. Sadly, much of this learning has disappeared as these traditional uses of language have diminished. For many Indigenous communities the critical role of Native language in children's development is challenged by the influence and presence of a larger, more dominant English language. Continued use is integral to the survival of Indigenous languages, as well as providing opportunities to learn and maintain them within their respective language communities. Those from smaller communities thus face the challenge of ensuring that Native students have access to Indigenous language learning opportunities to apply and use Indigenous languages alongside English.

Elders, tribal leaders, parents, and students themselves have long advocated for opportunities to learn their heritage languages as a regular part of their instruction in public schools, recognizing the critical nature of language erosion that is rapidly occurring in many tribes. Moreover, the 2003 Indian Education Act was clearly cited in the *Yazzie/Martinez* consolidated case as a major legislative act whose mandate had not been met, especially regarding support of Native language instruction.[4]

The continued existence of Indigenous languages is a critical aspect of many current efforts to stem the process of language shift that is occurring in all Native American communities in New Mexico. More broadly, this phenomenon impacts almost every Native American community throughout the United States. The replacement of Native languages by English in home and community life began more than a century ago when federal government schools were established for assimilation purposes. Schools were used as the conduit for ensuring that Native American children would leave behind their Indigenous languages and cultures through forced repression and painful consequences for speaking in their mother tongue. The legacy left behind by decades of oppressive and harmful school practices resulted in the loss of language over generations in many Native American tribes. While the vitality of Native languages and cultures in New Mexico has remained relatively strong for a longer period of time compared to Indigenous languages in other regions of the United States, the progression of language shift observed by tribal leaders, elders, and older generations shows that even here, in New Mexico, Indigenous languages are not immune to these processes. The integral tie between

Indigenous language use and cultural ways of life is therefore at stake when these languages are not learned or acquired by younger generations, especially school-age generations. Preschool and school-age Native children, who represent the most vulnerable age group for Native language loss, now spend almost all of their waking hours in English language school environments surrounded by an even wider English-speaking society. (In section 2, key issues in English language education for Native American students in New Mexico are addressed.)

These recent developments of language shift also bring to mind existential questions for all Indigenous communities. Will Indigenous languages be learned early enough in children's lives to allow for continued growth and maintenance so that they, too, become the next generation contributing to and upholding unique cultural traditions and ways of life? In many tribes and Indigenous Nations, Native language use is a significant aspect of a community's internal sociocultural practices, customs, and oral traditions. In addition, for many Pueblo Indian tribes in New Mexico, language is a critical aspect of socioreligious life and traditional self-governance systems, which entail a lifetime of cultural learning, mentoring, and practicing cultural traditions in daily life.

Providing an early foundation for children's language learning is therefore key to developing positive self-identity—as well as tribal identity—as children comprise the next generation of leaders and contributing members in their respective communities. Loss of language potentially compromises the very existence of Native cultures.[5] If Indigenous children from these language communities do not have support for learning their ancestral languages early on, there is no guarantee they will be able to sustain the important aspects of cultural ways that depend on use of the Native tongue. In an effort to address these issues, many tribes have taken it upon themselves to initiate community-based language programs or have advocated for classes in local schools where students will have the opportunity to spend a portion of their instructional day learning in their heritage language.

For many Native students today, however, it is more frequently the case that they are limited to the exclusive use of English throughout the instructional day, leaving no substantive time or opportunity to be immersed in an Indigenous language or in culturally relevant learning. The absence of substantive opportunities to learn their heritage language was an especially significant aspect of plaintiff testimonies in the *Yazzie/Martinez* consolidated case.[6] Similar learning environments devoid of Native language use in preschool and early childhood programs are especially detrimental because these learners are in the most critical stages of their social, emotional, cognitive, and linguistic development. Internal community surveys conducted by several tribes over the last two decades have shown increasing numbers of monolingual English speakers among Native preschool and school-age generations.[7] Learning their ancestral language as a second language has now become the more common situation among many Native American preschool children as well as students participating in community or school-based language programs. The urgency of addressing this language shift has moved some tribes, such as Jemez Pueblo, to consider how existing educational programs for preschool children need to be altered to better support culture and language learning before they begin formal schooling. In other Native communities, Native educators such as Trisha Moquino, founder of the Keres Children's Learning Center in Cochiti Pueblo, have been committed to maintaining their Native language by developing alternative approaches to English-only education. These individuals have worked tirelessly to establish their own Native language immersion schools.

While schools cannot be depended on as the only solution to Indigenous language regeneration, institutional support of tribal efforts to develop Native language initiatives may make a difference in the lives of Native children. As noted in the court's findings and conclusions in the *Yazzie/Martinez* consolidated court case, the supportive role schools can play in providing the services needed for Indigenous language learning is an important one for all New Mexico Native American students.[8] However, this raises the question of whether schools are willing to reach out and work in partnership with tribes to initiate and sustain programs in ways that will best fit tribal needs and goals for educating children in their Native language. The increased concern expressed by many tribal leaders and elders to support greater efforts for teaching language and culture to preschool and school-age children in Pueblo, Apache, and Navajo communities has been noted in countless Indian education summits and convenings between tribes and New Mexico state education agencies.

For some New Mexico tribes, Native language teaching efforts have largely been initiated on a local level in day care or early childhood centers, Head Start programs, or public school classes. Full Native language immersion environments, where an entire school day is conducted in a Native language, however, are few. Thus far, only two New Mexico tribes—Jemez and Cochiti Pueblos—have initiated full Native language immersion programs, both representing promising potential for implementation in other language communities. In 2014, for example, Jemez Pueblo leadership authorized the transition of its federally funded Head Start Program to a full Walatowa language immersion Head Start.[9] The program is fully staffed by fluent Towa-speaking teachers and teaching assistants, as well as ancillary staff. In Cochiti Pueblo a pre-K to grade 6 Montessori school—the Keres Children's Learning Center, founded by Trisha Moquino in 2012—serves Cochiti children aged two-and-a-half to twelve and offers a Keres language immersion environment and dual-language instruction for children aged six to eight.[10] In these Native language immersion environments, culturally relevant materials and resources are used in instructional curricula, ensuring the critical link between language and culture is not lost. Moreover, parents and communities provide another critical link that promotes intergenerational learning, a key aspect of Indigenous ways of teaching and socializing children to be active members of their communities. In both initiatives the Native language is not an "add-on" component, as is often found in educational programs in schools. Instead, the Native language is prioritized through its use as a means of normal daily communication in all activities, as well as by its use in culturally based learning and culturally relevant pedagogy.

Within the Navajo Nation there has also been movement toward developing more Navajo language–teaching preschool programs. Navajo Technical University in Crownpoint, New Mexico, for example, has recently created a new Navajo-based early childhood teacher preparation program. Standards for teaching Navajo language and culture have also been developed by the Department of Diné Education for use in public schools where Navajo language classes are being taught.[11] Central Consolidated Schools in northwestern New Mexico is another example where a full Navajo immersion program has been initiated for elementary students. Efforts are also emerging within the Albuquerque area to develop a Navajo immersion program, the Saad

K'idilye Language Nest, for Navajo children and families residing in the Albuquerque urban area.[12]

As can be seen in these examples, the prioritization of Native language learning has forced movement in new directions to educate Native children in ways that are more closely aligned with tribal goals for maintaining and reinvigorating language use among children and families and within communities. The enduring hope among New Mexico tribes is that their children will be afforded more substantive opportunities to receive the benefit of learning their ancestral languages even as they are also learning English in schools. Substantive opportunities should involve more than a forty-five-minute class offered two or three times a week. This was identified as a key issue in the 2003 NMIEA, which supports the teaching of Native languages in New Mexico public schools. It is also one of three important legislative acts that were not being adequately addressed by the New Mexico Public Education Department, as cited in the *Yazzie/Martinez* court case findings.[13]

Indigenous Children in English Language Schools

In the 1970s, when the Office of Civil Rights defined ELs as Limited English Proficient (LEP), there were still many Indigenous children who spoke their heritage languages at home and in their communities. Despite the efforts of federal and state governments to do away with Indigenous languages, many communities persevered in the maintenance of their languages. Isolation from larger urban centers allowed Indigenous communities to continue using their language as their primary form of communication. The deplorable physical and educational conditions of schools serving Native children had meant less time spent on school grounds where English would be required. When amendments to the national Bilingual Education Act were passed and funded in 1978, many public, federal, and religious schools with large enrollments of Indigenous students began focusing on developing bilingual programs in English and Native languages, with a primary emphasis on English. Indigenous leaders lobbied to have their children included in this educational reform. Thus, Indigenous children were included in the definition of LEP students as:

a Native American or Alaska native or who is a native resident of the outlying areas and comes from an environment where a language other than
English has had significant impact on such individual's level of English
language proficiency.[14]

It is important to note the criteria "a native resident of outlying areas" and
"where a language other than English has had significant impact." The inclusion of both criteria is important for the discussion in this next section of the
chapter.

Much has changed in Indigenous communities since this original definition. The US government's efforts to eradicate Native languages have had
devastating effects, greatly weakening most Indigenous languages and resulting in few children claiming their Indigenous language as their first language.
Moreover, as fluent speakers age, there are fewer adults fluent in their Native
language, and thereby fewer people to pass the language on. Despite this
trend, many Indigenous communities are making heroic efforts to revitalize
their languages by teaching it to the young, as described in the previous section.

Some conditions, however, have changed little. Many communities are still
isolated and lack basic services of present-day life: electricity, potable running
water, and—most notably during the first year and a half of the COVID-19
pandemic—access to the Internet.[15] Public schools with higher enrollment of
Indigenous children are frequently underfunded and poorly staffed. Most
teachers and administrators are white and unfamiliar with the histories, cultures, and languages of their Indigenous students. Further, they have little to
no contact with the communities from where their students come. Teacher
and administrator preparation programs generally are devoid of any information about Indigenous students, thereby maintaining the status quo. Little
effort is made to recruit Indigenous students to the teaching field, except for
Indigenous colleges and universities. The latest statistics in New Mexico
report less than 2 percent of teachers are Indigenous, despite the fact Indigenous children make up almost 12 percent of the student population in the
state. In several school districts in New Mexico where Native students make
up almost 95 percent of the total enrollment, there may be only a handful of
Indigenous teachers, if any. District and school-level administrators mirror

teachers' ignorance and often disregard or are unaware of the educational wishes of the tribes.

Adding to these difficulties is the fact most teacher and administrator education programs rarely include any information on the specific needs of ELs or the federal laws that protect them.[16] Only a handful of states (Arizona, Florida, New York, and California) require all teachers to have some preparation for working with ELs. New Mexico does not require this training for teachers. In cases where teacher preparation programs include the needs of ELs, they often focus on immigrant students who are in the early stages of English language development. It seems many teacher education programs are not aware that most ELs are Native born and have middle-level proficiency in English.[17]

In the last fifteen years there has been great concern over EL students enrolled in US public schools for at least six years who lag behind their English-fluent classmates academically.[18] In many large school districts these students may make up between 30 and 60 percent of the total EL population.[19] The term for these students—long-term English learners (LTELs)—and their academic circumstances have been the focus of much debate. Many scholars consider the term LTEL disparaging and one that blames the student rather than the education they have received.[20] Research has identified many reasons for the low achievement of this group of students, including inconsistent programming in schools, student mobility, teachers' ignorance about language development, deficit thinking on the part of school personnel, and racial and linguistic biases.[21] In the specific case of Indigenous children in New Mexico, because they only enroll in US schools and often lag behind white students academically, they are readily given the moniker of LTEL. But what does this really mean? What are the circumstances of their language development? How can their English be described?

Indigenous children have learned English in the context of their families and their communities as they listen to older adults speaking their heritage language. They have developed deep understandings of the ways in which they must interact with different people—their families, elders, and community leaders. They have been immersed in their cultures and know how to navigate those worlds. The interactional styles of their families and communities have been learned by participating in everyday life and listening at family and community gatherings. Although their parents and grandparents may be literate in English, the oral traditions of their cultures persist and require children to listen to long stretches of discourse, socializing them to listen respectfully without interruptions or questions.

Generally, Indigenous children have less experience interacting in more urban settings and using different registers of English. *Register* is a linguistic term used to define and explain the differences found in language (both spoken and written) based on the topic being discussed, the relationship of interlocutors or readers/writers, and the mode used (spoken or written).[22] The social and physical isolation of students' communities has been mentioned previously both as a benefit to heritage-language maintenance and as a detriment to the development of English, particularly the development of different registers in English. This isolation has existed for many generations. Across the years, schools serving Indigenous students have introduced basic literacy and numeracy using the routine in which the teacher asks a question with one right answer, a student responds, and the teacher evaluates the response.[23] However, for the most part and across generations, school personnel and curricula have conceived of Indigenous education as remediation, severely limiting Native students' access to different registers and more robust and intellectually stimulating content. The famous Meriam Report, published in 1928, identified many of the problems in the education of Indigenous students that persist today and called for "a change in point of view."[24] Despite this report and many more reports undertaken since, little has changed for Indigenous children. Rarely have Indigenous students had access to advanced studies. Instead, they have been tracked into programs for "underachievers," where content is introduced piecemeal and greatly simplified. The result has been a lack of access to the curriculum and materials that would allow them to develop greater academic and literacy skills.[25]

Scholars have argued that expectations for the use of language in schools are based on white, middle-class language models.[26] Expectations for participation, power relationships, and the ways of using language for school-based tasks are often very different for children from other social backgrounds. Indigenous children's understanding of how to participate in these tasks may not match those of their teachers.[27] Further, as children move from one grade to another, expectations for language use become more and more dependent on literacy and the ways in which language is used in written form. At the third-grade level, children are no longer expected to "learn to read" but rather to "read to learn." Texts and textbooks become the central focus of all classroom activities. Moreover, the curriculum begins to branch out into different subjects—social studies, science, and math—each with their own way of using language to explain and describe their fields. While vocabulary certainly differs in these fields, it is critical to understand how the grammatical and textual forms differ as well. Each subject area constructs knowledge through texts that reflect the ways of thinking in that field, and most children—especially those children who have not had access to more advanced levels of written material—need support in learning how to read and understand complex texts in different fields. Differences exist in "how the disciplines create, disseminate, and evaluate knowledge, and these differences are instantiated in their use of language."[28] Shanahan and Shanahan and others argue that "the literacy demands on students are unique depending on the discipline they are studying."[29] Further, they argue instruction that considers text structure as well as genre must be provided so students can enter these fields with a baseline understanding.

Research conducted for the *Yazzie/Martinez* case confirmed that the program most widely offered for Native American ELs was remedial reading.[30] When asked what was being done to assist Native American ELs, most educators pointed to remedial reading classes. In visits to remedial reading classes, children were observed to read a few lines of simplified texts, first individually and then aloud to the reading teacher. The content of the texts was equally simplified, making for a very uninspiring experience for the children. Many children had been placed in remedial classes since the first grade and continued on this track through the fifth grade. While some of these children may have been having difficulties with basic literacy skills, their lack of exposure to different genres, more sophisticated uses of language, and interesting content condemned them to many years of remedial education that kept them from developing greater academic and language skills. Further, this constant attention to skills and absence of interesting content relayed the message that "reading" was an exercise empty of meaning. Because most of the teachers interviewed lacked knowledge about how language develops and the relationship between language and literacy, whatever difficulties Indigenous children had were immediately diagnosed as reading difficulties, and placement in remedial reading classes followed.

Scholars have argued that teachers need an understanding of the role language plays in learning, particularly for those developing English as a second language.[31] Fillmore and Snow identify critical topics that should be included in teacher education programs so teachers can assist children in their linguistic and literacy development. These include an understanding of linguistics as it relates to educational considerations—specifically how language is structured and how those structures create meaning; first-language and second-language development; the languages of academic discourse; and how to analyze textual structures so new ways of using written language can be explained and understood by children.[32]

After studying the literacy difficulties faced by multilingual learners, Fillmore and Fillmore urged educators to provide access to complex texts while offering specific supports.[33] This became known as "juicy sentence" work and was further refined by Maryann Cucchiara when she worked with Wong Fillmore and New York City Schools.[34] The Fillmores argued for teachers to call out the *"grammatical structures and devices* for framing ideas, indicating relationships, and structuring arguments that create *substantial differences between spoken and written language."*[35] This is not an argument for teaching grammar; rather, through questions and conversations with students, attention is drawn to a particular structure or device, teachers and students talk about it, and later, students can utilize these structures in their own writing.

An example from the Indigenous Wisdom Curriculum, developed for the Indian Pueblo Cultural Center by Pueblo scholars and educators, is offered below.[36] This particular lesson is in a unit for grade six on the movement of Pueblo people to urban areas. An informational text taken from a local newspaper about the experiences of one person who moved to the city includes this sentence:

> As a migrant to the city long before the steadily growing wave of young Indians leaving the reservation, Mrs. Moquino on her own had to contend with problems of cultural shock, transportation, housing, and health.[37]

This sentence begins with important information about Mrs. Moquino, the subject of the sentence, with the phrase *As a migrant to the city*. The phrase *long before* refers to her moving to a city prior to the movement of most young people—*the steadily growing wave of young Indians leaving the reservation*. The phrase *Mrs. Moquino on her own* provides information concerning her possible isolation from family and community, as well as the difficulties of dealing with *cultural shock, transportation, housing, and health*.

Here are some suggested questions that could be asked of this sentence so that students become aware of the different parts of the sentence and how they come together to convey a particular message:

By breaking long and complex sentences into chunks and walking students through each section, teachers and students begin to build awareness of how written language works and how these structures and features can be used in their own writing. This provides teachers and students with the means to access difficult material that is often intellectually challenging and interesting. When these conversations become routine, children become aware of differences in register and genre. As teachers call out these structures and features and ask students to include them in their own writing, students realize there is no secret to reading and writing about complex material. They can own the language for their own purposes.

The Fillmores' "juicy sentence" work has been adopted by several school districts and by EL Education, an open-source English Language Arts curriculum. ELs of all levels, but especially those at intermediate stages of

Table 2. Suggested Questions to Build Awareness of Different Parts of the Sentence

as a migrant	[Who is a migrant in this sentence?]
to the city	[Where did the migrant go, or where is the migrant?]
long before	[When did the migrant (Mrs. Moquino) go to the city?]
the steadily growing wave	[What happened after Mrs. Moquino went to the city?]
of young Indians leaving the reservation	[How does the author describe the young Indians?]
	[Why would the author use "steadily growing wave?]
Ms. Moquino on her own	[Why is this phrase used?]
	[What does it say about Mrs. Moquino?]
had to contend	[What other verbs do you know that could substitute for contend?]
with cultural shock, transportation housing, and health	[Why would these issues be difficult for Mrs. Moquino?]

development, have made great strides in their reading and writing. Indigenous children are as gifted, intellectually curious, and able as any other group of children and can access this kind of material with the proper supports. It only takes "changing the point of view" of teachers and administrators to help Indigenous children experience the success in schools that they deserve. Clearly, implementing such improvements in teaching English to Native American students would begin to address the academic challenges that so many students face in New Mexico schools.

Conclusion

As we have discussed in this chapter, New Mexico's Native American students face daunting challenges in learning both their own ancestral languages and the academic English of schools. It is a formidable challenge given current circumstances in which the unique language needs of students are still unmet, as cited in the court's ruling in the *Yazzie/Martinez* consolidated case. This includes the lack of substantive opportunities for culturally and linguistically responsive education and failure to plan, design, and develop culturally relevant curricula and instructional materials that acknowledge and reflect the rich cultural backgrounds of these students.[38] It includes the lack of substantive instructional support and practice students need to be able to navigate through academic subject matter in a language completely different from their ancestral mother tongue.[39] The *Yazzie/Martinez* consolidated case has shown that significant educational disparities exist for Native students, especially when teachers are unprepared or unaware of how teaching practices must change. School administrators who are unaware of the limitations and inappropriateness of placing Native students in remedial programs contribute to this dilemma. They may also fail to see the significance and importance of reaching out to tribes to understand how schools can do a better job of supporting their efforts to teach and maintain Native languages.

While there is much discussion about the accountability of schools, which is merited, more attention must be paid to teacher and administrator preparation, inadequate staffing, and underfunded programs and services that still exist in districts serving Native American students. Accountability for ensuring these students receive a uniform and constitutionally sufficient education also rests in the hands of the New Mexico legislature, which must bear the responsibility for exercising its leadership in resolving and addressing the failures of the state's education system, its agencies, and its policies. Sadly, with the exception of a few committed legislators, the New Mexico legislature has thus far done little to address the needs of Indigenous children. Without an in-depth understanding of language issues affecting Indigenous students, as identified in the *Yazzie/Martinez* consolidated case and evidenced by the hesitancy of state policy makers, administrators, and legislators to make a strong commitment to transforming the current education system, these issues of inequity and insufficiency will unfortunately continue to exist for many Indigenous students.

Student Learning Objectives

1. Students will be able to distinguish between remedial reading and the kind of learning needed by ELs.
2. Students will recognize the importance of the New Mexico Bilingual Multicultural Education Act.

Discussion Questions

1. Identify the challenges of language learning that New Mexico's Indigenous students face according to the authors, and how these challenges can be addressed in your district, your school, or your own classroom.
2. Discuss what assumptions teachers and school administrators might make about Indigenous students when they are misinformed or lack knowledge about language issues. Reflect upon your own assumptions and what information would be helpful in your professional development as well as the preparation of future teachers.

Notes

1. Lev Vygotsky, *Thought and Language* (Boston: MIT Press, 1962).

2. Rebecca Blum Martínez and Preston Sanchez, "A Watershed Moment in the Education of American Indians: A Judicial Strategy to Mandate the State of New Mexico to Meet the Unique Cultural and Linguistic Needs of American Indians in New Mexico Public Schools," *American University Journal of Gender, Social Policy and the Law* 27, no. 3 (2019): 325.

3. Bambi B. Schieffelin and Elinor Ochs, eds., *Language Socialization across Cultures* (New York: Cambridge University Press, 1986), 2.

4. *Yazzie/Martinez v. State of New Mexico*, Court's Findings of Fact and Conclusion of Law and Order re Final Judgment.

5. Regis Pecos, "The Gift of Language from One Pueblo Perspective," in *The Shoulders We Stand On*, ed. Rebecca Blum Martínez and Mary Jean Haberman López (Albuquerque: University of New Mexico Press, 2020), 13–24.

6. *Yazzie/Martinez v. State of New Mexico*, Court's Findings of Fact and Conclusion of Law and Order re Final Judgment.

7. Donna Boynton and Christine P. Sims, "A Community-Based Plan for Acoma Language Retention and Revitalization," unpublished paper prepared for the Pueblo of Acoma, Acoma, NM, 1997; Tiffany Lee and Daniel McLaughlin, "Reversing Diné Language Shift, Revisited," in *Can Threatened Languages Be Saved? Reversing Language Shift Revisited: A 21st Century Perspective*, ed. Joshua A. Fishman (Clevedon, UK: Multilingual Matters, 2001), 69–98; Regis Pecos and Rebecca Blum Martínez, "The Key to Cultural Survival: Language Planning and Revitalization in the Pueblo de Cochiti," in *The Greenbook of Language Revitalization in Practice*, ed. Leanne Hinton and Ken Hale (San Diego: Academic Press, 2001), 75–85; Paul Platero, "Navajo Language Study," in Hinton and Hale, *Greenbook of Language Revitalization in Practice*, 86–97; Christine P. Sims, "Native Language Planning: A Pilot Process in the Acoma Pueblo Community," in Hinton and Hale, 251–68.

8. *Yazzie/Martinez v. State of New Mexico*, Court's Findings of Fact and Conclusion of Law and Order re Final Judgment.

9. Lana Garcia, discussion with author, November 17, 2021.

10. Trisha Moquino, email message to author, December 7, 2021.

11. Navajo Nation Division of Diné Education, *Navajo Nation Education Standards with Navajo Specifics* (Window Rock, AZ: Office of Diné Culture, Language, and Community Services, 2003).

12. Danielle Lansing, discussion with author, October 12, 2021.

13. *Yazzie/Martinez v. State of New Mexico*, Court's Findings of Fact and Conclusion of Law and Order re Final Judgment.

14. Bilingual Education Act of 1978, Pub. L. no. 95-561, 92 Stat. 2143, (1978), https://www.govinfo.gov/content/pkg/STATUTE-92/pdf/STATUTE-92-Pg2143.pdf.

15. Ledyard King and Mike Stucka, "In New Mexico, Many Still Lack Broadband Access," Deming Headlight, July 13, 2021.

16.   Council of the Great City Schools, *English Learners in America's Great City Schools: Demographics, Achievement and Staffing*, Washington, DC, April 2019, https://www.cgcs.org/cms/lib/DC00001581/Centricity/domain/35/publication%20docs/CGCS_ELL%20Survey%20Report.pdf; Tamara Lucas and Ana María Villegas, "Preparing Linguistically Responsive Teachers: Laying the Foundation in Preservice Teacher Education," *Theory into Practice* 52, no. 2 (2013): 98–109.

17.   Council of the Great City Schools, *English Learners in America's Great City Schools*; Kristen Bialik, Alissa Scheller, and Kristi Walker, "6 Facts about English Language Learners in U.S. Public Schools," Pew Research Center, October 25, 2018, https://www.pewresearch.org/fact-tank/2018/10/25/6-facts-about-english-language-learners-in-u-s-public-schools/.

18.   Laurie Olsen, *Reparable Harm: Fulfilling the Unkept Promise of Educational Opportunity for California's Long-Term English Learners* (Long Beach, CA: Californians Together, 2010).

19.   Council of the Great City Schools, *English Learners in America's Great City Schools*.

20.   Amanda Kibler and Guadalupe Valdés, "Conceptualizing Language Learners: Socioinstitutional Mechanisms and Their Consequences," *Modern Language Journal* 100 (Supplement 2016): 96–116.

21.   Kate Menken and Tatyana Kleyn, "The Long-Term Impact of Subtractive Schooling in the Educational Experiences of Secondary English Language Learners," *International Journal of Bilingual Education and Bilingualism* 13, no. 4 (2010): 399–417; Nelson Flores, Tatyana Kleyn, and Kate Menken, "Looking Holistically in a Climate of Partiality: Identities of Students Labeled Long-Term English Language Learners," *Journal of Language, Identity, and Education* 14, no. 2 (2015): 113–32.

22.   M. A. K. Halliday, *An Introduction to Functional Grammar* (New York: Routledge, 1985), 44; Mary Schleppegrell, *The Language of Schooling: A Functional Linguistics Perspective* (New York: Lawrence Erlbaum, 2004): 51–75; Pauline Gibbons, "Classroom Talk and the Learning of New Registers in a Second Language," *Language and Education* 12, no. 2 (1998): 99–118.

23.   Courtney Cazden, *Classroom Discourse: The Language of Teaching and Learning* (Portsmouth, NH: Heinemann, 2001). This common routine, often referred to as the IRE, has been studied extensively, particularly as it inhibits student participation.

24.   Lewis Meriam, *The Problem of Indian Administration* (Washington, DC: Institute for Government Research, 1928), 349.

25.   Rebecca Blum Martínez, *Basic Elements and Resources Necessary to Implement Quality English Language Learner Educational Programs and Educational Services for Native American Students*, unpublished report based on research conducted for New Mexico Center on Law and Poverty, last modified 2016.

26.   Schleppegrell, *Language of Schooling*; Susan Urmston Phillips, *The Invisible Culture: Communication in Classroom and Community on the Warm Springs Indian Reservation* (Long Grove, IL: Waveland Press, 1983); Ronald Scollon and Suzanne B. K. Scollon,

Linguistic Convergence: An Ethnography of Speaking at Fort Chipewyan, Alberta (New York: Academic Press, 1979).

27.   Donna Dehyle, "Constructing Failure and Maintaining Cultural Identity: Navajo and Ute Leavers," *Journal of American Indian Education* 31, no. 2 (1992): 21–47.

28.   Timothy Shanahan and Cynthia Shanahan, "Teaching Disciplinary Literacy to Adolescents: Rethinking Content-Area Literacy," *Harvard Educational Review* 78, no. 1 (Spring 2008): 48.

29.   Schleppegrell, *Language of Schooling*; Zhihui Fang and Mary J. Schleppegrell, "Disciplinary Literacy across Content Areas: Supporting Secondary Reading through Functional Language Analysis," *Journal of Adolescent and Adult Literacy* 53, no. 7 (2010): 587–97; Shanahan and Shanahan, "Teaching Disciplinary Literacy to Adolescents."

30.   Blum Martínez, "Basic Elements and Resources Necessary"; Sanchez and Blum Martínez, "Watershed Moment."

31.   Schleppegrell, *Language of Schooling*; Leo van Lier and Aida Walqui, "Language and the Common Core State Standards," in *Commissioned Papers on Language and Literacy Issues in the Common Core State Standards and Next Generation Science Standards* (Stanford, CA: Stanford University Press, 2012), 44–94; George C. Bunch, Amanda Kibler, and Susan Pimentel, "Realizing Opportunities for ELLs in the Common Core English Language Arts and Disciplinary Standards," in *Understanding Language: Language, Literacy, and Learning in the Content Areas*, conference proceedings, Stanford University, 2012, https://ul.stanford.edu/sites/default/files/resource/2021-12/01_Bunch_Kibler_Pimentel_RealizingOpp%20in%20ELA_FINAL_0.pdf; Lily Wong Fillmore and Charles J. Fillmore, "What Does Text Complexity Mean for English Learners and Language Minority Students?," in *Understanding Language: Language, Literacy, and Learning in the Content Areas* (Stanford, CA: Stanford University Press, 2012), 64–74; Lily Wong Fillmore and Catherine E. Snow, "What Teachers Need to Know about Language," in *What Teachers Need to Know about Language*, ed. Carolyn Temple Adger, Catherine E. Snow, and Donna Christian (Washington, DC: Center for Applied Linguistics, 2003), 8–51.

32.   Fillmore and Snow, "What Teachers Need to Know," 44–46.

33.   Fillmore and Fillmore, "What Does Text Complexity Mean."

34.   Fillmore and Fillmore.

35.   Fillmore and Fillmore, 1.

36.   Indian Pueblo Cultural Center, *Indigenous Wisdom Curriculum* (Albuquerque, NM: Indian Pueblo Cultural Center, 2020), https://indianpueblo.org/indigenous-wisdom-curriculum-downloads-2/.

37.   Indian Pueblo Cultural Center, *Indigenous Wisdom Curriculum*.

38.   *Yazzie/Martinez v. State of New Mexico*, Court's Findings of Fact and Conclusion of Law and Order re Final Judgment.

39.   *Yazzie/Martinez v. State of New Mexico*, Court's Findings of Fact and Conclusion of Law and Order re Final Judgment.

Figure 15. This image captures a pedagogical exercise through the Diné Language Teacher Institute (DLTI) designed by Tiffany Lee, Vincent Werito, and Melvatha R. Chee to bring together a cohort of Diné language teachers. Their program is designed to remedy one of the *Yazzie/Martinez* findings, which calls for incorporating "the cultural strengths of its diverse student population into the curriculum." Navajo students make up over 53 percent of American Indian students, according to the Albuquerque Public Schools. Photo Credit Tiffany Lee.

CHAPTER ELEVEN

Diné Language Teacher Institute and Language Immersion Education

TIFFANY S. LEE, VINCENT WERITO,
AND MELVATHA R. CHEE

IN THIS CHAPTER WE summarize a collaborative educator preparation project and demonstrate the state of Diné language today as affected by Western
schooling practices, followed by a strong justification for language immersion
education as a compelling remedy for the *Yazzie* rulings. We then conclude
with a reflection of current successes, challenges, and aspirations for the program. The collaborative project is an initiative informed by language experts
and practitioners, not policy makers, to provide a remedy for the *Yazzie* case.
This project, called the Diné Language Teacher Institute (DLTI), is aimed at
increasing the number of Diné language immersion teachers through a teacher
preparation program at the University of New Mexico (UNM). The purpose of
DLTI is to support the unique needs of Diné communities to revitalize and
sustain their languages by increasing the number of Diné language teachers
in community and school-based settings.

Beginning in fall 2020, UNM's Language, Literacy, and Sociocultural Studies, Native American Studies, and Diné Language Program started offering
eighteen hours of UNM college-level coursework and winter and summer
institutes with a specific focus on using language immersion methodologies
for Diné language revitalization. The activities at the summer institutes specifically address Diné language immersion teaching that draws upon the
strengths of Diné communities that utilize Diné-centered, community-based

($k'\acute{e}$) approaches to language teaching methodologies, pedagogies, and research.

In 1998–1999 co-author Lee conducted her dissertation research with Diné teenagers at five high schools across the Navajo Nation. She intended to understand the influences on Diné students' language attitudes and language use. She found that while the home-based influences were the strongest predictors of Diné teens' language use, school-based influences also had a significant impact. In fact, in many interviews with Diné youth, they strongly desired, if not demanded, to have more effective opportunities to learn their language. They felt the expectation to learn and speak Diné from Diné leaders and family members, and they pushed back on this expectation by questioning the prospects for consistent access to learning Diné. One student summed up this sentiment well when she said, "If they want Navajo to be learned, then they should require it in all schools."[1]

More than two decades have passed since that study, and the language shift from Diné to English among each new generation of Diné children is firmly taking hold. While there have been efforts in schools and communities to maintain and revitalize the Diné language, there is still tremendous need for a broader, comprehensive approach. Such approaches can serve as a direct remedy to address the ruling determined by Judge Sarah Singleton in the *Yazzie/Martinez v. State of New Mexico* case, in which Judge Singleton cited the State of New Mexico for failing to provide an adequate and sufficient education to Native American learners.[2] Diné language education and revitalization prioritizes the heritage, worldview, and knowledge that is embedded in the language, thereby making education culturally sustaining and relevant. The Navajo Nation still has a large number of Diné speakers among the adult and elderly population, so there are resources for building the Diné language teaching capacity. In 2010 the US Census counted approximately 170,000 self-reported speakers of Navajo.[3] However, as Benally and Viri have suggested, Diné language is at a crossroads where it can either be revived or continue to decline rapidly.[4] A 2017 *Navajo Times* article reported that Ethnologue estimated 7,600 Navajo-only speakers and 171,000 fluent speakers of Diné Bizaad.[5] Ethnologue also estimated the number of Diné Bizaad first-language and second-language speakers combined to be between ten thousand and one million (which is considered midsized). However, Navajo children are no longer learning Diné Bizaad as their first language in the home, which shows that Navajo is much more endangered than previously thought, a conclusion based on fieldwork by Chee.[6] Similarly, Ethonologue rates the vitality of Diné Bizaad as endangered because Navajo children are no longer learning and using the language.[7] We also know from the American Community Survey that, from 2012 to 2017, 65 percent of children in New Mexico reported English as their home language.[8] Community members from across the Navajo Nation are becoming aware of the shift to English among Diné children. In an article from the *Navajo Times*, a community member states, "My kids are not going to know what a (Blessingway ceremony) is. They're not going to know what a Ndaa' is, a Yei Bi Cheii [Yé'ii Bicheii] is, because all that's going to be dead by the time these guys are my age."[9] There is growing awareness and concern over the vitality of Diné Bizaad and culture. It is DLTI's mission to revive Diné Bizaad by working with Diné speakers, helping them become teachers of their language.

This chapter shares the efforts by three University of New Mexico Diné faculty, Dr. Vincent Werito (College of Education and Human Sciences, Department of Language, Literacy, and Sociocultural Studies), Dr. Tiffany Lee (College of Arts and Sciences, Department of Native American Studies), and Dr. Melvatha Chee (College of Arts and Sciences, Department of Linguistics Navajo Language Program), who are working to create an interdisciplinary program to raise the Diné language teaching capacity by training speakers to become Diné language immersion advocates and educators who address their students' desire and demand for more language-learning opportunities in community and school-based settings. This program, established in 2020, is called the Diné Language Teacher Institute (DLTI). DLTI recruits a cohort of prospective and experienced Diné (Navajo) language teachers from across Arizona, New Mexico, and Utah. Using a community-engaged approach to capacity building and local empowerment for parents and teachers, the primary goal of this project is to greatly increase the number of Diné language immersion teachers and influence a new generation of young Diné speakers in Diné communities across the Navajo Nation through ongoing, sustained professional learning via college courses, summer/winter language institutes and immersion camps, onsite instructional support, and curriculum development. The eighteen-hour UNM coursework developed for DLTI primarily focuses on Diné language revitalization through Diné language teacher preparation, recruitment, mentoring, and sustained professional learning. The courses come from UNM's Language, Literacy, and Sociocultural Studies Department, Native American Studies Department, and the Navajo Language Program in Linguistics. These courses can be counted toward degrees in each of these departments or a certificate of completion. Additionally, the cohort members will create learning activities to inspire Diné youth to relearn their language through community language advocacy initiatives.

As already mentioned, DLTI provides a direct remedy to address the ruling by Judge Sarah Singleton in the *Yazzie/Martinez v. State of New Mexico* case. The ruling responded to the state's violation of the state constitution to provide programs and services that prepare students for college and careers. These programs and services include culturally and linguistically relevant education. DLTI aims to significantly increase the number of Diné language educators who can teach Diné using immersion methodologies in schools, communities, and homes, and to change the paradigm of existing Diné language teachers to embrace more transformative approaches to revitalizing Indigenous languages. This type of education is culturally and linguistically relevant and sustaining as well as informed largely by Diné pedagogy and Diné critical theory. In the following sections we share the context for this need by describing the state of Diné language today, why we utilize an immersion approach, the specific delivery of the program, and our observations of its impact thus far.

State of Diné Language Today

Research has demonstrated that language shift occurs when two or more generations do not relearn a language.[10] Currently, in the Navajo Nation, families and communities are in the second or third generation of children who have limited capacity for understanding and speaking the Diné language. This language change is increasing at an alarming rate. A variety of factors contribute to the situation. These include the enforced cultural assimilation policies of US federal and state governments, the ethnocentric social and cultural attitudes of non-Native educators and policy makers, the high status of the English language, and the enticement of modern popular culture through media and technology that privileges the use of English.[11] There is also much complacency among Diné speakers themselves who do not use and teach the language to the youth. Additionally, school-based programs are unclear about their goals and/or instructional approaches.[12] As a result, Diné youth are learning English as their first language or have been steered toward a preference for speaking English at the cost of losing their heritage language. These factors have severed the intergenerational transmission of the Diné language, resulting in few Diné child speakers and a lack of young Diné language teachers.

In Diné communities, like many other Indigenous language communities, the number of young people proficient in speaking Diné is eroding at an alarming rate. While the adult generation (those over forty years of age) use Diné extensively, the upcoming generations do not know and/or use the language. Each successive generation is less and less fluent and unable to communicate in their heritage language. Although Diné language is one of the most widely spoken of North American Indian languages, studies indicate it is diminishing at an alarming rate, to the point that it is now listed as an endangered language.[13] In order to minimize further diminishment and loss, community initiatives for language sustainability and stabilization must be prioritized. As Diné communities engage in language revitalization efforts, they must define clear goals for perpetuating the language to create a new generation of speakers and sustaining the language to serve community needs. More so, each community that works to revitalize its language must first understand how the language came to be threatened and identify ways to reverse language shift in home, school, and community settings.[14]

From the 1960s through the 1990s the majority of Navajo Nation adults were fully bilingual. To regain this language versatility, youth must become proficient in both Diné and English. The Navajo Nation intends to have their citizens be able to communicate effectively in both languages. Yet around twenty years ago, some educators began lamenting that about one-third of Diné children were monolingual English speakers. According to sociolinguist Joshua Fishman's eight stages of language shift, Diné society is at varying degrees or stages of language endangerment.[15] Even though almost all Diné citizens over forty years of age are proficient in Diné, there is a lack of data to show when and how the language is being used for transmission to younger generations. While many older adult speakers may still use Diné language in some areas of social, political, and economic activities, how are the younger generations being exposed to or immersed in the language? For example, local Navajo Nation chapter house officials rarely use Diné language extensively in their deliberations and in reporting back to their constituents. Regardless of these inconsistencies, with the wide use of Diné language among the older adult generations, Diné society is at an optimal point in their history to revitalize their language for the youth and to take steps to sustain their language.

The Navajo Nation's Department of Diné Education has been collecting data from the Oral Diné Language Assessment (ODLA) to test language proficiency among Diné students in Diné language programs. Not surprisingly, teachers report that the oral language assessment data reveals that very few Diné children tested proficient in the language. As noted earlier, the American Community Survey five-year estimates from 2012 to 2017 show that English is the primary language spoken at home for 65 percent of all students in New Mexico.[16] With the majority of the Diné population under age thirty, and with the increasing number of non-Diné-speaking children in each succeeding generation, the necessity of establishing a pool of highly qualified Diné language educators and teachers is apparent.

The State of New Mexico has policies and practices in place that allow for the teaching of Indigenous languages and cultures in the classroom by tribal members who are speakers of their language. In 2002 New Mexico developed the New Mexico 520 Alternative Certification for Native Language and Culture through the New Mexico Indian Education Act (NMIEA) of 2003.[17] With this act the state department of education transferred the certification process of Indigenous language teachers to the respective Indigenous Nations in New Mexico, allowing them to determine the overall process and credentials for certification. This certification process allows Diné language teachers to be both tribe and state certified. Currently, the Navajo Nation Department of Diné Education administers a language certification exam to prospective Diné language teachers. However, the pedagogical practice of teaching Diné language in the classroom is left to the teachers and schools. Preparing and training speakers of the language through DLTI to become instructors utilizing language immersion strategies will facilitate a process for streamlining effective language teaching and recruiting new teachers for the future.

Research on Indigenous Language Immersion

Immersion language education is a form of bilingual education in which at least 50 percent of content-area instruction takes place in the target (second) language. However, many established Indigenous language immersion (ILI) schools teach 70 to 90 percent of content through the Indigenous language.[18] First launched in a few schools serving Native Hawaiian and Diné students in the 1980s, the ILI approach was developed by grassroots teams of Indigenous and non-Indigenous practitioners and parents to respond to the dual realities of enduring achievement disparities and a growing trend toward Indigenous language and culture loss—the consequence of a long history of policies of linguistic and cultural suppression. Whereas previous generations of Native American students entered school speaking a Native American language, most Native students today speak English as their primary language. ILI is a unique form of bilingual/bicultural/biliteracy education in which all or most academic content is taught in the Indigenous language, along with a strong Native language and culture revitalization component. It has shown the most success in producing child speakers of the Indigenous language.[19] ILI is unique in the challenges it faces. Diminishing numbers of speakers and inequitable access to higher education mean that there are few Indigenous language speaking teachers and that teachers are often second-language learners themselves. ILI programs must therefore "grow their own" teaching staff and curricula—a long-term, resource-intensive process. However, among Diné communities, there are still many adult speakers, making this an opportune time to harness their language abilities into immersion teaching skills.

Research supports the effectiveness of Indigenous language immersion approaches. Longitudinal data from several ILI programs have demonstrated that they have been highly effective in strengthening students' bilingualism, self-confidence, and pride in their cultural heritage. Additionally, this research has shown increases in students' rates of academic matriculation, graduation, and college attendance. The impact of learning one's Indigenous language also does not negatively impact their English language performance in English-based courses and content. ILI students perform equally as well as their peers in English-based schools.[20] In particular, this was observed in a Diné language immersion school. The Tséhootsooí Diné Bi Olta' (Navajo School at the Meadow between the Rocks) started with children in grades K through 5 of forty-six parents. Fifteen years after the program's inception, school principal Marie Arviso and administrator/teacher Wayne Holm reported that immersion students "were doing almost as well as, or better than," comparable students in English-medium classrooms on standardized tests in math and English language arts.[21] The ILI school was not holding students back from progressing in Western-based academics, *and* they were becoming speakers of Diné.

ILI also offers a holistic approach to education, which is in line with Diné-centered values and philosophies. ILI is designed to promote learners' cognitive, affective, linguistic, and social-emotional development equally with their ethnic identity, thus contributing not only to students' academic development but also to the sustainability and well-being of their cultural communities.[22] ILI is an integrated pedagogical approach with a strong family and community component. In recent research examining the impact of ILI schools at sites across the United States, leaders at one Mohawk school that serves students in grades K–8 remarked on how the community benefits from the knowledge their students gain in their immersion setting. They explained how the community will call upon the students to open ceremonial and community events as the students know the protocols, the opening address and prayers, and the language in which to do all of it appropriately.[23]

Another example of this holistic quality can be seen in the Keres Children's Learning Center immersion program, whose vision states, "Keres Children's Learning Center (KCLC) strives to reclaim our children's education and honor our heritage by using a comprehensive cultural and academic curriculum to assist families in nurturing Keres-speaking, holistically healthy, community minded, and academically strong students."[24] This requires that children have access to community-based knowledge, including associated cultural practices and the language through which that knowledge is acquired.

Why DLTI?

In general, regardless of the 520 Alternative Certification for Native Language and Culture, institutions of higher education in New Mexico have faced challenges in providing long-term solutions for the lack of quality Diné language programming, community support, mentorship, and training. In other words, the State of New Mexico does not have a single institution that focuses solely on Diné language immersion instruction and methods for its Diné citizens. Therefore, preparing and training speakers of the language to become instructors utilizing language immersion strategies will facilitate a process for recruiting new teachers for the future. DLTI's goal is to increase Diné community efforts to train and prepare a new teaching force that implements Diné language immersion methodologies and pedagogical practices in school and community settings. Additionally, DLTI will help these teachers begin applying what they learned through the eighteen hours of course work and think differently about teaching in Diné across content areas like art, music, math, physical education, science, and social studies at the pre-K to third grade levels.

DLTI is cultivating a cohort of prospective and experienced Diné language immersion teachers. Using a community-engaged approach for capacity building and local empowerment for parents and teachers, the primary goal of this project is to support a cohort of Diné speakers who aspire to be teachers through ongoing, sustained professional learning via UNM college courses, summer/winter language institutes and family immersion camps, onsite instructional support, and curriculum development. In particular, the cohort members will be encouraged to put theory into action and practice by strategically planning for and participating in immersion-style teaching during the summer/winter family immersion camps and after-school/community events for parents, youth, and other community members. The eighteen-hour UNM coursework developed for DLTI primarily focuses on using language immersion methodologies for Diné language revitalization. Aside from the newly developed DLTI, there are no other institutions that provide such courses for Diné language teachers.

DLTI cohort members must complete eighteen credit hours of required course work. These courses specifically address Diné language immersion teaching that draws upon the tribal strengths of Diné communities that utilize Diné-centered, community-based (k'é) approaches to language teaching methodologies, pedagogies, and research. The eighteen-hour course work includes the following four core courses and electives:

Native American Studies (three credit hours)
- ◆ NATV 462 CORE: Native American Oral Tradition and Language Reclamation
- ◆ NATV 461: Community-Based Learning in Indigenous Contexts
- ◆ Diné Language/Linguistics (six credit hours)
- ◆ NVJO 401 CORE: Diné Linguistics
- ◆ NVJO 315/515: Advanced Navajo (Navajo for Speakers)
- ◆ Language, Literacy, and Sociocultural Studies (LLSS) (nine credit hours)
- ◆ LLSS 462/562 CORE: Teaching Navajo in Immersion and Community Settings
- ◆ LLSS 419/519 CORE: Issues in Navajo Language and Education
- ◆ LLSS 425/525: Issues in Navajo Language Curriculum Development
- ◆ LLSS 465/565: Navajo Pedagogy and Community Engagement

Cohort members are also encouraged to apply after the first semester to a BA or MA degree program in Native American Studies or Linguistics with a Diné Language or Language, Literacy and Sociocultural Studies minor.

In addition to the eighteen credit hours of courses, cohort members participate in self- or collectively created immersion camps, events, and activities during the summer and winter breaks. These camps provide DLTI cohort members the opportunity to apply their knowledge and skills with camp learners. Due to COVID-19, the first two symposiums were held virtually over Zoom: a winter symposium in January 2021 and a spring symposium in May 2021. Both symposiums showcased the cohort's work and knowledge acquired through their participation in DLTI. The theme for the winter and spring one-day symposiums was *With Our Language We Are Stronger*. Both symposiums highlighted DLTI students' work through twenty-minute presentations that they delivered to participants. The organization Dual Language Education of New Mexico (DLENM) supported the winter symposium with technological assistance by creating the platform for holding the symposium over Zoom with breakout rooms. The winter symposium included a workshop from an expert in Diné language immersion methods and approaches. A traditional storyteller also joined to share his knowledge and stories.

The spring symposium was organized by DLTI students, who presented their work in the Diné language. The symposium also featured the group Shimá Storytelling. The group consists of three Diné mothers who, in partnership with the Navajo Nation Library, offer a grassroots reading and storytelling program for youth of all ages featuring storytelling, singing, and interactive learning in the Diné language.

Because these symposiums were supported by the grant received through the New Mexico Public Education Department (NMPED), there was no registration fee.[25] As a result of working with DLENM, DLTI was featured in the summer 2021 newsletter *Soleado: Promising Practices from the Field*.

In the summer of 2021 DLTI was able to hold an immersion camp in person. This was the first in-person event held since the pandemic started the year before and was also the first time an immersion camp had been held on the UNM campus. Adding to the excitement over this event, the local news channel KOB 4's Colton Shone, a Diné morning news anchor and supporter of Diné language instruction, covered the camp in a news story. The three-day immersion camp was part of DLTI's summer course LLSS 493/593: Teaching Navajo in Immersion Settings. The course was an intensive eight-day event packed with selected readings and assignments focused on preparing to teach an immersive language activity. An invited expert guest lecturer, Jennie DeGroat, who specializes in immersion methodologies, taught DLTI students how to prepare a language activity. Specifically, students had to select a culturally relevant language activity, identify items they would need, organize their time with details about what to teach, write a Diné Bizaad dialogue, and practice their language activity prior to delivery. While preparing the language lesson, students had to seriously consider the language they planned to use with their learners so as to not confuse them. DLTI students also had to make their language activities fun and engaging. The language camp was a success. The most challenging issue was space, due to UNM's guidelines on limitations on the number of participants in each of the building's rooms to meet space capacity limits. DLTI immersion instructors had to move from class to class, rather than students moving from class to class as initially anticipated. The immersion camp was held free of charge, and lunch and parking passes were provided for all participants as an incentive.

We asked learners participating in the camp to complete a feedback survey to collect their impressions and suggestions. Of the thirty-three participants who completed the survey, twenty-nine indicated they would participate again, three said maybe, and one said no. The participants included a range of ages from elementary schoolers to older adults. They had important suggestions, such as asking teachers to slow down in their teaching, enunciate phrases and words more clearly, and frequently check for their understanding. But overall, most of the feedback was very positive in terms of the participants' enjoyment engaging in the activities created by DLTI cohort members. Participants loved the games, singing, and hand gestures, as well as traditional activities like learning to plant corn. They learned the Round Dance game and reportedly enjoyed hearing and learning about verbs. Importantly, they appreciated and learned a lot from repetition. This feedback is significant for showing how immersion can be adapted to Diné language learners.

Preparing DLTI participants to teach immersion methodologies using culturally appropriate material and activities in Diné Bizaad meets the ruling in the *Yazzie/Martinez* case. It also meets the expectations set forth in the NMIEA. Most importantly, DLTI instructors are taught and trained to use their knowledge of Diné Bizaad and their own Diné cultural expertise to become Diné language instructors within their homes, communities, and schools.

Planning Ahead

After reflecting on the 2021 year, DLTI made some changes to course offerings to facilitate cohort members' progress through the program. Fall and spring courses will remain, as well as a winter institute focused on traditional knowledge and storytelling. The capstone experience will take place the following summer of each academic year, so the students finish the program with this immersion camp in the summer. Going forward, immersion camps will be hosted in locations close to the Navajo Nation that are easily accessible for DLTI immersion instructors and participants. Possible locations are Gallup, Farmington, or a location in the Navajo Nation. The 2022 immersion camp also included the current students' final summer course; however, the class was over a longer period of time than the first camp in June 2021. The second cohort taught their language activities for about a week or more, rather than just a few days. This change is to support learners and cohort instructors with gaining a longer experience in Diné immersion. We know the immersion camp in June 2021 had an impact, even though it was held for a few short days. We observed children, families, and other participants using the language they had learned during and after the camp experience. They also used the gestures they learned to remember nouns and verbs used in short, simple sentences. This was observed in our own families who attended the three-day immersion camp.

One of the 2021 cohort members wrote a short reflection for the summer issue of *Soleado: Promising Practices from the Field*. She provides important testimony on the impact of DLTI for creating a community of Diné language immersion educators and people who are passionate about Diné language maintenance and revitalization:

The classes I participate in through DLTI have brought me together with other relatives (educators) in our Diné community who are helping children and adults reclaim our language. Some of my fellow students live, like I do, in the Navajo Nation, while others live in urban centers in Arizona and New Mexico. We study the research on language shift and colonization's effects on Indigenous communities all over the United States. We study land-based teaching practices that connect us with traditional ways of teaching and learning. We look at ways to understand how language is used in the various communities so that we can connect our teaching practices to community practices. We find ways to walk a fine line in regards to using the tools, materials, and strategies used by world language teachers and students and anchor ourselves in a Diné worldview and our traditions. And we learn to develop curriculum to use with our students that reflects who we are. Best of all, we have a forum to air our frustrations and our triumphs. We have access to DLTI's professors and instructors for help and advice as we face challenges in our school communities. We are also able to connect with the cultural resources that DLTI has introduced us to. Even as the COVID-19 pandemic has impacted both our community and our schools, we continue to encourage and support these efforts. We emphasize oral language development by using immersion strategies, even on our online platforms. [. . .] Sometimes the work to revitalize our language feels pretty overwhelming. There are so many challenges in a public-school setting. But I am committed to finding the research and strategies to make sure that the Diné language and way of life are passed on to future generations.[26]

Conclusion

Judge Singleton's rulings in the *Yazzie* case were intended to provide a more sufficient education for Native American learners. Defining a sufficient education should be left to those most invested in that education and those who have the expertise, passion, and capacity for providing that education. For Diné people this includes an education that privileges Diné language, culture, history, experiences, and perspectives. DLTI aims to provide a remedy for addressing the rulings by facilitating the development and increasing the number of educators who can provide an education centered in the most valuable Diné cultural characteristic—language. Young Diné speakers and teachers will help stem the tide of language shift. It is critical to have a sufficient number of trained and certified Diné language educators to reverse the current negative trend. The long-term goal of DLTI is to contribute to strong community and school-based programs like Diné language nests, Diné dual-language education, and Diné full-immersion programs. It is exciting to be a part of this significant work. As of 2023, thirty Diné speakers and educators have joined the DLTI cohorts since the program's implementation in fall 2020. The increase in the Diné language immersion teaching capacity by thirty individuals in three to four years shows the enormous potential for reinvigorating the Diné language and language education. But addressing the magnitude of issues presented in the *Yazzie/Martinez* case will take dedicated effort, many allies, and a shift in the public educational perspective on the role and application of culturally responsive and sustaining education. UNM, NMPED, and the Navajo Nation can and should provide strong support and resources as the revitalization of Diné language benefits each of them in terms of contributing to the success of Diné learners and educators. Diné language immersion educators can model the level of commitment, investment, collaboration, and support needed to truly implement and transform education in this manner.

Student Learning Objectives

1. Students will be able to articulate the definition of Indigenous language immersion teaching methods.
2. Students will examine the role a teacher preparation program can play in supporting Indigenous language immersion.

Discussion Questions

1. Why do you think language immersion methodologies are the most effective for Indigenous language revitalization, based on what you read in this chapter?
2. What ideas of activities do you have for DLTI or other language revitalization programs to engage participants in such programs?

Notes

1. Tiffany S. Lee, "'If They Want Navajo to Be Learned, Then They Should Require It in All Schools': Navajo Teenagers' Experiences, Choices, and Demands Regarding Navajo Language," *Wicazo Sa Review* 22, no. 1 (Spring 2007): 7–33.

2. "Yazzie and Martinez vs. State of New Mexico: July 20, 2018 Decision and Order," Legislative Education Study Committee, https://www.nmlegis.gov/handouts/ALESC%20081518%20Item%2012%20.1%20-%20Brief%20-%20Decision%20and%20Order-Yazzie%20and%20Martinez%20v%20State%20of%20NM.pdf.

3. Julie Siebens and Tiffany Julian, "Native North American Languages Spoken at Home in the United States and Puerto Rico: 2006–2010," *American Community Survey Briefs* (Washington, DC: US Census Bureau, 2011).

4. AnCita Benally and Dennis Viri, "Diné [Navajo Language] at a Crossroads: Extinction or Renewal?" *Bilingual Research Journal* 29, no. 1 (2005): 85–108.

5. Pauly Denetclaw, "Data Shows Huge Reductions in Diné Speakers," *Navajo Times*, November 16, 2017, https://navajotimes.com/reznews/data-shows-huge-reduction-in-dine-speakers/.

6. Melvatha R. Chee, "A Longitudinal Cross-Sectional Study on the Acquisition of Navajo Verbs in Children Aged 4 Years 7 Months through 11 Years 2 Months" (PhD diss., University of New Mexico, 2017).

7. "The Size and Vitality of Navajo," *Ethnologue: Languages of the World*, accessed January 5, 2022, https://www.ethnologue.com/size-and-vitality/nav.

8. United States Census Bureau, "American Community Surveys, 2012–2017 Five-Year Estimates: S1601 Language Spoken at Home," https://data.census.gov/table?t=Language+Spoken+at+Home&g=2520000US2430R.

9. Pauly Denetclaw, "Community Finds Loss of Diné Language 'Scary,'" *Navajo Times*, November 16, 2017, https://navajotimes.com/ae/culture/community-finds-loss-of-dine-language-scary/.

10. Lilly Wong Fillmore, "When Learning a Second Language Means Losing a First," *Early Childhood Research Quarterly* 6 (1991): 323–46; Michael M. Krauss, "Status of Native American Language Endangerment," in *Stabilizing Indigenous Languages*, ed. G. Cantoni (Flagstaff: Northern Arizona University Press, 1996), 16–21.

11. James Crawford, "Endangered Native American Languages: What Is to Be Done and Why?" *Bilingual Research Journal* 19, no. 1 (1995): 17–38.

12. Vincent Werito, "'Think in Navajo': Reflections from the Field on Reversing Navajo Language Shift in the Home, School, and Community Contexts," in *Honoring Our Students*, ed. J. Rehyner et al. (Flagstaff: Northern Arizona University Press, 2021), 39–52.

13. Benally and Viri, "Diné [Navajo Language] at a Crossroads."

14. Vincent Werito, "Pioneering Navajo Bilingual Education: Voices from History to the Present," in *Standing on Their Shoulders: A History of Bilingual Education in New Mexico*, ed. R. Blum Martínez and M. J. Haberman López (Albuquerque: University of New Mexico Press, 2020), 25–54.

15. Joshua Fishman, *Reversing Language Shift: Theoretical and Empirical Foundations of Assistance to Threatened Languages* (Clevedon, UK: Multilingual Matters, 1991).

16. US Census Bureau, "American Community Surveys, 2012–2017."

17. "Certification of Native American Language and Culture, K-12," New Mexico Public Education Division, accessed September 11, 2021, https://webnew.ped.state.nm.us/wp-content/uploads/2018/02/Certification-in-native-American-Language-and-Culture.pdf.

18. Serafin M. Coronel-Molina and Teresa L. McCarty, eds., *Indigenous Language Revitalization in the Americas* (New York: Routledge, 2016).

19. Leanne Hinton and Ken Hale, eds., *The Green Book of Language Revitalization in Practice* (San Diego, CA: Academic Press, 2001).

20. Marie Arviso and Wayne Holm, "Tséhootsooídi Ólta'gi Diné bizaad bihoo'aah: A Diné Immersion Program at Fort Defiance, Arizona," in Hinton and Hale, *Green Book of Language Revitalization in Practice*, 203–15; Mary Hermes, "'Ma'iingan Is Just a Misspelling of the Word Wolf'": A Case for Teaching Culture through Language," *Anthropology and Education Quarterly* 36, no. 1 (2005): 43–56; Teresa L. McCarty and Tiffany S. Lee, "Critical Culturally Sustaining/Revitalizing Pedagogy and Indigenous Education Sovereignty," *Harvard Educational Review* 84, no. (2014):101–24; William H. Wilson and Kauanoe Kamanā, "Mai loko mai o ka i'ini: Proceeding from a Dream: The 'Aha Pūnana Leo Connection in Hawaiian Language Revitalization," in Hinton and Hale, *Green Book of Language Revitalization in Practice*, 147–76; William H. Wilson and Kauanoe Kamanā,

"Insights from Indigenous Language Immersion in Hawai'i," in *Immersion Education: Practices, Policies, Possibilities*, ed. D. J. Tedick, D. Christian, and T. W. Fortune (Bristol, UK: Multilingual Matters, 2011), 36–57.

21.   Arviso and Holm, "'Tséhootsooídi Ólta'gi Diné bizaad bihoo'aah."

22.   Wilson and Kamanā, "Insights from Indigenous Language Immersion."

23.   Elvera Sargent, former school manager, interview with Tiffany S. Lee and Teresa L. McCarty for the Indigenous Language Immersion and Native American Achievement research study, October 19, 2019.

24.   "Welcome to Keres Children's Learning Center," Keres Children's Learning Center, accessed August 9, 2021, https://kclcmontessori.org/.

25.   While NMPED was named a defendant in the consolidated Yazzie and Martinez case, through their Indian Education Division they funded DLTI, demonstrating some progress toward rectifying the issues named as unconstitutional in the case.

26.   Valencia Edgewater, "My Language Journey with DLTI," *Soleado: Promising Practices from the Field* (Summer 2021): 4–5.

Figure 16. The First Judicial District Court located at 225 Montezuma Avenue, Santa Fe, NM, 87505. This is where the late Judge Sarah Singleton determined her judgement in the *Yazzie/Martinez* lawsuit. Photo credit Hondo Louis. Funded by UNM's Center for Regional Studies and Native American Studies Department.

CHAPTER TWELVE

Lessons from the Past

Fifty Years after Sinajini v. Board of Education of San Juan School District

CYNTHIA BENALLY AND DONNA DEYHLE

THIS CHAPTER RECOUNTS THE Utah court case *Sinajini et al. v. San Juan School District*, which began in the early 1970s and continued up to the *Yazzie/ Martinez* case. The *Sinajini* case was initiated by Navajo parents asserting educational sovereignty.[1] In both the *Sinajini* and *Yazzie/Martinez* cases, Diné parents and communities challenged schooling systems and structures that inadequately provided funding, programs, and resources to meet the unique educational needs of Native students. The main goal of this chapter is to offer lessons learned from the last half a century of advocating for educational equality in a settler public schooling system.[2] Our hope is that this discussion of the Utah case will assist with implementing the New Mexico court orders in a timely and effective manner.

Seeking Educational Equity: The Racialized Landscape

We begin with an abbreviated account of how the Diné in San Juan County (SJC), Utah, have demonstrated resistance against white settlers' determination to subjugate Diné and their lands.[3] This story takes place on the high desert landscape of southeastern Utah, on the traditional homelands of the Utes, Paiutes, and Diné, located about three hundred miles from present-day

Albuquerque, New Mexico. The history of this contested area is entrenched in American exceptionalism, revisionist histories, and the struggle for democracy. As Dan McCool, a political scientist who researched these communities, explains, "It is difficult today to fathom the degree of racial animosity and hostility that has historically characterized the relationship between Navajo and Anglos."[4]

The colonial invasion of what is now known as New Mexico began over three hundred years prior to the occupation of the SJC area by members of the Church of Jesus Christ of Latter-Day Saints (LDS).[5] Yet the patterns of subjugation in economic and educational opportunities for Native peoples were similar in both places. In 1878 the leader of the LDS sent a group of 236 settlers "to establish a colony that would cultivate better relations with the Indians [. . .] and expand Mormon control into the area."[6] One of their first actions was to build a fort in Bluff, Utah, which in 2015 was rebuilt with funding from the LDS to honor and remember "the struggles and glory [the Mormon settlers] endured."[7] This area the Mormons sought to control is where the Diné have lived since time immemorial.

Native assertions of dignity and sovereignty and settler assertions of their perceived superior rights to the land have framed Native and settler interactions ever since first contact. The settlers forcefully removed Diné from their ancestral homelands to Hwéeldí, otherwise known as Fort Sumner. They were held in captivity from 1864 to 1868.[8] Since then, the Diné continue to fight illegal claims to their homeland. Almost ninety years after the removal to Hwéeldí, in 1952, white men carrying guns and whips forced the Diné off their ancestral homelands across the San Juan River while burning down Diné homes and confiscating their livestock.[9]

The Nuche, or otherwise known as the Utes, have also fought to maintain their homelands in the SJC area and keep it from encroachment by white settlers. In 1914 settlers in Blanding, Utah, wrote the commissioner of Indian affairs requesting the Indians be removed to Colorado.[10] Suspicion and distrust came to a head in 1923 in what the press called the "Posey War," described as the last war between Indians and whites in the United States. The *Salt Lake Tribune* headlines screamed, "Paiute Band Declares War on Whites at Blanding."[11] Local historian McPherson claimed the last "white uprising against Indians" was more accurate. Posey, a Paiute leader, appealed to the US government for the right to remain on Ute traditional land. Concerned that any trouble might jeopardize the Utes' struggles to stay in Utah, Posey attended a trial in Blanding of two Ute boys accused of minor crimes. The boys escaped from the jail and a posse was formed by the local sheriff, who declared, "Every man here is deputized to shoot. I want you to shoot everything that looks like an Indian."[12] Posey was wounded and fled with his people into the canyons west of Blanding. Eighty Native people were imprisoned inside a hundred-square-foot square compound made of cattle fencing topped with barbed wire located in the center of town. The Ute and Paiute prisoners of war would spend a month, until Posey's death, in this stockade. Even in death Posey could not escape the hatred of some of the local settlers. They found his grave, dug up his body, and much like the familiar photographs of hunters and their game, they posed for photographs with Posey's corpse.[13] Generations later, children of the settlers go in search of "Old Posey's grave" and sing the lyrics of the song titled "Posey": "He stirred up trouble in a Mormon town. They were ready his game to play."[14] Shortly after his death the Utes were granted permission to remain in Utah.

The disrespect of the bodies and possessions of "dead Indians" continued into the twentieth century.[15] In the mid-1980s, federal agents raided homes and stores in Blanding, searching for Native pottery, jewelry, and sellable objects stolen from ancient burial sites. Two of the three then county commissioners were arrested, yet no charges were ever filed against any of the detainees.[16] In 1996 two white settlers accused of grave robbing at one of the over thirty thousand Anasazi sites found in SJC were said to have thrown bones aside to dig a deep trench in search of pots and other possessions buried with the deceased. The court decided in favor of the white defendants, finding that a bone did not constitute a "dead human body" because the court determined the site was not in a proper grave.[17] Other county residents reported that looting ancient sites was a deeply engrained cultural practice of settler families. Indeed, "It's the American way. If you go against them, you are going against the rights of the people here in the west. They believe it is their right as American citizens to dig these Indian graves."[18]

The most recent illustration of the Diné struggle for equity and democracy in SJC is a voting rights case. In 2012 the Navajo Nation and Diné plaintiffs filed a suit against SJC, alleging that the election process for the county commissioner seats and school board positions violated the Equal Protection Clause of the Fourteenth Amendment of the United States Constitution and the Voting Rights Act of 1965. The district court decided in favor of the Navajo Nation and ordered the county to redraw the election districts. The county offered a plan for redrawing the district lines, but the court rejected the proposed plan due to racial gerrymandering.[19] In the newly created districts the Diné had the majority in two districts: District 1 with 11.1 percent Diné, District 2 with 65.6 percent Diné, and District 3 with 79.9 percent Diné.[20] In the 2018 special election, after the court-ordered redistricting, two Diné were elected to the three-seated county commissioner positions, basically giving "power" to the majority-Native county for the first time ever. This monumental achievement came after a long and arduous endeavor, yet the victory celebration was short-lived. The white residents of the county attempted *again* to change the county government and regain power by altering the three-member county commission to include five members.[21] This effort failed.

The relationship between Native and non-Native peoples was continuously contested, as settlers claimed ownership of land and all social, educational, and economic institutions in the area. The cultural practices of the settler-colonial society to dehumanize Natives frame current community interactions. The *Sinajini* case emerged from this contentious racial landscape, which is profoundly evident in the resistance to the provision of equal schooling to Native students.

Unequal Schooling in a Divided Landscape

Settlers in Utah created the San Juan School District (the District) to serve and uphold the values and dispositions of the white settler community. The District is geographically the largest school district in the United States and the only school district in SJC. The county and school district are located on 7,884 square miles (equivalent to Connecticut, Delaware, and Rhode Island combined) of southeastern Utah (see map 2). The first District school opened in 1880 in Montezuma Creek to serve white children. By the early 1890s sixty to eighty white children attended schools in the county; by 1894 the number had

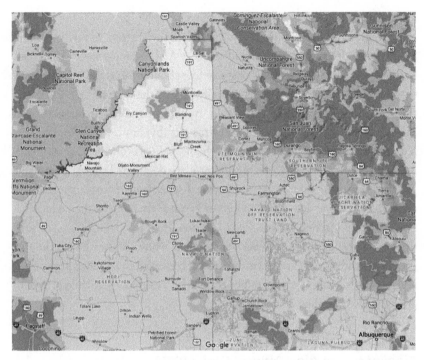

Map 2. San Juan County School District. Published by Google Maps.

doubled. By 1914 both Monticello and Blanding enrolled white students in high school programs. As more rural and isolated communities demanded local schools, more than two dozen single-room schools were opened for white children from the 1920s to the 1940s. Access to local public schools for Native students did not systematically occur until the late 1950s, more than sixty years after their white peers enjoyed a public education near their homes and years after the landmark *Brown v. Board of Education* desegregation case was decided in 1954.[22]

Despite resistance to Native students in classrooms in the District, Native youth started attending public schools in the 1950s.[23] White parents fought hard to maintain their sons' and daughters' exclusionary white setting, arguing that the Indian children would bring the diseases of glaucoma and tuberculosis into their healthy schools and expressing the fear that Indian students would disrupt student discipline, dilute academic scholarship, and cause the decay of student morale.[24] In an analysis of education in the District, researcher Donna Smith concluded simply that "prejudice in the Anglo communities of San Juan County proved to be a difficult obstacle for school integration."[25] The persistence of one Navajo parent, Hugh Benally, started the dismantling of segregation in the San Juan School District. In the 1950s Benally purchased land in Montezuma Creek and paid property tax on this land, which by law was required to be used to fund the local school—schools to which his own children were denied access for being Indians. He demanded the right as a taxpayer to have his children attend the local schools his taxes supported. He challenged the practices that required Indian students to seek their education only in boarding schools outside of SJC schools. He wanted his children to have the same rights of access to public education as white children had in the District. After three denied requests the district conceded to Benally's arguments, and in 1964 his son, Clyde Benally, became the first non-foster-child Native to graduate from a public school in SJC.[26]

Sinajini v. San Juan County, Utah (1975)

Prior to the 1970s, the prevailing views toward Native students among educators and administrators in public education across the United States were framed by deficit thought and a model of assimilation. In an environment where Native languages and cultures were viewed as educational barriers, Native parents were understood as apathetic and unsupportive of schooling. Indian intelligence was seen as inferior, and terms such as "culturally deprived," "handicapped," "empty," and "cultural vacuum" were used to describe Native students.[27]

As Diné parents fought to have their children attend public schools in the late 1960s, teachers and administrators in the District were following a century-old model of assimilation that viewed Navajo culture and language as the reasons for school failure. This educational ideology remains in schooling practices even today and stands as an obstacle to the educational equity demanded by the court cases we discuss in this chapter. As one English as a Second Language (ESL) teacher explained, "These kids we get are learning disabled with their reading. Because they speak Navajo, you know. The Indian students need to learn English and basic skills to survive in the Anglo world. That bilingual and bicultural stuff is not important for them."[28] Educational research, however, supports just the opposite—cultural and linguistic affirmation enhances school success.[29] These racially driven views were also used to adjust educational and economic opportunities downward, providing a vocationalized curriculum for semiskilled jobs deemed "appropriate" for Navajo students. It was against this backdrop that Navajo parents sued the San Juan School District.

In 1970 the population in the northern portion of the county was mostly white while the southern portion was 90 percent Navajo; the District had 47 percent Native student enrollment.[30] *Sinajini v. San Juan School District* found there were inequities in the distribution of resources, financing, equipment, and supplies. Additionally, similar to *Yazzie/Martinez*, the school district lacked provisions of educational services and programs for Native students.

Before the 1975 *Sinajini* case, the only two high schools were located in Monticello and Blanding, in the county's northern portion. There were no secondary schools in the southern half of the District, the section that overlapped with the Navajo Nation. The *Sinajini* case demonstrated how bus routes were illustrative of this disparity. During the school year, Navajo students traveled an average of fifteen thousand miles to and from the only two high schools in the county—four times as far as the average non-Native student—and spent the equivalent of 120 school days "physically sitting on a bus."[31] The court found that "the busing [. . .] is burdensome and negatively affects the quality of education received by these children, and [. . .] disrupts their family life."[32] Due to the court order, an elementary school and two high schools were constructed in the southern section of the District.

The court agreement additionally stipulated the District should practice equality in expenditures on equipment, supplies, and other resources between the primarily white and primarily Native portions of the school district. The District agreed to "allocate operational expenditures and expenditures for equipment to all schools in the northern portion as compared to schools in the southern portion on a substantially equal basis [. . .] [and] the District will allocate instructional expenditures to all schools on a substantially equal basis."[33]

Finally, the 1975 court agreement addressed the lack of provision for educational services and programs that were beneficial to Native students, including bilingual and bicultural education. The decree, supporting bilingual education, declared,

> The parties agree to the following general concepts:
>
> (a) That an educational program should be based upon the principle that a child should have pride in his cultural heritage; that he should have the opportunity to learn in school [. . .] through the language with which he is best able to learn; and that such an approach improves the self-image of the child and facilitates learning.
>
> (b) That an effective bilingual-bicultural program is necessary in order that Indian students who speak little or no English, can have the opportunity fully and effectively to participate in the educational process.
>
> (c) That all students benefit from a basic curriculum and special programs which reflect the diversity of cultures and heritages of the students within the District.
>
> Defendant District Board of Education shall develop and use:
>
> (a) A bilingual-bicultural plan which will utilize both Navajo and English languages as media of instruction.
>
> (b) A cultural awareness plan for all students consisting of a study of the Navajo history and culture.[34]

Unlike the *Yazzie/Martinez* court order to create a culturally relevant education that included Native language instruction for Native students, the District was ordered to develop a bilingual/bicultural curriculum for *all* students, including the predominantly white students in the Northern portion of the district. The *Sinajini* case is significant because it defined the state and district's educational responsibilities to meet the unique needs of Native students and argued for the importance of a culturally specific curriculum for the local community. We focus the rest of the chapter on the culturally specific curriculum mandated by the court, in particular the curricular contestations.

The Early Bilingual-Bicultural Curriculum: Visions of Inclusion

The first court-ordered educational curriculum was created by district teachers and parents with an effort to incorporate suggestions from Diné parents and the Navajo Tribal Educational Office in Window Rock, Arizona. The director of the Navajo Division of Education was laudable in his support for the curriculum: "Our evaluation is that the publication is an excellent document and a viable guide and requirements for Navajo bilingual-bicultural curriculum. [. . .] Hopefully, programs such as this will aide [sic] the other educational agencies in more humane and intrinsically interesting education for the Navajo and other children."[35] The plan indicated two primary purposes. The first was to create a bilingual curriculum that would help limited-English speaking students "make a smooth transition to the English language with a minimum of frustration" and avoid "academic retardation caused by language barriers."[36] The bilingual program was installed in grades K–3 in schools with significant Navajo student enrollment in 1977 and was planned to be expanded in 1978 to grades 4–6. Although the court-ordered curriculum for all students included Navajo history and culture, the second purpose of the educational plan stated, "Through the use of culturally oriented curriculum materials, the child will be assisted in the development of a positive self-image and the development of pride in *his heritage*, which will lend meaning to the educational environment."[37] The wording seemed to focus on the Native students studying their cultures, rather than all students being taught the bicultural curriculum, as required by the consent agreement.

The cultural awareness part of the curriculum was to take effect in K-12 during the 1976–1977 school year. All teachers received the curriculum guides.[38] Under the guidance of the bilingual staff, school staff, and "interested community concerns," the cultural awareness curriculum was to be integrated into the school curriculum in all grades in all schools in the District.[39] The curriculum guide explained to teachers, "In this way, 'culture' becomes a part of the curriculum rather than a separate entity 'tacked' onto the regular curriculum."[40] Teachers were given examples such as: "Health problems on the reservation are discussed during the health class; tribal government is discussed during social studies; 'Coyote and Toad' is part of the math program; Native American arts are dealt with during art; Navajo literature will be discussed during English classes."[41] Cultural lessons were printed on orange paper for teachers to insert into their lesson plans to "simplify the identifying of cultural programs in any curriculum guide."[42]

For the next decade, the newly created *Dinéjí Dóó Bilagáanají Íhoo'aah: A Bilingual-Bicultural Education Design* curriculum "gathered dust in the district's material center."[43] The lawsuit, rather than the support of white administrators or teachers, was the reason for even the existence of a formalized bilingual plan. In 1984 the superintendent explained that although he was concerned about equal educational opportunities for Navajo students,

> There is no real bilingual program in place now. The use of a model that uses the native language first is not enforced here in the district. There were not enough Navajo-speaking teachers, and later cutbacks led to reducing Navajo teacher aides. We have a decentralized district here; principals have total control over their schools. And they don't support bilingual education. [. . .] There is no interest in their involvement with Navajo language. We need to bring kids up to grade level to avoid any future court cases; then we will have done our job.[44]

The cultural awareness curriculum was suppressed, as the director of the District Curriculum Center explained: "Here is a copy of the plan we developed after the court case. Look at it carefully. It says that we will provide cultural awareness for all students; that means the whites too. But that never happened. Their parents would never let it happen."[45] John Hopkins, author of *Indian Education for All*, argues that Native and non-Native community members need to engage in open and honest dialogue about reasons for mistrust before school reform for Native students can occur.[46] Such honest and open dialogue did not exist between Native and non-Native SJC community members and the District.

In defiance of the *Sinajini* court order, the District did not implement a uniform bilingual-bicultural program. This refusal was framed by an educational ideology that blames the perceived educational failure of Navajo students on their Navajo language and culture. Current educational research, however, affirms that embracing the identities of these youth—young Native peoples with vibrant cultural communities and bilingualism—enhances school success. In other words, denying Native youth their history, language, and culture in school increases their chances of educational failure. On an individual basis, some elementary teachers attempted to minimally integrate Navajo words and cultural information in their classrooms. In some classes an alphabet lining a classroom wall used Navajo words for letters. Navajo clan names were printed neatly on the side of a chalkboard in several classrooms. Occasionally, Navajo elders visited classrooms. At the school level, yearly "cultural days" included Navajo songs and dance, Navajo food, and speeches from Navajo educators and politicians. In the high schools, the inclusion of Navajo culture and language was rare. Walking through the halls and classrooms at night gave no clues that the schools would be filled with young Native men and women in the morning.[47] These touristic attempts at multicultural education that focus on food, festivals, and fun are superficial at best.[48]

Back in Court: Resistance to Educational Equity

In the decades since Navajo parents fought for educational change in court, the District's educational practices and programs produced dismal statistics for Diné students: low graduation rates, high pushout rates, and low standardized test scores. Little academic improvement had occurred since the case against the District started in 1974. For example, as measured by the California Test of Basic Skills, Native students at the eighth-grade level made minimal gains in a decade from 1977, when the average score was a fifth-grade level equivalent, to 1987, when the average was 5.6-grade level equivalent.[49] In both mathematics and reading, Native students scored an average of two and a half years behind their white peers. In 1990 the District moved to the Stanford Achievement Test, which reports national percentile figures, with the national mean being 50 percent. Native students at the two southern schools with the largest Native populations scored in the seventh and tenth percentile in reading at the eighth-grade level. In the eleventh grade, Native students showed some improvement, scoring in the twentieth percentile in math, but still scoring in the seventh percentile in reading. In the early 2000s, Utah changed its form of student assessment to Criterion-Referenced Testing (CRT), used to assess the knowledge, skills, and abilities of students as outlined in the Utah Core

Curriculum. From the years 2005 to 2009, almost 50 percent of the Native students failed to test proficient in both math and language arts. In 2014 Utah changed from CRT to SAGE as a form of assessment. Native students scored below 10 percent in language arts, mathematics, and science. Current Native student proficiency results continue a record of little academic success as measured on tests. From 2014 to 2019, less than 10 percent tested proficient in language arts, mathematics, and science. Though assessment measures have changed significantly over the years, test scores have yet to demonstrate a closure in the academic disparity gap between Native students and their white counterparts. The test scores told a story of the District's failure to provide Native students educational experiences equivalent to those of their white peers.[50]

Some District personnel blamed the dismal testing record on Native students and their families. In a 1990 interview, a white woman from the community explained:

> It's so cultural! As soon as one of them bobs above the water a bit they pull him back down. It's innate! It's so destructive. They [Navajo families] pull everyone down if one tries to succeed. Some people give me that line, "They walk in beauty stuff"—it is certainly a good part of the traditional stories and culture—but this other is so negative. They are such a negative people. They make sure most don't succeed.[51]

Native families blamed low academic achievement in part on racism and inadequate schooling. A Navajo student's description of her experiences in high school illustrated what this looked like:

> The teachers really don't listen to the Indians much. Like an Indian would raise up their hands. These white teachers don't want to take the time to work with Indians. Then they just look at them and they ignore their hands and stuff like that. But when a white person, a white student raises up their hand, they'll go to them first. So, it's like whites, they get first served and then the Indians last [. . .] probably because they want the Indians to be dumb [. . .] they probably think that the Navajos don't know much.[52]

Navajo parents have continually demanded quality education, including bilingual education, for their children. These efforts have been resisted or ignored by the white settlers of SJC. These Navajo parents' concerns were verified with the findings of an investigation by the US Department of Education.

Namely, in 1991, seventeen years after the *Lau v. Nichols* decision, the US Department of Education's Office for Civil Rights (OCR) cited the District for violation of federal ESL requirements. In 1993 the District's proposed alternative bilingual education curricular plans were unacceptable by OCR.[53] The OCR found the District had not developed plans for identifying and assessing the language proficiency of students who have a primary home language other than English; had not implemented an alternative language program with qualified teachers and staff who would provide services to Limited English Proficiency (LEP) students in the District; had not ensured appropriate staffing and materials for alternative language programs; and had not adopted procedures to ensure that LEP students are not placed in special education classrooms because of their lack of proficiency in English.[54]

A "New" Beginning: *Sinajini, et al. v. San Juan County School District* (1997)

The *Sinajini* case became active again in 1994. The OCR joined the case to address the inadequate language support. Another component of the case was to build a high school at Navajo Mountain. The District argued they would not build another school because the original *Sinajini* settlement did not stipulate that order. The school construction claim was dismissed as part of the *Sinajini* case.[55] However, Navajo parents filed the *Meyers v. Board of Education* case, alleging the school district racially discriminated against the Diné because the District constructed schools in smaller white areas. The District argued they were not responsible for educating Diné students living within the Navajo Nation. This case is significant because the court declared the District has an obligation to provide educational opportunities to Native students despite their living on Native lands; it further reiterated that the state constitution mandates free public education for children living within the state.[56]

An examination of the curriculum across the District's schools and admissions provided by district administrators confirmed Navajo parents' concerns that the District denied their children the same educational opportunities provided to white students. The two southern schools with a Navajo student majority, Monument Valley and Whitehorse High Schools, had more limited curriculum offerings than the two northern white-majority schools, San Juan and Monticello High Schools. The southern schools focused on vocational education, unlike the northern schools that offered college readiness courses. As one principal of Whitehorse High School explained, "I'm interested in equal educational opportunity. [. . .] We need to recognize the needs of the people in this local area. I'm not saying we should ignore the academic classes. But the vocational training is where the jobs are for the local Navajo people."[57]

Of the District's twenty-one course offerings in social studies, only three were offered at Whitehorse High School—US History, World Geography, and US Economics. Of the thirty-two different English/reading courses offered by the District, only basic Language Arts 7, 8, 9, 10, 11 and eleven different sections of Basic Reading were offered to students at Whitehorse High School. Additionally, the high school only offered Math 7, 8, and General Math Review in ten different classes. Only two classes in higher math courses were offered— a combined Algebra/Geometry class. Unlike students at the other district high schools, Whitehorse High School Navajo students lacked access to Algebra I, Algebra II, Calculus, and Trigonometry. Earth Science, Physics, and Chemistry were also missing from the schedule. Due to a lack of higher math and science courses, high-achieving students from Whitehorse could not gain admission to the state flagship university, even with a diploma. As a result, some Navajo parents exerted educational sovereignty and went to extraordinary means— including driving their children to other schools outside the District—to provide college readiness courses for their children.

The District again came to a court-approved decree. They agreed to formulate a bilingual or Limited English Proficiency program that "shall take into account the spirit" of the commitment to the implementation of a bilingual/bicultural curriculum and "incorporate a Native American cultural awareness plan" in *all* schools in the District.[58] Three committees—bilingual education, curriculum, and special education—were formed to develop new district instructional plans. These compliance teams consisted of three school-appointed and three Navajo Nation/OCR-appointed educational experts. Dr. Donna Deyhle served as one of the Navajo Nation–appointed experts on the curriculum committee. The three committees developed detailed curriculum and language plans: Heritage (Navajo and Ute) language classes were finally available to all students in all grades at all appropriate schools. Navajo and Ute language teachers were hired at each school site. Elementary schools required thirty minutes per day of Navajo literacy instruction and fifteen minutes per day of content area instruction in Navajo. Secondary schools offered two levels of Navajo language classes. All English and Navajo teachers became English as a Second Language (ESL) endorsed and certified.

Over the course of five years, the consensus teams monitored the District's implementation of the various plans. However, the curriculum team witnessed resistance to the use of school funding for Navajo language and cultural instruction in daily discourses. Local historian Robert McPherson captured these feelings and what they meant for the consensus plan in his 2001 book, *Navajo Land, Navajo Culture: The Utah Experience in the Twentieth Century*:

> While this plan was implemented in various stages in 1998, there are some people who still voice complaints. They argue that the system hinders the acquisition of English-language skills for those who need the help the most; that the whole plan is politically and legally motivated and does not consider the welfare of the children; that the Navajo tribe, which has a voice in the adoption of the curriculum, is foisting family responsibility for teaching language and heritage onto the schools, where it does not belong; and that there are not enough staff to implement a true bilingual model. After listening to these arguments, a Navajo man serving on the school board countered: "I think we should withdraw every Navajo student from the San Juan School District. That's when you will be happy. Take care of it once and for all. Just sweep the floor and go home. You have no interest in educating Navajo students in San Juan School District."[59]

In 2002 the District informed the curriculum compliance team that due to the 2001 No Child Left Behind Act, they were ceasing to fully implement the court agreement. A district administrator argued that discontinuing the bilingual curriculum complied with federal policies regarding English-only instruction. Additionally, he argued the issue of an instructional need for the Navajo language was a "past problem," and once again, the educational demands from Navajo parents in the *Sinajini* case were dismissed as unimportant for Navajo students. Furthermore, the administrator contended that continuing to follow the outdated curriculum negatively impacted teacher retention and recruitment and resulted in the loss of certain programs for white students.

District administrators, as well as classroom teachers, interpret and implement policies according to "their own schemes of interest, motivation, and action."[60] In this case, an educational ideology that views the Navajo language as impeding the learning of English guided the District's actions. The District chose to maintain language practices—English only—that existed prior to the *Sinajini* case. The reauthorization of the federal Elementary and Secondary School Act known as No Child Left Behind eliminated federal support for bilingual education and thus provided justification for neglecting the court order.

During the 2003–2004 academic school year, the District and the Navajo Nation again came to a consensus over the revisions of the 1997 plan. At the unwavering insistence of the Navajo Nation, the Navajo language was again a mandatory district-wide course offering.[61]

The Current Curriculum: Navajo, Ute, Hispanic, and Pioneer Cultures

In 2004 the District adopted a new curriculum—the "Cultural Literacy Social Studies Curriculum"—that from the District's perspective was the final requirement of the Consent Decree in the *Sinajini* case.[62] In the eyes of the court, however, the *Sinajini* case is still active. The court still "retained jurisdiction," meaning the case is available for monitoring and enforcement of the terms and mandates of the decree. The District must provide "equal educational opportunity" over time that ensures the court that "equal educational opportunity" exists.[63]

The latest curriculum includes a "menu" of Navajo, Ute, Hispanic, and

Pioneer cultural objectives for teachers to use for discussions and to further their ideas.[64] The plan tells teachers to insert cultural lessons in place of some Utah Social Studies Standards, such as "Perform a dance: Round Dance [. . .] to a Navajo Song, Dance to Ute Songs, Dance to Mexican Folklorico Songs, and Dance a Pioneer social dance" or "Host a guest Navajo, Ute, Hispanic, Pioneer story teller."[65] This curriculum plan included white settlers, going against the original agreement that stated the District "shall develop and use [. . .] a cultural awareness plan for all students consisting of a study of the Navajo history and culture."[66] According to the educational consultant hired by the District to compile the curriculum, it is also the first plan that spoke reflectively about the neglect of previous cross-cultural inclusion:

> Some of the references in the cultural curriculum name the harsh actions which have occurred in Navajo-Ute-Hispanic and Pioneer history. Had educators before us taken on the difficult task of adding the Navajo-Ute-Hispanic and Pioneer cultural points of view to Social Studies, we would be more at ease in discussing these historical phenomena and less daunted by the historical subject matter of coercion.[67]

The curriculum writers removed the Navajo language from the required curriculum offered at most Navajo schools in favor of one that is optional, dependent on the number of Navajo students registered for the class. In a district that had a history of reducing Navajo teachers and Navajo language and culture classes, this is an ominous echo of the past. Once again, Navajo language, culture, and history are seen as impediments to academic success or as a frill that may be removed during times of budget tightening or when more time is needed for PE, health, technology, social studies, or extracurricular activities. In Dr. Cynthia Benally's research on the status of the Arizona mandate that requires the instruction of Native history in all schools in Arizona, she found that Native content was erased, made palatable, and deemed unnecessary to educational programs and achievement. In an interview, an assistant superintendent of a school district in Arizona described how peripheral activities practices are meaningless. "It's almost like we will have a Native month or we will have a Native dance or we will have a Native art show and it's like, it's almost better not to do that because lip service is almost like nothing at all."[68]

Over time the presence of Navajo language and culture has faded from the District's priorities. An administrator with thirty-five years of experience in the District explained:

> There are no longer any cultural programs. Several of the Navajo language and culture teachers were kicked out of the district. They fired some excellent teachers. Now they use the Rosetta Stone Navajo language program. It is just work on the Internet. There is no face-to-face interaction with a teacher. Our classes have little cultural knowledge in them now. Or language. They [district administrators] said, "We are done with that." Bringing the community into the school is important for their learning. The district did not like that. They have eliminated all of the classes where we had elders and community members coming to the classroom. We have no Native language and history class now.[69]

In a critique of the curricula used and a reflection on limited student success over the past three decades, the administrator stated:

> The district just moves from [one] canned curriculum to another. They are all designed without regard to the student population. They try them for a few years. And then they change to another. [. . .] What I know is that the important key issue is the relationship between the teachers and students. It is not a pre-programmed curriculum.[70]

This administrator talked about "best practices of respect and inclusion" that were important for Native student success. "We were a community at the school. We would talk. We would have potlucks. We were working together for the kids."[71]

Over a period of fifty years, the *Sinajini* case has remained an unfinished challenge for educational equity. During this time, Navajo parents have continually demanded quality education, including bilingual education, for their children. These efforts have been resisted or ignored by the white settlers of SJC. Bearing in mind the current state of affairs in the county, would the court-ordered curriculum that included Diné perspectives and assets have reduced the ongoing racial tensions if the District had implemented it in 1975? Would

Native students have felt respected, included, and been more academically successful? Would white students have accepted their Native peers if they learned about them? Would the inclusion of Native culture, language, and history into the curriculum have helped more Native students to stay in school?[72]

Significance to Education

There are lessons to be learned from *Sinajini. v. San Juan School District* and hope for educational change envisioned in *Yazzie/Martinez v. State of New Mexico*, as well as implications for improving educational practices for Native and other marginalized students. As we have illustrated, Navajo parents consistently supported their children's education, even if it meant using the judicial system to force educational equality. The parents fought to build schools in their community so their children did not have to travel long distances or leave home for boarding schools. Schools were built but the physical structures did not translate into higher graduation rates or higher academic success. For almost fifty years and through three generations of school-aged children, Navajo parents sought to have Native histories, cultures, and languages included on an equal basis in the District's curriculum. This has not happened. Resistance from white community members and school officials blocked these efforts. Centuries of racial conflict do not end with court decisions. This has profound implications for educational efforts in *Yazzie/Martinez v. State of New Mexico*. The educational changes required by the *Sinajini v. San Juan School District* were carefully monitored and enforced by compliance teams outside of the District. Policy maker and administrator buy-in is critical. Benally wrote, "A change in culture—from beliefs and norms to practice—is needed for successful implementation of policies that are vastly different from existing policies and practices. [. . .] To effect such sweeping change, teachers need supportive networks of administrators, mentors, and facilitators."[73]

A study of *Sinajini v. San Juan School District* can be useful in guiding curricular and policy recommendations for similar cases. In New Mexico the *Yazzie* plaintiffs alleged the New Mexico Public Education Department and the state were "failing to provide a sufficient and uniform system of education to all New Mexican children,"[74] specifically Native American students. Similar to the *Sinajini* ruling, the New Mexico state education department must create and implement a culturally relevant curriculum for Native students. The defendants are required to set aside funding to address the court decisions. Similarly, the San Juan School District was required to allocate funding to alleviate the issues in the District; however, those conditions still exist in 2023. Money, although useful, does not solve systemic and institutional inequities that are deeply embedded in schools that serve Native students. Time dedicated to developing respectful and reciprocal relationships is needed to create an environment with mutually beneficial conditions. Caring and respect—expressed in the relationships between Native students and their teachers—is another critical factor in a successful educational experience. Native students know when their teachers dismiss their lives and language, impacting dropout rates and academic achievement. Benally's research speaks to the issue of sovereignty and education. She argues that "due to numerous broken promises, it is imperative that Native communities act for them/ourselves by expressing our sovereignty in educating our children with our perspectives, truths, and knowledges."[75] It could be that getting control of schools—educational sovereignty—for the inclusion of specific tribal epistemologies, culturally sustaining pedagogy, and cultural specific curricula might be one of the solutions to address the academic neglect Native students too often experience in public schools.

Student Learning Objectives

1. Students will be able to compare the two court cases to identify similarities and differences.
2. Students will be able to identify lessons learned from the *Sinajini v. San Juan School District* case.

Discussion Questions

1. Would the court-ordered curriculum that included Diné perspectives

and assets have reduced the ongoing racial tensions had it been implemented in 1975?

2. In what ways can the *Sinajini v. San Juan School District* case assist with similar cases that implement Native content instruction for all students?

Notes

1. Note on the use of terms: We use Diné when referencing people and Navajo as an adjective for land, government, and entities related to the Diné. Native is used to refer to the original inhabitants of what is currently known as the continental United States. Indians is used in conjunction to its use in primary sources.

2. The data sources are from Dr. Donna Deyhle's personal archive collected between 1984–2004.

3. Our use of white in lowercase is the rejection of the "hegemonic grammatical norms" of whiteness (Jessica C. Harris and Lori D. Patton, "Un/Doing Intersectionality through Higher Education Research," *Journal of Higher Education* 90, no. 3 [2019]: 368). Our definition of settlers: "Settlers come with the intention of making a new home on the land, a homemaking that insists on settler sovereignty over all things in their new domain."

4. Daniel McCool, Expert Witness Report in the Case of *Navajo Nation v. San Juan County*, UT Case no. 2:12-cv-00039-RS (2015), 13.

5. Members of the Church of Jesus Christ of Latter-Day Saints are commonly known as Mormons.

6. Donna Deyhle, *Reflection in Place: Connected Lives of Navajo Women* (Tucson: University of Arizona Press, 2009).

7. McCool, Expert Witness, 29; Beth King and Donna Deyhle, "Rebuilding the Fort: Historical Denialism and Reterritorialization in the Modern Southwest," presentation at a meeting of the Society for Applied Anthropology, Portland, Oregon, March 19–23, 2019.

8. David E. Wilkins, *The Navajo Political Experience*, rev. ed. (Lanham, MD: Rowman and Littlefield, 2003).

9. Beth King, "The Utah Navajos Relocation in the 1950s: Life along the San Juan River," *Canyon Echo*, February 9, 2002 (originally published July 1996), https://canyonechojournal.com/category/archive-1993-1997/.

10. Robert McPherson, "Paiute Posey and the Last White Uprising," *Blue Mountain Shadows* 4 (1989), https://issuu.com/utah10/docs/uhq_volume53_1985_number3/s/150346.

11. Deyhle, *Reflection in Place*, 41.

12. McPherson, "Paiute Posey."

13. Steven Boos, "San Juan County Utah. Lessons for Everyone to Learn from San Juan County, Utah. What's the Future for San Juan County after Litigation?" presentation at the First Nations Voting Rights—Planting for the Future Conference, Salt Lake City, Utah, September 25–29, 2019.

14. Stanley Bronson, "Posey," in *Blue Mountain Shadows* 23 (2000): 46.

15. McPherson, "Paiute Posey."

16. Joe Mozingo, "A Sting in the Desert," *Los Angeles Times*, September 21, 2014, https://graphics.latimes.com/utah-sting/.

17. Deyhle, *Reflection in Place*, 50.

18. Deyhle, *Reflection in Place*, 49.

19. *Navajo Nation, et al. v. San Juan County*, United States District Court, D. Utah, Central Division, Case no. 2:12-cv-00039, 2017.

20. Christopher Smart, "San Juan County Readies for Political Shift following Federal Court Ruling on Voting Districts," *Salt Lake Tribune*, December 22, 2017.

21. Zak Podmore, "San Juan County Heads into Another Controversial Special Election—and Possibly the First Step to a New Form of Government," *Salt Lake Tribune*, October 14, 2019.

22. Donna Deyhle, Expert Witness Report for Dr. Donna Deyhle, *Navajo Nation, et al., v. San Juan County*, Civil No. 2:12-cv-00039-RS. 2015.

23. Donna Smith, "The Integration of the San Juan County School District," *Blue Mountain Shadows* 21 (1999).

24. Deyhle, Expert Witness, 13.

25. Smith, "Integration," 32.

26. Smith, "Integration," 33; Gary Shumway, "Blanding: The Making of a Community," in *San Juan County Utah: People, Resources, and History* (Salt Lake City: Utah State Historical Society, 1983), 149.

27. Brewton Berry, *The Education of American Indians: A Survey of the Literature* (Washington, DC: US Government Printing Office, 1968); Donna Deyhle and Karen Swisher, "Research in American Indian and Alaska Native Education: From Assimilation to Self-Determination," in *Review of Research in Education*, vol. 22, ed. Michael W. Apple (Washington, DC: American Educational Research Association, 1997), 113–94; K. Tsianina Lomawaima and Teresa L. McCarty, *"To Remain an Indian:" Lessons in Democracy from a Century of Native American Education* (New York: Teachers College Press, 2006).

28. Donna Deyhle, "Navajo Youth and Anglo Racism: Cultural Integrity and Resistance," *Harvard Educational Review* 65, no. 3 (1995): 418.

29. Teresa L. McCarty, "The Holistic Benefits of Education for Indigenous Language Revitalization and Reclamation (ELR2)," *Journal of Multilingual and Multicultural Development* 42, 10 (2020): 927–40.

30. *Sinajini v. Board of Education of the San Juan School District*, Agreement of Parties, United State District Court for the District of Utah Central Division, 1975.

31. Deyhle, *Reflection in Place*, 62.

32. *Sinajini v. Board of Education of the San Juan School District,* Agreement of Parties, 9.

33. *Sinajini v. Board of Education of the San Juan School District,* Agreement of Parties, 13.

34. *Sinajini v. Board of Education of the San Juan School District,* Agreement of Parties, 15–16.

35. Letter from Director Dillon Platero, Navajo Division of Education, Navajo Nation, May 18, 1976.

36. San Juan School District, *Dinéjí Dóó Bilagáanají Íhoo'aah: A Bilingual-Bicultural Education Design* (1977), 3 (emphasis added), author's archive.

37. San Juan School District, *Dinéjí Dóó Bilagáanají Íhoo'aah,* 3.

38. San Juan School District, *Dinéjí Dóó Bilagáanají Íhoo'aah.*

39. We do not name teachers and administrators in the District. Structural racism is systematic and larger than individuals.

40. San Juan School District, *Dinéjí Dóó Bilagáanají Íhoo'aah,* 46.

41. San Juan School District, *Dinéjí Dóó Bilagáanají Íhoo'aah,* 46.

42. San Juan School District, *Dinéjí Dóó Bilagáanají Íhoo'aah,* 46.

43. Donna Deyhle, "Journey towards Social Justice: Curriculum Change and Educational Equity in a Navajo Community," in *Narrative and Experience in Multicultural Education,* ed. J. Phillion, M. Fang He, and F. C. Connelly (Thousand Oaks, CA: Sage, 2005), 62.

44. Deyhle, *Reflection in Place,* 92.

45. San Juan School District, *Dinéjí Dóó Bilagáanají Íhoo'aah,* i.

46. John P. Hopkins, *Indian Education for All: Decolonizing Indigenous Education in Public Schools* (New York: Teachers College Press, 2020).

47. This observation is based on Deyhle's twenty years of ethnographic research in San Juan County.

48. Troy Richardson, "At the Garden Gate: Community Building through Food: Revisiting the Critique on 'Food, Folk and Fun' in Multicultural Education," *Urban Review* 43 (2011): 107–23.

49. Deyhle, Expert Witness Report.

50. Deyhle, Expert Witness Report.

51. Deyhle, *Reflection in Place,* 187.

52. Deyhle, *Reflection in Place,* 187.

53. Deyhle, "Journey towards Justice"; Deyhle, "Reflection in Place."

54. Letter from Cathy H. Lewis, regional director, Region VII, US Department of Education, Office for Civil Rights, October 20, 1993.

55. Larry R. Baca, "Meyers v. Board of Education: The Brown v. Board of Indian Country," *University of Illinois Law Review,* 5 (2004): 1155–80.

56. Baca, "Meyers v. Board of Education."

57. Deyhle, *Reflection in Place,* 151.

58. *Sinajini v. Board of Education of the San Juan School District,* 1997 Order and

Consent Decree, United States District Court for the District of Utah Central Division, 1997, 4–5.

59.   Robert McPherson, *Navajo Land, Navajo Culture: The Utah Experience in the Twentieth Century* (Norman: University of Oklahoma Press, 2001).

60.   Bradley A. Levinson, Teresa Winstead, and Margaret Sutton, "Theoretical Foundations for a Critical Anthropology of Education Policy," in *The Anthropology of Education Policy: Ethnographic Inquiries into Policy as Sociocultural Process*, ed. Angelina A. Castagno and Teresa L. McCarty (New York: Routledge, 2018), 28.

61.   Deyhle, Expert Witness Report.

62.   San Juan School District, *Cultural Literacy Social Studies Curriculum K-12 Scope and Sequence* (Blanding, UT: San Juan School District, 2004).

63.   *Sinajini v. Board of Education of the San Juan School District*, Agreement of Parties, 3.

64.   Terms used in the San Juan School District's *Cultural Literacy Curriculum*.

65.   San Juan School District, *Cultural Literacy Curriculum*, 7, 9.

66.   *Sinajini v. Board of Education of the San Juan School District*, Agreement of Parties, 16.

67.   San Juan School District, *Cultural Literacy Curriculum*, 2.

68.   Interview conducted by Cynthia Benally on November 30, 2012.

69.   Deyhle, Expert Witness Report, 79.

70.   Deyhle, Expert Witness Report, 79.

71.   Deyhle, Expert Witness Report, 81.

72.   Deyhle, "Navajo Youth and Anglo Racism."

73.   Cynthia Benally, "'You Need to Go beyond Creating a Policy': Opportunities for Zones of Sovereignty in Native American History Instruction Policies in Arizona," *Journal of American Indian Education* 58, no. 3 (2019): 21.

74.   New Mexico Center on Law and Poverty, "Yazzie/Martinez v. State of New Mexico Decision," January 7, 2022, http://nmpovertylaw.org/wp-content/uploads/2018/09/Graphic-Yazzie-Martinez-Decision.pdf.

75.   Benally, "'You Need to Go beyond Creating a Policy,'" 30.

Figure 17. A photo of Karen Sanchez-Griego, superintendent of Cuba School District in Cuba, New Mexico. She called upon UNM faculty to support developing initiatives to remedy the *Yazzie/Martinez* lawsuit in the Cuba School District. Photo credit Hondo Louis. Funded by UNM's Center for Regional Studies and Native American Studies Department.

CHAPTER THIRTEEN

Promoting Solidarity for Social Justice and Indigenous Educational Sovereignty in the Cuba Independent School District

LEOLA TSINNAJINNIE PAQUIN, SHIV R. DESAI,
VINCENT WERITO, NANCY LÓPEZ,
AND KAREN SANCHEZ-GRIEGO

Education in New Mexico is at a crucial tipping point. Now, at this moment, we have a heightened opportunity to fix what is broken. Decades of underfunding, coupled with longstanding systemic racism in our society and institutions, have left our education system with some of the worst educational inequities in the nation. Opportunity gaps have never been wider for far too many New Mexico students. Our families come to schools with diverse cultures, languages, and heritages, and yet these cultural assets are routinely ignored.

TRANSFORM EDUCATION NM

This paradoxical legacy—schools serving both to promote equity and reproduce inequities—was on full display in spring 2020 as COVID-19 forced schools online (while, at the same time, the murder of George Floyd ignited a national reckoning with anti-Black racism and violence). On one hand, educators all over the country made superhuman efforts to continue their work. On the other hand, large numbers of students—Black and brown, and many who live in rural parts of our country, these students, especially—were unable to participate in their newly virtual K-12 classrooms, their absence serving as yet another painful reminder that not every child has secure access to computers and Wi-Fi, much less to food, housing, counselors and social workers for social emotional needs, and other necessities that would allow them to stay focused on school during a national emergency.

DE ROYSTON ET AL. 2020

Introduction

The opening passages describe the backdrop of an opportunity to exercise community empowerment and Indigenous sovereignty through Indigenous education for structural change given the national attention to social justice and the devastation wrought by the COVID-19 pandemic on BIPOC (Black, Indigenous, People of Color) communities. [1] When we began our partnership with the Cuba Independent School District (CISD) in the first few months of 2020, it was approximately one and a half years after the ruling of *Yazzie/ Martinez v. State of New Mexico*. CISD served as one of the plaintiffs, and now the district is poised to serve as a model for transformational change, tasked with the mission of providing quality and sufficient educational services to hard-hit Diné (Navajo) communities trying to withstand traumatic assaults on their livelihood. The pandemic quickly changed the dynamics of our collaboration as issues of social inequities, educational and health disparities, a housing crisis, under/unemployment, and racial injustice became exacerbated and highlighted in the national spotlight. As lockdowns were implemented, no one knew how long they would last. However, the pandemic also invited teachers into students' homes and families into teachers' classrooms. The collaborative work with CISD and BIPOC professors gave us glimpses into the possibilities of how educators can work in union with families and communities to address key educational disparities. The idea of building on students' lived experiences and honoring our communities was no longer a foreign concept. The deaths of George Floyd, Ahmad Arbery, and Breonna Taylor; the devastation COVID-19 brought to Native Nations and other communities of color; and the critical attention given to issues of equity and inclusion became more pronounced as communities demanded that schools pay attention to the racial reckoning that was at hand, along with the increasing number of deaths resulting from COVID-19. Teachers needed to be attentive to which students and families were facing housing and food insecurities. Students needing access to counselors and social workers became a top priority. Furthermore, while social-emotional learning has always been a key aspect of Indigenous education, it became ever more prominent among our concerns. Issues of inequality and diversity were not inconsequential but in fact were the center of focus. We witnessed the challenges as well as the new possibilities.

Ultimately, we were forced to ask: What is our *kuleana* (responsibility) to our community, to each other, to our land, to our families and loved ones, to our children, to our ancestors, and to our progeny? [2]

The purpose of this chapter is to describe our team's efforts to work with CISD to promote Indigenous education, equity, racial justice, and culturally sustaining/revitalizing pedagogies that embrace healing and wellness, connecting the mind, body, and spirit and fostering intercultural community by advocating for a critical consciousness lens. As a team, in partnership with the school district, we created student distance-learning modules in the wake of COVID-19, implemented two sets of virtual professional development series for educators, and worked with groups of students from seventh to twelfth grade in sets of Zoom workshops. More importantly, in this chapter we tell the story of these efforts to weave together race and social justice theory, Indigenous education, policy, pedagogy, solidarity, and community well-being amid the backdrop of the double pandemic of COVID-19 and racial injustice.

Background

In this section, we share demographic information on Cuba schools, highlight the participation of CISD as a plaintiff in the *Yazzie/Martinez* lawsuit, contextualize our work in terms of the initial response of the State of New Mexico to Judge Singleton's ruling, and provide background on each of the authors. While this chapter is primarily narrated from the perspective of the University of New Mexico scholars, we have worked collectively with Dr. Sanchez-Griego to produce this piece.

DEMOGRAPHICS

While the majority of the administrators, faculty, and staff are non-Native, the schools in the district serve a predominantly Native student population coming from local Diné communities. CISD is located in the town of Cuba, New Mexico, in Sandoval County in the north-central part of the state on US Highway 550. According to CISD demographic data, Navajo students comprise almost 71 percent of the student population of 672 students. Most of the

Navajo students come from the surrounding and neighboring communities of Counselor, Ojo Encino, and Torreon. In conversations with students and families, we learned that bus rides can take over two hours one way from the furthest homes to the school. Given the strength of the Native presence, the location of the schools, and the history of structural challenges embedded in these dynamics, CISD embodied the need for New Mexico to adhere to its responsibility of equal access to education.

THE LAWSUIT

As described by the New Mexico Center on Law and Poverty, which represented the *Yazzie* plaintiffs, a collection of families and school districts brought their lawsuit against the State of New Mexico for failure to "meet its constitutionally mandated responsibility to provide all public school students the programming and supports necessary to succeed."[3]

Specifically, as written in the *Yazzie* Plaintiff's Closing Brief (2018):

> The Yazzie Plaintiffs include ten Native American and Hispanic children from low-income families who have been neglected by New Mexico's public education system. They come from Gallup-McKinley (Yazzies), Albuquerque (Martinezes), Grants-Cibola (Lenos), Gadsden (Sanabrias), and Peñasco (Dominguezes). Each would like the opportunity to attend college or pursue a career. Each would like to better understand how to participate in New Mexico's political and economic life as adults. But unless there is a dramatic change now in New Mexico's educational system, they will likely finish their educations without sufficient skills and knowledge to allow them to achieve these fundamental goals. The Yazzie Plaintiff children are but 10 out of over 200,000 children who are suffering substantial educational harm in New Mexico's deficient public educational system.
>
> The Yazzie Plaintiffs also include six school districts that are denied the funds and services they need to provide students, especially economically disadvantaged, English language learner, and Native American ("at-risk") students, the basic educational opportunities necessary for them to attend college, pursue a career and participate fully in political and economic life. Gallup-McKinley, Santa Fe, Moriarty-Edgewood, Rio Rancho, Cuba, and

Lake Arthur have struggled just to keep the doors open and the lights on over the past seven years, and cannot provide a sufficient education to their at-risk students with current funds. [4]

In joining forces and voices with the collective plaintiffs in the lawsuit, CISD was able to shed a powerful light on the dire circumstances of the countless families who have, over decades, persistently attempted to obtain access to schooling. While there have always been those who fight on behalf of Indigenous education locally and globally, the *Yazzie/Martinez v. State of New Mexico* case has engendered the opportunity to position family experiences in the context of structural inequalities that contrast with federal and state political responsibilities. We must continue to build upon the efforts of the plaintiffs, the lawyers, those who provided expert testimonials, the ruling of Judge Singleton on behalf of the plaintiffs, and all those who have worked toward true, transformational change. As already stated, quality educational opportunities are needed in order to access political and economic life. This is key to the well-being of our children and their pathways to adulthood. In our work we believe quality education is grounded in pedagogy that honors student identity, family history, and critiques of the structures and the legacy of inequality (genocide, racism, colonization, greed, destruction of land, violence against culture, etc.).

RESPONSE

Unfortunately, the overall response of the State of New Mexico to the ruling has been insufficient. On October 30, 2019, the *Yazzie* plaintiffs filed a motion with the First Judicial District Court, citing the lack of basics necessary for a constitutionally sufficient education and calling for a long-term plan. Co-author and Cuba Superintendent Karen Sanchez-Griego was quoted by the New Mexico Center for Law and Poverty as saying, "Cuba Schools serves predominantly Native American Students but we still lack the funds to provide culturally relevant curriculum and language support." Further, she said, "We also can't provide adequate programming for our students with disabilities or transportation services to get students to and from tutoring, summer school, and after school programs. We need to make real changes to our education system now to give all our children—and our state—an opportunity to succeed."[5]

Nonetheless, the state has taken some steps toward responding to the ruling in the *Yazzie/Martinez* case. For example, Cuba was able to take advantage of the state's Indigenous Education Initiative Funding. In November 2019 CISD was one of eight northern New Mexico schools awarded an Indigenous Education Grant from the New Mexico Public Education Department (NMPED). Fortunately, Cuba was able to pool sources of funding (federal, state, and grant) to channel school and community-based energies toward Indigenous education initiatives.

In late 2019 and early 2020, Superintendent Sanchez-Griego began discussions with our group of University of New Mexico (UNM) professor colleagues: Dr. Vincent Werito, Dr. Leola Tsinnajinnie Paquin, Dr. Shiv R. Desai, and Dr. Nancy López. We identified the overall initiative as fostering intercultural dialogue and promoting racial healing for the district. As a team, in partnership with the school district, we began to explore how the district could take steps to move toward social justice and Indigenous education. Subsequently, we created student distance-learning modules in response to the closure of in-person schooling due to the rise of COVID-19 cases. Next, we implemented two sets of virtual professional development series for educators that took place from March to December and worked with groups of students from seventh through twelfth grade through Zoom online workshops from January to April 2021. The team continued to work with CISD in the 2021–2022 school year.

BACKGROUND OF UNM COLLEAGUES

The background of each UNM team member is important to share as the dynamics of our working group play a major role in how we have developed our approach to engaging with the administrators, teachers, staff, students, and community. As four professors of color with differentiated and valued cultural perspectives, we strive not only for solidarity and representation but also for a balance informed by both scholarship and lived experiences. In the work we do with Cuba staff, faculty, and students, we openly share how our identities inform our understanding of education and thus how important it is to recognize who we are in spaces of learning.

Vincent Werito is an associate professor of Language, Literacy, and Socio-cultural Studies and is a member of the Institute for American Indian Education (IAIE) at UNM. He is originally from Na'Neelzhiin (Torreon, New Mexico). His scholarship and research are centered in the following areas: teacher education, Indigenous pedagogy, Diné (Navajo) education, Navajo language/cultural revitalization, Indigenous Nation building, and cultural sustainability. Specifically, some of his recent research has focused on the experiences of Indigenous youth in education, identifying exemplary practices in the education of this demographic and defining community well-being and community-engaged research.

Leola Tsinnajinnie Paquin is an assistant professor of Native American Studies and is also a member of IAIE. Her maternal grandparents emigrated from the Philippines to the Hawaiian island of Oahu. Her mother was born and raised in Waipahu and eventually moved to New Mexico. Leola's paternal grandparents raised their children in Na'Neelzhiin (her grandmother's home community), where they served as educators. Leola's dad graduated from Cuba High School in 1967. Dr. Tsinnajinnie Paquin is a former president of the American Indian Studies Association, former co-chair of the Diversity Council Curriculum Subcommittee, and is actively engaged in faculty fellowships across UNM. Her community-engaged scholarship is centered on Indigenous educational sovereignty.

Shiv R. Desai is an associate professor of Teacher Education and Educational Leadership. He is the co-chair of the Diversity Council Curriculum Subcommittee, among other race and social justice activities. He is a former elementary and high school teacher and as such has extensive experience working with community youth and school districts in multiple states. He identities as an immigrant, English language learner from the South Asian diaspora.

Nancy López is a professor of Sociology as well as associate vice-president for Equity and Inclusion. She is the co-founder and director of the Institute on the Study of "Race" and Social Justice and was integral to the implementation of UNM's US and Global Diversity and Inclusion graduation requirement for undergraduates at the University of New Mexico. She is a Black Latina, born and raised in New York City, and daughter of Dominican immigrants who never had the opportunity to pursue formal schooling beyond the second grade and were rich in funds of knowledge. Spanish is her first language.

BACKGROUND OF CO-AUTHOR AND PARTNER, DR. KAREN SANCHEZ-GRIEGO

Dr. Karen C. Sanchez-Griego, Ed.D. is the superintendent of Cuba Independent Schools. She is leading district-wide redesign and support in the landmark case of *Yazzie/Martinez*, working on ensuring that the students in CISD receive an equitable academic education using a systems approach in the pre-K through 12 educational system. Her work centers on preparing students for successful college and career trajectories from the first day they enter CISD schools. She is an experienced teacher, administrator, and educational reformer who has worked statewide and across the country on educational issues. She is a native New Mexican and loving wife, mother, and grandmother to her family.

The Objectives of Our Partnership

Overall, our goal was to promote social justice, ethnic studies, and Indigenous education in CISD using the context of the local history of long-standing racial conflict and the *Yazzie/Martinez v. State of New Mexico* court ruling. The district's board of education was forward thinking in its participation as a plaintiff in the *Yazzie/Martinez* case, as the board saw the negative effects of not having in place either funding or a plan that supported equity for students in the Cuba district. Here, we discuss the four objectives that continue to guide our work: promoting community-based schooling, confronting deficit notions by building a community cultural wealth consciousness, centering ethnic studies, and identifying equity and equality. These objectives were born out of heavy conversations with CISD leadership, discussions of our community-based experiences, the intersections of our commitments to decolonization and antiracism scholarship, and the understanding that we would be honoring the immeasurable contributions countless entities made to ensure the successful outcome of the case against the State of New Mexico. In the words of our mentor, colleague, and leader, former UNM professor Dr. Joseph Suina:

> There has never been a come-together of the two entities, the school and the tribe, the family. We have never enjoyed what middle class America has

always enjoyed, and that is a continuation of home language, home values, home knowledge in the school. It's always been a severing—our home experience is at the doorstep of the school, and I think right now tribes are looking to find that connection.[6]

As scholars and community members with diverse family backgrounds that echo Professor Suina's description of the American Indian experience in Westernized education, we are personally invested in these objectives. We want to make contributions to the CISD communities that would help address the histories of injustice that produced the dire circumstances experienced by students and their families, generation after generation.

PROMOTE COMMUNITY-BASED SCHOOLING

As community engaged scholars, we draw upon BIPOC core values of reciprocity, responsibility, and respect that inform our work with communities of color. For example, we believe that we have the *kuleana* to work with schools to promote schooling that is community based, honors diverse cultural perspectives, views families and communities as key partners, and centers students' cultures and identities to strive for equitable social change.[7] Therefore, one of the chief objectives of our work with teachers, administrators, staff, and students included using concepts like *k'é* (acknowledgement of all relations) and *kéyah* or *'āina*—"the land that feeds you"—to understand how land shapes our identity, our community.[8] Through a connection with land, a strong sense of community is developed and the maintenance of language, culture, traditions, and values is reinforced.

Several key aspects of Indigenous education provide culturally relevant/responsive pedagogy and the idea of educating "the inner self through enlivenment and illumination from one's own being and the learning of key relationships."[9] Thus, even if students are not strongly informed about their cultural traditions or if they don't speak their Native languages, culturally responsive educators can still guide and mentor them to embrace innate cultural characteristics essential for learning, which have already been planted within them through their ancestors' blood and teachings (i.e., genetic memory). In this way, culturally responsive educators tap into the lived experiences of

Indigenous youth coming from different cultural backgrounds who bring with them different perspectives based on their own cultural lifeways, values, and beliefs. Therefore, Indigenous knowledge is "community cultural wealth" that teachers and students must acknowledge, recognize, and utilize in teaching and learning.[10] Moreover, embedded within the idea of culturally sustaining/revitalizing pedagogy is the practice of educators themselves coming to realizations about who they are, where they come from, and why they are teaching.[11] This process of consciousness raising through professional, sustained learning allows educators to strive to learn more about their own cultural knowledge and draw upon their lived experiences, including Indigenous languages, stories, rituals, songs, and traditional ecological knowledge. Finally, a deeper understanding of integrating Indigenous languages and culture into students' learning experiences requires acknowledging oppression and a culturally sustaining/revitalizing and social justice–oriented pedagogical approach that gives ownership and responsibility for learning back to Indigenous communities and youth.[12]

CONFRONT DEFICIT NOTIONS

Another chief objective was helping teachers, administrators, staff, and students to confront cultural-deficit thinking and recognize community cultural wealth and funds of knowledge as a strength that exists in Cuba.[13] Valencia (1997) notes how various scholars have employed different models to help explain the achievement gap between minority students and mainstream ones. For example, some scholars have utilized "communication process" models to emphasize misunderstandings between students and teachers due to different verbal and communication styles. Other scholars have argued the "caste theory" model, wherein involuntary minorities (i.e., Latinos, Native Americans, and African American students) create an "oppositional identity" to battle a racist, oppressive society that does not value them. Lastly, some scholars have proposed "structural inequality" models that contend that school failure for low socioeconomic status (SES) students can only be understood by analyzing political, economic, and cultural contexts. Each of these models alludes to the conceptualization of Valencia's notion of deficit thinking, which he defines as:

an endogenous theory—positing that the student who fails in school does so because of internal deficits or deficiencies. Such deficits manifest, it is alleged, in limited intellectual abilities, linguistic shortcomings, lack of motivation to learn and immoral behavior. [. . .] We shall see that genetics, culture, and class, and familial socialization have all been postulated as the sources of alleged deficits expressed by the individual student who experiences school failure.[14]

What is important in Valencia's explanation of deficit thinking is how new terms are developed in each historical period to explain student failure. Thus, we move from earlier models of genetic explanations to later models that place blame on cultural and family values. However, a major weakness in all these models is that student and community perseverance, resolve, and agency are often ignored. In addition, ancestral knowledge, home language, traditions, and beliefs are judged based on Western ideologies, which ignore the worldviews of communities of color.[15]

BUILD A COMMUNITY CULTURAL WEALTH CONSCIOUSNESS

Given the wealth of Indigenous cultural resources embedded in the communities of the school district, we have made it a core objective to direct energy toward building a consciousness of this richness. Our theory of change includes the understanding that to facilitate system-level transformations, critical reflection on one's own positionality in grids of power is a necessary first step for advancing understanding about unjust power relations and the possibilities for equity and justice through practicing solidarity. One important mechanism that can facilitate this transformation is reframing the narrative about Indigenous and other marginalized communities so that it is anchored in asset language that recognizes the resources and funds of knowledge in these communities.[16] Like Valencia, critical race theorist Tara J. Yosso (2005) recognizes that traditionally marginalized groups are not always acknowledged for the many forms of capital they possess.

We learn from her work that honoring community cultural wealth can be done through the recognition of aspirational, navigational, social, linguistic, familial, and resistant capital. Yosso writes:

These forms of capital draw on the knowledges Students of Color bring with them from their homes and communities into the classroom. They are not conceptualized for the purpose of finding new ways to co-opt or exploit the strength of Communities of Color. Instead, community cultural wealth involved a commitment to conduct research, teach and develop schools that serve a larger purpose of struggling toward social and racial justice.[17]

Essentially, we wanted to use Yosso's community cultural wealth framework to build a ground on which educators and learners could find ways of absorbing and nourishing the roots of knowledge stemming out of each family in all local communities.

According to the Transform Education NM Coalition ("Our Platform," 2021), creating a public education school system that "embraces, reflects, and incorporates the cultural and linguistic heritage of our diverse communities as a foundation for all learning" is integral to fixing the current education system that has failed Native students.[18] Building a community cultural wealth consciousness based within the communities of the CISD is key to creating this foundation.

IDENTIFY EQUITY AND EQUALITY

One of the last objectives we wanted to focus on was helping educators and community members differentiate between equity and equality. Because CISD is such a small district, it can respond to the needs of the community fairly quickly. For instance, when the lockdown occurred in 2020, district staff would go door-to-door to drop off school materials and other resources, such as meals. They also dropped off jetpacks that would help with Internet services. Equality would have meant every student receiving such a device irrespective of need. Equity brings these devices to students who do not have access. More importantly, CISD worked in concert with providers to identify areas with the most connectivity issues to ensure jetpacks were needed. A major goal during the pandemic was helping the district examine what students needed and how we could alleviate that challenge rather than getting every student the same items. This meant recognizing that some students had to travel on gravel roads to get home, other students had to go to an outhouse even on cold winter nights, and yet other students had difficulty accessing clean water.

Building Our Collective Framework

The core of our framework has been to bring CISD educators together as a community to practice and explore Indigenous education as a foundation for cultivating community wellness and intergroup, flexible solidarity. Indigenous education is a holistic approach that centers community wellness through land, language, core values, community identity, and ethics. More so, Indigenous education encompasses an integrated holistic approach to teaching and learning that makes content knowledge relevant and the act of teaching and learning a conscious act and/or practice for decolonization and empowerment.[19] While our approach is largely grounded in diverse Indigenous and Diné perspectives, the applied values benefit the entire CISD community in preparing all students for college, career, and life readiness. This approach also complements a Chicano/a-based approach. Our sessions have focused on identity, storytelling/testimonio, community, and solidarity. They have included presentations, discussions, activities, personal reflection projects, and opportunities to workshop lesson plans and/or cocurricular ideas. Our team is committed to Indigenous education, ethnic studies, and project-based learning that examines systemic inequalities, including settler colonialism/tribal status, structural racism/race, patriarchy/gender, ableism/disability, and other sites of overlapping, simultaneous, and systemic inequalities and resistance in order to cocreate solutions that advance social justice.

A key part of this work has been building a deep understanding of the concept of flexible solidarity, or what Patricia Hill Collins (2019) describes as a political praxis (action and reflection on power relations) grounded in a commitment to cultivating healthy, loving, and more just communities (see also transversal politics and political solidarity).[20] This means creating bridges of understanding, empathy, and unity in our communities while we struggle for justice with others who are different among and across political communities. To catalyze flexible solidary, we asked students, teachers, and administrators to give examples of other social justice solidarity projects anchored in human rights for liberation and built on bridging differences. Using our own lived experiences as well as the current political climate and racial reckoning, we described the difference between a bystander, upstander, and whistleblower. We also assigned an essay where students could talk about issues to family/community and/or teachers/administrators. We integrated the arts into our examples of flexible solidarity.

During the Black Lives Matter solidarity demonstrations that took place in downtown Albuquerque in spring of 2020, we saw signs that affirmed Indigenous solidarity with Black Lives Matter, most notably a sign that said, "I can't be silent, no justice no peace, 400+ years end now!" This example effectively conveys what flexible solidary could look like by literally walking the talk and practicing solidarity:

> [This] emphasizes coalition building that takes into account the specific location of "political actors" [. . .] based on principles of rooting and shifting—this is being centered in one's own experience while being empathetic to the differential positioning of the partners in the dialogue. [. . .] The boundaries of the dialogue will be determined by the message rather than the messengers.[21]

On-the-ground examples of flexible solidarity can provide concrete evidence of the types of unity that can be cultivated when people engage in long-term, organized struggle for liberation and decolonization, even when they come from different communities and lived experiences.[22] Collectively, our work is grounded in ethnic studies (ES) pedagogy. Tintiangco-Cubales et al. (2015) state that such a pedagogy has four main traits: (1) it exhibits a dedication to decolonization; (2) privileges culturally responsive pedagogy; (3) honors student lived experiences via community responsive practices that focus on working with families and communities; and (4) affirms positive racial/ethnic identity formation.[23] In addition, Acosta (2007) discusses how ES pedagogy emphasizes the use of love as a guiding principle to understand students and their lived experiences.[24] Moreover, this pedagogical love encompasses a form of care that acknowledges students' barriers while embracing and problematizing their experiences, honoring their identities, and encouraging them to draw on their strengths. Thus, we have sought to do this work out of love and a deep commitment to students, their families, and their communities.

Lastly, we have also incorporated testimonio pedagogy with the goal of healing and wellness.[25] Testimonios emphasize that participants engage in critical reflection of their lived experiences and connect them to sociopolitical realities.[26] Testimonios empower the voiceless and enable the marginalized to be at the center through microaffirmations and by challenging deficit-oriented narratives about our communities and shifting them to asset framing.[27] Testimonios lend themselves to a form of teaching and learning that brings mind, body, spirit, and political urgency together to help orchestrate social change. Even more importantly, "through testimonio pedagogy we are able to hear and read each other's stories through voices, silences, bodies and emotions and with the goal of achieving new *conocimientos*, or understandings."[28] By sharing these stories, we learn about each other in-depth and discover new ways of being and other worldviews. Simultaneously, we are able to be vulnerable and coalesce in different ways by sharing our connections. By listening to marginalized stories, we move people to action and transcend pain, moving toward a space for healing and societal transformation. We ground these stories into the lived realities of students who are better equipped to study themselves, their communities, and their world to create solutions and empowerment for communities that have survived injustices across generations.

The Stories of our Efforts

We originally designed a program where we would talk to students about the issues occurring in Cuba through community circles. Using Freiran concepts, each community circle would empower youth to share what they considered key issues happening in their community, why these issues were occurring, and how we could address them. As society locked down and quarantined, we had to come up with a new plan to engage students. Thus, we pivoted to developing virtual learning modules for CISD students. In particular, the modules were created for the senior students, as Dr. Karen Sanchez-Griego wanted to prioritize their access to the lessons before they graduated from the district. As various discussions proceeded within CISD, an overwhelming consensus emerged to create enrichment-providing modules for students. All seniors at CISD were allowed to use the modules to support the work in their other regular education classes (i.e., English, history, etc., as all work was aligned with Common Core standards). CISD worked to deliver the modules online or through paper copies.

We created four modules: what is race and intersectionality, counterstory-telling/testimonio, ethnic studies, and Indigenous well-being. In the ethnic studies module, we began with Luis Valdez's (1973) poem "In Lak'ech."[29] This poem has been a consistent tool in all our work because it emphasizes con-nectedness, the Spirit that we are all united with, and notions of looking beyond empathy and seeing the humanity in each other, the wholeness in each other. We even translated the poem into Diné (fig. 18).

The modules provided students with the opportunity to experience educa-tion in ways that centered their identities, cultures, and languages, and bridged the mind, body, and spirit. They also provided teachers with an opportunity to see how education could be reimagined. Too often schools want a curricu-lum that is easy to pick up and implement—a curriculum that is vanilla and does not stir any complaints from parents. But such notions ignore the harsh realities and truths our students face daily. In this case, a virus that ravaged the Navajo Nation put students' families at risk of losing housing, employ-ment, and access to food. The modules introduced learning that is multimodal, fosters student creativity, and helps them engage in self-reflexivity. Student testimonios were put at the forefront.[30] These modules also shaped what activities we would do with teachers. They allowed Cuba students to think critically about the issues of race, class, language, and culture and how all these identities affect them as students going out into the workforce and the community as adults. Students were able to connect with professors via Zoom and to have meetings among themselves to further discuss and write about the content in the modules. Each module demonstrated the possibilities of education not determined by testing and/or scripted curricula. Instead we illustrated the power of culturally sustaining pedagogy, which empowered students to engage in counterstorytelling and reflect on their intersectional identities and the meaningful impact of Indigenous education.[31]

The summer institute focused on identity, storytelling/testimonio, solidar-ity, and community. We began with identity because we believe that if

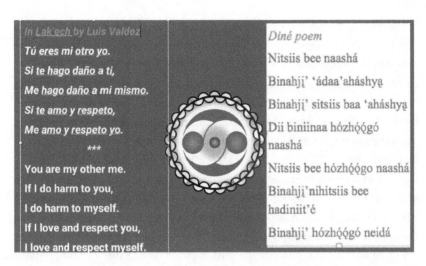

Figure 18. Poem by Luis Valdez (1973), "In Lak'ech," translated into the Diné Language. Credit: Leola Tsinnajinnie Paquin, Shiv R. Desai, Vincent Werito, Nancy López, and Karen Sanchez-Griego.

teachers are not attuned to their identities, then they will not be able to properly advocate for students. One of the most important activities we did during the first week was titled the "River of Life."[32] Specifically, the "River of Life" is a pictorial autobiography of your life, which uses the river as a metaphor for how our lives are always moving (forward and sometimes backward). It shows the highs and lows, the joys and the hurt, the happiness and pain, the good and bad. Through this activity teachers got to reflect on what key experiences have shaped them. They reflected on what traumas they still carry and how their weight might impact their teaching. They reflected on what brings them joy and how this might inspire them to change their teaching. Most importantly, the teachers experienced the power of humanizing education by traversing the deep crevices of their lives. In other words, they experienced testimonio pedagogy firsthand and the power of sharing one's stories.[33] It was a reminder for them that by centering students' lived experiences we can create enriching educational experiences that empower them. Moreover, they got to witness what common experiences they shared with their colleagues and where they differed.

Other activities explored how well teachers know their communities. One of the unique features of CISD is that students come from various communities, from Navajo communities such as Torreon or Pueblo Pintado to smaller New Mexican communities such as La Jara and Regina. We asked educators to draw their school district and then indicate from where CISD students came. Next, we asked them to discuss what resources the various communities had, such as access to healthcare, groceries, public services, and so forth. Then we asked educators to consider how much time it took for students to travel to school. Through this process we helped educators unpack issues of equity and consider community cultural wealth as well as the challenges each community faces. In doing so we were able to connect to the "Community River" activity, which mapped where each community has been and where the collective wanted it to go. Typically, this is an individual activity done as a way of sharing one's biography with a group (the "River of Life" activity mentioned earlier). The flow, bends, rocks, and splits in the river indicate major events and turning points, as well as destinations. We added the community component to deepen a sense of group/school community. These activities, which were often emotional, illustrate how we were able to create solidarity with teachers, staff, and administrators.

We continued to work along the same lines with teachers, staff, and administrators in the fall. While we were able to bring in speakers as well, the focus was on how to translate the four module themes into the classroom. We stressed the importance of embracing students' lived experiences and utilizing the classroom as a space to discuss these issues. Students were living in fear of uncertainty. There was a contested election, more and more citizens were dying, and the economy had slowed tremendously. BIPOC communities continued to suffer, being disproportionately impacted by COVID. Therefore, the four themes were vitally important in terms of reassuring students, opening space for their testimonios, finding new ways to create community, and realizing the importance of creating solidarity to defeat various forms of oppression.

In working with students, we focused on identity. Specifically, we wanted students to reflect on who they are, how their family shapes their identity, how their community molds their identity, and how they practice solidarity. It was not easy, as challenges of connectivity and engaging students in a virtual environment presented themselves. We experienced looking at black screens and trying to engage students who seemed reluctant to speak with us. However, once we got students to share their stories, even though their screens were still black, more voices were heard. Students revealed lessons learned from their families, their communities, and elders who guided them, where they felt safe and where they did not, and what they loved most about their community. In the end they demonstrated how they practice solidarity and reported what they see as the strengths of their communities. Students were able to express what they need from schools to be more successful.

Reflections and Lessons Learned

Working with CISD to create change is an ongoing process. There are no short-cuts or easy answers. In an environment where half the country is divided over vaccines and even more so on issues of equity, change takes time. We have seen the backlash against critical race theory (CRT) and the 1619 Project, which has led to several states banning and/or censoring CRT. However, we also know that we cannot afford to be patient any longer, as our children attend schools that don't value their humanity. We know that several teachers in the district were invested in creating change and valued the elements of Indigenous pedagogy, while other teachers wanted to preserve the status quo. We learned that a few hours with teachers is not enough to affect change. Instead, if we had time and more resources, working with teachers over multiple days and in the classroom would be more effective. Observing student-teacher interactions would be invaluable.

We also learned how critical it is to have support from the leadership. In addition to teachers, school leaders were also present in our trainings. Engaging teachers, school leaders, and community members in dialogue was invaluable. Each participant brought a critical lens that fostered rich dialogue and helped unpack different nuances.

The pandemic conditions were challenging, but they also created an opportunity to consider creative solutions to enduring inequalities. On one hand, having a virtual space was freeing. We could log on in the comfort (or not) of our homes. We could catch a glimpse of our families. Students all received computers, Internet access, and other materials that could support their education. We felt intimate connections because we were in each other's homes. Yet it was a disconcerting experience because we know that the mortality rates of COVID in New Mexico (like in the rest of the country) disproportionately impacted Indigenous and other marginalized communities.[34] It was also challenging to create community and unity when speaking to blank screens. This was especially true when working with students, because only one or two had their cameras on. Even putting aside Internet connectivity issues that come with poor broadband access in rural communities, it was hard to get students to talk and engage when some may not have wanted others to see the privacy of their home life. We also recognize that we were presenting new material and approaching education differently by engaging in conversations that were challenging, uncomfortable, and difficult. We remain hopeful that these engagements did contribute to creating community and cultivating solidarity.

Imagining the Future

Twenty years from now how will we know that we have been successful? What would be different for success to be measurable? It may be worth imagining what a day in the life of a CISD student could be in our transformational future. At the state level, ethnic studies and intersectionality would be a core requirement for all credentialed teachers. At the same time, all graduating high school seniors would be required to take a year-long ethnic studies course. Paid summer opportunities for students to intern in the career of their choice would be a matter of course. Finally, parents, grandparents, and families would feel at home in the school and be instrumental partners. From students to families to staff to teachers to administrators, all members of the community would practice flexible solidarity. Educators engaging in critical reflection on their own positionalities in grids of power, as well as shifting and creating bridges of empathy, would build unity with Indigenous families and their worldviews.

In this future the dreams of the *Yazzie/Martinez* ruling have come to fruition. Instead of overwhelming resistance there is now endless support. The State of New Mexico has upheld its own laws and created structures of accountability that advance equity, and when there is a failure of compliance it is quickly resolved. The NMIEA is the governing policy that ensures Native youth are fully supported and language loss is no longer an issue. The collective fearless voices that fought for so long are no longer silenced; our ancestors' and elders' dreams of what it means to be fully engaged in Indigenous education is fulfilled. The harm that institutions inflicted on Native children, families, and communities has transitioned into hope, healing, and wellness.

Conclusion

Together with CISD our group has continued to move toward realizing the power of solidarity for social justice and Indigenous education and enacting system-level transformations despite the continuing obstacles. We believe in the power of transforming the relationships of families from community to community through their relationship to the lands, the honesty of our stories, the experiences and dreams of our ancestors, and a commitment to change the structures of the institution from within to advance equity and justice.

As we shared earlier, our objective in this partnership has been to promote community-based schooling, confront deficit notions by building a community cultural wealth consciousness, center ethnic studies, and identify equity and equality. We understood from the beginning that transformational change occurs on many levels and true investment in change takes strong leadership from many actors. Our hope is that we have assisted in the motion for this change already set forth by the Cuba Independent School District and the families of its rich communities. In conclusion, we seek to connect the spirit of our work to the final ruling in the case of *Yazzie/Martinez v. State of New Mexico*.

In summarizing Judge Singleton's ruling in favor of the *Yazzie/Martinez* plaintiffs, the NM Center on Law and Poverty noted four key points. The first point is: "The state has failed to comply with state and federal laws regarding the education of Native American and ELL students, including the NMIEA, Bilingual Multicultural Education Act, and the Hispanic Education Act, which has resulted in an inadequate education system for New Mexican students.[35]" The first purpose of the Indian Education Act amended in 2005 was to "ensure equitable and culturally relevant learning environments, educational opportunities and culturally relevant instructional materials for American Indian students enrolled in public schools."[36] In the virtual learning modules we created and in the Zoom sessions we had with the students, we shared lessons that were grounded in social justice and reflected the histories of the students. Furthermore, we facilitated activities that recognized and honored students' family backgrounds, no matter what communities they represented. In our work with the school faculty and staff, our lessons and activities again were centered on social justice as well as each of their respective backgrounds. We did this to model what culturally engaged pedagogy looked like in practice. We facilitated workshop-style activities that had educators connect their lessons to the communities of the students.

The second point is: "In violation of the state constitution, the state has failed to provide students with the programs and services that it acknowledges prepare them for college and career. Such programs and services include: quality pre-K, K-3 Plus, extended learning, dual language, culturally and linguistically relevant education, social services, small class sizes, and sufficient funding for teacher recruitment, retention, and training."[37] All educators and families deserve support that results in college and career readiness for their children. Through creating a partnership-oriented model for working toward district-specific initiatives, we have demonstrated that state investment in the Indigenous Education Grant provided quality and thoughtful programming through public education, from the elementary level to higher education. This was not a research initiative but a community-engaged partnership. This chapter serves as the first academic manuscript to document our efforts. Furthermore, we are composing two additional documents that will be written (1) for school leadership and educators and (2) for the families of the communities. We hope to contribute to the understanding that policies intended to serve those who have been historically marginalized must be backed by support for each and every school district in a sustainable way that provides time and space to build relationships.

The third point in Judge Singleton's ruling is: "Lack of funds is not an excuse for denying New Mexico's students a sufficient education. The state must come up with the necessary funding to meet New Mexico students' right to a sufficient education."[38] We continue to highlight the resilience of

Native families despite the histories of oppression and the ongoing denial of educational rights reserved in federal treaties and state policies. The onslaught of the pandemic deepened the issues of access to technology, healthcare, food, safe work, a healthy economy, and education. Although families continued to persevere, many lives were lost and ways of being were once again destroyed by inequalities. The state cannot afford to continue to fail in its regard for its own laws at the cost of Indigenous well-being. Our workshops, lessons, presentations, activities, and discussions will always be grounded in anti-racism, decolonization, and social justice. Key to this work is reminding our participants that they are all deserving of funding to meet their rights to a sufficient education. We do this through critical education and promoting solidarity.

Finally, the fourth summarizing point of the ruling read that the New Mexico Public Education Department (NMPED) "has failed to meet its oversight functions to ensure that all students are receiving the programs and services they need."[39] As BIPOC scholars, community members, teachers, family members, friends, and partners, we have been honored to have the trust of CISD leadership in developing programming funded in part by NMPED to begin to remedy its failure. In particular, we have been able to align our core values as educators and the focus areas of our scholarship to the NMIEA, amended in 2005 as discussed in the first point. While our connections were limited by time, space, and availability in the context of a constantly shifting global pandemic, we experienced the heart of the educators and students who shared their truths with us. We hope that by celebrating their identities and connecting them to their cultural wealth they can do the same for themselves and for each other. This is what every student in New Mexico should experience at every level, every day, and in every space of learning.

Student Learning Objectives

1. Students will be able to identify key characteristics that help cultivate school-university partnerships.
2. Students will be able to demonstrate Indigenous education and anti-

racist practices through centering students' lived experiences and cultural identities and building solidarity.

Discussion Questions

1. What elements of this partnership and/or this work provide support to families who want to engage in New Mexico's political and economic life?
2. How does centering Indigenous education and anti-racist practices promote students' cultural identities, solidarity, and challenge dominant narratives?

Notes

1. The epigraphs for this chapter come from "The Platform for Transformation—Transform Education NM," Transform Education NM, accessed January 25, 2022, https://transformeducationnm.org/our-platform/ and M. M. de Royston, C. Lee, N. I. S. Nasir, and R. Pea, "Rethinking Schools, Rethinking Learning," *Phi Delta Kappan* 102, no. 3 (2020): 8.

2. We utilize Hawaiian concepts to promote the idea of universal concepts found in Indigenous education, like connection to the land, the responsibility to promote culture and sovereignty, and connections with each other. See R. J. Ka'anehe, "Ke a 'o Mālamalama: Recognizing and Bridging Worlds with Hawaiian Pedagogies," *Equity and Excellence in Education* 53, nos. 1–2 (2020): 73–88.

3. New Mexico Center on Law and Poverty, "Education Lawsuit against State of New Mexico Seeks Justice for New Mexico's School Children," New Mexico Center on Law and Poverty, January 7, 2022, https://transformeducationnm.org/wp-content/uploads/2019/01/Flyer-Overview-of-NMCLPs-education-lawsuit-2017-08-05.docx.pdf.

4. *Yazzie/Martinez v. State of New Mexico* (2018), Plaintiffs Closing Brief.

5. New Mexico Center on Law and Poverty, "Yazzie/Martinez v. State of New Mexico Decision," New Mexico Center on Law and Poverty, January 7, 2022, http://nmpovertylaw.org/wp-content/uploads/2018/09/Graphic-Yazzie-Martinez-Decision.pdf.

6. *Yazzie/Martinez v. State of New Mexico*, 2018, *Id.* at 57:14–58:9.

7. Ka'anehe, "Ke a 'o Mālamalama."

8. V. Werito and L. Belone, "Research from a Diné-Centered Perspective and the Development of a Community Based Participatory Research Partnership," *Health Education and Behavior* 48, no. 3 (2021): 361–70; Ka'anehe, "Ke a 'o Mālamalama."

9.   G. Cajete, *Look to the Mountain: An Ecology of Indigenous Education* (Durango, CO: Kivaki Press, 1994).

10.   Tara J. Yosso, "Whose Culture Has Capital? A Critical Race Theory Discussion of Community Cultural Wealth," *Race Ethnicity and Education* 8, no. 1 (2005): 69–91.

11.   T. McCarty, and T. S. Lee, "Critical Culturally Sustaining/Revitalizing Pedagogy and Indigenous Educational Sovereignty," *Harvard Education Review* 84, no. 1 (2014): 101–24.

12.   McCarty and Lee, "Critical Culturally Sustaining/Revitalizing Pedagogy."

13.   Luis C. Moll et al., "Funds of Knowledge for Teaching: Using a Qualitative Approach to Connect Homes and Classrooms," *Theory into Practice* 31, no. 2 (1992): 132–41.

14.   Richard R. Valencia, ed., *The Evolution of Deficit Thinking: Educational Thought and Practice* (Abingdon, UK: Routledge, 2012), 2.

15.   Angela Valenzuela, *Subtractive Schooling: US-Mexican Youth and the Politics of Caring*, 2nd ed. (Albany: State of New York Press, 2010).

16.   Moll et al., "Funds of Knowledge."

17.   Yosso, "Whose Culture Has Capital?" 82.

18.   "The Platform for Transformation."

19.   G. Cajete, *Look to the Mountain*; V. Werito, "Education Is Our Horse: On the Path to Critical Consciousness in Teaching and Learning," in *Going Inward: The Role of Cultural Introspection in College Teaching*, ed. S. D. Longerbeam and A. F. Chavez (New York: Peter Lang, 2016), 66–73.

20.   Patricia H. Collins, *Intersectionality as Critical Theory* (Durham, NC: Duke University Press, 2019); N. Yuval-Davis, "What Is 'Transversal Politics?'" *Soundings* 12 (Summer 1999): 88–93; A. Hancock, *Solidarity Politics for Millennials: A Guide to Ending the Oppression Olympics* (New York: Springer, 2011).

21.   Collins, *Intersectionality as Critical Theory*, 245.

22.   P. H. Collins, *Black Feminist Thought* (New York: Routledge, 2009); Collins, *Intersectionality as Critical Theory*.

23.   Allyson Tintiangco-Cubales et al., "Toward an Ethnic Studies Pedagogy: Implications for K-12 Schools from the Research," *Urban Review* 47, no. 1 (2015): 104–25.

24.   Curtis Acosta, "Developing Critical Consciousness: Resistance Literature in a Chicano Literature Class," *English Journal* (2007): 36–42.

25.   Kathryn Blackmer Reyes and Julia E. Curry Rodríguez, "Testimonio: Origins, Terms, and Resources," *Equity and Excellence in Education* 45, no. 3 (2012): 525–38.

26.   Bernal Delgado, Dolores, R. Buriaga, and J. Flores Carmona, "Chicana/Latina Testimonios: Mapping the Methodological, Pedagogical, and Political," *Equity and Excellence in Education* 45, no. 3 (2011): 363–72.

27.   D. L. Brunsma and J. Padilla Wyse, "The Possessive Investment in White Sociology," *Sociology of Race and Ethnicity* 5, no. 1 (2019): 1–10; D. Paris and H. S. Alim, "What Are We Seeking to Sustain through Culturally Sustaining Pedagogy? A Loving Critique Forward," *Harvard Educational Review* 84, no. 1 (2014): 85–100.

28.   Delgado, Buriaga, and Flores Carmona, "Chicana/Latina Testimonios," 367.

29.   Luis Valdez, *Pensamiento Serpentino: A Chicano Approach to the Theater of Reality* (n.p.: Cucaracha Publications, 1973).

30.   Reyes and Curry Rodríguez, "Testimonio: Origins, Terms, and Resources."

31.   Paris and Alim, "What Are We Seeking to Sustain"; Delgado, Buriaga, and Flores Carmona, "Chicana/Latina Testimonios"; Collins, *Intersectionality as Critical Theory.*

32.   Engage for Equity, "Creating a River of Life: Ethnic Studies, Education, and Health Partnership, University of New Mexico and Albuquerque Public Schools, Partnership River of Life Examples," YouTube video, 2017, https://www.youtube.com/watch?v=-K_saoYQdDo. For more River of Life examples visit: https://engageforequity.org/tool_kit/river-of-life/partnership-river-of-life-examples/.

33.   Reyes and Curry Rodríguez, "Testimonio: Origins, Terms, and Resources."

34.   J. M. Feldman and M. T. Bassett, "Variation in COVID-19 Mortality in the US by Race and Ethnicity and Educational Attainment," *JAMA Network Open* 4, no. 11 (2021): e2135967–e2135967.

35.   New Mexico Center on Law and Poverty, "Education Lawsuit against State of New Mexico."

36.   New Mexico Center on Law and Poverty, "Education Lawsuit against State of New Mexico."

37.   New Mexico Center on Law and Poverty, "Education Lawsuit against State of New Mexico."

38.   New Mexico Center on Law and Poverty, "Education Lawsuit against State of New Mexico.

39.   New Mexico Center on Law and Poverty, "Education Lawsuit against State of New Mexico."

Figure 19. 1973 local newspaper photo of Larry Casuse testifying in Santa Fe, New Mexico, against the appointment of Emmett Garcia as a University of New Mexico board regent. Larry's legacy is a reminder of the continued struggles in the fight to battle violence and racism in border town communities such as Gallup, New Mexico. Photo credit Special Collections/Center for Southwest Research.

Constructing Critically Conscious Race Policy for our State

The Case for a Re-racialization and Indigenizing of Our Education Policies

WENDY S. GREYEYES AND FORMER NAVAJO NATION
PRESIDENT JONATHAN NEZ

How much longer do our children have to fail for us to get this Right?
—NEW MEXICO STATE REPRESENTATIVE DERRICK LENTE,
D-SANDIA PUEBLO, LEGISLATIVE HEARING, JULY 2021

We've had a mindset shift at PED.
—RYAN STEWART, SECRETARY OF EDUCATION, NEW MEXICO PUBLIC
EDUCATION DEPARTMENT (NMPED), LEGISLATIVE HEARING, JULY 2021

AS A TRIBAL NATION it is impossible for us to fully lean upon the state for all the policy necessary to empower our students and our tribal communities.[1] State policy must remove itself as a hurdle to tribal nations' authority and right to create their own tools of governance, which would fulfill the government-to-government relationship within the State of New Mexico. When these policies are implemented the state must acknowledge and recognize that it will enforce and require its schools to fall in line. To fulfill the original intent of the dream of a government-to-government reality, the State of New Mexico must recognize that tribal nations and tribal leaders know what is best for their own people, communities, and children. To fulfill this hope the State of New Mexico must protect and defend calls for racial equality and Indigenized policies as part of the state's architecture. It is important to understand how state laws and policies continue to perpetuate a colonized and hierarchical structure implicitly built in the state's architecture. In this chapter we first discuss the current debate around the changing tides and shifts of conservative, non-Indigenous policies toward more liberal, Indigenous-focused policies. Conservative views have constrained the support of tribal sovereignty in favor of the sovereignty of the State of New Mexico. In contrast, liberal views continue to honor the sovereignty and rights of tribal nations. Next, we examine policies focused on Indigenous rights in New Mexico, then follow with state policies that support tribal decision-making, and finally provide an overview of existing tribal policies that promote a self-determination agenda.

The State of New Mexico's ideological split between conservative and liberal perspectives is best understood through the recent debates around critical race theory (CRT), which embodies understandings of tribal sovereignty. Teaching CRT would force the State of New Mexico to confront its settler-colonial history with Native Americans. Born in the mid-1970s, CRT evolved to address how laws create and maintain a discriminatory system that perpetuates the suppression of certain groups of people.[2] The importance of the evolution of this field stems from the understanding that racism is prevalent in our society and is so deeply entrenched into our values, outlooks, and institutions that it becomes invisible. Currently, many believe that a transition is occurring—a movement away from conservative approaches in national and state policies to articulating the support for and acceptance of Indigenous decision-making, with limitations. Hollie J. Mackey points out the historic tension found in federal Indian education laws and policies that have on the one hand "purposely and systematically worked to eradicate Native languages, religions, beliefs, and practices" and on the other "provide resources and infrastructure to support indigenous control and cultural self-determination."[3] This language of Indigenous responsiveness is captured in terms like "government-to-government" or "tribal consultation." Former US president Barack Obama articulated this relationship in his memorandum to the heads of executive departments and agencies on November 5, 2009, as follows: "Pursuant to Executive Order 13175 of November 6, 2000, executive departments and agencies (agencies) are charged with engaging in regular and meaningful consultation and collaboration with tribal officials in the development of Federal policies that have tribal implications, and are responsible for strengthening the government-to-government relationship between the United States and Indian tribes."[4] The meaning behind these terms must be met with caution and an awareness that there will never be true government-to-government relations, meaning that Pueblo governors and tribal presidents must find additional tools in their tribal nations to empower the laws to work in their favor. Still, it is important to understand the history and continuous project of creating meaningful tribal consultation with the states and federal government. The history of tribal consultation is reflected in table 3.

The question remains: What is the systematic payoff for the State of New

Table 3. Tribal Consultations and Policy Changes, State of New Mexico (2003–2021)

TRIBAL CONSULTATION YEAR	POLICY CHANGES
2003	Governor of the State of New Mexico and Indian Tribes of New Mexico adopted the 2003 Statement of Policy and Process to "establish and promote a relationship of cooperation, coordination, open communication and good will, and work in good faith to amicably and fairly resolve issues and differences."
2005	Governor Bill Richardson issues Executive Order 2005-004 mandating the executive agencies adopt pilot tribal consultation plans with the input of the twenty-two New Mexico tribes.
2009	Governor Bill Richardson signed SB 196, the State Tribal Collaboration Act (STCA) into law. The STCA reflects the statutory commitment of the state to work with tribes on a government-to-government basis. The STCA establishes in state statute the intergovernmental relationship through several interdependent components and provides a consistent approach through which the state and tribes can work to better collaborate and communicate on issues of mutual concern.
2021	Three-three departments and offices are in operation throughout the State of New Mexico and each have approved tribal consultation policies and procedures in place, including the Public Education Department, Higher Education Department, and the Indian Affairs Department.*

* State of New Mexico, "33 Tribal Consultations Policies and Procedures," accessed May 1, 2021, https://www.iad.state.nm.us/tribal-collaboration/state-tribal-consultation-collaboration-and-communication-policies/.

Mexico? Government-to-government relations means recognizing that tribes and pueblos know best how to address the social and educational challenges in their own communities. The Harvard Project on American Indian Economic Development (2008) offers its own analysis, in which it states, "New models of cooperation and dispute resolution, bolstered by some states' explicit recognition of tribes as governments, are helping alleviate tensions without litigation. A number of states are beginning to acknowledge that supporting tribal sovereignty is advantageous since sustained economic development on Indian lands benefits all state residents."[5] The Harvard Project's analysis shows that while one end of the pendulum contains an element of high risk for the state—a loss through litigation—the other side of the coin comprises possible gain through economic development. But it is clear that in the relationship between the many departments of the New Mexico government and the twenty-three tribal nations and pueblos, the state has created structured and uniform policies and procedures to protect the interests of the state. Sadly, the State of New Mexico, with its diversity and unique heritage, continues to utilize colonial hegemonic tools to maintain the authority of the state.

We must voice our determination to fight for our freedom from oppressive bonds. Paulo Freire, a philosopher of critical pedagogy, argues that "the oppressed, having internalized the image of the oppressor and adopted his guidelines, are fearful of freedom. Freedom would require them to eject this image and replace it with autonomy and responsibility [. . .] freedom is acquired by conquest, not by gift."[6] It is incumbent upon us, the Indigenous citizens in this state, to raise the consciousness and awareness of the harmful impact of state educational laws and policies that continue to reinforce and embed racial hegemony into our system. We also must examine the entire structure of the educational hierarchy and recognize when decision-makers cherry-pick policies that work for them. The state must recognize the unique position of Indigenous peoples in New Mexico. Here, we utilize a framework developed by Bryan Brayboy, with additional consideration for the work of Hollie Mackey, to examine the unique positionality of Indigenous policy. Brayboy points out the nine tenets of a tribal critical race theory, which, when enhanced by a tenth recommendation from Hollie Mackie, read as follows:

1. Colonization is endemic to society.

2. US policies toward Indigenous peoples are rooted in imperialism, white supremacy, and a desire for material gain.

3. Indigenous peoples occupy a liminal space that accounts for both the political and racialized natures of our identities.

4. Indigenous peoples have a desire to obtain and forge tribal sovereignty, tribal autonomy, self-determination, and self-identification.

5. The concepts of culture, knowledge, and power take on new meaning when examined through an Indigenous lens.

6. Governmental policies and educational policies toward Indigenous peoples are intimately linked to the problematic goal of assimilation.

7. Tribal philosophies, beliefs, customs, traditions, and visions for the future are central to understanding the lived realities of Indigenous peoples, but they also illustrate the differences and adaptability among individuals and groups.

8. Stories are not separate from theory; they make up theory and are, therefore, real and legitimate sources of data and ways of being.

9. Theory and practice are connected in deep and explicit ways, such that scholars must work toward social change.[7]

10. The focus should be on the effect of tribal self-determination rather than its policy goals.[8]

The nine points developed by Brayboy and the tenth by Mackey recognize the contributions an Indigenous tribal critical race theory may make to the unique terrain of the State of New Mexico's educational policies and realities. In what follows, we examine, in light of this book's findings, what race means in New Mexico and apply this model to our analysis.

Race in New Mexico

In New Mexico, race features as a central part of the community: 49.3 percent of the population is Hispanic and Latino, while 8.7 is American Indian and Alaska Native (as depicted in table 4).

Table 4. 2019 American Community Survey Demographic and Housing Estimates, Table DP05: New Mexico

Race	Percent
Hispanic or Latino	49.3
White	36.8
Black or African American	1.9
American Indian and Alaska Native	8.7
Asian	1.6
Two or more races	1.6

The data shows New Mexico is a majority-minority state, meaning minority groups are more numerous than the white population. NMPED reports that there are approximately thirty-five thousand American Indians students in public schools and that 5 percent of statewide district staff identifies as American Indian. In addition to the public school population, approximately six thousand American Indian students attend one of the twenty-eight Bureau of Indian Education–operated and tribally controlled schools.[9] However, the data points from the National Center for Education Statistics (NCES) show different numbers, described in figure 20.

It is important to also contextualize how New Mexico stacks up in comparison to the other forty-nine states. New Mexico's educational terrain has one of the highest numbers of American Indian students in the United States as well as all-Indian schools (BIE-funded schools). In 2019 the National Congress of American Indians conducted a cross-comparison of twenty-eight states, including New Mexico. In their *Becoming Visible* report they state that only nine states allocate funding to implement Native American education curricula. New Mexico was one of eight top states in this regard, allocating beyond the amount of one hundred thousand dollars.[10] The report discusses the number of staff needed to fulfill the state's educational objectives related to Native students. New Mexico ranked third after Hawaii (sixteen full-time employees [FTE]) and Montana (eight FTE), with seven FTE dedicated to implementing Native American education.[11] Third, the study examined states that required schools to include Native American education standards and

Figure 20. American Indian or Alaska Native (2020–2021), "State Nonfiscal Public Elementary/Secondary Education Survey Data, Preliminary" (released on June 28, 2021). Source: Dataset, American Indian or Alaska Native, (2020-2021), State Nonfiscal Public Elementary/Secondary Education Survey Data, Preliminary (released on June 28th, 2021). Accessed September 14, 2021. https://nces.ed.gov/ccd/files.asp#FileNameId:15, VersionId:27,FileSchoolYearI d:35,Page:1

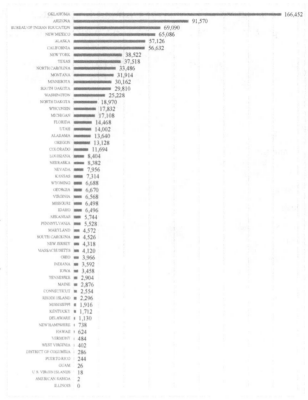

curricula. New Mexico was among the eleven states committed to ensuring these were required by schools.[12] Finally, the report assessed tribal engagement with the state, finding that a high level of tribal engagement reflects a state's strong political will to work with tribes, as opposed to low engagement, which reflects low state interest.

The study situates states in a comparative analysis to show their commitment to Native American education and brings to light the minimal contributions being offered by all states combined. The report's title, *Becoming Visible*, captures with empirical evidence the lack of visibility around Native American education. The dominant narrative reveals that the value of Native American education across the country is minuscule. Although this type of comparison shows that New Mexico ranks in the top tier compared to other states,

Table 5. Extent of Tribal Government Engagement in Advocacy and Support for Native Education and Curriculum by State Respondents*

STATE	A HIGH AMOUNT	A MODERATE AMOUNT	A SMALL AMOUNT	NOT AT ALL	I DON'T KNOW
Arizona			x		
California					x
Colorado	x				
Connecticut			x		
Florida					x
Hawaii	x				
Idaho	x				
Illinois (Chicago only)				x	
Indiana			x		
Kansas					x
Louisiana			x		
Maine		x			
Massachusetts					x
Minnesota		x			
Mississippi					x
Montana		x			
Nebraska		x			
Nevada		x			
New Mexico		x			
New York			x		
North Dakota	x				
Oklahoma		x			
Oregon		x			
Utah				x	
Virginia		x			
Washington		x			
Wisconsin					x
Wyoming	x				

* Source: National Congress of American Indians, *Becoming Visible: A Landscape Analysis of State Efforts to Provide Native American Education for All*, Washington, DC, September 2019, https://www.ncai.org/policy-research-center/research-data/prc-publications/NCAI-Becoming_Visible_Report-Digital_FINAL_10_2019.pdf.

it disguises the continued systematic neglect of Native American children. As this book closes out the discussion around the *Yazzie/Martinez* consolidated lawsuit, it is imperative we urge awareness and caution regarding how states are imagined to be pivotal educational decision-makers, such that even if they inform tribal leaders that they don't have all the answers, they are unwilling to relinquish their authority or power to tribal nations. This is the next step post-NCLB and post-tribal consultation: the need for states to give up the authority, power, and funding to allow tribal nations to become the primary decision-makers instead of hosting tribal consultations where tribal leadership dictates to state education agencies what must be done. This practice has had the unintended consequence of creating larger and more powerful state agencies that continue to build the behemoth of the bureaucracy.

In this next section we dig deeper to examine specifically the New Mexico Indian Education Act (NMIEA) as a potential tool to build a true government-to-government responsiveness.

A Tribal Capacity-Building Indian Education Act

There must be a deep analysis of existing laws that continue to perpetuate a guardianship mindset. In this case, we must examine the NMIEA,[13] passed in 2003, which recognizes the unique relationship between the State of New Mexico and American Indians and Alaska Natives. The law itself must be understood in its value in shaping government-to-government projects. The following analysis deconstructs and shows that the law is not constructed around the true meaning of self-determination, which derives its strength from "doing it for ourselves." Instead, we see a slate of expectations required of NMPED built on enhancing the state's bureaucratic advantage over tribes. Here we utilize table 6 to examine the main tenets of the law.

The NMIEA is a powerful set of laws that supports New Mexico Native American tribes and pueblos. At times it exceeds the powers granted to Native American tribes of other states throughout the United States. But for tribal nations to have their say and exert their own self-determination it is imperative the language of capacity building be included and clarified with the following:

Table 6. New Mexico Indian Education Act*

IEA STATES	STATE CONTROLLED	TRIBAL SELF-DETERMINATION
A. **Ensure** equitable and culturally relevant learning environments, educational opportunities and culturally relevant instructional materials for American Indian students enrolled in public schools.	NMPED and local education agencies retain oversight and implementation by hiring staff, receiving funding, providing grants, and making primary decisions on the shape and form of "culturally relevant."	Nonexistent. Tribes are only brought to the table to review or comment on completed projects; if tribes are provided opportunities at all, these come in the form short-term grants. There is no longevity or commitment from the state to support true sustainable outcomes for tribal self-determination. The sense of doing it for ourselves so that tribes become expert-primary drivers is lost.
B. **Ensure** maintenance of native languages.	NMPED offers grants (STL) that operate on a short-term basis. They control the duration, length, and program design of language programs.	Tribal nations need long-term and continuous funding to build their internal infrastructure to promote their languages.
C. **Provide** for the study, development, and implementation of educational systems that positively affect the educational success of American Indian students.	Research and studies of Indigenous communities have never been from the view of tribes or pueblos. Also, tools of analysis are moving toward indices, which are collections of variables that truncate the experiences and complexity of Indigenous peoples' views into categories. Indices give clean numerical support and are a disadvantage to tribes.	It is important to reiterate that tribal philosophies, beliefs, customs, traditions, and visions for the future are central to understanding the lived realities of Indigenous peoples, but they also illustrate the differences and adaptability among individuals and groups;[†] stories are not separate from theory; they make up theory and are, therefore, real and legitimate sources of data and ways of being;[‡] inclusion of Institutions of Higher Education;[§] research should be conducted by the tribal members themselves.[‖]
D. **Ensure** that the department of education [public education department] partners with tribes to increase tribal involvement and control over schools and the education of students located in tribal communities.	The department becomes the intermediary between the schools and the tribal education departments. These create frustrating situations for both entities that continues as elected school board members argue they are the decision makers for their schools.	Tribes must build their capacity to begin transferring the power and authority from the department to ensure school control and oversight. This may include building the tribal educational codes to include language regarding the transfer of state rights over education to help build the capacity and strengthen the arm of tribal nation governance.
E. **Encourage** cooperation among the educational leadership of Arizona, Utah, New Mexico, and the Navajo Nation to address the unique issues of educating students in Navajo communities that arise due to the location of the Navajo Nation in those states	States become the main policy decision makers in this relationship, with tribes continuing to operate as reviewers at the tail end. It is also clear from the NCAI study, *Becoming Visible*, that states have differing commitments and priorities for Native American education.	Tribes must be the main drivers in this relationship. In the past, the Navajo Nation has called for the status of a state education agency. They have proposed this to Congress in past testimony but it is clear that congressional representatives from these states struggle to relinquish the funding, authority, and power to the tribe.

F. **Provide the means** for a formal government-to-government relationship between the state and New Mexico tribes and the development of relationships with the education division of the Bureau of Indian Affairs and other entities that serve American Indian students.

Government-to-government requires a clearer statement that includes the idea that decisions made by leaders will be followed by executive orders.

Each tribe and pueblo operates its own unique governing system. The government-to-government meetings must consider the need to meet with tribes and pueblos individually.

G. **Provide the means** for a relationship between the state and urban American Indian community members to participate in initiatives and educational decisions related to American Indian students residing in urban areas.

The urban Native community is a larger constituency. This is one component in which there isn't strong engagement from the department.

Tribes do not acknowledge the reality of the larger urban constituency. According to a recent American Community Survey report, nearly 70 percent of self-reported American Indians or Alaska Natives live off Indian territories. Students attending public schools off reservations are subjected to discriminatory practices as reflected in the *Yazzie/Martinez* lawsuit.

H. **Ensure** that parents, tribal departments of education, community-based organizations, the department of education [public education department], universities, and tribal, state, and local policymakers work together to find ways to improve educational opportunities for American Indian students.

Many of these groups are not included in the government-to-government sessions, which hinders a holistic conversation about American Indian students.

Tribal self-determination efforts are constrained as many of these players are not included in the dialogue.

I. **Ensure** that tribes are notified of all curricula development for their approval and support.

This is where it gets problematic because tribes or their expert staff should be part of the development of curricula.

Tribes must gather teams of Native educators to help develop these curricula.

J. **Encourage** an agreement regarding the alignment of the Bureau of Indian Affairs and state assessment programs so that comparable information is provided to parents and tribes.

The department continues to operate as the intermediary between these relationships.

Tribes must begin building their own internal assessment teams to evaluate student learning and progress using their own Indigenous tools and methods.

K. **Encourage** and foster parental involvement in the education of Indian students.

The department continues to limit the inclusion of a parent advocate or individuals in groups.

Tribes must include parents in these proceedings as well.

---

* New Mexico Indian Education Act, accessed September 10, 2021, https://webnew.ped.state.nm.us/bureaus/indian-education/ie-act-rules/.

† Bryan McKinley Jones, "Toward a Critical Race Theory in Education," *Urban Review* 37, no. 5 (December 2005): 428.

‡ Brayboy, "Toward a Tribal Critical Race Theory," 428.

§ Robin Zape-tah-hol-ah Minthorn, Lorenda Belone, Glenabah Martinez, and Christine Sims, "Indigenous Research Perspectives in the State of New Mexico: Implications for Working with Schools and Communities," Journal of American Indian Education 58, nos. 1 and 2 (Spring–Summer 2019): 113.

‖ Christine P. Sims, "Langauge Planning inAmerican Indian Pueblo Communities: Contemporary Challenges and Issues," *Current Issues in Language Planning* 7 (2006): 251–68.

- *Transfer of authority and power to tribal nations.* Tribes must consider building their internal infrastructure and codes to match the expectations to control schools. This is not a journey taken lightly because there is a need to unify existing curricula, assessments, and instructional practices to manage these responsibilities. States will need to be willing to give up their state education agency authorities to tribal nations, which requires an act of the state and Congress.
- *Transfer of knowledge and experience to tribal nations.* Tribes need time to build their governance and oversight of these schools. This requires human expertise and knowledge. There is also a need to give tribes the time to hone and refine the craft of governance. Therefore, states must be willing to provide this knowledge and experience.
- *Transfer of resources and funding to tribal nations.* This will be a difficult move for states as there is always a shortfall of funding for schools, school districts, and state education agencies. The Central Consolidated School District, which encompasses over five thousand students with a majority American Indian or Alaska Native, receives $74,720,942. This includes the total expenditure of federal, state, and local funds.[14]
- *Recognition of tribal and pueblo educational codes.* Tribal nations and pueblos have their own sovereign governing bodies. They create and offer their own tribal educational codes that are relevant for public schools and BIE-funded schools. There is also a tremendous amount of funding coming from the federal level through the US Department of the Interior and the US Department of Education to support administrative capacity building, including the development and implementation of tribal educational codes. These are reflected in the State Tribal Education Partnership (STEP) grant and Tribal Education Department (TED) grant encoded within federal law.

Overall, the NMIEA is one small step toward supporting the self-determination of tribal nations. The next step is to strengthen the capacity of the latter to take on the full capacity of operating their own state education agency responsibilities. At the same time, it is important to understand what is occurring at the tribal level that supports this desire and interest. Here, we examine tribal codes from the Navajo Nation as a case study.

Tribal Education Action

Tribal codes are part of the architecture of tribal governance. These are rules and laws codified into statutes for tribal nations. The Native American Rights Fund (NARF) has developed a guidebook to support tribes, titled *Tribalizing Education: Tribal Governance in Education*.[15] In fact, tribes and pueblos are legally empowered to strengthen their partnership with schools and state education agencies. The Navajo Nation government has made the effort to strengthen their Title X language around education. Here are some cases in which the Navajo Nation has worked to build its oversight and control of schools:

- *Strengthening tribal oversight of education.* During the period of the No Child Left Behind Act of 2001, the Navajo Nation moved to transform its existing tribal code to take control and clarify the oversight of schools. It also established a decision-making body, the Navajo Nation Board of Education. It reorganized three school board associations into one body and scaled up the position of the executive director to that of a superintendent of schools for Navajo schools. The tribe's Title X changes went through several years of extensive public hearings.
- *Strengthen tribal authority over school boards.* In 2022 the Navajo Nation government reapportioned BIE-funded school boards from seventy-eight boards into sixteen boards, which gives the Navajo Nation government the ability to strengthen tribal authority over school initiatives. From this point on the Navajo Nation will organize and structure school boards and the mechanisms that run them. In the past there were seventy-eight school boards going in different directions, and efforts are being undertaken to create a more unified system. Reducing the number of school boards means they can be held accountable, especially when it comes to improving academic and student achievement. This follows similar actions by the Hopi Tribe, which removed school boards. Another example is the Mississippi Choctaw, who replaced their school board with the tribal council. The smaller the board, the more accountability is strengthened.
- *Strengthen tribal executive powers over public schools.* The response

to COVID-19 is a great example of how school boards resist tribal sovereignty. Arizona schools are more willing to work with the Navajo Nation compared to New Mexico, which has been less responsive. In New Mexico the state public schools continue to move in their own direction and ignore the Navajo Nation's authority and health orders, keeping the schools open in defiance of the Nation's directives.

◆ *Strengthen accountability measures over all schools through tribal consultation.* Tribal consultation guides should be developed and should include Title I funding and more as part of the consultation process. Federal legislative changes must be made and the NMIEA must be amended so that schools develop a needs assessment and accountability tool. Schools must provide this information as part of the school districts' budget review process.

◆ *Manage assessments that dictate learning.* The Navajo Nation created the Diné School Accountability Plan, which provides directions on how to assess Navajo student learning. This effort to assess, evaluate, and control the metrics underlying student learning is a must have for tribal nations as they continue to use colonial metrics of growth and learning. These should be determined by the tribal nation and not the states.

These are just a few examples of how the NMIEA can support tribal nations. Currently, the Navajo Nation is restricted to oversight of tribally controlled schools, which are BIE-funded. If the state permitted the transfer of authority to tribes, this would send a powerful message and signal a historical shift in the government-to-government relationship.

Conclusion

Overall, we must begin building and constructing critically conscious race policy for our state. The case for Indigenizing our education policies is clear. As the *Yazzie/Martinez* lawsuit has proven, the state considers our children a mere variable in a stream of quantitative interpretations of success. The language of critical consciousness must transform the use of the NMIEA

Table 7. Soft Action Compared to Direct Action Terms*

Soft Action Terms (Used by the Indian Education Act)	Direct Action
Engage	Build tribal capacity to make decisions
Provide	Give tribes the means resources to enact decisions
Ensure	Transfer authority to tribes to empower their decision making
Encourage	Uphold tribal decision making

* New Mexico Indian Education Act, accessed September 10, 2021, https://webnew.ped.state.nm.us/bureaus/indian-education/ie-act-rules/.

terminology from soft action to direct action. A model of action is illustrated in table 7.

This table shows how terminology and vocabulary can limit and constrain state behavior toward tribal responsiveness, betraying the larger goal of government-to-government relations. The state's self-interest is protecting its own longevity, a phenomenon long documented in organizational analysis research. The state itself operates like an organization with goals, processes, hierarchies, and rules to guide its decision-making and outcomes. In this case, the state does operate like an organism (organization) that strives for its only survivability. The state is a vexed institution that holds both our freedoms and unfreedoms. Therefore, it is imperative for us as scholars, activists, and community members to consider what it means to take the power back. We have observed over the decades that as we continually demand the state be held accountable, the state's response has been to become bigger, more expansive, and more intrusive into our educational decision-making.

It is important we consider what the type of discourse presented in table 7 means in terms of the survivability of our tribal communities. The threat is not as clear as it would be if the military were enacting violence on a community. Instead, the tactics of invisibility and coded language disguise the continued project of colonization. It is important we pay close attention to the meaning of these concepts and reject the passiveness of soft action and, instead, think about big action that is directed at true self-determination projects that build tribal nations up to a level of equivalence of authority and power. Words mean everything, and in a world where attorneys and courts are stepping in to protect the future of our education and the opportunities for our children, we must pay particular attention to the subtleness of language, which is the pathway to building a mightier nation. The logic of the state is to protect and defend its own interests. We must continue to demand more from the state in order to produce a future invested in our own lifeways.

Notes

1. The epigraphs for this chapter both cite the Albuquerque Journal editorial board, "Editorial: How Is Failure an Option," *Albuquerque Journal*, August 1, 2021, https://www.abqjournal.com/2415284/how-is-failure-an-option.html.

2. Bryan McKinley Jones Brayboy, "Toward a Tribal Critical Race Theory in Education," *Urban Review* 37, no. 5 (December 2005): 425–46.

3. Hollie J. Mackey, "The ESSA in Indian Country: Problematizing Self-Determination through the Relationships between Federal, State, and Tribal Governments," *Educational Administration Quarterly* 53, no. 5 (2017): 782–808.

4. President Barack H. Obama, "Memorandum on Tribal Consultation," the White House, November 5, 2009.

5. The Harvard Project on American Indian Economic Development, *The State of Native Nations: Conditions under U.S. Policies of Self-Determination* (Oxford: Oxford University Press, 2008).

6. Paulo Friere, *Pedagogy of the Oppressed* (New York: Continuum, 1998), 29.

7. Brayboy, "Toward a Tribal Critical Race Theory," 430.

8. Mackey, "The ESSA in Indian Country," 784.

9. New Mexico Public Education Department, *2019–2020 Tribal Education Status Report (TESR)*, November 2020, https://webnew.ped.state.nm.us/wp-content/uploads/2021/01/TESR2020.pdf.

10. *Becoming Visible: A Landscape Analysis of State Efforts to Provide Native American Education for All*, National Congress of American Indians, Washington, DC, September 2019, 17.

11. *Becoming Visible*, 18.

12. *Becoming Visible*, 20.

13. See the New Mexico Indian Education Act at https://webnew.ped.state.nm.us/wp-content/uploads/2019/03/NM-Indian-Education-Act.pdf.

14.   New Mexico Public Education Department, "Finance—Total Expenditure, Central Consolidated Schools, Shiprock, New Mexico," accessed September 10, 2021, https://newmexicoschools.com/districts/67/finance.

15.   Melody McCoy, "Tribalizing Education: Tribal Governance in Education," Native American Rights Fund, October 1994, http://www.narf.org/wordpress/wp-content/uploads/2015/01/red.pdf.

Figure 21. Xavier Yazzie graduating from high school, May 6, 2021, Gallup, New Mexico. Photo credit Hondo Louis. Funded by UNM's Center for Regional Studies and Native American Studies Department.

Appendix A

Teaching Recommendations for This Book

State and Tribal Educational Policy Resources

Fletcher, Matthew L. M. *American Indian Education: Counternarratives in Racism, Struggle, and the Law*. New York: Routledge, 2008.

McCoy, Melody L., Staff Attorney. *Tribalizing Indian Education: Compilation of State Indian Education Laws*. October. Boulder, CO: Native American Rights Fund, 2005.

Eagle Shield, Alayna, Django Paris, Rae Paris, and Timothy San Pedro, eds. *Education in Movement Spaces: Standing Rock to Chicago Freedom Square*. New York: Routledge, 2020.

Curriculum and Standards Development Resources

Martinez, Glenabah. *Native Pride: The Politics of Curriculum and Instruction in an Urban Public School*. Cresskill, NJ: Hampton Press, 2010.

Dalton, Stephanie S., and Daniel G. Youpa. "Standards-Based Teaching Reform in Zuni Pueblo Middle and High Schools." *Equity and Excellence in Education* 31, no. 1 (April 1998): 55–68.

Culturally Relevant Teaching Resources

Sims, Christine. "Language Planning in American Indian Pueblo Communities: Contemporary Challenges and Issues." *Current Issues in Language Planning* 7, nos. 2 and 3 (2006): 251–58.

McCarty, Teresa L., and Tiffany S. Lee. "Critical Culturally Sustaining/Revitalizing Pedagogy and Indigenous Education Sovereignty." *Harvard Educational Review* 84, no. 1 (Spring 2014): 101–24.

Lee, Tiffany S. "The Significance of Self-Determination in Socially, Culturally, and

Linguistically Responsive (SCLR) Education in Indigenous Contexts." *Journal of American Indian Education* 54, no. 1 (Spring 2015): 10–32.

Paris, Django, and H. Samy Alim. "What Is Culturally Sustaining Pedagogy and Why Does It Matter?" In Django and Alim, eds., *Culturally Sustaining Pedagogies: Teaching and Learning for Justice in a Changing World*, 1–17. New York: Teachers College Press, 2017.

Critical and Decolonization Educational Theory Resources

Sabzalian, Leilani. *Indigenous Children's Survivance in Public Schools*. New York: Routledge, 2019.

Grande, Sande. *Red Pedagogy: Native American Social and Political Thought*. Lanham, MD: Rowman and Littlefield, 2015.

Villegas, Malia, and Sabina Rak Neugebauer, eds. *Indigenous Knowledge and Education: Sites of Struggle, Strength and Survivance*. Cambridge, UK: Harvard Education, 2008.

Tuhiwai Smith, Linda, Eve Tuck, and K. Wayne Lang, eds. *Indigenous and Decolonizing Studies in Education: Mapping the Long View*. New York: Routledge, 2019.

Battiste, Marie. *Decolonizing Education: Nourishing the Learning Spirit*. Saskatoon, SK: Purich Publishing, 2013.

Martinez, David G., Oscar Jiménez-Castellanos, and Victor H. Begay. "Understanding Navajo K-12 Public School Finance in Arizona through Tribal Critical Theory." *Teachers College Record* 121, no. 5 (May 2019): 1–34.

Appendix B

Yazzie/Martinez v. State of New Mexico Lawsuit Timeline

March 19, 2014
New Mexico Center for Law and Poverty files a lawsuit in the 11th Judicial District Court, Gallup McKinley County. The suit, filed on behalf of families, seeks to increase funding for public education, especially for at-risk students, including Native Americans and Latinos. The case is known as *Yazzie v. State of New Mexico.*[1]

July 20, 2018
The First Judicial Court rules that the State of New Mexico violated students' fundamental rights by failing to provide a sufficient public education, as required under the state constitution. Judge Sarah Singleton rules that all New Mexico students have a right to be college and career ready and that the state is failing to meet this obligation, enjoining the state to take immediate steps to create an educational system that ensures New Mexico's at-risk student will have the opportunity to prepare for their future.[2]

December 20, 2018
Judge Singleton files the Court's Findings of Fact and Conclusions of Law and Order regarding final judgement. Principle in its findings is that the educational inputs are inadequate and that at-risk students can benefit from adequately funded programs.[3]

February 14, 2019
The court files its final judgement in favor of the plaintiffs. There are no appeals.[4]

March/April 2019
The New Mexico legislature passes a landmark budget that increases public
education spending by $446 million to $3.2 billion.[5]

October 22, 2019
New Mexico Public Education Department (NMPED) releases a memo outlin-
ing the four-part strategy to fulfill the court's decision and order.[6]

October 30, 2019
The court allows the Mexican American Legal Defense and Educational Fund
as Martinez's attorneys to take discovery and learn what steps the state has
taken to comply with the injunction. The filing also requests the court set a
schedule for further proceedings to enforce the injunction.[7]

November 22, 2019
NMPED releases a memo to superintendents and charter school leaders out-
lining requirements for equity councils. The memo includes guidance on the
formation of equity councils.[8]

December 18, 2019
The court schedules a hearing for March 27, 2020, at the Martinez attorneys'
request to take additional discovery and schedule proceedings for the enforcement of the injunction.[9]

February/March 2020
NMPED hosts equity council webinars to guide districts and charter schools
through the equity council formation process.[10]

March 2020
NMPED hosts the Equity Council Summit in Albuquerque, New Mexico.[11]

March 13, 2020
The state moves to dismiss the lawsuit, claiming the requirements of the
court's injunction have been satisfied.[12]

March 23, 2020
As a result of the COVID-19 public health emergency, the court postpones the hearing scheduled for March 27, 2020, until June 29, 2020.[13]

April 26, 2020
Attorneys for the Martinez plaintiffs file motion to strike the state's March 13, 2020, motion to dismiss on procedural grounds, claiming it is an untimely supplemental response to Martinez's plaintiff's motion for entry of schedule for discovery and enforcement proceedings.[14]

May 1, 2020
Attorneys for both the Yazzie and Martinez plaintiffs respond in opposition to the state's motion to dismiss the lawsuit, claiming the state has not yet satisfied the requirements of the court's injunction.[15]

May 11, 2020
The state responds to the Martinez plaintiff's motion to strike the state's motion to dismiss, noting procedural differences between that motion and the Martinez plaintiff's motion for discovery, noting that denying the plaintiff's motion would not have the same effect as granting the state's motion to dismiss.[16]

May 26, 2020
Attorneys for the Martinez plaintiffs reply to the state's response to Martinez plaintiff's motion to strike the state's motion to dismiss and request a hearing on their motion to strike.[17]

June 5, 2020
Attorneys for NMPED file the State's Replies to Plaintiff's Responses to the State's Motion to Dismiss.[18]

June 29, 2020
There is a hearing on the motions before the court.[19] The state's motion to dismiss is denied.

August 9, 2021
Release of the Draft Action Plan Response to Judge Singleton Decision: *Yazzie/Martinez v. State of New Mexico.*

Notes

1. "Martinez v. New Mexico Timeline," Mexican American Legal Defense and Education Fund, October 30, 2019, https://www.maldef.org/2019/10/martinez-v-new-mexico-timeline/.
2. "Martinez Yazzie Consolidated Lawsuit—Since the Time of the Court's Orders," New Mexico Public Education Department, June 2020, https://webnew.ped.state.nm.us/wp-content/uploads/2020/06/M-Y-timeline-since-the-Orders-June-2020.pdf.
3. "Martinez Yazzie Consolidated Lawsuit—Since the Time of the Court's Orders," 1.
4. "Martinez Yazzie Consolidated Lawsuit—Since the Time of the Court's Orders," 1.
5. "Martinez Yazzie Consolidated Lawsuit—Since the Time of the Court's Orders," 1.
6. "Martinez Yazzie Consolidated Lawsuit—Since the Time of the Court's Orders," 1.
7. "Martinez Yazzie Consolidated Lawsuit—Since the Time of the Court's Orders," 1.
8. "Martinez Yazzie Consolidated Lawsuit—Since the Time of the Court's Orders," 1.
9. "Martinez Yazzie Consolidated Lawsuit—Since the Time of the Court's Orders," 1.
10. "Martinez Yazzie Consolidated Lawsuit—Since the Time of the Court's Orders," 1.
11. "Martinez Yazzie Consolidated Lawsuit—Since the Time of the Court's Orders," 1.
12. "Martinez Yazzie Consolidated Lawsuit—Since the Time of the Court's Orders," 1.
13. "Martinez Yazzie Consolidated Lawsuit—Since the Time of the Court's Orders," 1.
14. "Martinez Yazzie Consolidated Lawsuit—Since the Time of the Court's Orders," 1.
15. "Martinez Yazzie Consolidated Lawsuit—Since the Time of the Court's Orders," 1.
16. "Martinez Yazzie Consolidated Lawsuit—Since the Time of the Court's Orders," 1.
17. "Martinez Yazzie Consolidated Lawsuit—Since the Time of the Court's Orders," 1.
18. "Martinez Yazzie Consolidated Lawsuit—Since the Time of the Court's Orders," 1.
19. "Martinez Yazzie Consolidated Lawsuit—Since the Time of the Court's Orders," 1.

Selected Bibliography

Acosta, Curtis. "Developing Critical Consciousness: Resistance Literature in a Chicano Literature Class." *English Journal* (2007): 36–42.

Adams, David Wallace. *Education for Extinction: American Indians and the Boarding School Experience 1875–1928.* Lawrence: University Press of Kansas, 1995.

"Addressing the Urgent Needs of Our Tribal Communities: Full Committee Hearing before the United States House of Representatives Committee on Energy and Commerce, 116th Cong. (2020) (statement of Jonathan Nez, President of the Navajo Nation)." https://energycommerce.house.gov/sites/democrats.energycommerce.house.gov/files/documents/Testimony-Nez-Tribal%20Communities%20Hearing_070820.pdf.

Advancement via Individual Determination. "Cultural Relevance." Accessed September 11, 2021. https://www.avid.org/cultural-relevance.

Aguilera, Dorothy E. "Who Defines Success: An Analysis of Competing Models of Education for American Indian and Alaska Native Students." PhD diss., University of Colorado, 2003.

Aguilera-Black Bear, Dorothy, and John W. Tippeconnic III, eds. *Voices of Renewal: Indigenous Leadership in Education.* Norman: University of Oklahoma Press, 2015.

Albuquerque Journal Editorial Board. "Editorial: How Is Failure an Option." *Albuquerque Journal,* August 1, 2021. https://www.abqjournal.com/2415284/how-is-failure-an-option.html.

Albuquerque Public Schools. *2020–2021 Tribal Education Status Report.* September 2021. https://www.aps.edu/indian-education/documents/tesr.

———. *Equity Plan.* Office of Equity, Instruction, Innovation, and Support, 2017.

———. Office of Equity and Engagement website. Accessed February 18, 2022. https://www.aps.edu/office-of-equity-and-engagement.

Anderson, Kim. *A Recognition of Being: Reconstructing Native Womanhood.* Toronto, ON: Sumach Press, 2000.

Annie E. Casey Foundation. *Kids Count Data Book: State Trends in Child Well Being.* Baltimore: Annie E. Casey Foundation, 2014–2020.

Apple, Michael. *Knowledge, Power, and Education: The Selected Works of Michael W. Apple.* New York: Routledge, 2013.

Arviso, Marie, and Wayne Holm. "Tséhootsooídi Ólta'gi Diné bizaad bihoo'aah: A Diné Immersion Program at Fort Defiance, Arizona." In Hinton and Hale, *Green Book of Language Revitalization in Practice*, 203–15.

Baca, Larry R. "Meyers v. Board of Education: The Brown v. Board of Indian Country." *University of Illinois Law Review* 5 (2004): 1155–80.

Barro, S.M. "New Mexico's 2019–20 Education Funding Still Less Than in 2007–08" (January 27, 2020).

Battiste, Marie Ann. *Decolonizing Education: Nourishing the Learning Spirit.* Saskatoon, SK: Purich Publishing, 2013.

Beach, Robert H., and Ronald A. Lindahl. "A Discussion of Strategic Planning as Understood through the Theory of Planning and Its Relevance to Education." *Educational Planning* 22, no. 2 (2015): 5–16.

Benally, AnCita, and Dennis Viri. "Diné [Navajo Language] at a Crossroads: Extinction or Renewal?" *Bilingual Research Journal* 29, no. 1 (2005): 85–108.

Benally, Cynthia. "'You Need to Go Beyond Creating a Policy': Opportunities for Zones of Sovereignty in Native American History Instruction Policies in Arizona." *Journal of American Indian Education* 58, no. 3 (2019): 11–33.

Berry, Brewton. *The Education of American Indians: A Survey of the Literature.* Washington, DC: US Government Printing Office, 1968.

Bialik, Kristen, Alissa Scheller, and Kristi Walker. "6 Facts about English Language Learners in U.S. Public Schools." Pew Research Center, October 25, 2018. https://www.pewresearch.org/fact-tank/2018/10/25/6-facts-about-english-language-learners-in-u-s-public-schools/.

Bilingual Education Act of 1978. Pub. L. no. 95-561, 92 Stat. 2143 (1978). https://www.govinfo.gov/content/pkg/STATUTE-92/pdf/STATUTE-92-Pg2143.pdf.

Bird, Carlotta Penny. "Building Partnerships for Native American Languages: A Study of MOA between State and Tribes." PhD diss., University of New Mexico, 2007.

Blum Martínez, Rebecca. "Basic Elements and Resources Necessary to Implement Quality English Language Learner Educational Programs and Educational Services for Native American Students." Unpublished report based on research conducted for New Mexico Center on Law and Poverty, last modified 2016.

Blum Martínez, Rebecca and Preston Sanchez. "A Watershed Moment in the Education of American Indians: A Judicial Strategy to Mandate the State of New Mexico to Meet the Unique Cultural and Linguistic Needs of American Indians in New Mexico Public Schools." *American University Journal of Gender, Social Policy and the Law* 27, no. 3 (2019): 317–55.

Boynton, Donna, and Christine P. Sims. "A Community-Based Plan for Acoma Language Retention and Revitalization." Unpublished paper prepared for the Pueblo of Acoma, Acoma, NM, 1997.

Brayboy, Bryan McKinley Jones. "Toward a Tribal Critical Race Theory in Education." *Urban Review* 37, no. 5 (December 2005): 425–46.

Bronson, Stanley. "Posey." *Blue Mountain Shadows*, 23 (2000): 46.

Brown, Cynthia G., Frederick M. Hess, Daniel K. Lautzenheiser, and Isabel Owen. *State Education Agencies as Agents of Change: What It Will Take for the States to Step Up Education*. Washington, DC: Center for American Progress, July 27, 2011.

Brunsma, D. L., and J. Padilla Wyse. "The Possessive Investment in White Sociology." *Sociology of Race and Ethnicity* 5, no. 1 (2019): 1–10.

Bunch, George C., Amanda Kibler, and Susan Pimentel. "Realizing Opportunities for ELLs in the Common Core English Language Arts and Disciplinary Standards." In *Understanding Language: Language, Literacy, and Learning in the Content Areas*. Conference proceedings, Stanford University, 2012. https://ul.stanford.edu/sites/default/files/resource/2021-12/01_Bunch_Kibler_Pimentel_RealizingOpp%20in%20ELA_FINAL_0.pd.

Cajete, Gregory. *Look to the Mountain: An Ecology of Indigenous Education*. Durango, CO: Kivaki Press, 1994.

Campisteguy, Maria Elena, Jennifer Messenger Heilbronner, and Corinne Nakamura-Rybak. "Research Findings: Compilation of All Research." *First Nations Development Institute*, June 2018. https://www.firstnations.org/wp-content/uploads/2018/12/FullFindingsReport-screen.pdf.

Castagno, Angelina E., and Bryan McKinley Jones Brayboy. "Culturally Responsive Schooling for Indigenous Youth: A Review of the Literature." *Review of Educational Research* 78, no. 4 (2008): 941–93.

Cazden, Courtney. *Classroom Discourse: The Language of Teaching and Learning*. Portsmouth, NH: Heinemann, 2001.

Chavez, G. Christine et al. *Quick Response of Implementation of Indian Education Act*. New Mexico Legislative Finance Committee, Report #06-04, 2006, 1.

Chee, Melvatha R. "A Longitudinal Cross-Sectional Study on the Acquisition of Navajo Verbs in Children Aged 4 Years 7 Months through 11 Years 2 Months." PhD diss., University of New Mexico, 2017.

Child, Brenda J. *Boarding School Seasons: American Indian Families 1900–1940*. Lincoln: University of Nebraska Press, 2000.

——. "Homesickness." In *Boarding School Seasons: American Indian Families 1900–1940*, 43–54. Lincoln: University of Nebraska Press, 1998.

Chin, Jeremiah, Brian Mckinley Jones Brayboy, and Nicholas Bustamante. "Carceral Colonialisms: Schools, Prisons, and Indigenous Youth in the United States." In *Handbook of Indigenous Education*, edited by Elizabeth Ann McKinley and Linda Tuhiwai Smith, 575–604. Singapore: Springer, 2019.

Collins, Patricia H. *Black Feminist Thought*. New York: Routledge, 2009.

——. *Intersectionality as Critical Theory*. Durham, NC: Duke University Press, 2019.

Coronel-Molina, Serafin M., and Teresa L. McCarty, eds. *Indigenous Language Revitalization in the Americas* (New York: Routledge, 2016).

Council of the Great City Schools. *English Learners in America's Great City Schools: Demographics, Achievement and Staffing*. Washington, DC, April 2019. https://

www.cgcs.org/cms/lib/DC00001581/Centricity/domain/35/publication%20docs/
CGCS_ELL%20Survey%20Report.pdf.

Crawford, James. "Endangered Native American Languages: What Is to Be Done and
Why?" *Bilingual Research Journal* 19, no. 1 (1995): 17–38.

Dalton, Stephanie S., and Daniel G. Youpa. "Standards-Based Teaching Reform in Zuni
Pueblo Middle and High Schools." *Equity and Excellence in Education* 31, no. 1
(April 1998): 55–68.

Delgado Bernal, Dolores, R. Buriaga, and J. Flores Carmona. "Chicana/Latina Testimonios:
Mapping the Methodological, Pedagogical, and Political." *Equity and Excellence in
Education* 45, no. 3 (2011): 363–72.

Deloria, Vine, Jr. *Indian Education in America.* N.p.: American Indian Science and Engineering Society, 1991.

Deloria, Vine, Jr., and Daniel Wildcat, eds. *Power and Place: Indian Education in America.*
Golden, CO: Fulcrum Resources, 2001.

Denetclaw, Pauly. "Community Finds Loss of Diné Language 'Scary.'" *Navajo Times*,
November 16, 2017. https://navajotimes.com/ae/culture/community-finds-loss-of-
dine-language-scary/.

———. "Data Shows Huge Reductions in Diné Speakers." *Navajo Times*, November 16,
2017. https://navajotimes.com/reznews/data-shows-huge-reduction-in-dine-
speakers/.

Denetdale, Jennifer Nez. "Representing Changing Woman: A Review Essay on Navajo
Women." *American Indian Culture and Research Journal* 25, no. 3 (2001): 1–26.

DeVoe, Jill Fleury, and Kristen E. Darling-Churchill. *Status and Trends in the Education of
American Indians and Alaska Natives: 2008.* Washington, DC: National Center for
Education Statistics, 2008.

Dewees, Sarah, and Benjamin Marks. "Twice Invisible: Understanding Rural Native
America." Research note, First Nations Development Institute, April 2017, 5.
https://www.usetinc.org/wp-content/uploads/bvenuti/WWS/2017/May%20
2017/May%208/Twice%20Invisible%20-%20Research%20Note.pdf.

Deyhle, Donna. "Constructing Failure and Maintaining Cultural Identity: Navajo and Ute
Leavers." *Journal of American Indian Education* 31, no. 2 (1992): 21–47.

———. "Journey towards Social Justice: Curriculum Change and Educational Equity in a
Navajo Community." In *Narrative and Experience in Multicultural Education,* edited
by J. Phillion, M. Fang He, and F. C. Connelly, 62. Thousand Oaks, CA: Sage, 2005.

———. "Navajo Youth and Anglo Racism: Cultural Integrity and Resistance." *Harvard
Educational Review* 65, no. 3 (1995): 403–44.

———. *Reflection in Place: Connected Lives of Navajo Women.* Tucson: University of Arizona Press, 2009.

Deyhle, Donna, and Karen Swisher. "Research in American Indian and Alaska Native
Education: From Assimilation to Self-Determination." In *Review of Research in
Education,* vol. 22, edited by Michael W. Apple, 119–94. Washington, DC: Ameri-
can Educational Research Association, 1997.

Duarte, Marisa Elena. *Network Sovereignty: Building the Internet Across Indian Country*. Seattle: University of Washington Press, 2017.

Eagle Shield, Alayna, Django Paris, Rae Paris, and Timothy San Pedro, eds. *Education in Movement Spaces: Standing Rock to Chicago Freedom Square*. Indigenous and Decolonizing Studies in Education. New York: Routledge, 2020.

Edgewater, Valencia. "My Language Journey with DLTI." *Soleado: Promising Practices from the Field* (Summer 2021): 4–5.

"Education Legislative Study Committee." Prepared by Joseph W. Simon, July 14, 2020. https://www.nmlegis.gov/handouts/ALESC%20071520%20Item%203%20-%20 Brief%20-%20Martinez%20and%20Yazzie%20Lawsuit.pdf.

Eid, Troy A., Chairman Affie Ellis, Tom Gede, Carole Goldberg, Stephanie Herseth Sandlin, Jefferson Keel, and Ted Quasula. *A Roadmap for Making Native America Safer: Report to the President and Congress of the United States*. Washington, DC: Indian Law and Order Commission, 2013.

Emerson, Larry W. *Indigenization: A Working Definition for American Scholars and Collaboration Program*. San Diego, CA: San Diego State University, 2005.

Engage for Equity. "Creating a River of Life: Ethnic Studies Education and Health Partnership." University of New Mexico and Albuquerque Public Schools Partnership. Summer Institute, 2017. YouTube video. https://www.youtube.com/watch?v=-K_sa0YQdD0.

———. "Creating a River of Life Examples." Last updated 2022. https://engageforequity.org/tool_kit/river-of-life/partnership-river-of-life-examples/.

Esposito, Luigi, and Victor Romano. "Benevolent Racism and the Co-Optation of the Black Lives Matter Movement." *Western Journal of Black Studies* 40, no. 3 (Fall 2016): 161–73.

Fang, Zhihui, and Mary J. Schleppegrell. "Disciplinary Literacy across Content Areas: Supporting Secondary Reading through Functional Language Analysis." *Journal of Adolescent and Adult Literacy* 53, no. 7 (2010): 587–97.

Families United for Education. "Open Letter to APS." June 15, 2020. https://docs.google.com/forms/d/e/1FAIpQLScD4NUhNHm1Bam0mKYUa_TLpaBMa5PuDFH-vrQJpgC1JADm6kw/viewform.

Feldman, J. M., and M. T. Bassett. "Variation in COVID-19 Mortality in the US by Race and Ethnicity and Educational Attainment." *JAMA Network Open* 4, no. 11 (2021): e2135967.

Fillmore, Lily Wong. "When Learning a Second Language Means Losing a First." *Early Childhood Research Quarterly* 6 (1991): 323–46.

Fillmore, Lily Wong, and Catherine E. Snow. "What Teachers Need to Know about Language." In *What Teachers Need to Know about Language*, edited by Carolyn Temple Adger, Catherine E. Snow, and Donna Christian, 8–51. Washington, DC: Center for Applied Linguistics, 2003.

Fillmore, Lily Wong, and Charles J. Fillmore. "What Does Text Complexity Mean for English Learners and Language Minority Students?" In *Understanding Language:*

Language, Literacy, and Learning in the Content Areas, 64–74. Stanford, CA: Stanford University Press, 2012.

Fishman, Joshua. *Reversing Language Shift: Theoretical and Empirical Foundations of Assistance to Threatened Languages*. Clevedon, UK: Multilingual Matters, 1991.

Fletcher, Matthew L. M. *American Indian Education: Counternarratives in Racism, Struggle, and the Law*. New York: Routledge, 2008.

Flores, Nelson, Tatyana Kleyn, and Kate Menken. "Looking Holistically in a Climate of Partiality: Identities of Students Labeled Long-Term English Language Learners." *Journal of Language, Identity, and Education* 14, no. 2 (2015): 113–32.

Friere, Paulo. *Pedagogy of the Oppressed*. New York: Continuum, 1998.

Fryberg, Stephanie A., Rebecca Covarrubias, and Jacob A. Burack. "Cultural Models of Education and Academic Performance for Native American and European American Students." *School Psychology International* 34, no. 4 (August 2013): 439–52.

Fryberg, Stephanie A., and Sarah S. M. Townsend. "The Psychology of Invisibility." In *Commemorating Brown: The Social Psychology of Racism and Discrimination*, edited by G. Adams, M. Biernat, N. R Branscombe, C. S. Crandell, and L. S. Wrightman, 173–93. Washington DC: American Psychology Association, 2008.

Garcia, Jeremy. "Critical and Culturally Sustaining Indigenous Family and Community Engagement in Education." In *The Wiley Handbook of Family, School, and Community Relationships in Education*, edited by Steven B. Sheldon and Tammy A. Turner-Vorbeck, 71–90. Hoboken, NJ: Wiley-Blackwell, 2019.

Gibbons, Pauline. "Classroom Talk and the Learning of New Registers in a Second Language." *Language and Education* 12, no. 2 (1998): 99–118.

Gilbert, Matthew Sakiestewa. *Education beyond the Mesas: Hopi Students at Sherman Institute, 1902–1929*. Lincoln, Nebraska: University of Nebraska Press, 2010.

Goldberg, Julia. "NM Grapples with 'Staggering' Teacher Shortage." *Santa Fe Reporter*, September 22, 2021.

Grande, Sandy. *Red Pedagogy: Native American Social and Political Thought*. Lanham, MD: Rowman and Littlefield, 2015.

Greyeyes, Wendy S. *A History of Navajo Nation Education: Disentangling Our Sovereign Body*. Tucson: University of Arizona Press, 2022.

Halliday, M. A. K. *An Introduction to Functional Grammar*. New York: Routledge, 1985.

Hancock, A. *Solidarity Politics for Millennials: A Guide to Ending the Oppression Olympics*. New York: Springer, 2011.

Harris, Jessica C., and Lori D. Patton. "Un/Doing Intersectionality through Higher Education Research." *Journal of Higher Education* 90, no. 3 (2019): 347–72.

Harvard Project on American Indian Economic Development. *The State of Native Nations: Conditions under U.S. Policies of Self-Determination*. Oxford: Oxford University Press, 2008.

Heine, Bernd, Gunther Kaltenböck, Tania Kuteva, and Haiping Long. "Cooptation as a Discourse Strategy." *Linguistics* 55, no. 4 (2017): 813–55.

Hermes, Mary. "'Ma'iingan Is Just a Misspelling of the Word Wolf': A Case for Teaching

Culture through Language." *Anthropology and Education Quarterly* 36, no.1 (2005): 43–56.

Hinton, Leanne, and Ken Hale, eds. *The Green Book of Language Revitalization in Practice.* San Diego, CA: Academic Press, 2001.

Hopkins, John P. *Indian Education for All: Decolonizing Indigenous Education in Public Schools.* New York: Teachers College Press, 2020.

Hornby, Garry. *Parental Involvement in Childhood Education: Building Effective School-Family Partnerships.* New York: Springer, 2011.

Horvt, Erin McNamara, Elliot B. Weininger, and Annette Lareau. "From Social Ties to Social Capital: Class Differences in the Relations between Schools and Parent Networks." *American Educational Research Journal* 40, no. 2 (2003): 319–51.

Huff, Delores J. *To Live Heroically: Institutional Racism and American Indian Education.* Albany: State University of New York Press, 1997.

Indian Education Act (New Mexico). https://webnew.ped.state.nm.us/wp-content/uploads/2019/03/NM-Indian-Education-Act-1.pdf.

Indian Pueblo Cultural Center. *Indigenous Wisdom Curriculum.* Albuquerque, NM: Indian Pueblo Cultural Center, 2020. https://indianpueblo.org/indigenous-wisdom-curriculum-downloads-2/.

Indian Self-Determination and Education Assistance Act. Pub. L. no. 93-638. https://www.bia.gov/sites/bia.gov/files/assets/bia/ots/ots/pdf/Public_Law93-638.pdf.

Institute for American Indian Education. *2020 Post-Summit Executive Report.* University of New Mexico, May 2020. https://iaie.unm.edu/docs/iaie_post_summit_report_final_2020v3.pdf.

———. *2021 Post-Summit Executive Report.* University of New Mexico, May 2021. https://iaie.unm.edu/news-events/summit/2021-iaie-post-summit-report6236.pdf.

Jojola, Theodore, Tiffany Lee, Adelamar N. Alcántra, Mary Belgarde, Carlotta Bird, Nancy López, Beverly Singer, et al. *Indian Education in New Mexico, 2025.* Ohkay Owingeh, NM: Indigenous Education Study Group, 2010.

Jones, Sosanya. "Subversion or Cooptation? Tactics for Engaging in Diversity Work in a Race-Adverse Climate." *Journal of Educational Leadership and Policy Studies* 3, no. 2 (January 2019). https://files.eric.ed.gov/fulltext/EJ1233799.pdf.

Juneau, Carol, and Denise Juneau. "Indian Education for All: Montana's Constitution at Work in Our Schools." *Montana Law Review* 72, no. 1 (Winter 2011): 111–25.

Ka'anehe, R. J. "Ke a 'o Mālamalama: Recognizing and Bridging Worlds with Hawaiian Pedagogies." *Equity and Excellence in Education* 53, nos. 1–2 (2020): 73–88.

Kibler, Amanda K., and Guadalupe Valdés. "Conceptualizing Language Learners: Socioinstitutional Mechanisms and their Consequences." *Modern Language Journal* 100 (Supplement 2016): 96–116.

King, Beth. "The Utah Navajos Relocation in the 1950s: Life along the San Juan River." *Canyon Echo,* February 9, 2002 (originally published July 1996). https://canyonechojournal.com/category/archive-1993-1997/.

King, Ledyard, and Mike Stucka. "In New Mexico, Many Still Lack Broadband Access." *Deming Headlight,* July 13, 2021.

Kober, Nancy. "Why We Still Need Public Schools: Public Education for the Common Good." Center on Education Policy, Washington, DC, 2007.

Kochan, Donald J. "You Say You Want a (Nonviolent) Revolution, Well Then What? Translating Western Thought, Strategic Ideological Cooptation, and Institution Building for Freedom for Governments Emerging out of Peaceful Chaos." *West Virginia Law Review* 114, no. 3 (Spring 2012): 897–936.

Krauss, Michael M. "Status of Native American Language Endangerment." In *Stabilizing Indigenous Languages,* edited by G. Cantoni, 16–21. Flagstaff: Northern Arizona University Press, 1996.

Lee, Tiffany S. "'If They Want Navajo to Be Learned, Then They Should Require It in All Schools': Navajo Teenagers' Experiences, Choices, and Demands Regarding Navajo Language." *Wicazo Sa Review* 22, no. 1 (Spring 2007): 7–33.

———. "The Significance of Self-Determination in Socially, Culturally, and Linguistically Responsive (SCLR) Education in Indigenous Contexts." *Journal of American Indian Education* 54, no. 1 (Spring 2015): 10–32.

Lee, Tiffany, and Daniel McLaughlin. "Reversing Diné Language Shift, Revisited." In *Can Threatened Languages Be Saved? Reversing Language Shift Revisited: A 21st Century Perspective,* edited by Joshua A. Fishman, 69–98. Clevedon, UK: Multilingual Matters, 2001.

Levinson, Bradley A., Teresa Winstead, and Margaret Sutton. "Theoretical Foundations for a Critical Anthropology of Education Policy." In *The Anthropology of Education Policy: Ethnographic Inquiries into Policy as Sociocultural Process,* edited by Angelina A. Castagno and Teresa L. McCarty, 28. New York: Routledge, 2018.

Lomawaima, K. Tsianina, and Teresa L. McCarty. *"To Remain an Indian": Lessons in Democracy from a Century of Native American Education.* New York: Teachers College Press, 2006.

Lozano, Roberto. "Las Cruces Public Schools: Addressing Educational Equity for All Students." *Las Cruces Sun News,* August 29, 2020. https://www.lcsun-news.com/story/news/education/lcps/2020/08/29/lcps-addressing-educational-equity-all-students/5667452002/.

Lucas, Tamara, and Ana María Villegas. "Preparing Linguistically Responsive Teachers: Laying the Foundation in Preservice Teacher Education." *Theory into Practice* 52, no. 2 (2013): 98–109.

Mackety, Dawn M., and Jennifer A. Linder-VanBerschot. *Examining American Indian Perspectives in the Central Region on Parent Involvement in Children's Education.* Washington, DC: US Department of Education, 2008.

Mackety, Dawn M., Susie Bachler, Zoe Barley, and Lou Cicchinelli. *American Indian Education: The Role of Tribal Education Departments.* Report produced for the Institute of Education Sciences, May 2009. https://sites.ed.gov/whiaiane/files/2012/04/The-Role-of-Tribal-Education-Departments.pdf.

Mackey, Hollie J. "The ESSA in Indian Country: Problematizing Self-Determination through the Relationships Between Federal, State, and Tribal Governments." *Educational Administration Quarterly* 53, no. 5 (2017): 782–808.

Markstrom, Carol A. "North American Indian Perspectives on Human Development." In *Empowerment of North American Indian Girls: Ritual Expressions at Puberty*, 46–84. Lincoln: University of Nebraska Press, 2008.

Martinez, David G., Oscar Jiménez-Castellanos, and Victor H. Begay. "Understanding Navajo K-12 Public School Finance in Arizona through Tribal Critical Theory." *Teachers College Record* 121, no. 5 (May 2019): 1–34.

Martinez et al. v. State of New Mexico et al., No. D-101-CV-2014-00793 and *Yazzie et al. v. State of New Mexico et al.*, no. D-101-CV-2014-02224. Final Judgment and Order (NM February 14, 2019).

Martinez et al. v. State of New Mexico et al., No. D-101-CV-2014-00793 and *Yazzie et al. v. State of New Mexico et al.*, No. D-101-CV-2014-02224. Yazzie Plaintiffs' Response to State's Motion to Dismiss (NM May 1, 2020).

Martinez, Glenabah. *Native Pride: Politics of Curriculum and Instruction in an Urban High School*. Cresskill, NJ: Hampton Press, 2010.

Martinez v. State of New Mexico. Yazzie Plaintiffs' Expedited Motion for Further Relief Concerning Defendants' Failure to Provide Essential Technology to At-Risk Public School Students, no. D-101-CV-2014-0079, 2020 WL 10223955 (NM Dist. Ct. Dec. 14, 2020), 2–3.

McCarty, Teresa L. "The Holistic Benefits of Education for Indigenous Language Revitalization and Reclamation (ELR2)." *Journal of Multilingual and Multicultural Development* 42, 10 (2020): 927–40.

———. *A Place to Be Navajo: Rough Rock and the Struggle for Self-Determination in Indigenous Schooling*. Mahwah, NJ: Lawrence Erlbaum Associates, 2002.

McCarty, Teresa, and Tiffany S. Lee. "Critical Culturally Sustaining/Revitalizing Pedagogy and Indigenous Educational Sovereignty." *Harvard Education Review* 84, no. 1 (2014): 101–24.

McCool, Daniel. *Expert Witness Report in the Case of Navajo Nation v. San Juan County, UT Case no. 2:12-cv-00039-RS* (2015).

McCoy, Melody. "Tribalizing Education: Tribal Governance in Education." Native American Rights Fund, October 1994. http://www.narf.org/wordpress/wp-content/uploads/2015/01/red.pdf.

McGowen, Kay G. "Weeping for the Lost Matriarchy." In *Make a Beautiful Way: The Wisdom of Native American Women*, 53–68. Lincoln: University of Nebraska Press, 2008.

McKay, Dan. "Top Legislative Staffer Who Was Censured Quits." *Albuquerque Journal*, September 1, 2021. https://www.abqjournal.com/2425258/gudgel-top-legislative-staffer-submits-resignation.html.

McPherson, Robert. *Navajo Land, Navajo Culture: The Utah Experience in the Twentieth Century*. Norman: University of Oklahoma Press, 2001.

———. "Paiute Posey and the Last White Uprising." *Blue Mountain Shadows* 4 (1989). https://issuu.com/utah10/docs/uhq_volume53_1985_number3/s/150346.

Menken, Kate, and Tatyana Kleyn. "The Long-Term Impact of Subtractive Schooling in the Educational Experiences of Secondary English Language Learners." *International Journal of Bilingual Education and Bilingualism* 13, no. 4 (2010): 399–417.

Meriam, Lewis. *The Problem of Indian Administration.* Washington, DC: Institute for Government Research, 1928.

Mihesuah, Devon A. *American Indians: Stereotypes and Realities.* Atlanta, GA: Clarity, 1996.

Miller, Robert J. "Consultation or Consent: The United States' Duty to Confer with American Indian Governments." *North Dakota Law Review* 91, no. 1 (October 2015): 37–98.

Minthorn, Robin Zape-tah-hol-ah. "Indigenous Motherhood in the Academy, Building Our Children to Be Good Relatives." *Wicazo Sa Review* 33, no. 2 (2018): 62–75.

Minthorn, Robin Zape-tah-hol-ah, Lorenda Belone, Glenabah Martinez, and Christine Sims. "Indigenous Research Perspectives in the State of New Mexico: Implications for Working with Schools and Communities." *Journal of American Indian Education* 58, nos. 1–2 (Spring–Summer 2019): 108–23.

Moll, Luis C., Cathy Amanti, Deborah Neff, and Norma Gonzalez. "Funds of Knowledge for Teaching: Using a Qualitative Approach to Connect Homes and Classrooms." *Theory into Practice* 31, no. 2 (2993): 132–41.

Mondragón, John B., and Ernest S. Stapleton. *Public Education in New Mexico.* Albuquerque: University of New Mexico Press, 2005.

Montana et. al. v. United States et al., 450 U.S. 544 (1981).

Mozingo, Joe. "A Sting in the Desert." *Los Angeles Times,* September 21, 2014. https://graphics.latimes.com/utah-sting/.

Mullan, Dillon. "State Moves to Dismiss Yazzie/Martinez Lawsuit." *Santa Fe New Mexican,* March 17, 2020. https://www.santafenewmexican.com/news/local_news/state-moves-to-dismiss-yazzie-martinez-lawsuit/article_99ec76a8-6865-11ea-bf86-1b6eec7938c7.html.

National Center for Education Statistics. *The Nation's Report Card.* National Assessment of Educational Progress, 1983–2019. nationsreportcard.gov.

National Congress of American Indians. *Becoming Visible: A Landscape Analysis of State Efforts to Provide Native American Education for All.* Washington, DC, September 2019. https://www.ncai.org/policy-research-center/research-data/prc-publications/NCAI-Becoming_Visible_Report-Digital_FINAL_10_2019.pdf.

———. "The List of Federal Tribal Consultation Statutes, Orders, Regulations, Rules, Policies, Manuals, Protocols and Guidance." January 2009. https://www.ncai.org/resources/consultations/list-of-federal-tribal-consultation-statutes-orders-regulations-rules-policies-manuals-protocols-and-guidance.

Native American Budget and Policy Institute, New Mexico Center on Law and Poverty, and Jonathan Sims. "When Access Is Remote: The Digital Divide for Native

Students." YouTube video, December 17, 2020. https://www.youtube.com/watch?v=9MMAXc1GXSA.

Navajo Nation Code. 2 N.N.C. § 1005(C)(14).

Navajo Nation Commission on Emergency Management. CEM 20-03-11, March 11, 2020.

Navajo Nation Council. *Sovereignty in Education Act*, CJY-37-05, 2005.

Navajo Nation Department of Diné Education. *Alternative Accountability Workbook.* https://www.navajonationdode.org/wp-content/uploads/2021/01/NN_DSAP_Final.pdf.

Navajo Nation Department of Health. *Dikos Ntsaaígíí-19 (COVID-19).* https://ndoh.navajo-nsn.gov/covid-19.

Navajo Nation Division of Diné Education. *Navajo Nation Education Standards with Navajo Specifics.* Window Rock, AZ: Office of Diné Culture, Language, and Community Services, 2003.

Navajo Nation et al. v. San Juan County, United States District Court, D. Utah, Central Division. Case no. 2:12-cv-00039. 2017.

Navajo Nation Office of the President and Vice President. *Executive Orders*, EO 011-20, EO 012-20, EO 002-21, and EO-003-21.

Navajo Nation Sovereignty in Education Act of 2005. The Navajo Nation Education Code Title X (as amended), Navajo Nation Tribal Council, 2005.

New Mexico Center on Law and Poverty. "Education Lawsuit against State of New Mexico Seeks Justice for New Mexico's School Children." New Mexico Center on Law and Poverty, January 7, 2022. https://transformeducationnm.org/wp-content/uploads/2019/01/Flyer-Overview-of-NMCLPs-education-lawsuit-2017-08-05.docx.pdf.

———. "Yazzie/Martinez Education Lawsuit Moves Forward!" June 29, 2020. http://nmpovertylaw.org/2020/06/yazzie-martinez-education-lawsuit-moves-forward/.

———. "Yazzie/Martinez v. State of New Mexico Decision." New Mexico Center on Law and Poverty, January 7, 2022. http://nmpovertylaw.org/wp-content/uploads/2018/09/Graphic-Yazzie-Martinez-Decision.pdf.

New Mexico Legislative Finance Committee. *Progress Report: Indian Education Act Implementation.* Program Evaluation Team, January 2021.

———. *Report of the Legislative Finance Committee to the Forty-Seventh Legislature, First session, January 2005 for Fiscal Year 2005–2006*, vol. 1. https://www.nmlegis.gov/Entity/LFC/Documents/Session_Publications/Budget_Recommendations/2006RecommendVolI.pdf.

———. *Spotlight: Learning Loss Due to COVID-19 Pandemic.* Program Evaluation Team, June 10, 2020. https://www.nmlegis.gov/Entity/LFC/Documents/Program_Evaluation_Reports/Spotlight%20-%20Learning%20Loss%20Due%20to%20COVID-19%20Pandemic.pdf.

New Mexico Public Education Department (NMPED). *2019–2020 Tribal Education Status Report (TESR).* November 2020. https://webnew.ped.state.nm.us/wp-content/uploads/2021/01/TESR2020.pdf.

———. "Equity Council Brief." Summer 2021. Author archive (Natalie Martinez).

———. *Equity in Action Equity Councils 2020.* Accessed August 21, 2021. https://webnew.ped.state.nm.us/wp-content/uploads/2020/12/EquityInAction_Equity-Councils_2020.pdf.

———. "Finance—Total Expenditure, Central Consolidated Schools, Shiprock, New Mexico." Accessed September 10, 2021. https://newmexicoschools.com/districts/67/finance.

———. *Internet Connectivity Concerns on Tribal Lands: Guidance Document.* June 25, 2020. https://webnew.ped.state.nm.us/wp-content/uploads/2020/04/Revised-Tribal-Guidance-Document_FINAL_6.25.2020.pdf.

———. *Martinez and Yazzie Consolidated Lawsuit.* February 2, 2021. https://webnew.ped.state.nm.us/bureaus/yazzie-martinez-updates/.

———. "Readiness Assessment: Purpose of the Martinez/Yazzie Readiness Assessment Tool." April 21, 2020. https://webnew.ped.state.nm.us/bureaus/yazzie-martinez-updates/readiness-assessment/.

———. *Request for Application.* Indian Education Act Funding RFA # 21–92400–00002, April 16, 2021.

———. *School District Report Card 2016–17: Albuquerque Public Schools.* July 12, 2018. https://webed.ped.state.nm.us/sites/conference/2017%20District%20Report%20Cards/Forms/AllItems.aspx.

New Mexico State Legislature. "2021 Legislative Finance Meeting." September 21, 2021. http://sg001-harmony.sliq.net/00293/Harmony/en/PowerBrowser/PowerBrowserV2/20210922/-1/67947.

New Mexico State-Tribal Collaboration Act. https://www.iad.state.nm.us/wp-content/uploads/2019/11/SB0196.pdf.

Oakes, Jeannie, Daniel Espinoza, Linda Darling-Hammond, Carmen Gonzales, Jennifer DePaoli, Tara Kini, Gary Hoachlander, et al. *Improving Education the New Mexico Way: An Evidence-Based Approach.* Palo Alto, CA: Learning Policy Institute, 2020.

Obama, Barack H. "Memorandum on Tribal Consultation." The White House, November 5, 2009.

Ocasio, William, and John Joseph. "Rise and Fall—or Transformation?: The Evolution of Strategic Planning at General Electric Company, 1940–2006." *Long Range Planning* 41, no. 3 (June 2008): 248–72.

Olsen, Laurie. *Reparable Harm: Fulfilling the Unkept Promise of Educational Opportunity for California's Long-Term English Learners.* Long Beach, CA: Californians Together, 2010.

Organization of American States. "American Declaration on the Rights of Indigenous Peoples." https://www.oas.org/en/sare/documents/DecAmIND.pdf.

Oxford, Andrew. "Pueblo Leaders Decry Public Education Chief's 'Manifest Destiny' Comment." *Santa Fe New Mexican,* December 22, 2017. http://www.santafenewmexican.com/news/education/pueblo-leaders-decry-public-education-chief-s-manifest-destiny-comment/article_da7cd5bf-4102-5f2f-9bf0-c5692dc49e73.html.

Paris, Django, and H. Samy Alim. "What Are We Seeking to Sustain through Culturally
    Sustaining Pedagogy?: A Loving Critique Forward." *Harvard Educational Review*
    84, no. 1 (2014): 85–100.
———. "What Is Culturally Sustaining Pedagogy and Why Does It Matter?" In *Culturally
    Sustaining Pedagogies: Teaching and Learning for Justice in a Changing World*,
    edited by Django Paris and H. Samy Alim, 1–17. New York: Teachers College Press,
    2017.
Pecos, Regis. "The Gift of Language from One Pueblo Perspective." In *The Shoulders We
    Stand On*, edited by Rebecca Blum Martínez and Mary Jean Haberman López,
    13–24. Albuquerque: University of New Mexico Press, 2020.
Pecos, Regis, and Rebecca Blum Martínez. "The Key to Cultural Survival: Language Plan-
    ning and Revitalization in the Pueblo de Cochiti." In *Greenbook of Language Revi-
    talization in Practice*, edited by Leanne Hinton and Kenneth Hale, 75–85.
Pewewardy, Cornel, and Patricia Cahape Hammer. "Culturally Responsive Teaching for
    American Indian Students." *ERIC Digest*, December 2003. https://files.eric.ed.gov/
    fulltext/ED482325.pdf.
Phillips, Susan Urmston. *The Invisible Culture: Communication in Classroom and Commu-
    nity on the Warm Springs Indian Reservation*. Long Grove, IL: Waveland Press, 1983.
Platero, Paul. "Navajo Language Study." In *Greenbook of Language Revitalization in Prac-
    tice*, edited by Leanne Hinton and Kenneth Hale, 86–97.
Podmore, Zak. "San Juan County Heads into Another Controversial Special Election—
    and Possibly the First Step to a New Form of Government." *Salt Lake Tribune*,
    October 14, 2019.
Prucha, Francis Paul. *The Churches and the Indian Schools, 1888–1912*. Lincoln: Univer-
    sity of Nebraska Press, 1979.
Ramirez, Renya K. *Native Hubs: Culture, Community, and Belonging in Silicon Valley and
    Beyond*. Durham, NC: Duke University Press, 2007.
Reyes, Kathryn Blackmer, and Julia E. Curry Rodríguez. "Testimonio: Origins, Terms, and
    Resources." *Equity and Excellence in Education* 45, no. 3 (2012): 525–38.
Reyhner, Jon A., and Jeanne Eder. *American Indian Education: A History*. Norman: Uni-
    versity of Oklahoma Press, 2006.
Richardson, Troy. "At the Garden Gate: Community Building through Food: Revisiting
    the Critique on 'Food, Folk and Fun' in Multicultural Education." *Urban Review* 43
    (2011): 107–23.
Robinson-Zañartu, Carol, and Juanita Majel-Dixon. "Parent Voices: American Indian Rela-
    tionships with Schools." *Journal of the American Indian Education* 36, no. 6 (Fall
    1996): 33–54.
Roessel, Robert A., Jr. "An Overview of the Rough Rock Demonstration Schools." *Journal
    of American Indian Education* 7, no. 3 (May 1968): 2–14.
———. *Indian Communities in Action*. Tempe: Arizona State University, 1967.
———. *Navajo Education, 1948–1978: Its Progress and Its Problems*. Rough Rock, AZ:
    Navajo Curriculum Center, 1979.

Roth, Guenther, and Claus Wittich. *Economy and Society: An Outline of Interpretative Sociology*. Berkeley: University of California Press, 1978.

Royston, M. M. de, C. Lee, N. I. S Nasir, and R. Pea. "Rethinking Schools, Rethinking Learning." *Phi Delta Kappa* 102, no. 3 (2020): 8–13.

Sabzalian, Leilani. *Indigenous Children's Survivance in Public Schools*. New York: Routledge, 2019.

San Juan School District. *Cultural Literacy Social Studies Curriculum K-12 Scope and Sequence*. Blanding, UT: San Juan School District, 2004.

Sanchez, Preston, and Rebecca Blum Martínez. "A Watershed Moment in the Education of American Indians: A Judicial Strategy to Mandate the State of New Mexico to Meet the Unique Cultural and Linguistic Needs of American Indians in New Mexico Public Schools." *Journal of Gender, Social Policy and the Law* 27, no. 3 (2019): 183–221.

Schieffelin, Bambi B., and Elinor Ochs, eds. *Language Socialization across Cultures*. New York: Cambridge University Press, 1986.

Schleppegrell, Mary J. *The Language of Schooling: A Functional Linguistics Perspective*. New York: Lawrence Erlbaum, 2004.

Scollon, Ronald, and Suzanne B. K. Scollon. *Linguistic Convergence: An Ethnography of Speaking at Fort Chipewyan, Alberta*. New York: Academic Press, 1979.

Shanahan, Timothy, and Cynthia Shanahan. "Teaching Disciplinary Literacy to Adolescents: Rethinking Content-Area Literacy." *Harvard Educational Review* 78, no. 1 (Spring 2008): 40–59.

Shepardson, Mary. "The Gender Status of Navajo Women." In *Women and Power in Native North America*, edited by Laura F. Klein and Lillian A. Ackerman, 159–76. Norman: University of Oklahoma Press, 2000.

Shotton, Heather J., Stephanie J. Waterman, and Shelly C. Lowe. *Beyond the Asterisk: Understanding Native Students in Higher Education*. Sterling, VA: Stylus, 2013.

Shumway, Gary. "Blanding: The Making of a Community." In *San Juan County Utah: People, Resources, and History*, 149. Salt Lake City: Utah State Historical Society, 1983.

Siebens, Julie, and Tiffany Julian. "Native North American Languages Spoken at Home in the United States and Puerto Rico: 2006–2010." *American Community Survey Briefs*. Washington, DC: US Census Bureau, 2011.

Sims, Christine P. "Language Planning in American Indian Pueblo Communities: Contemporary Challenges and Issues." *Current Issues in Language Planning* 7, nos. 2–3 (2006). 251–68.

———. "Native Language Planning: A Pilot Process in the Acoma Pueblo Community." In Hinton and Hale, *Greenbook of Language Revitalization in Practice*, 251–68.

Sinajini v. Board of Education of the San Juan School District. Agreement of Parties. United State District Court for the District of Utah Central Division, 1975.

"The Size and Vitality of Navajo." *Ethnologue: Languages of the World*. Accessed January 5, 2022. https://www.ethnologue.com/size-and-vitality/nav.

Smart, Christopher. "San Juan County Readies for Political Shift following Federal Court Ruling on Voting Districts." *Salt Lake Tribune*, December 22, 2017.

Smith, Donna. "The Integration of the San Juan County School District." *Blue Mountain Shadows* 21 (1999).

Smith, Graham Hingangaroa. "The Politics of Reforming Maori Education: The Transforming Potential of Kura Kaupapa Maori." In *Towards Successful Schooling*, edited by Hugh Lauder and Cathy Wylie, 73–87. London: Routledge, 2012.

Smith, Linda Tuhiwai, Eve Tuck, and K. Wayne Lang, eds. *Indigenous and Decolonizing Studies in Education: Mapping the Long View*. 2019. New York: Routledge.

Spruhan, Paul. "COVID-19 and Indian Country: A Legal Dispatch from the Navajo Nation." *Of Note* (blog), *Northwestern University Law Review*, May 5, 2020. https://northwesternlawreview.org/uncategorized/covid-19-and-indian-country-a-legal-dispatch-from-the-navajo-nation/.

State of New Mexico. "33 Tribal Consultations Policies and Procedures." Accessed May 1, 2021. https://www.iad.state.nm.us/tribal-collaboration/state-tribal-consultation-collaboration-and-communication-policies/.

Stewart, Ryan. "Memorandum: Expansion of In-Person Learning—Tribal Consultation." NMPED, January 29, 2021.

Tapahonso, Luci. "It Has Always Been This Way." In *Sáanii Dahataał: The Women Are Singing: Poems and Stories*, 17–18. Tucson: University of Arizona Press, 1993.

Tintiangco-Cubales, Allyson, Rita Kohli, Jocyl Sacramento, Nick Henning, Ruchi Agarwal-Rangnath, and Christine Sleeter. "Toward an Ethnic Studies Pedagogy: Implications for K-12 Schools from the Research." *Urban Review* 47, no. 1 (2015): 104–25.

Torres-Velásquez, E. Diane, Christine E. Sleeter, and Augustine F. Romero. "Martínez v. State of New Mexico and Multicultural Education: Divide and Conquer? We Don't Think So!" *Association of Mexican American Educators Journal* 13, no. 3 (December 2019): 170–94.

Tribal Education Alliance. *Pathways to Education Sovereignty: Taking a Stand for Native Children Summary Report*. Presented December 2020.

United Nations. "United Nations Declaration on the Rights of Indigenous Peoples." September 13, 2007. https://www.un.org/development/desa/indigenouspeoples/declaration-on-the-rights-of-indigenous-peoples.html.

United States Census Bureau. "American Community Surveys, 2012–2017 Five-year Estimates: S1601 Language Spoken at Home." https://data.census.gov/table?t=Language+Spoken+at+Home&g=2520000US2430R.

United States Department of Education. Every Student Succeeds Act. P.L. 114-95, December 10, 2015.

———. "Improving Basic Programs Operated by Local Education Agencies (Title I, Part A)." https://www2.ed.gov/programs/titleiparta/applicant.html.

———. *Tribal Leaders Speak: The State of American Indian Education, 2010 Report of the Consultations with Tribal Leaders in Indian Country*. 2010. www2.ed.gov/about/inits/ed/indianed/consultations-report.pdf.

Valdez, Luis. *Pensamiento Serpentino: A Chicano Approach to the Theater of Reality.* N.p.: Cucaracha Publications, 1973.

Valencia, Richard R., ed. *The Evolution of Deficit Thinking: Educational Thought and Practice.* New York: Routledge, 2012.

Valenzuela, Angela. *Subtractive Schooling: US-Mexican Youth and the Politics of Caring.* 2nd ed. Albany: State of New York Press, 2010.

Vallejo, Pedro, and Vincent Werito. *Transforming Diné Education: Innovations in Pedagogy and Practice.* Tucson: University of Arizona Press, 2022.

van Lier, Leo, and Aída Walqui. "Language and the Common Core State Standards." In *Commissioned Papers on Language and Literacy Issues in the Common Core State Standards and Next Generation Science Standards,* 44–94. Stanford, CA: Stanford University Press, 2012.

Villegas, Malia, Sabina Rak Neugebauer, and Kerry R. Venegas. *Indigenous Knowledge and Education: Sites of Struggle, Strength, and Survivance.* Cambridge, MA: Harvard Educational Review, 2008.

Vygotsky, Lev S. *Thought and Language.* Boston: MIT Press, 1962.

Walker, Anthony. "Culturally Relevant Pedagogy, Identity, Presence, and Intentionality: A Brief Review of Literature." *Journal of Research Initiatives* 4, no. 3 (2019): Article 11.

Werito, Vincent. "Education Is Our Horse: On the Path to Critical Consciousness in Teaching and Learning." In *Going Inward: The Role of Cultural Introspection in College Teaching,* edited by S. D. Longerbeam and A. F. Chavez, 66–73. New York: Peter Lang, 2016.

———. "Pioneering Navajo Bilingual Education: Voices from History to the Present." In *The Shoulders We Stand On: A History of Bilingual Education in New Mexico,* edited by Rebecca Blum Martínez and Mary Jean Haberman López, 25–54. Albuquerque: University of New Mexico Press, 2020.

———. "'Think in Navajo': Reflections from the Field on Reversing Navajo Language Shift in the Home, School, and Community Contexts." In *Honoring Our Students,* edited by J. Rehyner et al., 39–52. Flagstaff: Northern Arizona University Press, 2021.

Werito, Vincent, and Lorenda Belone. "Research from a Diné-Centered Perspective and the Development of a Community Based Participatory Research Partnership." *Health Education and Behavior* 48, no. 3 (2021): 361–70.

White House, Office of the Press Secretary. Executive Order 13592. "Improving American Indian and Alaska Native Educational Opportunities and Strengthening Tribal Colleges and Universities." December 2, 2001.

Whittington, Richard, and Ludovic Cailluet. "The Crafts of Strategy: Special Issue Introduction by the Guest Editors." *Long Range Planning* 41, no. 3 (June 2008): 241–47.

Wilkins, David E. *The Navajo Political Experience.* Rev. ed. Lanham, MD: Rowman and Littlefield, 2003.

Wilson, William H., and Kauanoe Kamanā, "Insights from Indigenous Language Immersion in Hawai'i." In *Immersion Education: Practices, Policies, Possibilities,* edited by

D. J. Tedick, D. Christian, and T. W. Fortune, 36–57. Bristol, UK: Multilingual Matters, 2011.

——. "Mai loko mai o ka iʻini: Proceeding from a Dream": The ʻAha Pūnana Leo Connection in Hawaiian Language Revitalization." In *Green Book of Language Revitalization in Practice*, edited by Leanne Hinton and Kenneth Hale, 147–76.

Yazzie/Martinez v. State of New Mexico. Courts Findings of Face and Conclusions of Law, 2018-12-20; 553.

Yosso, Tara J. "Whose Culture Has Capital? A Critical Race Theory Discussion of Community Cultural Wealth." *Race Ethnicity and Education* 8, no. 1 (2005): 69–91.

Yuval-Davis, N. "What Is 'Transversal Politics?'" *Soundings* 12 (Summer 1999): 88–93.

Contributors

Georgina Badoni, PhD (Diné), is an assistant professor of Native American Studies at New Mexico State University. She has served as a Native American consulting teacher for Seattle Public Schools; her collaborative work includes series of professional development for teachers to strengthen culturally responsive teaching. She has taught K-12 for twelve years and Native American studies for two years. She works with charter and public schools in southern New Mexico as an equity council member. She teaches upper division undergraduate courses including key offerings in Native American studies and graduate courses.

Cynthia Benally, EdD (Diné), is Nát'oh Dine'é Tachiiní and born for Ma'íí Deeshgiizhnii. She is an assistant professor of Native American Education in the Department of Education, Culture and Society at the University of Utah. She was recently a guest editor for a special issue, "Indigenizing the Curriculum: Putting the 'Native' into Native American Content Instruction Mandates," in the *Journal of American Indian Education*. Her research focuses on the intersections of educational policies, curriculum and instruction, and Native Nations and histories.

Rebecca Blum Martínez, PhD, was an expert witness during the *Yazzie/ Martinez* trial, testifying before the court about her findings concerning the lack of appropriate language instructional support for Native students in New Mexico public schools. She is a professor emerita in the Department of Language, Literacy and Sociocultural Studies. Her work has focused on bilingualism, second-language development, and language revitalization.

Nathaniel Charley (Diné) is an American Indian Professional Educators Collaborative (AIPEC) graduate and currently serves as an advisory board member of the Institute for American Indian Education. Mr. Charley received a BA in Secondary Education with teaching endorsements in English, history, TESOL, mathematics, and physical education from the University of New Mexico and Eastern New Mexico University. He completed a Master's in Educational Leadership from the University of New Mexico in May 2019. His research has been published in *The Need for Indigenous Education: Promoting Equality, Respect, and Post-Secondary Opportunities for Urban Native American Students in New Mexico*. Nathaniel's background and qualifications as a coach, public school educator, and former student in the College of Education allowed him to share his experience, knowledge, and expertise to the UNM members of IAIE and the College of Education and Human Services. Mr. Charley provided insight to IAIE about the current state of Native American education, curriculum, and school settings. Nathaniel believes that every child deserves the best educational experience.

Melvatha R. Chee, PhD (Diné), is Tsé Nahabiłnii, Kin Łichíi'nii, Hooghan Łání and Áshįįhí, originally from Lake Valley, New Mexico. Dr. Chee's research focuses on the linguistic analysis of Navajo child speech. Through the analysis of child speech, Chee studies how children understand information that is packaged into a single word and what patterns are recognized at different stages of linguistic development. Dr. Chee's research interests include the first language acquisition of morphophonology, polysynthesis, semantics, and morphology, as well as the intersection between culture and linguistics, and language sustainability. Her secondary research goal focuses on building a Navajo language database consisting of literature, conversations, narratives, and child speech for corpus-based studies. Dr. Chee is a United States Marine Corps veteran and maintains a connection to her culture to enrich her Navajo language skills, knowledge, and well-being. She is an assistant professor of Linguistics and director of the Navajo Language Program at the University of New Mexico.

Shiv R. Desai, PhD, is an associate professor of Teacher Education and Educational Leadership at the University of New Mexico. He is the co-chair of the

Diversity Council Curriculum Subcommittee, in addition to engaging in various other race and social justice activities. He has extensive experience in working with community youth and school districts in multiple states.

Donna Deyhle, PhD, is a professor emeritus at the University of Utah in the Departments of Education, Culture, and Society and Ethnic Studies. Over the past four decades her research has focused on social justice and the education of Native and Indigenous peoples. She was awarded the Distinguished Career in Educational Anthropology Award from the American Anthropology Association and the Distinguished Scholar for Diversity and Outstanding Scholarship and Research Awards from the University of Utah.

Terri Flowerday, PhD (Swiss/Lakota), is a professor of Educational Psychology and faculty member in the Institute for American Indian Education (IAIE) at the University of New Mexico. She has been designated the Chester C. Travelstead Distinguished Fellow, an award that recognizes excellence in teaching and scholarship. Born and raised on the northern plains, she earned her doctoral degree in Psychological and Cultural Studies from the University of Nebraska and came to New Mexico in 2001 to realize her goal of working with Indigenous college students. She teaches courses in cognition, learning, and motivation; her passion is mentoring graduate students, especially those from underrepresented populations. Dr. Flowerday was acknowledged in the 2016 book *"All The Real Indians Died Off" and 20 Other Myths about Native Americans*, where co-author Dina Gilio-Whitaker, a graduate of UNM, says, "Pilamiya to Terri Flowerday in the College of Education for daring to indigenize educational psychology." Research interests include academic motivation and Indigenous education.

Wendy S. Greyeyes, PhD (Diné), is an assistant professor of Native American Studies at the University of New Mexico and a former research consultant with the Department of Diné Education. Dr. Greyeyes formerly worked as the Arizona governor's tribal liaison for the Arizona Teacher Excellence Program and Homeland Security, a grassroots manager for the Indian Self Reliance Initiative in Arizona, a statistician/demographer for the Department of Diné Education, and a program analyst/chief implementation officer for the Bureau of Indian Education. She currently is the Navajo representative member for the New Mexico Indian Education Advisory Council (IEAC), president of Diné Studies Conference, Inc., president of the American Indian Studies Association (AISA), and faculty advisor for the Kiva Club and UNM Native American Alumni Chapter. Dr. Greyeyes received her MA and PhD in Sociology from the University of Chicago and BA in Native American studies from Stanford University. Her research is focused on political sociology, organizational analysis, Indigenous education, tribal sovereignty, and nation building. Recent publications include an article for *Wicazo Sa Review* titled "The Paradox of Tribal Community Building: The Roots of Local Resistance to Tribal State Craft" (2021) and a book titled *A History of Navajo Education: Disentangling Our Sovereign Body* (2022).

Alexandra Bray Kinsella is a student at Harvard Divinity School, pursuing a master's in Divinity. She was the education attorney with the Navajo Nation Department of Justice from 2018–2021, focusing on educational sovereignty and nation building. Prior to working with the Navajo Nation, Alex worked as the special assistant to Dean James Anaya, former special rapporteur on the rights of Indigenous Peoples at the University of Colorado Law School, where she practiced international Indigenous human rights law, advocating for Indigenous inclusion at the United Nations and supporting the Maya Leaders Alliance in foreign-domestic litigation for their collective land tenure in Southern Belize. Alex's research focuses on feminist/womanist philosophy, Indigenous human rights, and sacred care.

Lloyd L. Lee, PhD, is an enrolled citizen of the Navajo Nation. He is a professor of Native American Studies and the director of the Center for Regional Studies at the University of New Mexico. He is the editor of *Wicazo Sa Review*, former president of the Native American Alumni Chapter of the University of New Mexico, a council member on the American Indian Studies Association (AISA), and a faculty member in the Institute for American Indian Education (IAIE). He is the author of *Diné Identity in a 21st Century World* (2020), *Diné Masculinities: Conceptualizations and Reflections* (2013), co-author of *Native Americans and the University of New Mexico* (2017), and editor of *Diné Perspectives: Reclaiming and Revitalizing Navajo Thought* (2014) and *Navajo*

Sovereignty: Understandings and Visions of the Diné People (2017). His research focuses on American Indian identity, masculinity, leadership, philosophy, and community building.

Tiffany S. Lee (Dibé Łizhiní [Blacksheep] Diné) is from Crystal, New Mexico, and Oglala Lakota from Pine Ridge, South Dakota. Dr. Lee is a professor and the chair of Native American Studies at the University of New Mexico in Albuquerque. Her research examines educational and culturally based outcomes of Indigenous language immersion schools, Native youth perspectives on language reclamation, and socioculturally centered education. Her work has been published in journals such as the *American Journal of Education, Harvard Educational Review,* the *Journals of Language, Identity, and Education,* and *American Indian Education,* and in books such as *Culturally Sustaining Pedagogies: Teaching and Learning for Justice in a Changing World, Diné Perspectives: Revitalizing and Reclaiming Navajo Thought* and *Indigenous Language Revitalization in the Americas.* She is currently working with colleagues to open a Diné language nest in Albuquerque and to prepare Diné language immersion educators.

Nancy López, PhD, is a professor of sociology. Dr. López cofounded/directs the Institute for the Study of "Race" and Social Justice and is the founding coordinator of the New Mexico Statewide Race, Gender, Class Data Policy Consortium (race.unm.edu). Dr. López currently serves as associate vice-president for the Division of Equity and Inclusion (DEI) at the University of New Mexico. Her scholarship and teaching are guided by the insights of intersectionality—the simultaneity of tribal status/settler colonialism, race/structural racism, gender/heteropatriarchy, class/capitalism, ethnicity/nativism, and sexuality/heterosexism as systems of oppression/resistance across a variety of social outcomes (education, health, employment, wealth, and housing)—and the importance of developing contextualized solutions that advance justice. Dr. López has been recognized for her contributions to engaged scholarship through the American Sociological Association William Foote Whyte Distinguished Career Award for Sociological Practice and Public Sociology. Dr. López's current research, funded by the WT Grant Foundation and Hewlett Foundation, includes a mixed-method study in three research practice partnerships that examine the role of ethnic studies curriculum and culturally relevant pedagogy in reducing complex intersectional inequalities in high school. She received funding from the Robert Wood Johnson Foundation for a project titled "Employing and Intersectionality Framework in Revising Office of Management and Budget Standards for Collecting Administrative Race and Ethnicity Data." She has served on over seventy-five PhD/MA committees and has given over 130 seminars at national conferences, invited lectures, and community gatherings.

Glenabah Martinez, PhD (Taos Pueblo/Diné), was raised in Taos Pueblo and is an associate professor in the Department of Language, Literacy, and Sociocultural Studies at the University of New Mexico and director of the Institute for American Indian Education (IAIE). Dr. Martinez's research focuses on Indigeneity, youth, and education with a particular emphasis on Indigenous youth, critical pedagogy, and the politics of social studies curriculum. She captures these research areas in her book *Native Pride: The Politics of Curriculum and Instruction in an Urban, Public High School* (2010). She continued this scholarship in a narrative ethnographic study titled "An Examination of Educational Experiences of Indigenous Youth in a New Mexico Bordertown." She taught high school social studies for fourteen years and Native American Studies for three years at the Youth Diagnostic Development Center in Albuquerque. She works with the schools and districts throughout New Mexico on projects directly related to the histories of Indigenous peoples of the United States and Southwest. She has led several curriculum projects targeting K-12 education. At UNM, Dr. Martinez teaches graduate and undergraduate courses in education theory, policy, and praxis.

Natalie Martinez, PhD (K'awaika-meh), is a professional educator in New Mexico. She is a former administrator and teacher at the tribally controlled middle school in her Pueblo Nation. Her teaching career has included middle school, high school, and higher education in public, private, charter, and tribal schools in New Mexico. Dr. Martinez worked with teams to create Indigenous-centered curriculum projects, including Indigenous Wisdom, Indigenous New Mexico, and the curriculum guide to accompany the adaptation of An Indigenous Peoples' History of the United States for Young People. Her recent publications include a chapter in *Luminous Literacies* on the *Yazzie-Martinez* court case. Dr. Martinez teaches at the University of New Mexico. Her research focus is education for Indigenous youth, professional curriculum development, and education policy.

Jonathan Nez, former president of the Navajo Nation (2019–2023), was born in Tuba City, Arizona, and raised in Shonto, Arizona. He is married to Phefelia H. Nez, and they have two children, Christopher and Alexander. He is the son of John H. Nez and Mabel H. Nez. His grandfather, H. T. Donald, was the former Navajo Nation Council delegate for Shonto Chapter, and his grandmother was Mae Donald from Shonto. Nez began his public service after being elected as Shonto Chapter vice president. He was later elected to serve three terms as a Navajo Nation Council delegate, representing the chapters of Shonto, Oljato, Tsah Bi Kin, and Navajo Mountain. He was also elected to the Navajo County Board of Supervisors for District 1 and served two terms. In 2015 Nez was elected Navajo Nation vice president. He is currently a doctoral student in Political Science and completed research on local empowerment and mobilizing local communities of the Navajo Nation to reinstate their inherent local way of governance. His research focuses on the reduction of dependence on the central tribal government, upholding and enhancing the local inherent sovereignty of the chapter areas. He is an alumnus of Northland Pioneer College and Northern Arizona University. He earned a bachelor's degree in Political Science and a master's degree in Public Administration from Northern Arizona University.

Carlotta Penny Bird, EdD (Santo Domingo Pueblo), has worked in the field of education for over forty years in the Bureau of Indian Affairs (at the time), higher education, and the public school systems. Most recently, she worked as senior program manager for the American Indian Language Policy Research and Teacher Training Center and the Institute for American Indian Education in the College of Education at the University of New Mexico. Prior to that she served as the first assistant secretary for American Indian education in New Mexico and was a coprincipal investigator in the Indigenous Education Study Group that examined and conducted research in public education for American Indian students. She continues to work with tribes, schools, and organizations providing technical assistance in Native language and classroom instruction, educational planning and development, and policy study and analysis, and facilitating workshops, discussions, and professional development for Native American teachers. She currently serves as an officer in the New Mexico Tribal Language Consortium, comprising teachers, tribal education directors/coordinators, tribal leaders, and advocates for Native language and cultural maintenance and survival.

Preston Sanchez (Jemez Pueblo, Laguna Pueblo, and Diné) is a 2012 graduate of UNM's School of Law. From 2013 to the present, Preston has served as colead counsel in *Yazzie/Martinez v. State of New Mexico*. In 2019 Preston became the Indigenous justice attorney for the ACLU of New Mexico, where he directs litigation and policy efforts that challenge the disparate and discriminatory treatment of New Mexico's Indigenous peoples. Outside of his profession Preston spends most of his time with friends, family, and his two Labradors and floating on the Rio Grande by paddleboard.

Karen C. Sanchez-Griego, EdD, is the superintendent of Cuba Independent Schools (CISD). She is leading district-wide redesign, supporting the landmark case of *Yazzie/Martinez*, in which CISD is a plaintiff, and working on ensuring Pre-K–12 grade students in CISD receive an equitable academic education through a systems approach that supports holistic efforts to prepare students for college and careers. She was hired as an adjunct professor in August 2016 to teach a multitude of courses preparing principals and other leaders in education. She is also working on two books: *From the Boardroom to the Classroom* and *Latina Leadership: Born to Lead*. She completed a master's in Educational Leadership from the University of New Mexico and completed her doctorate in Educational Leadership in May 2010. Her dissertation title is "The Power of Their Voice: Promoting Equal Respect and Redistributing Power in Hierarchically Differentiated Groups."

Christine Sims, PhD (Acoma Pueblo), is an associate professor in the Department of Language, Literacy, and Sociocultural Studies and Bilingual Program at the University of New Mexico. She established the American Indian Language Policy Research & Teacher Training Center in 2008 and provides technical assistance to tribes and training support for Native speakers and Native language teachers.

Leola Tsinnajinnie Paquin, PhD (Diné/Filipino), is an assistant professor of Native American Studies at the University of New Mexico. She is a member of the Institute for American Indian Education and former president of the American Indian Studies Association (AISA). She grew up in Torreon, a community within the Cuba Independent School District (CISD). In addition to her recent work with CISD, she has been actively engaged with the Bernalillo Public School District since 2017.

Vincent Werito, PhD (Diné), is an associate professor in the College of Education and Human Sciences at the University of New Mexico in the Department of Language, Literacy, and Sociocultural Studies. Dr. Werito is originally from the Na'neelzhiin community. His past and current research examines the experiences of Indigenous youth in education, identifying exemplary practices in the education of Indigenous youth and using community engaged approaches to create research partnerships with a community health research focus. He continues to work with schools in New Mexico to promote culturally responsive approaches to education for Indigenous youth and collaborate with Indigenous communities in their language revitalization efforts.

Wilhelmina Yazzie (Diné) is from the eastern region of the Navajo Nation, where she grew up in the small rural community of Casamero Lake, New Mexico. She and her significant other, who is of the Lakota Tribe of South Dakota, are parents of three beautiful children. Wilhelmina is one of the key plaintiffs in the landmark education lawsuit, *Yazzie/Martinez v. State of New Mexico*, who sued the state for its failure to uphold its legal obligation to give all students a sufficient education, especially for Native Americans, Hispanics, English language learners, low-income students, and children with disabilities. Like all parents, Wilhelmina wants her children to have a better-quality education and an equal opportunity to succeed. She also values her culture and language and views all children as sacred. Aside from being a courageous parent, Wilhelmina is also a licensed law advocate practicing before tribal courts and has been a paralegal for over ten years.

Index

Printed in the USA
CPSIA information can be obtained
at www.ICGtesting.com
LVHW051946280124
770114LV00018B/481